THE ARTS
MAN'S QUEST FOR BEAUTY

General Editors
J. M. PARRISH, M.A. (Oxon.)
JOHN R. CROSSLAND, F.R.G.S.

"TO THE GREATER GLORY OF GOD."

Exeter Cathedral, of which this is the nave, is a magnificent piece of twelfth century Gothic architecture. The roof is an especially beautiful example of early English vaulting.

The Times.

THE ARTS
MAN'S QUEST FOR BEAUTY

PAINTING : DRAWING AND DESIGN
SCULPTURE : ARCHITECTURE : MUSIC
DRAMATIC ART

Advisory Editor (Art)
SIR WILLIAM ROTHENSTEIN, D. Litt.

Advisory Editor (Music)
SIR HENRY J. WOOD, F.R.A.M., F.R.C.M.
Mus. Doc. (Cantab.), D. Mus. (Oxon.)
Conductor of the Queen's Hall Promenade
Concerts and of the B.B.C. Symphony Concerts

Edited by
R. D. COOLE, B.A. (Oxon.)

ODHAMS PRESS LIMITED
LONG ACRE, LONDON, W.C.2

INTRODUCTION

AN overcrowded, dimly lit café in Chelsea; at a rickety table, covered with a blue-checked cloth, sits a heavily bearded, swarthy man dressed in a virulent green polo sweater and a thick red cloak. He is lolling idly in his chair, listening absent-mindedly to a Russian-looking girl with flat, jet hair who is wearing long green earrings. In a deep bass voice she is explaining just why a fashionable sculptor will never be really great : " Too many inhibitions, my dear fellow. Quite impossible, really." It is 2 a.m., and they are sipping coffee as black as it can be bought in what they call " this benighted country." He, of course, is a well-known painter ; she a model, or " something on the stage."

This picture, or one very similar, is conjured up in many people's minds at the sound of the word " Art," and it is undoubtedly responsible for much of the prejudice against that subject, even while it endows it with a degree of false but exciting romance. It is, however, by no means a true picture. When the actors in the scene described were playing their characteristic parts, the real artists, with whose work this book is concerned, were almost certainly in bed and asleep after a hard day's labour. A crystal-clear brain and a rock-steady hand are essential for most kinds of art and neither of them is acquired on a diet of black coffee, alcohol, and nicotine.

In whatever form art may express itself—as painting, drawing, music, singing, or acting—it is subject to certain definable principles, and, in addition, it requires in the artist mastery of a technique. The first article in this book— *The Glory and Good of Art*—attempts to set out in simple, clear language those underlying principles of all art which form the difficult but enthralling subject known as " æsthetics." It also enters briefly into some of the classical controversies on the subject, and touches on the problems set for us by the " moderns " of our own time.

HOW THE BOOK IS ARRANGED.

THE rest of the book consists of articles on the main forms of art, first the visual arts (those that depend on the use of the eyes), painting, drawing, sculpture, architecture; then the applied arts, design, illustration, advertisement, lettering; thirdly, there are articles on music and singing; and, finally, we have the art of the drama, ending with the newest form of all, cinema and photography.

In each case the authors have taken care to explain the limits within which the artist must work. They have set out what may fairly be asked of a painting, for instance, and what should not be expected of a drawing. Similarly, in writing of music, they have shown that the musician does not try to write either poems or dramas without words, but that his task is to weave sound into satisfactory, expressive forms and patterns. In this way a sound, rational basis is prepared, both for criticism and appreciation.

Each article contains an historical survey of its subject, down to the present day, and practical advice on how to master its technique. The various " Schools " of painting are considered, with their individual characteristics; the main movements in sculpture, architecture, music, and drama are outlined, while attention has been given, in every branch of art, to modern developments.

At the end of each article, or—in the case of music and drama—each section, guidance is given to those who wish to earn a living in the art under discussion, and annotated lists of books help the reader in the next steps of his reading.

It is not necessary to start this book at the beginning and work through to the end. All readers are strongly advised to begin with the first article, but after that each should choose the subject that interests him most. Each article, while forming part of a coherent whole, is complete in itself. In time, it is hoped, interest in one article will lead to interest in another, until the whole book has been read and enjoyed.

The editors' thanks are due in particular to Mr. Fred Stratton and to Mr. Hilary Stratton for their frequent assistance when the book was being planned, and for many suggestions which have helped considerably to improve it during preparation.

CONTENTS

7

"THE GLORY AND GOOD OF ART"

by PAUL CHADBURN, B.A., B.Litt.(Oxon)

THE amateur with his paint-box in the park, Michelangelo cramped on the scaffolding under the ceiling of the Sistine Chapel; the boy whittling a figure from a tree-branch, Donatello shaping Madonnas out of stone; Kreisler with his Stradivarius and the shepherd with his pipe—what are they trying to do? Artists are notoriously touchy people. As a rule, it is not wise to ask them what they are trying to do. Explanations are best left to the critics; and the explanations in the end always amount to this: artists are out to capture, to create or to interpret beauty, and to communicate it. In the past the inquirer might have remained content with this explanation. To-day, perhaps, he looks about him, puzzled. The modern critics themselves are sometimes puzzled. " Can beauty survive in a democratic world? " they cry.

This question strikes at the very root of the matter, raising the problem of the nature of art and its relation to life; so we shall begin by examining it. What exactly do the critics mean when they ask: " Can beauty survive in a democratic world? " By a democratic world, they mean—quite apart from political upheavals in various countries since the World War—a condition of affairs which shows an increasing tendency to alter the physical appearance of the entire globe. They mean the startling transformation of town and countryside which goes on apace, and which is due to the invasion on all sides, into every sphere of life, into every home and hamlet and colonial outpost, of science and its inseparable attendant, the machine. They mean pylons, railways, factory chimneys sprouting from the fields, petrol tanks, garish cafés, road-houses; they mean " beauty spots " littered with refuse, loud with gramophones and radio, cocktail parties on the Pyramids and monsters in Loch Ness.

This is what the people who express their anxiety about the survival of beauty mean by a democratic world. And what do they mean by beauty? That is a question they would find more difficult to answer. Let us say, at a rough guess, they mean that "something"—we can define it no more exactly than that—which resides in nature and human life as a kind of intermittent tracery behind the surface of things, which we see dimly, which the artist sees more clearly—something the artist recreates for us which gives us pleasure, and which, recognising, we call beauty.

BEAUTY CAPTURED AND HELD BY ART

ART—to be distinguished from craftsmanship, which is the making of an object perfectly adapted to practical uses, as, for instance, a chair—art captures beauty. It brings out, stamped with the artist's individuality, that underlying harmony and form we all perceive in Nature, dimly or clearly, as we are sensitive to such things. It is all one whether the work of art finds immediate response in our experience, or whether the artist's representation of the underlying harmony is strange to us at first, as was Epstein's figure of Rima, for example. It is art, nevertheless, if, sooner or later, its significance appears and enriches our perception of nature, our experience of life.

The art Jeremiahs, then, have a case against a democratic world ; they prophesy the death of beauty because the forms we have been accustomed to perceive in nature are speedily becoming extinct—and not only that : beautiful old buildings are rapidly being demolished to make way for new buildings which, if they be beautiful—and this we shall discuss later—are certainly not so in the way, let us say, that a Gothic church is beautiful. The answer to the question whether beauty can survive in a democratic world can only be given when we have examined what art is, the nature of the impulse which goes to create it, and the connection of art with life.

THE RELATION BETWEEN LIFE AND ART

IN order to raise some of the issues inseparable from a discussion on the nature of art, let us imagine ourselves present in a picture gallery when two very different kinds of person are making a tour of the exhibits. We shall call them Mrs. Brown and Miss Languish, and suppose them to be standing before a picture illustrating the Bible story of the woman taken in adultery. It is necessary to bear in mind that the points raised are applicable to art generally, and not only to painting. The following conversation ensues :

MRS. BROWN. Don't those people look real ! They might be living to-day—except for their clothes, of course !

MISS LANGUISH. That doesn't make a good painting. Art isn't photography. As a matter of fact, this isn't art at all—it's all out of drawing, the colours are crude, and the composition is as rudimentary as it could be !

MRS. BROWN. I call it fine. I like a picture that has a story to it, a picture that illustrates something grand and moving. This kind of picture makes the past come to life—and I'm sure it has a great influence for good. You can feel that woman's story, and sympathise with her.

MISS LANGUISH. Art is art and a story is a story. Art doesn't teach—or preach, either.

MRS. BROWN. If a picture pleases me, and makes life seem finer, then I say it's beautiful. I have my taste, and you can have yours.

MISS LANGUISH. What you appreciate has nothing whatever to do with art. Art is a selection and arrangement into æsthetic forms which cause a certain indefinable pleasure in those who are sensitive to beauty. There is a significance in form, which has nothing to do with meaning in the everyday sense.

The two visitors continue their tour of the gallery. Miss Languish stops and admires a picture which does not convey anything to Mrs. Brown, seeming to her like nothing so much as a jig-saw puzzle scrabbled haphazard together by a fretful child. But Miss Languish insists that this is beautiful, that this has " significant form."

Lastly, the two visitors come to a picture before which both stop and exclaim simultaneously : " Beautiful ! " But Miss Languish goes on to remark on the technical excellencies of the picture, while Mrs. Brown observes there is feeling in it, that the artist has caught the character of the flowers, which seem to be living, growing things.

PROBLEMS THAT LIE IN THE THEORY OF BEAUTY

IT may be as well to summarise the points raised in this conversation, because they lead on to some of the chief questions in what is called Æsthetics, or the theory of beauty. The points are :

(1) Is beauty only subjective, that is to say, purely a matter of individual taste ?

(2) What is the relation, if any, between life and art?

(3) What is the connection between the subject of a work of art and the form it assumes?

(4) What is "meaning" in art?

(6) Has art a function?

(7) Is art connected in any way with religious creeds and moral codes?

All these issues are really only developments of the fundamental question concerning the relation between life and the pleasure we obtain from visiting museums, concerts, and theatres, or from reading books.

The first thing to do is to try and restore beauty, which the diametrically opposed tastes of the two visitors would seem to have divided, to a decent unity. For if this cannot be done, if beauty is only a term used to describe anyone's pleasurable responses to any picture or poem or sonata, then nothing further can be said about art; no principles can be established, no criteria; and the edifice created by all the artists since the world began must turn out to be no more than a tower of Babel.

Mrs. Brown and Miss Languish, representing respectively the ordinary person and the "highbrow," made their approach to art from opposite directions. Mrs. Brown, admittedly sentimental, required art to awake in her and embellish for her certain perceptions, certain emotions, certain ideas which had come to mean much to her. Because she had no training in the appreciation of art, these things were best interpreted to Mrs. Brown through a treatment which idealised and did not violate her everyday conception of life. Accordingly, Mrs. Brown was apt to mistake prettiness for beauty, sentimentality for pathos, and, in short, romance for art.

Miss Languish, on the other hand, approached art from a lofty abstraction from life, from an "ivory tower"; a picture to her was an arrangement of lines, forms, tones, causing an indescribable ecstasy in the chosen few, though it interpreted nothing in one's emotional experience. Her appreciation was intellectual, born of a study of art, a knowledge of the principles of art.

THE CONSTANT QUALITY OF BEAUTY

THERE is no denying that tastes do vary: what is exquisite music to one person is fiddle-di-dee to another. Yet beauty, as it is caught and interpreted by great artists, remains constant ; it is brought into being in accordance with the same unvarying laws, whatever may be its medium. There are all kinds and conditions of men, whose tastes all differ ; generations succeed one another ; fashions, in art as in all else, come and go ; civilisations rise and fall ; east is still east and west is west. But the beauty that has been created, anywhere, at any time, in any medium, remains—to be responded to by all those who have developed the faculty of appreciating it.

To develop this faculty, one must bring to art not only the range of emotional experience possessed by the one visitor to the gallery, but the intellectual experience of the other ; one must both have felt those things the artist felt, and have some understanding of the medium through which he expresses himself. Mrs Brown and Miss Languish were appreciating the picture of flowers from different angles, and they could only half appreciate it, because its beauty was one and in-divisible.

Though there is none to whom it is given to respond to all the arts equally, appreciating every example in each kind, nevertheless the sum total of every artist's contribution to the temple of art since civilisation began, all the beauty painter, sculptor, architect, musician, poet have reclaimed from life, all this is absolute and constant. Though most people appreciate—and, indeed, see—no more than a narrow facet, a cornice here, a frieze there, some have made the journey round about and learned to understand the underlying laws which govern the structure of the whole.

"THE HIGHEST SUMMIT OF ALL ART AND LIFE"

BEAUTY, then, though difficult to capture and not always easy to appreciate, is no mirage appearance, evoked by individual desires for a life beyond life ; it is no escape, no opium dream. For, though the artist's creation may be appreciated by people of different cultures and countries, it must be founded solidly on realities underlying the surface conditions of life. And so the fundamental question arises : what exactly has art to do with life ?

The answer is : everything and nothing. Nothing in respect of how most of all our lives are spent, in what trivialities of intercourse, futilities of action. Yet if we have experienced

something deeper, more permanent, then art has everything
to do with life, for it interprets the moments we have lived
most intensely; it is "emotion recollected in tranquillity."
And this is why there is no such thing as a combination of
forms or sounds or words that bears a significance unrelated
to our experience of life.

FORMS OF EXPRESSION THE SERVANTS OF IMPULSE

JUST as art is inseparable from life, so is the form which
any work of art assumes, into which it bodies itself forth
through the medium of the artist's individuality, inseparable
from the content, or what the artist wishes to express. True,
there are certain patterns, or forms, which the critic may
classify, apart from the subject or content which finds
expression through them. There are verse forms, for example,
such as the sonnet and blank verse; there are various kinds
of musical forms. But the form cannot be superimposed
on what the artist wishes to express, and it cannot be deliberately selected by him.

However skilfully an artist may make use of any form of
expression, with whatever grace he may adapt it to his
individual style, still he will not have produced any great and
lasting work if, combined with his mastery over technique,
he has not made that vital contact with reality which, as
even psycho-analysts have not helped us out here, we must
call by that old-fashioned, much abused term, inspiration.
To sum this matter up : *style*, which is the imprint of the
artist's individuality on his work, *content*, which is what he
wishes to express, and *form*, the shape his work assumes—
all merge together in great art; they are one and indivisible.

HOW THE ARTIST CONVEYS HIS MESSAGE

THE Japanese artist who considers the landscape he is about
to paint upside down between his legs does not do so
because he is afflicted by that "imp of the perverse" who
so often stimulates Bernard Shaw to produce his paradoxes. He
does it so that he may more easily contemplate his landscape
freed from those everyday associations which are apt to
detract from its deeper significance, the meaning which art
endeavours to capture. He makes this inverted examination
in order, for example, that a tree shall not appear to be merely
something growing out of the ground, bearing a certain kind

of fruit to which he is particularly partial, and which, despite the best creative will, he is not able completely to dissociate from matters irrelevant to his purpose as an artist. He wishes to contemplate the tree as it blends in with the composition of the landscape, irrespective of other considerations.

Examine a Chinese or a Japanese print, and you will often find that the artist has not indicated the ground at all. The figures might appear to a matter-of-fact person—one who requires art to represent, not to interpret—to be floating in the air ; and such a person would conclude that the only possible meaning was that the figures were meant to be super-natural. Actually, of course, the artist has taken from his subject some of its everyday meaning in order to bring out more clearly the significance he perceives beneath the surface.

THE ONLY MEANING THAT LIES IN ART

THE important point to remark is this : there are not two distinct kinds of meaning in art—an everyday one, and a mysterious one which has nothing to do with ordinary life. The truth is that the meaning art catches and interprets may be wholly conveyed through the presentation of associations, ideas, images which are familiar to us all every day, but that sometimes also, in some mediums, the artist is able to convey his meaning without making so much use, or without making any use, of these interpreters.

This brings us to the differences between the various arts. It is obvious that much music causes pleasure in the hearer purely and simply by the combination and variation of sounds, which, while they play upon chords of emotion, evoke no definite picture in the mind. Music has been called the most abstract of the arts ; it would be better to call it the most direct, for it causes that indefinable pleasure which all art conveys with less recourse to everyday meanings than do any of the other arts.

ARTS THAT MAY DISPENSE WITH EVERYDAY MEANING

A PICTURE also—though less easily—may not convey any idea of what it is a picture of—it may be parts taken from a number of objects, blended into composition.

Sculpture provides a good example of both ways of pre-senting the underlying significance of life. Go into the Grecian gallery of the British Museum. There you will see the human body idealised in its physical aspect. The Greek sculptors translated the classical conception of life into stone ; the human form is intellectualised in their sculpture ; the figures convey the *ideas* of physical fitness, womanly grace, sensual abandon, soldierly vigour.   Or if you examine examples of mediæval Christian sculpture you will see that the artist has draped and shaped his figures to express his belief, a belief which turned away from physical beauty towards spiritual regeneration.

Yet on the other hand, sculpture may also—as much modern work in this medium—express a significance dependent on no concept.   It may not look like any one, and it may not convey any idea, evoke any sentiment which may be defined by the beholder.   It pleases, but we cannot tell why, except that there is harmony in it arising from its shape, balance and design, and something which we too have felt.

It is clear, then, that three of the arts—music, painting and sculpture—may capture beauty in nature and communicate it, while dispensing with meaning in the everyday sense altogether.   What about the other two arts, literature and architecture ?

THE ARCHITECT'S AND THE POET'S MESSAGE

THE writer works with words, and though he may not always use the everyday meaning of words, there is no escape from the associations they evoke in the reader.   Even the fantastically compounded words in Lewis Carroll's *Jabberwocky :*

> 'Twas brillig, and the slithy toves
> Did gyre and gimble in the wabe :
> All mimsy were the borogroves,
> And the mome raths outgrabe.

convey a more or less definite image to the mind ; they are more than mere sound.   In the same way architecture is more than a tracing out of abstract pattern in stone or concrete.

The architect first considers the uses of the building he is to design ; the harmony of the structure is dependent on these uses ; the architect perceives the beauty latent in them and he shapes his material in accordance with these perceptions. A factory that looked like a church would be a sorry structure, and vice versa.   The architect, besides interpreting the spirit of an age—be it a machine age or a " golden age of Athens " —is concerned no less with the needs of the age and of the people who are to use the building, according as they are to live, work or pray in it. And for this reason architecture, like literature, is inseparable from everyday meaning. Yet art has not two meanings but one meaning, which may be conveyed either directly to our intuition or indirectly by way of our intellect.

ART AS A MEANS OF ESCAPE INTO LIFE

THERE are people who say: "Art is all very well for those who have a taste for it, but we really haven't time to make a study of art; we can get along very well without it." These people have already been answered in what we have said about the relation of art to life, and about the meaning of art. But to emphasise a point which is important, it may be as well to sum up. We must not only bring life to our appreciation of art, but, conversely, bring art to our experience of life. This is the function of art. Art is not an escape from life; if we call it an escape at all, it is an escape to life.

The test of great art is, precisely, that it does not lead away from reality. The artist selects, arranges, composes to a design we only vaguely sense, but which, nevertheless, is present in the artist's material and is responded to, more or less, by us all. As Walter Pater wrote:

> "In truth all art does but consist in the removal of surplusage, from the last finish of the gem-engraver blowing away the last particles of invisible dust, back to the earliest divination of the finished work to be, lying somewhere, according to Michelangelo's fancy, in the rough-hewn block of stone."

HOW APPRECIATION MAY GROW

LET us return once more to Mrs Brown and Miss Languish. Mrs Brown, a good citizen and a religious woman, we may believe, was struck with a picture because of the moral it pointed, the religion it upheld. Miss Languish, on the other hand, repudiated any connection between art and religion or morals. We have said that the function of art is to bring us back to life, to the underlying significance in human experience. Now, while the meaning in all our lives is undeniably connected with our ideals, with our beliefs, in short, with our values, these represent feelings which form into religion and moral codes on the one hand, and into works of art on the other. The effect on us of art which is inspired by the loftiest ideals, the most fervent belief, has nothing to do with religious and moral *teaching*—even though the painter may have been a monk, the poet a moralist.

What is required to appreciate a work of art fully is a share of the spiritual feeling that went into it, a share of the sentiment and belief. For while faith and fine qualities of the heart are constant, the forms of faith and behaviour vary from age to age, from civilisation to civilisation. Didactic art (or art which sets out to teach) and polemic art, which submits itself to the service of an idea or contemporary policy, die with the dogma or faction they support.

The test of great art is that it outlives what is transitory. The religious paintings of El Greco are beautiful in a large measure because of their creator's faith, but not because of the articles of that faith. In the same way the monstrous graven deities, half beast, half human, which gaze at each other majestically across the Egyptian corridors of the British Museum, were hewn out of the religious awe of the dawn of Mediterranean civilisation ; they were born of Egyptian mythology. Few understand, and no one believes in that mythology now. Yet the colossal figures still evoke awe in us ; they express a calm and sublime grandeur, conceptions of vastness and mystery to which we still respond, despite all the researches of our science, all the refinements of our belief.

The connection between religion, morals, and art, in brief, lies at the root, where all have their common origin, in the human spirit and in the human heart ; but the flowering is separate : religion and morality from the one stem, art from the other.

KNOWLEDGE THAT LEADS TO TASTE IN ART

"YOU should not say it is not good. You should say you do not like it ; and then, you know, you're perfectly safe." This witticism of Whistler's, the American painter, might well have been repeated by Miss Languish to Mrs. Brown. For while Mrs. Brown had spiritual and emotional experience, she could not have hoped to express a valuable opinion on any work of art until she had some knowledge of æsthetic principles, or, more plainly, of the nature of art. Until she had this she could not even begin to form a taste of her own. She had opinions and an idea of what a picture ought to look like ; what taste she had was formed by the " pretty-pretty " sentimental portraits of a Frank Dicksee or a Greuze.

Formation of individual taste in art is not nearly so common as it would seem from listening to the number of people who dogmatise about their likes and dislikes. A lady, herself a talented miniature painter, once pointed to a picture in the National Gallery with the observation that she had particular affection for it, because it was the only picture she had ever come to appreciate purely by herself, without any one else's opinion to influence her. Hers was not so meagre an achievement as it sounded. Taste, as distinct from opinion, is rare. To acquire it, it is not enough to be familiar with the principles of art, with art history ; nor does it even suffice to have walked through a great number of galleries all over the world.

SINCERITY THE ESSENCE OF APPRECIATION

TASTE should evolve in us with our own individuality ; it should start with real, sincere appreciation of something, even if it is not something wholly good. The important thing is that we should respond to what is sincere, what is beautiful in the poem or picture, on our own. The son of John Evelyn, the diarist, quoted the classics when he was five, but he would have shown more taste, the promise of a finer appreciation, had he thrown Virgil and Horace on the fire and gone of his own free will to a poem by Herrick ; if he had surprised his too cultured father by coming out with :

> Here a little child I stand,
> Heaving up my either hand ;
> Cold as paddocks though they be,
> Yet I lift them up to Thee.

Taste does not depend on a wide range of æsthetic experiences. One's taste may be excellent in a narrow compass. But it will be found that when one has really begun to appreciate anything for oneself—let us say Gothic architecture —then this will lead naturally by an evolution of taste to appreciation of other styles. Because art, though it is often exhibited in such sepulchral places as are most museums, and though books coldly lay it forth in examples and periods —art is not a number of objects arranged chronologically and exhibited in show cases. Art is alive, contemporaneous, continuous.

Once you have really identified yourself with a masterpiece, experienced the full pleasure, responded to the vital contact with reality which it expresses, you will not stop there ; for you will already in that one example have appreciated *motifs* which, while they are auxiliary to the main conception in that particular work, have been the dominant *motif* in masterpieces of later or earlier times.

THE DISCOVERY THAT ART "IS A HUMAN ACTIVITY"

APPRECIATION of kinds of art proceeds concurrently with the broadening of one's intellectual interests and the deepening of one's emotional experiences. Considering only European art—leaving aside Eastern and primitive art—two tendencies are perceptible, which come to the fore alternately, and which indicate the spirit of the age (for the artist's intuition precedes the critic's formula) in much the same way as the wooden mannikin and his wife swing to and fro from the doors of their chimney-piece cottage, foretelling wet or dry weather.

There is a kind of art which seems to be produced in a civilisation which has reached maturity ; a civilisation which is neither struggling to establish itself, nor is being wracked by wars, yet which has not reached a complacent condition where the vital flames—the belief in itself, the vigour in achievement—have burnt low. The best period of Greek art is an example. There is about such art a repose, a clearness, a calm intellectual ordering, as if the soul had made a perfect balance between the passions and the reason, and the artist a just compromise between the individual and society.

There is a tendency in this art, as it passes its meridian, for harmony of line, formal beauty, to predominate more and more over colour ; tradition over innovation ; generally accepted, intellectually formulated truths over bright flashes of intuition. Precepts begin to crystallise, and in literature, for example, we find rules for the drama formulated by Aristotle and for poetry by Horace. Because of the great periods of this kind of art in Greece and Rome it is generally referred to as classical art. But it is not confined to those civilisations. Both the seventeenth century in France and the eighteenth century in England were classical in spirit.

Classical art—be it a poem by Pope, a drama by Racine, a Queen Anne building—is not as a rule the first kind of art one appreciates. When we first adventure into the realms of art we are attracted by works which have more élan, less of the intellect and more of the fancy. The Elizabethan dramatists and Ibsen are more to our taste than Euripides and Corneille ; the aspiring Gothic arch traces the spirit of adolescence more closely than the tranquil architrave of the Greeks, and Wagner has at this period more to impart to our imagination than has Bach. Romantic art is individual ; it is revolutionary, glamorous, ardent, colourful. It attracts the eye sooner than the more restrained art of the classicists.

Yet there comes a time, as our appreciation widens, when we find that rigorous distinctions between kinds are misleading, and that they do not serve to describe much of the best art. When we have come in painting to appreciate equally a Botticelli, a Rubens, a Hogarth, and a Leonardo we cease to have much more use for such a rough distinction as that between classical and romantic art. And when this happens we have attained a knowledge of the nature of art ; we have formed a catholic taste—of our own.

ART IN AN AGE OF RECONSTRUCTION

WE cannot determine all the conditions which came together to produce such periods of artistic profusion as were the Golden Age of Athens, the Quattrocento in Italy, the Tudor Period in England. But, bearing in mind the identification of the creative impulse with the enduring values in human life—the spiritual and emotional, as well as the intellectual vitality of a people—this much may be certainly affirmed : that any form or kind of art requires of society that it shall possess a certain community of belief, a staunch and unified front to life ; that people shall be linked by some common tenets ; that their thought and their feeling and their belief shall have found some synthesis, some proportional balance. There must be values binding a people together. Otherwise the artist has nothing to work on, no means of communication.

There have been periods of upset and turmoil, periods, as they are called, of transition or of decadence, when the pre-requisites which buttress the artist have been absent. There has been a waste land, with one or two voices, still and small, crying in the wilderness. Such was the period of the barbarian invasion of the Roman Empire and the period in

English poetry between Chaucer and the Elizabethan dawn. Europe would seem to have undergone such a time in the years following the World War. Reconstruction is now under way, with what prospects for art we shall next consider.

POST-WAR CONFUSION THAT WITHERS BELIEF

THE World War, which shattered so many of our beliefs, had the effect at the same time of sending civilisation further forward than it would normally have gone in several generations. The result is that most of us—and the post-War generation is not exempt—are living in a world to which we cannot adjust ourselves. It is rather as though we had climbed into Wells's Time Machine and had been translated into a future age, bearing our pre-War background with us. We still believe in things which are dead—or we would persuade ourselves we believe. Alternately, faced with the problems of modern life, we turn aside, give ourselves up to the circus of machine age diversion, to the blaring accompaniment of the brazen voice :

> I am the Kallyope, Kallyope, Kallyope !
> Hoot toot, hoot toot, hoot toot, hoot toot,
> Willy willy willy wah HOO !
> Sizz, fizz. . . .[1]

And we believe in nothing at all.

What has this got to do with art ? A great deal ; because, as we have said, art requires for its creation and its communication that there should be cohesion in its material ; that there should be latent in life what Michelangelo divined in the rough-hewn block of stone, that intuition of the finished work to be. The artist must perceive the same prefigurement in the spirit of the age. He can make nothing of hollow men ; he can communicate nothing to them.

Nor is this only the case with literature. One has only to think of the impetus given to painting and sculpture and architecture, as well as to poetry, by the Renaissance, which was, in fact, a renaissance of man's belief in himself, and in the delight of living. The Middle Ages—murky though they were, cluttered with superstition, the sources of knowledge dammed by dogma—themselves provide an example. Wretchedly stunted and cramped as was the physical and intellectual life of those times, yet the people as a whole

[1] Vachell Lindsay : *The Kallyope Yell.*

possessed a spiritual vitality without which it would have been impossible for their cathedrals to have risen in such magnificent forms towards a haven beyond this world. The first ardour of the Communist régime in Russia might also be mentioned for the masterpieces of Eisenstein and Pudovkin.

The problem to-day is to find this driving force, this zest, this unity which provides the impulse to art. The machine age has come upon us with the rattle and roar of its engines. We are trying to recover from our bewilderment, to readjust ourselves. A problem faces the artist. To take a modern illustration : everybody knows that for the voice of the radio announcer to be reconstructed out of the vibrations it effects in the ether, in order that his message should come to us from our loud-speakers, contact must be made from an aerial and with the earth. In the same way, in order that the artist may communicate with us, he must first make contact with the spirit of the time, with the pulse of consciousness throbbing at the core of the age. Only then can the creative impulse operate strongly, without impediment.

Art cannot be produced by the intellect alone—as has been abundantly proved in the post-War era. Nor can one force feeling, as, for instance, some moderns have tried, who have played at being the wounded, raging, too often ranting D. H. Lawrence. Art cannot go back ; it cannot fight science. It would only shatter itself to pieces in that attempt. Art to-day must accept science, create an expression which shall include everything science has introduced into life. This, to some measure, has been accomplished, especially by architecture and the cinema.

THE PARTNERSHIP BETWEEN SCIENCE AND ART

IT is too early to say much about the cinema as a form of art, because films which may be called great art have been few and far between. All that one would say at present is that the cinema—a medium born of the machine age itself—would appear to provide quite exceptional possibilities for the artistic expression of these times. It combines all the arts ; it is far less exclusive than any of them—that is to say, it is within the reach, literally speaking, of everyone. Above all, the cinema is itself a machine. Science has here been accepted as a collaborator with art.

The other medium of art in the West to-day which would seem to have achieved a re-birth from the ruins effected by the World War is architecture. The very speed, the drive towards efficiency and economy of space and time, the general acceleration brought about to a considerable degree by the War, has tended to bring architecture close to the spirit of the times, to the current of the Age's consciousness. The design of modern life no longer permits of such florid ugliness as characterised buildings of the Victorian period. To be sure these continue to be built ; ugliness still abounds in our buildings. But modern architecture has to a large extent orientated itself.

This adaptation to the spirit of the times is especially noticeable in the New World and in countries like Italy, Germany, Austria and Soviet Russia—in countries, that is, where the traditional régimes have been overthrown. And it must be said that revolutions, however adversely they may work upon the other arts, have sometimes undoubtedly been beneficial to architecture. During the last few years entire towns have been built in Italy on land reclaimed from swamps, and great industrial cities have sprung up in Russia on what was before uninhabited, barren land. Colonies of working-men's houses in Berlin and Vienna were erected as a direct consequence of Social Democracy taking over power in these capitals after the War. These modern buildings to a large extent dictate their own form ; twentieth century speed sweeps them into clear, spare lines, frees them from the useless decorative ugliness of Victorian forms.

BEAUTY DIFFUSED INTO EVERYDAY LIVES

THIS new design, both created by and expressing modern life, is apparent in the crafts as much as in the arts. The advance has, of course, been due in the first place to changing conditions, dependent on the progress of scientific invention. We are not concerned here with old forms which persist— ugly mahogany furniture, horse-hair chairs, hideous " art " curtains, and wall-papers—but with those forms which, swiftly on some fronts, slowly on others, are more and more invading the domain of our everyday lives.

Considered in this way, it may be said that the old conception of a craft, the conception of William Morris with his " home beautiful," his hand-made objects, his refusal to accept machinery and standardisation—all this is not only impracticable (it was always that) but dead. And yet Morris's ideal—that every man should have pleasant surroundings in which to live—is actually nearer realisation now, *in consequence* of that very machinery, that very standardisation Morris decried. Only machines and only specialisation in industry can supply every man with pleasant, even with beautiful surroundings.

An example of the change which has come over the form of objects which are primarily not works of art, but articles of use, may be found by comparing a motor-car of the year 1900 with a motor-car of to-day. Motor-cars in the early period, though they possessed a kind of grotesque character, were ugly objects, gawky, stubborn-looking, mulish. To-day they are graceful. Speed, which resulted from the mastery of science over the principles of the internal combustion engine, and specialisation which perfected each separate part, have made a thing of beauty out of what was once a ramshackle adaptation of a horse carriage.

Though motor-cars, considered æsthetically, are far removed from the examples we have been discussing, we mention them as an illustration of what we have been chiefly concerned to point out in this introduction—the relation which art bears to life—in order to give a final familiar illustration of a point where this twentieth century life, which has so much to do with machines, is finding expression in æsthetic form. Poetry, music, painting, though they would seem to have little affinity with a locomotive or a factory, must, all the same, if they are to be living expressions of modern life, draw their material and shape their form in accordance with the same forces which have created our vast power plants, sky-scrapers and air liners.

PAINTING : "SILENT POETRY" RICH IN ELOQUENCE

by FRED STRATTON

THE story of painting begins in so remote a past that it is
difficult to surmise from what need or motive in primitive
man it arose. That there is a need inherent in his nature
for what is called beauty nearly all will agree, but the difficulty lies in the fact that there are so many manifestations of
it that agreement as to its precise appearance is not so general.
All through the ages, as far as we know, man has made some
effort to beautify his surroundings, and even himself. Nature
around him was so marvellous and varied that unconsciously
he would feel a blankness on the wall of his cave and take
some steps to decorate it.

One can imagine his attention being fixed by the accidental
similarity to a human or an animal head in some of the flints
he was trying to shape. It would interest him greatly and his
natural impulse would be to take it to his cave, and, for the
better display of it, place it on a projecting piece of rock,
some height above the ground. It would arouse interest and
that particular part of his cave would receive much attention
—much more than if nothing was there. The piece of flint
would decorate that particular spot and probably bring back
to him the pleasant feeling he experienced when he found
it—the warmth and brightness of the sun, the soft whiteness
of clouds and blue of sky, the sparkle of dew, and possibly
the affectionate caress of his dog.

Here, then, are two most important functions of painting
(and of all art)—to decorate, and to stimulate the imagination.
These interests and feelings might be generated by his sight
of the bit of flint, but they would be much more readily
aroused when the discovery of coloured earths had led him
to smear his walls with rude attempts to render the animals
that he hunted. Painting begins here and is one method by
which man has attempted to pass on to others his delight in
the appearance of things around him ; or the emotions that
stir his heart from sources within. That there may have
been further reasons for the work of the cave artist does not
concern us here.

ART A CONSOLATION AND DELIGHT

BUT the fact that even a slight scribble does make a piece of paper or canvas more interesting does not necessarily turn the scribble into a precious work of art. Other qualities are necessary, the qualities which make one turn to it for entertainment and delight, for consolation and for spiritual peace. What are these qualities and how are they produced ? One may give some clue to the former, but the emotions of the spirit are much more difficult to account for.

Entertainment and delight may certainly result in a painting from the artist's handling of his materials only. The relation of line, the balance of light and shade, the play and quality of his colours, the variety and beauty of his surface all contribute. These features may not be discerned by some, but even the most ignorant are influenced. The relation, the harmony of line, is difficult to explain, but it will frequently be found that important lines, the swing of a full-length figure in a composition for instance, will be repeated in another part of a picture. It will not necessarily have the same importance, but it takes up and repeats the " beat " as it were. One may say in explanation of this, that a doubled line is found to be more interesting than a single one.

It is easy to make an experiment. A line may contrast with another, or it may continue another to produce rhythm in the picture. Frequently it is necessary to give the principal interest to one feature, but it is not advisable that the eye should rest there, so, by a judicious arrangement of line, it is led over the whole. There must also be some relation to the enclosing shape of the painting.

The balance of light and shade is perhaps more obvious than the composition of line. There is the big mass of light and the big mass of dark, and they may impinge on each other in various ways and degrees. They may interpenetrate, and this interpenetration adds, or may add, much to the movement in a picture. Simple masses of light and dark produce calm and sombreness, but intricacy of interpenetration suggest movement and unrest. The illusion of movement in a picture may be given by a series of lines running in one direction, or by patches of light and dark so distributed over the picture that there is no rest for the eye, which is carried on from point to point.

UNBALANCED COLOUR THAT DISTURBS THE EYE

WITH regard to the distribution of colour, much the same may be said ; but it is more intricate and consequently the successful manipulation of a rich colour-scheme more rare. Balance is necessary in producing a successful colour effect. A want of balance produces an uncomfortable feeling. It is rather like a human being with one leg shorter than the other. The short leg may be perfect in shape, but one's vision is disturbed. Possibly it might be put right by taking a bit off the opposite arm, but that is an experiment one cannot try.

In painting, a mass of red on the right may be balanced by a smaller quantity of brighter red on the left. The amount of cold colour must be considered in its relation to the warm. Then, again, there must be interpenetration, and there is the whole range between the warm and the cold colours which can be brought into play. It is not as simple as all this, for the shape and pattern of the masses and patches of colour or light and shade have to be taken into consideration. Also the most appropriate colour to express the particular emotion desired must be decided upon.

There is also the *quality* of the colour to be chosen, and this is important in the final effect of the picture. We may strive for the luscious transparency of red wine in a decanter, or may prefer the opacity of Thames water in a medicine bottle. We may strive for the brilliance of thirteenth-century stained glass ; or may prefer the opacity of paint in a tin before it is applied to our door. There are two pictures in the National Gallery which illustrate very clearly this difference in the quality of the colour, No. 5727 by Pessellino, and No. 2490 by Ghirlandaio, both in Room 19.

The brilliance of the former was the aim of the great masters of the past and, to succeed, great knowledge, long practice, and experiment were necessary. In modern times the dull " matt " quality of the house-painter seems to be preferred. It is all very much a matter of individual taste and preference ; but the masters we have hitherto looked up to seemed to think it necessary to employ all the resources of their craft to enhance the emotion or sensation desired.

BEAUTY THAT LIES IN VARIETY OF TEXTURE

ANOTHER feature of paintings by the great masters is the extraordinary variety of surface and texture. In nature

1. " COMPOSITION " IN A GREAT PICTURE

*This analysis of " The Virgin of the Rocks," by da Vinci,
reveals that the group is kept together by a series of triangles
and a curved line. Note how the eye is led upwards by the
pillar of rock to a repetition of the curve.*

and in man's surroundings it is to be seen everywhere. Birds, beasts, flowers, trees, sky, plumage, hair, furs, stuffs, silk, glass, porcelain; polished or unpolished jewels and stones all display it. There is infinite variety, and the same may be said of many great paintings. Every conceivable surface may be found in pictures by Titian or Turner, for instance. It interests and it delights, this variety; and it is partly due to this that pictures which have no emotional value interest and please.

This explains why the coloured photograph is so unsatisfying, and also explains why the colour reproduction of to-day, marvellous as it is, fails to have anything like the effect of the original. There is an æsthetic delight given by the variety of surface alone which is lacking in the print or photograph. Their surfaces are comparatively monotonous and unstimulating to our sense of sight. Nature has this variety of surface; the texture of a clump of birch trees breaking into leaf is different from the silkiness of the grass below. The painter does not attempt to imitate this, but by the manipulation of his pigment and oil, he suggests it.

The coloured photograph and reproduction also lack the luscious transparency of varnish and oil, the jewel-like sparkle of transparent colours properly displayed and contrasting with the thick creaminess of the opaque pigments. Since these qualities are lacking, it is not surprising that the sum of the sensations in looking at a photograph or a reproduction is small.

A QUALITY PRESENT IN ALL GREAT WORK

ALL this relates mainly to the sensations of pleasure and delight one may receive from a painting; but there is another aspect which is more rare and much more important —the emotional. Again it is a matter of individual feeling. It is almost impossible to describe emotional quality, and it is impossible to say how it is produced, but it is undoubtedly present in the greatest work. The deep and powerful calmness of Egyptian sculpture, the placid serenity of the early Christian paintings and carvings, the humility that one feels before a Giotto or a Rembrandt, indicate that it is there in the highest degree. It depends neither upon drawing, light and shade, colour nor composition. It is present when most of these features are lacking, and it is present when all are there. In that great craftsman Rembrandt it is present frequently in an almost unbearable degree ; and in that curious combination of primitiveness and modernity, Modigliani, the volume is almost as great. It shows itself, spasmodically, here and there through the whole range of art. Great and accomplished works may entirely lack it ; and the slightest scribble by the rare master may possess it.

One cannot explain it, one cannot describe it, one can only know if it is there. The writer's theory is that, when the true *artist* touches his material—any material—he changes the rate of its vibrations. He transfers to it some of his own vibrations, some of his own life, and there it is, a living thing —no power of movement, no mechanism, but a living thing ; and there is in that bit of life some knowledge of which we are ignorant and which some of us would give much to possess. This quality is the rarest of all in works of art, and is the one we should most earnestly seek to know. It explains Giotto and the more modern Modigliani.

THE LITTLE KNOWLEDGE THAT PREVENTS UNDERSTANDING

How to discover this quality, how to get anything from a work of art, has not yet been developed into a science. Sit in front of it ; stroll in front of it ; if possible, stroll round it. Give it time. Do not take to it a preconceived idea of what a picture should be. Just submit to it. Turn out any knowledge you may think you possess. A little knowledge is a complete preventive to enjoying anything the picture may possess. A person with a little knowledge always seeks in a picture something to find fault with, and this will prevent enjoyment and understanding. On one occasion a portrait was condemned because the original had a small mouth. " Put it away," said the critic. " I hate anybody with a small mouth." There was much in that portrait besides the small mouth, but it was completely ignored.

MAN'S ADDITION TO THE BEAUTY OF NATURE

We must go to a work of art to look for and to feel the emotions of art, not the emotions of nature. They are different. Nature is wonderful, marvellous, and one's head is always bowed in front of her ; but art is wonderful too. It is man's addition to the beauty of nature, to the beauty of the world, and no amount of knowledge of nature will qualify a man either to judge or to appreciate a work of art. Art is a language. To acquire an understanding of a language

2

one must give time to the study of it, and matters will be speeded up if one lives for a time in the country where it is spoken. So it is with art. Because human beings, animals, landscapes, are used in a picture the artist is not necessarily trying to imitate them. He is more likely using them as symbols to pass on an idea or experience, or possibly to recall some pleasant aspect of life, or even an unpleasant one. Goya's prison scenes and street scenes frequently remind one of unpleasant incidents, but can give great pleasure as works of art. Again, the artist may not be trying to do anything more than to excite your eye agreeably, by his arrangement of form and colour.

Of course there are those who say that the object of the artist-painter is to imitate Nature. That is absurd. One cannot imitate Nature. One cannot imitate a human being without using flesh and blood, hair and skin, and so forth. One cannot imitate a tree without using leaves and bark and other materials, neither can one imitate or suggest the life within by slavish copying. In the effort to " get nearer to Nature " one may get farther away from art.

Ruskin taught that to be able to draw a tree one must first be able to draw a leaf. It does not follow at all. An accumulation of leaves does not necessarily make a tree. A tree is one simple thing. The same may be said of a flock of sheep. It is *one* flock, not a collection of four hundred sheep. If you bother yourself because you cannot see the tufts of wool you will never get the peaceful emotion of a flock in English meadowland. If realism is needed, then Madame Tussaud's is the place to seek it and not the National Gallery.

MOOD AS THE MISTRESS IN STUDYING ART

BEFORE entering a picture gallery it is well to analyse your own mood. If you feel a longing for the country and wish your imagination to be stimulated into taking you there, confine your attention to the landscapes. By seeking the costume or architectural pictures, you may find yourself in some remote period of history. By browsing among the Primitives you may realise how deep was their conviction that Christianity was true, and also what delicious means they employed to pass on that conviction. Do not, in a portrait, seek only for a suggestion of what the sitter was like. You may find colour, form, tone, line, texture, all combined to please you. Do not try too much at a time. The capacity

for feeling and enjoying is limited, and its indulgence
fatiguing.

THE PAINTER'S REALMS OF FANCY AND DELIGHT

BROADLY speaking, the object of the artist is to stimulate
us into enjoying what he has enjoyed, or into feeling what
he has felt. We may have beliefs which he can strengthen,
or we may love nature in its many aspects and moods, and
let him remind us of them. We may wish to remember the
appearance of friends and the feelings they create for us·
With the artist we may live in times past or be carried far
from this noisy, rushing world into realms of fancy and
delight. To convey all this the painter has invented many
methods and employed many mediums. The earliest which
has directly influenced European artists is the wall painting
of Egypt.

This was more in the nature of writing and was used,
primarily, to relate the adventures and acts of the kings, and
the important events of their reigns. It was not realistic or
representational in any way, but just diagrammatic. The
King and his great officers would be identified by the emblems
they wore, but the artist told the story at some length, and in
the course of it gave an insight into the habits, customs, and
beliefs of the mass of the people. The Egyptian artist could
be representative, and portraits—chiefly carvings—do exist
which must have borne a strong resemblance to the originals.
The famous bust of Nefertite, one is sure, was " like," and
one realises that the queen was an exquisite person physically :
but there is something more, that indefinable quality which
all works of art, especially portraits, must possess if they are
to endure.

There is very little left of Greek painting, but we can conclude what it was like from Græco-Roman efforts that have
come down to us. The story told of Appelles, that the birds
tried to peck his painting of a bunch of grapes, is significant
of its development in the direction of naturalism ; and one
can believe the story when the Greeks' capacity in sculpture is
considered. But the method they employed in painting
would be very restricting. There are interesting Græco-
Roman portraits in the National Gallery which give us a very
good idea of what Greek painting was like. They are full of

character but very simple in method—almost tinted drawings compared with what has since been done. Roman painting was similar, but the purely decorative and conventional floral design was developed to a greater extent.

With the Early Christians painting became much more pictorial. To tell the story was the great desire, and the human figure became the chief and almost the only motif. In the later religious paintings a new element appeared, for frequently they contained portraits of the donors. This, combined with the invention of oil painting by the brothers Van Eyck in the early fifteenth century, led to an expansion of vision and an increase in the range of subject, and portrait painting became an important part of the painter's activities. Landscape was attempted, but mainly as a background and an accessory.

WHAT SHOULD WE ASK OF THE PORTRAIT PAINTER?

WHAT can one expect, and what should one ask for, in a painter's portrait? First, the painting should be a good piece of decoration; second, it should remind everybody who knows the original of the original; thirdly, it might possess that indefinable quality which attracts and holds, not only the friends and relatives of the sitter, but generations and generations of men. The writer was standing a short time ago in front of the *Portrait of a Sculptor* by Andrea del Sarto in the National Gallery. A man and boy, obviously father and son, came up to the picture. " There it is," said the father, " one of the most wonderful things in the world. How I love that picture! How I love that picture!" Four hundred years after it was painted. . . . Likeness did not enter into this emotion, but that strange, arresting, and living quality to which reference has been made above, did. This is portrait painting at the top.

There are those who will say: " Yes, but I don't care a scrap about this quality you make so much of. What I want is a likeness." You cannot have it *like*; it is bound to be *unlike* somewhere; and in the pursuit of " likeness" where is one to stop? Sometime ago a painter examined his sitter through opera glasses. Why not a microscope? Where is one to stop? All that ought to be attempted is to *remind*—all that can be achieved is to remind.

A human being is probably different in appearance to each one of the people who know him, and it is impossible to represent all these different aspects on one canvas or piece of paper. If the painter attempts more than a reminder, if he forces the light, and paints up to that, if he over-accents the "lines," the tones and colour of the flesh, if he exaggerates generally the traits of the sitter, the result will be something dangerously near to a caricature, and without the amusing qualities that go to making a caricature tolerable.

THE PORTRAIT THAT ANNOYS

THIS type of portrait may be effective in an exhibition but becomes irritating beyond measure when placed in an ordinary living-room. It comes out from the wall and peers over the shoulder of any one sitting underneath. It is continuously shouting, " Look at me," until one feels inclined to say, " That fellow is so insistent in his craving for attention that he annoys me beyond endurance. Let's get rid of him." The writer has known of this type of portrait being banished to lumber rooms and coal cellars, and even being burnt.

One essential of any portrait is that it should keep its place on the wall. Look back over the work of the great masters of portrait painting, and we find them quiet and low in tone, far removed from the white which is so obvious in modern exhibitions. Take Moroni, for instance ; how wonderfully he renders the personality of his sitter and yet how quiet and unassertive the portrait is. The same may be said of the others, Rembrandt, Titian, Velasquez, El Greco, Holbein, Reynolds, Gainsborough, Raeburn, Whistler, and many besides. One sees in Raeburn and Gainsborough the beginning of the exhibition influence. Their portraits are sometimes " pitched " very high but they have other qualities which enchant. Who, with any feeling for beauty at all, would be without that delicious something that a Gainsborough portrait or picture exudes ?

The art of the portrait painter deteriorated during the nineteenth century. The painter became engulfed by the great wave of prosperity that passed over England and other countries. Dazzled by the wealth around him he aspired to a social importance equal to that of his patrons, and he became commercial. There are exceptions, of course. Whistler's portrait of his mother in the Louvre and his painting of Thomas Carlyle in Glasgow are great works. But most nineteenth-century pictures lack emotional and decorative value, a fact which is clearly shown by indications in the sale-rooms to-day.

HOW THE PAINTER EXPRESSES LOVE OF HIS WORLD

NEXT in importance, or in the affections of the people, are landscapes. In these not only does the painter delight his æsthetic sense but he displays his interest in, and love of, the world in which he lives. Trees, rivers, clouds, and sky ; meadowland and hills, the brown earth, the greens of grass and hedgerow ; man in his various activities associated with them, are motifs or symbols used by the landscapist to delight the spectator. Here again the question of imitation comes in. Does anybody on earth think it possible to imitate on canvas or paper the variety of forms, tone, and colour to be observed in even the simplest outdoor scene ? Does it not occur to everyone how ridiculous it is to try and render on a few square inches of paper or canvas what nature does on so large a scale ?

One must eliminate and simplify. A tree has a distinctive shape which, broadly speaking, no other object in nature possesses. We can distinguish the ploughed field from the green meadow by the colour of the earth or grass. By a certain shape the painter states cow, house, sheep, or human figure. Of course there is more than this, for it may be necessary to suggest action in either. If the canvas is large then a bald statement of a tree may need the addition of the masses of foliage to make that particular bit of the canvas interesting. Some painters go further, and by adding dabs of paint suggest the multiplicity of leaves. There is no reason why they should not if it does not detract from the decorative effect or the æsthetic delight. The decorative effect must be placed first ; but in addition the artist will express his own interest and delight in natural scenes and objects, and try to pass it on.

Who, enclosed by four walls in a dirty, noisy, modern town, will not be refreshed to be reminded of flying clouds and their shadows on hill and plain, of the sparkle upon water, or the transparent depth of a silent pool; the hush of dawn or the mystery of twilight ? A heart must be hard indeed not to be moved by the sight of the tired ploughman and his team. Then there are perhaps the memories recalled by the solemnity of a moonrise, or the placid stillness of the dawn. All this by his manipulation of the paint the artist can suggest, but he must not forget his effect as a piece of decoration.

THE FIRST LANDSCAPES : A DECORATIVE BACKGROUND

WHEN landscape motifs first appeared, in primitive pictures, they were merely used as decorative backgrounds to figure subjects, as in the pictures by Francesca in Room 1 in the National Gallery. Later, as the painter became more skilful in the handling of his medium, they were much more realistic but still only used as backgrounds. It was the possibilities opened up by the discovery of oil painting that led to its development as a separate art. Some of the little bits of landscape in the early Dutch and Flemish pictures are exquisite. One of the earliest, treated for the landscape itself, is Patinir's (1485–1524) *Landscape : River Scene* in Room 15, National Gallery.

Later Rubens, Rembrandt and others produced great landscape pictures, and the French painter Claude made it his chief motif. The landscape with him was the main theme and the figures accessory. Look at the two pictures by him in Room 20 in the National Gallery. Was ever greater dignity and serenity displayed by such rich, glowing colour ? The art developed beautifully all over lower Western Europe. France, England, and Holland can produce a list of great names, but Italy and Spain were not so prolific. The great wave of inspiration which spread over both countries during the Renaissance seems completely to have exhausted itself by the end of the eighteenth century. England and France, however, showed virility during the greater part of the nineteenth century, though the influence of photography and commercialism had completely overwhelmed the art when the century drew to its close. To-day there is amongst the younger generation a violent reaction against this influence.

THE ART OF TELLING A STORY IN PAINT

THE art of telling a story, describing an incident, or conveying an emotion in paint by means of the human figure, or group of human figures as symbols, first appears in the East, and through Egypt was passed on to the peoples of Europe. The earliest and most interesting development was under the influence of the Byzantine kings, especially Constantine the Great (288 ?–337), when the story of the New Testament occupied men's minds and hearts.

The human figure in these early compositions is very stiff and archaic in appearance, but placed in the particular space it has to occupy in the most effective position to tell the story. Very little obvious attempt at arrangement is to be seen. When the number of figures was large, a certain amount of scheming had to be done to make the figures fit into the space they were to occupy, and certainly the shape of the outside line—whether a square, rectangle, circle, or semi-circle—would influence the direction and position of them. From this developed that elaborate art of composition, of which Rubens, perhaps, was the most memorable exponent. Stiff and still, archaic and architectural at first, one can trace the whole evolution until one arrives at the grace and movement of Rubens, who seemed to play with the human figure as a boy does with a handful of marbles. Even with him chance and accident counted for very little and there is always to be found a definite scheme on which those elaborate compositions are based.

Pictures of this kind have been painted by the great Italians and Spaniards, Titian, Michelangelo, Tintoretto, Veronese, El Greco, Velasquez, Goya; and by the Frenchmen in their delightful compositions of frivolous subjects during the eighteenth century. There are also the elaborate religious pictures of Germany, Holland, and Flanders, and the later, freer movement of Rembrandt and Hals. Even in the more homely subjects of the lesser Dutch Masters there is definite order in the placing of the figures on the canvas or panel. England has been almost sterile in this particular branch of the artist's craft, but there is a ceiling in the painted hall at Greenwich which demonstrates that Hogarth's father-in-law Thornhill was not without great ability. Hogarth himself seemed to handle masses of figures with ease, but the English painters confined themselves principally to portrait groups or single figures. We must not forget, nevertheless, that great master of drawing and composition, Rowlandson, who, on a smaller scale, handled his groups with a skill second to none.

During the nineteenth century there were many, both English and French painters, who were extremely skilful in composing an important figure subject, but the influence of the photograph, especially in England, became more and more pronounced, and the decorative aspect of a picture was forgotten and the enduring charm was gone.

SIMPLER SUBJECTS FOR THE LESSER ARTISTS

MANY artists who have found painting an interesting occupation, a fascinating one, but who realised they had not the talent for the greater themes, have occupied themselves with simpler subjects—flowers and still life, and birds and beasts. The craft of the painter was never displayed to greater advantage and beauty than by the Dutch painters of " Still Life." " Still Life " is a term applied originally to objects such as fruit, flowers, and vegetables, which have life but no mechanism, but eventually it came to include other things which are frequently associated with these, the pots and pans that hold and cook the vegetables, the vase that contains the flowers, the knives and forks and platters and things connected with the table. Every conceivable quality and texture is shown in the Dutch " Still Life " paintings ; and in some of the Dutch and Flemish flower painting there is great skill in arrangement and beauty of colour. The decorative aspect was not forgotten. By the Flemish painter Hondoecoeter the domestic fowl was used as a motif, and much beauty resulted. His pictures possessed emotional value, too, for he has been called a " great painter of motherhood." He included the chicks as well as the hens.

Some of the French painters of the eighteenth century put together large compositions of birds, landscape, and architecture with great skill and very satisfying decorative effect. Chardin with a technique that was perfect was a rare master in the simpler forms of still-life painting, as may be seen from his pictures in the National Gallery. In the later schools of France still-life subjects are an important feature ; and following the example of Cézanne and Van Gogh, the living representatives of the modern school have produced a plethora of still-life subjects.

With Cézanne and Van Gogh one feels reasonably sure that these subjects were produced when inspiration in other directions was low, but whatever the reason many beautiful works resulted, works beautiful in composition and technique. Cézanne has left numerous canvases just commenced—slight, tinted things full of charm, but the charm of water colour. Probably he never meant them to be left like this. There is one in the Stoop Bequest at the Tate Gallery which is full of " music "—a delicious " prelude "—but echoes of it are to be heard from all directions.

RACIAL TRAITS REVEALED IN PAINTING

IN the development of painting it is quite natural that racial characteristics and temperament should be displayed and should modify considerably the various forms and ways by which painters express themselves. We should expect to find the high spirits and passion of the Latin, the serious solidity of the Teuton, the unemotional complacency of the Anglo-Saxon, all modifying the appearance of the works they have produced. This has given rise to the use of the term " School " to define the painters of various nations and also groups of painters within one nation.

The " Italian School," for instance, includes many groups of painters who, in their turn, were " labelled " according to the town or district in which they worked, and where, influenced by similar circumstances and environment, the manner of their expression was naturally similar. There are the Florentine, the Venetian, the Sienese Schools, and many others, all included in the term Italian School, but each having characteristics of its own. It is often difficult to differentiate, and even the expert sometimes fails to place a particular work. It is then defined as Italian School, and when the master cannot be identified it is given the label of the local School. The term " School " used in this sense never applies to a training institution.

EARLY ART INSPIRED BY THE BIBLE

IT is impossible here to describe in detail the characteristics of the various Schools of the different countries. In Italy alone there are about twenty Schools, so one can do no more than refer to the general characteristics of the Italian School, and perhaps to a particular master as being representative of his " School." With other nations one must adopt the same course. One can only hope to stimulate a sufficient interest in the reader to impel him to seek further, when his vision may be enlarged and his life enriched.

One feature that all the early Schools of Europe had in common was their almost complete preoccupation with the story of the New Testament. Of course the Old Testament inspired much, but the early painters were chiefly interested in all that related to Jesus. That marvellous story, which has enriched the world so much not only in painting but in all the other artistic activities of man, became, until the end of the fourteenth century, almost the only theme from which painters took their inspiration. The paintings and carvings were part of the means employed by the religious and learned people of that period to pass on the story. Few people could read or write, but all could understand the painted or carved illustration ; and how wonderfully it was presented to them by those early artists, with what beauty and tenderness, and with what conviction.

GLOOM IMPOSED BY EARLY CHRISTIANITY

WHEN one says how tenderly and beautifully they rendered the story, one refers more particularly to the Early Italian painters who, towards the end of the thirteenth century, began to cast off the rigidity and grimness of Byzantine influences. To the early Christian all forms of decoration were wicked, and so when, for the sake of fixing upon the memory of his fellows the reminding images of the great actors in the story of Jesus, he consented to their representation upon the walls of his churches, their types were hard, rigid, and unyielding—stiff, gloomy, upright figures, types who never had a graceful movement, or the necessity for controlling an erring thought. The limitation of the medium, mosaic (in which small pieces of coloured glass are embedded in underlying plaster), imposed this to a certain extent, but it was also the result of the violent reaction of the early Christian from the joyous paganism of Greece and the bestial sensuousness of the later Rome.

In the placing of the figures there was no attempt at design or arrangement. There was just a certain balance and symmetry—Jesus or the Virgin in the centre, and two or more figures on the right and on the left. In the big decorations of the churches a background might possibly be patterned with very conventional trees, and here and there a symbol might be introduced, surrounded by a conventional border. This was all. The emotional aspect was violent, and certainly calculated to terrify the ignorant masses into obedience.

All through that dark and gloomy period, from about the third to the thirteenth century, very little was created either in architecture, sculpture, or painting but that it showed the influence of Byzantine thought. The Cathedral of Vezeley in France (about A.D. 1100), the decorations in mosaic at St. Vitale at Ravenna, and Santa Paolo Fuori le Mura in Rome

(A.D. 1220) all indicate their origin in Byzantium, the capital of the Empire of Constantine, the first Christian ruler. In the later period of Byzantine influence, towards the ninth and tenth centuries, there was much greater variety in the treatment of metal and the carving of ivory for the decoration of the altars ; but the same dismal presentation of the theme held sway in the mosaic and in the painted picture, until the end of the thirteenth century. See *Madonna and Child* by Duccio (1260–1399), *Jesus on the Cross* by Buonaventura (working 1305–1326), Sienese School, Room 3, National Gallery.

It was only after the teaching and the influence of St. Francis of Assisi had spread across the face of Europe that gentler and more lovable types became general. An atmosphere of loving kindness, sympathy, and understanding breathed from all the characters of the story and quiet pleading took the place of the rigid threat. *Two Apostles* by Spinello Aretino (1333–1410), Florentine School, Room 3, National Gallery, will illustrate this.

The easel picture at this period came into general use and the closer relation between the painter and his medium allowed of a far more subtle expression of the most varied and intimate feelings. Side by side with the easel picture, fresco painting for large wall decorations was carried on and developed. The character of the Italian Gothic buildings was such that large spaces were provided on walls, vaults, and ceilings for mural decoration. Great skill was necessary for this kind of painting, and the whole composition had to be very definitely fixed. A small portion of the wall was prepared, as much as could be completed in the day, and the subject was painted on the wet plaster. As the effect was entirely different when dry, it is not difficult to realise what vision and practice were necessary. Fresco painting reached its greatest period under Raphael and Michelangelo during the early sixteenth century. It gradually fell into disuse as the popularity of oil painting (invented about 1500) and of the easel picture increased.

A SAINT'S LIFE FOSTERS THE GENIUS OF GIOTTO

THE interest in St. Francis, his life and teaching, naturally developed the desire to pass on to the mass of people an account of the incidents of his life and death. This gave scope for the genius of the great Giotto. Freed from the

ecclesiastical direction which previously had ruled choice and
treatment of everything, artists now gave play to their own
imaginations and desires.   Natural objects and scenes were
brought into use to embellish the story, and to give colour to
it.   St. Francis was not far removed in time, so actual scenes
that formed the background for the events of his life could
easily be used.   There was no great display of representational
skill, proportions were wrong, and there was little attempt
at local colour ; but there was a breakaway from the conventional gold background and the rigid attitudes of the figures
of the Byzantine School, and this led to much as the century
unrolled.   Giotto died in Florence in 1337.   His greatest
work is to be found at Assisi, at Padua, and at Florence.
Contemporaneously, Duccio, Buonaventura and others, with
gifts as rare but perhaps less great, were working at Siena.

As the century developed, the influence of the Dominican
order began to make itself felt and subjects became more
complex.   Allegories and symbolic subjects on a large and
elaborate scale were undertaken.   Every conceivable motif
was included to make the story effective.   A certain capacity
for naturalistic representation began to appear, but was still
far removed from the development in more recent times.
It was a beginning, however, and the greatness, complexity,
and variety of subject, with the multiplicity of materials
employed to relate and embellish the story, led to that increase of skill in the handling of the medium which became
so marked at the beginning of the fifteenth century.

A GALAXY OF GLORIOUS NAMES

THE fifteenth century in Italy was a period of great discovery, adventure, and material prosperity.   The pomp
and ceremony of the Church and State, the luxury and
sumptuousness of the works of man, added to his increasing
consciousness of the beauty of nature, carried the painter
further and further in the direction of skilful representation.
When the fifteenth century closed he was much more concerned with the beauty of the body than of the soul within.
Think of Venice and all that pertained to it in the later fifteenth
and early sixteenth century, and it becomes easy to comprehend that wonderful company of artist painters who are the
great glory of the Venetian School.   The list of great names
includes Bellini, Crivelli, Giorgione, Titian, Palma, Carpaccio,
Tintoretto, Veronese, Moroni, Guardi, Zuccarelli, and Tiepolo.

Tiepolo died in 1769, and with him the days of great Italian painting came to an end.

The other states and cities of Italy developed along lines similar to those of Venice, with various modifications according to environment and conditions ; but no other produced that wonderful mass of sensuous beauty which goes to the make up of what we know as the Venetian School.

COOLNESS AND SOFTNESS IN FLORENTINE ART

OF all the other Schools of Italy perhaps the Florentine is the most important. Its great men had equal skill in composition and drawing, but as colourists perhaps not the same range as the Venetians. It was a different range, with a preference for colour inclining to coolness, such as rose-colour, crimson, and purple blues, while with the Venetians the range went in the direction of orange. There was also a difference in the types chosen. The Florentines favoured a softness and tenderness which was in great contrast to the fulness and vigour of the Venetian men and women.

Michelangelo, that powerful, restless, unhappy spirit, with the knowledge of a god and the power of a Titan ; Leonardo, artist, scientist, everything ; who can tell what source of knowledge, of information, these " supermen " had ? There must have been something vast flowing into the spirit of Michelangelo, some conception of the magnitude of the universe, or a knowledge of the purpose and destiny of man. There was something he could not express in spite of the wonderful command of his means. He was always troubled, always in labour, though at times he attained serenity. In the National Gallery the picture *Madonna and Child, St. John and Angels* approaches a certain brightness, and *The Entombment* is serene and calm ; but usually his figures are weighed down with the burden of their knowledge. The prophets and sibyls which go to make up the decoration of the Sistine Chapel in Rome are terrifying and overpowering. They are magnificently designed. The figures in *The Entombment*, which has already been referred to, are beautiful in drawing and modelling, and the contrasting poses most interesting. The delicate colour-scheme gives great pleasure. Michelangelo is one of the great sculptors of the world and his fame as a poet is enduring. He died in Rome in 1564.

Leonardo, like Michelangelo, was a great experimenter who sought to probe the secrets of every phenomenon, and who certainly succeeded in rendering on canvas that veiled sensuousness which gives to woman so much of her power and charm. Titian, Rubens, and others have displayed the beauty of colour and form, the softness of flesh ; Leonardo rendered that curious " something " within, more powerful than all. The picture at the National Gallery, *The Virgin of the Rocks*, is typical, but does not display his most subtle qualities. He was probably one of the greatest men the world has seen.

The Umbrian School claims Raphael, whose greatness cannot be realised outside of Italy, but whose tenderness and charm can be felt in nearly all the important galleries of the world. There is also Ucello, Cimabue, Orcagna, Angelico, Fillipo Lippi, Pesillino, Botticelli, Ghirlandaio, del Sarto, Bronzino, Perugino, Signorelli, Francesca, Baltraffio, Luini, Correggio, Tura, and a host of others, each one worthy of separate study. Examples of the work of all of these are to be found in the National Gallery, and in the Wallace Gallery. There are several lovely pictures of this School at Hampton Court Palace.

FRANCE FLAVOURS PAINTING WITH THE ESSENCE OF HER SOIL

IT has been stated that France had no indigenous school of painting until towards the end of the seventeenth century. If that is the case, if many outside ingredients went to the making of the cake, then it was highly flavoured with an essence extracted from the soil of that wonderful country. If early frescoes showed the influence of Byzantine Art and were akin to those of Florence and Siena, the early panel pictures were related to French miniatures and illuminations, and even in the frescoes there sometimes appeared a character and charm that could be given by no other nation in the world. So, for instance, the wall decorations at Avignon in the " Chambre de la Garde Robe." But even before the thirteenth century the frescoes had a simplicity of arrangement and mass, and a delicacy of colour not to be found in any other country of Europe. The French artist was more interested in the decorative aspect of his picture than in the realistic, and the flat simple treatment of masses and background continued well on into the sixteenth century, and often reappeared much later.

A very beautiful and impressive example of this treatment
is given in the Villeneuve *Pietà* now in the Louvre. All
will be able to appreciate the effectiveness of the simple
silhouette against the background, the flatness of the dark
masses and of the half tones and lights. They are not empty
by any means, but whatever modelling and drawing there is
is quite unassertive. Expression of figure, pathos of facial
expression, beauty of drawing, colour and craftmanship, all
combine to make it one of the most beautiful pictures of the
world. One cannot leave this picture without referring
especially to the " drawing " and modelling of the body of
the dead Saviour. The date of this picture is given as the
latter half of the fifteenth century.

Various reasons have been given to explain and account
for this flat and simple treatment, but there is little doubt
that the masses of carved panels that are to be found in the
cathedrals and churches in France, combined with the stained
glass, would affect the vision of the painter of pictures. Much
could be said about that wonderful stained glass and about
the impression it creates. Seldom has a group of men more
enriched the world than did those wonderful people who
produced the miracles in glass at Chartres.

FRENCH PAINTING MAKES A QUIET BEGINNING

IT is curious and interesting to observe that although the
glass gives evidence of the French artist's capacity as a
colourist, the early paintings are very quiet. An ivory tone
seems to give the key and is especially to be noticed in the
early portraits almost to the end of the sixteenth century.
Look at the group in the National Gallery and see what a
delightful portraitist is Clouet (1510–1572), how genial and
human Corneille de Lyon (1530–1575) makes his sitters.
Fouquet (1465–1480), a rare artist, and with whom the
decorative quality is of the greatest importance, was earlier.
He was an exception, perhaps, and certainly ivory could not
be said to give the key to the colour schemes of that great
colourist, Le Maitre de Moulins (working 1470). The little
picture in Room 20 of the National Gallery illustrates this,
and the more important work in the cathedral at Moulin-sur-
Allier shows other great qualities.

There is also in the same building a large picture by the
famous Ingres (1780–1867). Was ever talent employed to
produce anything more dull ? The early picture moves one

profoundly. The one of the nineteenth century produces
only yawns. It is, to begin with, very large. The figures
are all life-size. They are all posed obviously, they all do
their job with precisely the right expression and gesture,
as if they had been taught to do it at a dramatic school ; and
they are very serious about it all. The " drawing " is very
accurate, the painting very thin, and the colour limited and
respectable. There is nothing spontaneous about it and
nothing so vulgar as the indication of an impulse anywhere.
It is wholly intellectual, conceived in the brain and rendered
by the hand. Neither spirit, nor heart, nor the senses had
anything to do with its production. Ingres was a great
draughtsman but a dull painter.

Of the work of the various early groups of painters who
have been classed as Schools—the Brea School, whose pictures
are to be found at Nice, Eze, and Monaco ; the Avignon
School and the Lyon School—not much remain, and although
French traits are always there, Italian or Flemish influences
dominate and it is difficult to say that a native school of
painting really existed. Perhaps one of the most typically
French pictures of this early period is the altar-piece at
Gréolières (before 1450). Two small panels in the National
Gallery may be studied, Nos. 1302 and 1303 in Room 20.
The Wilton diptych in Room 1 is disputed, but it appears
French in character, and is certainly very beautiful.

AN OUTBURST OF ACTIVITY AMONG FRENCH PAINTERS

WITH the unfolding of the seventeenth century there was
    very great activity, but as most of the painters studied
and lived in Italy, a typically French school was not developed.
One must not, however, omit to mention Claude (1600–1682),
the great painter of classical landscapes, and Nicholas Poussin
(1594–1665) whose charming figure and landscape compositions are a delight. See Room 20, National Gallery, for
examples.

The succession to the throne of Louis XIV. and his patronage
of the arts, changed all this. The work he instigated on such
an enormous scale necessitated the employment of many
artists and craftsmen, and the whole of the talent of France
seemed to be concentrated around Versailles. The need
created the supply, and artists appeared in great numbers.
Since they were working under the same influence and with
the same motive, it was natural that a distinct style should be

evolved. This style was not so much a manifestation of the vision or inspiration of the artists as a rendering of the character and activities of the King. The vast galleries were decorated with huge representations of every conceivable subject in which the King was interested, or which would display his importance and power. Never before in the history of modern Europe had a king surrounded himself with such pomp and magnificence, and the works of the artists were wholly devoted to displaying it. The portraits, packed with all the richness of stuffs, also went to display the pomposity and self-importance of the sitters, rather than their character or charm. While these tendencies may not seem very admirable from the standpoint of to-day, they had the effect of concentrating native talent, and when Louis XIV. died the French school was fully established, and took the lead that up till then had been held by Italy.

In portraiture Rigaud (1659–1743) is perhaps most typical of this period, and Charles le Brun (1619–1690) led the way for the army of painters who executed the decorative pictures.

With the death of the King, life became less fixed and was followed more according to natural impulse and desire, rather than to forms and manners set by the Court. The aristocratic patrons went their own way and, encouraged and stimulated, artists painted according to their own taste. The reaction that took place was complete, and not only manner but scale was changed. The vastness on which everything had been conceived at Versailles was altered to an interest in the comparatively small, and the mould was complete for Watteau (1684–1721) and the Romanticist School that followed him. To this School—a School which dealt with scenes far removed from the everyday activities of life—belong Watteau, Lancret, Pater, Nattier, Fragonard, Bondur, and others. Who does not know that delicious School of the eighteenth century France which, after the formality and heaviness at Versailles, created a world of lightness, gaiety, and charm ? Masters of life, great masters of technique, these artists played with both, and the result was a delicious mélange that still delights and enchants. Fragonard died in 1806.

FRIVOLITY GIVES WAY TO SIMPLICITY

PORTRAITS of the eighteenth century reflected very much the life and manners of the time. Nattier, perhaps, led the way, followed by his stepson Louis Toque. (Picture 4679,

Room 26, National Gallery, is very typical of the period.)
There were many others, and the pastelists, Carrière and
Latour, added to the renown of the century. Towards 1780
the writings of Rousseau brought about a change in the
values of the French people. Simple people and simple
things became the chief interest, and painters, playwrights,
authors, found their success in the rendering of themes based
on the activities of the poorer classes. From being frivolous
and self-indulgent they strove to impress that it was better
to be moral and good and to walk uprightly. The response
to all this in painting was Greuze (1725–1805).

After the French Revolution the Roman republic became
the ideal, and the mantle of antiquity was over all. Roman
heroes and patriots were extolled, held up as examples and
their mighty deeds illustrated. David (1748–1825) and
Prudhon (1758–1823) led to Ingres and Delacroix and the
hosts of others who, during the middle of the nineteenth
century, were engaged either in the effort to represent a
scene or to illustrate a story. In the midst of all this there
came first, that earnest and inspired group of men, the Barbizon
School, whose chief members were Millet, Rousseau, Corot,
Diaz, Daubigny. Their work was characterised by an
acceptance of nature as a source of inspiration, and they only
modified her appearance inasmuch as it was necessitated by
the shape of the canvas or for the presentation of the scene or
incident. They were accomplished craftsmen, and although
their composition is ordered and sometimes dramatic, a deep
emotion is often rendered.

EARNESTNESS THAT FOUND OUTLET IN IMPRESSIONISM

THEN came the " Impressionists "—Manet, Monet, Degas,
Sisley, Renoir, Berthe Morrisot, and others, who again in
great earnestness took inspiration from the aspect of life and
nature around, an aspect modified by the light and colour
or atmosphere they wished to suggest. By atmosphere is not
meant " composed of oxygen, hydrogen, and nitrogen," but
the " psychic " atmosphere. The picture now in Room 21 of
the National Gallery by Manet, *The Bar at the Folies Bergères*,
illustrates what is intended. Apart from its representative
effect, one does in an amazing way very definitely feel the
whole content of the life of that exotic place of entertainment.
The picture in the same room by Renoir also conveys much.
Round about these two groups were many individualists

of distinction, Boudin, Daumier, Courbet, and others, and after them came the various groups which have resolved themselves into the bewildering mélange that exists to-day. One cannot conclude this section without some reference to the amazing fecundity of France in all that pertains to the arts. It seems that everything that has been fresh and original in painting during the last hundred years, with but a few individual exceptions, has come from that country. Other nations have followed on, but the new inspiration always seems to come to France.

THE LATE BLOSSOMING OF HOLLAND'S GENIUS

WHAT is known as the Dutch School of Painting begins at the opening of the seventeenth century. The character of whatever had existed previously had been determined by the influence of Italy, or by the direction of the Roman Catholic Church. The struggle for independence both in government and religion had occupied the minds and energies of the people so much that any need for art and any expression of it had been submerged. There are at the National Gallery, in Room 15, two little pictures of great interest. One, No. 4081, a *Nativity* by Gurtgen Tot Sint Jin (1465–1493), and the other, No. 3459, a " School " picture, *Lot and his Daughters* (1510). They show definitely the Dutch temperament and character breaking through. In the latter, one can feel a certain amount of Italian and Flemish influence, but there is in the other the Dutch character unmistakably asserting itself.

In the seventeenth century, when the Spanish domination had been cast off and there was a prospect of a period of peace and serenity, it was natural that this strong national character should show itself. It was a period of great prosperity and satisfaction for Holland. The Dutch were pleased with, and very conscious of themselves, and what more natural than that this happy state should be reflected in the work of the artists who appeared in response to the needs of the people ? The whole character of the Dutch School of painting is given by the Dutchman's interest in, and contentment with himself, his own particular bit of the earth and all that therein is, the sea that surrounds it, and the ships that ride thereon. Even the fishes of that sea must be a satisfaction to him also. Painting with him begins at home and stays at home, and all the material that goes to the making of his wonderful art he finds at home.

EARNEST CONVICTION BEAUTIFULLY EXPRESSED

THERE was one exception, and that was the great master Rembrandt. He sometimes looked further afield for a theme, into Roman History or elsewhere ; but he was never so good as when he confined himself to his own vision and experience. His rendering of religious subjects can be included as part of the result of his own experience, for frequently they are so deeply moving that his conviction of the truth of his Bible must have been very strong.

Rembrandt was a great draughtsman, a great painter, and a great etcher. He saw accurately, he felt deeply, and he painted beautifully. He missed nothing that was picturesque and beautiful in the aspect of his fellow-men. He felt and sympathised with them in their sorrows and their troubles, and he painted it all so beautifully, so subtly, that the paint disappears to leave his figures suspended in a rich, luscious atmosphere that has no beginning and no end. There they sit, thinking and brooding, knowing, understanding, a little weary perhaps, suspended in that wonderful luminous darkness into which they will presently dissolve. The picture at the Wallace Gallery, *Cornelius, the Centurion*, illustrates this well. The three figures on the right always give the writer the impression that they are about to go. The little picture in the Louvre, *The Supper at Emmaus*, must be one of the most moving in the world. The figure of Jesus just breathes tenderness and kindness, it exudes volumes of that spirit which, in spite of so much misrepresentation, has enabled His teaching to endure for two thousand years.

It is said that Rembrandt was the first to paint light ; but it would be more correct to say that he was the first to paint darkness. His lights only appear light inasmuch as they occupy a very small space amidst much dark. His lights are luminous, perhaps, but so are his darks ; so much so that all objects that normally would disappear become visible in his luminous darkness. He made his lights " sing " by contrast with his dark ; but he did not concern himself with light as some of the Impressionists did—Monet, for instance, who sometimes seemed to paint with " luminiferous ether."

In addition to his paintings, Rembrandt has left us some

fine etchings. They make any one who can appreciate the peculiar quality of the etched line almost shout with delight. There is a wonderful collection at the British Museum. Rembrandt died in poverty in 1669.

Another great artist of this period, Hals, born a little earlier, perhaps represents the spirit of his time and country more than Rembrandt. Rembrandt belongs to the world, but Hals to the Dutch School of the seventeenth century. He was essentially a portrait-painter, and with amazing dexterity he has passed on the satisfaction that his obviously prosperous sitters and he himself felt in the changed conditions of their country. He has well rendered the pomposity and self-esteem of those over-nourished merchants, masquerading in the uniforms of the arquebusiers. He can also tell us what good-humoured homely people their womenfolk were. A smiling, mischievous boy looks out from his canvas at times, or a grinning, toothless beggar; so he could be interested in poverty as well as riches. This doubtless saved him from becoming a slippery-slimy painter of likenesses to which there was a tendency later in his career.

His chief work is at Haarlem, where his skill in composition and characterisation amazes one. There is a "swagger" about these pictures that one much enjoys. He is well represented in the National Gallery, and the earlier portrait at the Wallace Gallery, *The Laughing Cavalier*, ought to be seen. "The Wizard of Haarlem," he used to be named, and it is only there one can realise his great capacity. He died in 1666.

DUTCH ARTISTS WHO LOVED THEIR NATIVE SCENERY

OUTSTANDING at this period was the Dutchman's love of the natural scenery of his country, and many and well-known are the names of those who recorded it—Van Goyen, Ruisdael, Wouwerman, Cuyp, Birchem, Potter, Van de Velde, and perhaps the greatest of all, Hobbema, who saw and rendered with a bigness of vision that was denied to the others. Vermeer must be included, but his fame as a landscapist rests on one picture, the famous *View of Delft*.

The Dutch landscapists are distinguished chiefly by their interest in the multiplicity of objects which go to the make-up of the ordinary scene. Here, as in the "genre" pictures, their technical skill tempted them to overcrowd in order to display it. ("Genre" is a name applied to the small subject pictures, usually interiors with figures. It was first applied to the Dutch " Little Masters " but became general in its application to that type of subject.) The colour scheme was limited, the russets and brown of autumn prevailing, and there is always coolness in the sky. There is no attempt to render the fresh yellow and greens of spring, nor the fullness of early summer. The form and tone is good, but the colour according to recipe. Here, again, Hobbema was different. Look at *The Avenue* in the National Gallery. Wynants also approached a green grey, and Cuyp was sometimes rich and strong.

Of the " little " Dutch Masters, Vermeer, like Rembrandt, holds a place by himself. His skill is equal to that of the others, but there is a bigness of mass, a simplicity of tone colour, and a preciousness of texture, that one can find no words to describe and with which to express one's pleasure. After him, the first place must be given to Terborch. There can be nothing more exquisite than the two portraits in Room 12 of the National Gallery. His vision was similar to Velasquez's, and his technique quite as accomplished. The face in the *Portrait of a Gentleman* is beyond criticism. Very different is Ostade, but in his rendering of Inn scenes and similar subjects he takes a high place. Teniers and Jan Steen also were masters, and Maes and Fabritius, Gerrard Dou and Mieris contained something " common," but their dexterity was amazing.

Belonging to this class, but whose pictures were more in the nature of " conversation " portraits, were Dirk Hals, Duyster, De Kuyser, Codde, and others. Honthorst, not quite in the highest rank, but near, is very moving in his picture of *Jesus before Pilate* in the National Gallery. It is difficult to place De Hooch. Although he painted large pictures, the greater number come between those with " lifesize " figures and the very small. He is somewhat of an individualist, although he could belong to no other School. His interiors of well-kept houses, with pleasant, kindly people placed exactly where they ought to be and dressed in velvets of black and crimson-red ; his tidy courtyards in sunlight and shadow, with red bricks or whitewashed walls, could be associated with no other country. Lacking the brilliance of touch of his contemporaries, he more than compensates by his rich transparent colour and his quality of light.

In marine painting there are many names that are famous. Vlieger, Van de Velde the Elder, Bakhuysen, Van de Velde the Younger, and Van de Cappelle. Here again is astonishing technical skill. There is nothing more difficult than to give the " airiness " and softness, the depth of a morning sky, but these artists did it beautifully. Van de Cappelle's skies are full of loveliness, sometimes almost unbearably so. The colour was limited, confined to browns and umbers, with nothing stronger than a tender yellow or gold in the sky. As a colourist in the Dutch School, Cuyp was an exception. His range was far greater and stronger, and he must have been one of the first to attempt to paint light itself. He is perhaps a connecting link between Rembrandt's " light " and the later French " Impressionists." Rembrandt's light is still ; Cuyp's moves ; it steals quietly over the landscape and figures. In the " Impressionists " it " buzzes " around everything.

We cannot wander into the Dutch Rooms of the National Gallery without being attracted by the still-life and the flower paintings. They also are characterised by a beauty of craftmanship that has never been excelled. The paintings by Heem, Treck, Van Os, Heda, and Kalf well repay attention. As a painter of the domestic fowl and chicken and other picturesque birds, Hondecoeter charms us. All these artists lived and worked in the seventeenth century ; they conferred glory on Holland, and left a great heritage for the whole world. At the end of the century the inspiration had exhausted itself. In the latter half of the nineteenth century there was another throb, and Josef Israels and the brothers Maris were not unworthy representatives of the Dutch School and of their great predecessors.

THE HEYDAY OF FLEMISH PAINTING

ALTHOUGH the churches and other ecclesiastical buildings of Flanders, down to the tenth century, must have been decorated with paintings and mosaics, nothing seems to have remained. Therefore, to understand the wonderful Flemish primitives one must refer to the miniaturists or the makers of the illuminated manuscripts in which Flanders is so rich, and without a knowledge of which the painting of the early Flemings must be quite incomprehensible in its technical skill. Simply explained, the illuminated manuscripts are illustrated manuscripts, and the earliest examples in Europe

2. DECORATED LETTERS WHICH INFLUENCED
FLEMISH ART

Examples of Celtic and early Flemish initial letters. Later, as the skill of the artists increased, the initial became simple and plain while the decoration was elaborated into exquisite miniature paintings, of which the influence may be traced in the early work of the Van Eycks.

are the Bibles and Gospels and works dealing with Church History.

In the earlier examples the greatest skill and care was bestowed upon the initial letters, and the decorations consisted entirely of conventional floral ornament, Celtic or Romanesque in type. Later, the spaces between the limbs of the initial letters were occupied with figures, ill drawn and Byzantine in character. Finally, as the skill of the artist increased, the letters were left as simple initials, and elaborate miniature paintings occupied spaces in the text. There are many beautiful specimens to be seen at the British Museum. By the end of the fifteenth century the art had arrived at a state of great perfection. In composition the spacing, the drawing and expression were excellent, and so advanced was the representational skill that its real object had been forgotten.

There is evidence that the practice of panel painting had

been carried on concurrently with illuminating since the thirteenth century, and by the end of the fourteenth century works of much beauty and skill were produced. Two shutters of a reredos by Melchior Broederlaus (completed 1399) are in the Museum at Dijon. The composition is excellent. The balance between architecture, landscape, and figure, perfect. The figures are graceful and the draperies beautifully cast. Although the work is delicate the emotional effect is great.

TWO BROTHERS WHO CARRIED OIL PAINTING TO PERFECTION

As inheritors of this tradition came the Van Eycks, who are said to have invented oil painting, and who certainly were the first to carry it to perfection—Hubert Van Eyck, born between 1370 and 1380, and Jan Van Eyck, born between 1380 and 1390. Their names are great in the history of Art, and their work epitomises all that is great and best in early Flemish painting. The picture *The Adoration of the Lamb* in the church of St. Bavon, at Ghent, displays the work of both. Hubert is said to have been responsible for the composition, but only partly for the execution. He died before it was finished and Jan completed it. It is wholly perfect in execution, but certain figures and groups of figures show a devotional aspect which is absent from the later work of Jan, and therefore they are with every probability given to Hubert. The famous picture of the *Three Maries at the Sepulchre* in Sir Herbert Cook's collection is generally admitted to be by Hubert. There is an imaginative quality and artistry in the treatment of the landscape that is not often found in early Flemish pictures.

The painters of the early Flemish school are characterised by an intense earnestness in the presentation of the subject, combined with a technical skill that is marvellous, but there is little evidence of any imaginative capacity. They are completely contented with, and interested in, their surroundings. Satisfied that nothing can be better than their comfortable interiors, and that the landscape at hand needs no arranging, they settle down to render them as well they know how. In portraiture it is the same. In Jan Van Eyck's famous picture, *Jan Arnolfini and His Wife*, in the National Gallery, there is the man on the left and the woman on the right, and the very comfortable room for a background. The artist decided to paint them like that, and proceeded to do so with no further bother, but the result is perfection.

An artist of great merit and perfection of representational skill, and with great charm, was Rogier Van Der Weyden. There were also Campin, Dierick Bouts, Memlinc, Christus, Van der Goes, and later Matsys and Mabuse, Ghuraert, Gerard David, and Bosch. They all so obviously belong to the same School that little need be said of them individually. They each added a flavour to the canvas they worked on, but brought about no change and were in no sense innovators. They can all be studied in Room 15 at the National Gallery, and in the *Adoration of the Kings*, by Mabuse, the latest development of the style can be seen. This is a picture that creates wonder but no affection, and the skill with which all the accessories are represented tends to irritate instead of delight. It may almost be said, in fact, that the figures in these pictures are merely used to hang the draperies on, and to surround with elaborate architecture or landscape, in order that the painter may show his skill. Memlinc is an exception, for there is in his work a tenderness and a sweetness that is above mere skill.

It is difficult to associate Breughel with any School. He is alone. A craftsman, a draughtsman, he was somewhat of an illustrator rather than a painter, and to emphasise his story he tended to caricature. A caricaturist in paint, perhaps, but a colourist. There is no caricature, however, in his treatment of landscape, which was impelled by a love and understanding that is unique in his period. He was born in 1525 and even he, as was the custom of his time, travelled in Italy. Italian influence had no visible effect on him, but it was responsible for the change in the Flemish style of painting after the sixteenth century and the fusion of the two produced that great wonder of the world, Rubens.

AN ARTIST WHO EXCELLED IN EVERY ASPECT

BORN in 1577, Rubens inherited all that was great from his fellow-countrymen, and he acquired by his seven or eight years of study and labour in Italy all that was rare and wonderful in the Italians. His work represents a remarkable fusion of the best of the two nations. He is so accomplished, so great, that it is almost presumption to talk about him. In every aspect of the artist's work he excelled. Drawing, tone, colour, composition, quality, characterisation, sentiment, he possessed all. Perhaps there is a lack of spiritual emotion, but one does find occasionally in his pictures great depth of feeling. His canvases, frequently of enormous size, teem with figures in every conceivable position, and all rendered with no sign of effort at all. He seemed to play with the human figure as a juggler plays with his knives, and he plays with his medium in the same way. The fat Silenus is changed from rolls of greasy flesh to a mass of luscious paint, and the bulky Sabine women to the ripe peach or mother-of-pearl.

In landscape, the rear trees or rocks, the patterned middle distances, the blue of hills and the varied sky are all rendered with the same ease and beauty. Rubens died in 1640. His pictures are to be seen, one might say, " Everywhere ! " There is an interesting portrait of himself at Windsor.

The genius of Rubens somewhat overshadows that of Vandyck, who was almost as prolific and perhaps as accomplished. He lacks in vigour, but makes up in charm and devotional feeling. A pupil of Rubens, in his draughtsmanship and in his handling of his medium he was the equal of the older man, and possibly as a portraitist he was superior. One cannot conceive of anything more perfect than his portraits of the Italian and English aristocracy. He is well represented at the National Gallery, and his portraits are to be found in nearly all the big collections in England. At Wilton they are numerous and important, but there are indications that even in the seventeenth century the portrait painter did too much and allowed his vision to be obscured by the vanity of his patrons. Vandyck died in London in 1641. A contemporary was Jordaens, whose work retained its Flemish character, but which was later modified by the influence of Rubens. With a fluency and beauty of technique he treated a large range of subjects. Evidently a " bon viveur," his pictures display his interest and delight in the more material side of life, as well as his independence of character.

Of a different type, but one of the most gifted of the Flemish School, is Adrien Brower. His small pictures of village life, of tavern scenes, festivities, orgies, dancings, quarrels, and of every sordid activity of which his rustic compatriots were capable are rendered with such a freedom of touch and such a sparkle of light and colour that one ignores the squalor of the scene in the beauty of the paint. There is an example in Room 10 of the National Gallery. David Teniers, also a painter-in-small of peasant subjects, which he treated from a more wholesome and homely point of view, was of great fame at one time, but he seems lately to have become almost obscure.

Of Still Life painters perhaps De Heems was the most eminent, and Jan Liberechts was the best of the landscapists. The architectural subjects of Neeffs are full of interest technically. Examples of all these are to be found in the National Gallery.

The eighteenth century was sterile and one finds it difficult to name a Flemish painter of outstanding merit and individuality. There was skill in abundance, but all inspiration was gone. The pseudo-classicalism of the French painter, David, ushered in the nineteenth century. This waned, and in the middle of the century a movement in the direction of Romanticism was led by Wappers. Stevens, Leys, and Wauters, whose works one had heard spoken of with praise, were influenced by, or succumbed to, the commerical spirit that prevailed at this time in Belgium, as elsewhere.

DRAMA AND FIDELITY IN THE SPANISH SCHOOL

EARLY Spanish painting followed much the same course as early painting in other countries. The political situation prevented its free development, and the complete domination of the Church determined its character. There was the same effort to pass on to the people the Christian story, but in Spain the illustration was designed with much greater force and dramatic power than in any other country, even in Italy. There must be no missing the point of the story, and the parts taken and played by the actors must be definitely suggested by the types selected. The result was a certain crude realism, a certain photographic quality even in the religious pictures. There is evidence that in some cases the early artist clothed his subject with a mystic beauty of his own, and the few remains of mural paintings illustrate this. Figures, stiff in attitude, angular in pattern, and flat in tone, but with a delicacy and sweetness of colour, show a strong relationship with Cimabue and Orcagna. See *The Crucifixion* in Room 18 in the National Gallery.

During the fifteenth century the influence was entirely Flemish. Jan Van Eyck had visited Madrid about 1428, and great interest was aroused in the works of the Flemish painters. Pictures of this period and later followed very much the pattern of the Flemish school. The same interest in accessories and surroundings, almost the same skill in presenting them was there. See *Adoration of the Magi*, by an unknown artist, in Room 18 of the National Gallery. Towards the end of the century national characteristics began to assert themselves, and there is a departure from Flemish influence. During the sixteenth century it became the custom for Spanish painters to study in Italy, and the result was the largeness of composition and handling of Italy used to present unmistakable Spanish types. There are numerous painters of this period whose work can be studied at the Prado in Madrid, but they are only interesting as forming the matrix from which the great masters sprang. One of the few names of this century that is widely known is Morales. He died in 1586. There is a small picture by him in the National Gallery.

The sixteenth century is accented by the fame of El Greco. Now one of the most famous artists of the world, he was until recent years very little known, at any rate in England. Although individuals have succumbed to his influence from time to time, it seems to have needed the " modern movement " to enable his peculiar genius to be appreciated. Gautier, in his *Voyage en Espagne*, which took place in 1840, says, " Few pictures have interested me so much as those by Greco, for the worst of them have always something unexpected and impossible which surprises us and makes us dream and ponder." There, it seems, is the great quality of Greco. He makes us dream and ponder. We may not like him but we cannot pass him by. That is art at the top.

Born in Crete in 1545, he is supposed to have been a pupil of Titian. He migrated to Spain and lived in Toledo where he spent the rest of his life in trying to demonstrate that he owed nothing to Titian's influence. The picture in the National Gallery, No. 1457, certainly has a strong flavour of Venice, but the various Greco types already appear, and in the *Agony in the Garden* Venice is forgotten.

It is a strange juxtaposition that of Greco and Velasquez at the beginning of the sixteenth century. The latter was probably the greatest realist of the world of painters, and Greco the greatest mystic. The one was concerned wholly with the aspect without, the other profoundly moved by the life and turmoil within. Velasquez employed the very perfection of technical skill to render the formal life that he saw. Greco, with similar skill, was driven to distraction in his efforts to express the cravings and longings, the doubts and uncertainties and the agonies, that we feel in our experiences of life.

All those curious distortions, expressions, elongations; those twists and twirls, those dramatic skies and restless rocks, are manifestations of his consciousness that man is a troubled spirit. His attitude is the same when he is a portraitist. The sitters of Velasquez are unemotional automatons, those of Greco have lived and thought and suffered and doubted, and the portraits show it. Here is the very quintessence of portrait painting. " A madman," some will say on seeing his pictures for the first time. May he not be extra sane ? Very little is known about his life, which is to be regretted.

PORTRAITURE UNTROUBLED BY IMAGINATION

How different was Velasquez ! Here is the courtier painting, an artist interested only in the life of the Court. Those impassive beings who look as if they never felt, and who certainly never showed a human emotion ; who never walked, but seem as if they were pushed along on little trolleys —marvellously he has sent them down to us. Even his soldiers and sailors have no impulses ; they never rush into the fight, but always walk with measured tread. The children, poor little things, have never romped ; from the first they must have been told to behave with dignity. Velasquez lived so much at the Court that his attitude appears to have become as fixed and immovable as that of Philip IV. himself. His manners are perfect and his technique is perfect. He applies his paint as he regulates his life—perfectly, and that is all there is to be said about it. He sees exactly what there is to be done and he knows how to do it. There is no imagination to bother him and suggest that it might be better this way or that. His subject is there, in front of him, and he paints it as skilfully as he painted masses of still-life in his early days, and just as unemotionally. Even in the picture in the National Gallery, *Christ at the Column*, there is no emotion. Technically it is superb, but emotionally it does not count at all. Landscape seems to move him more.

The same remark might almost apply to *The Dead Christ*, by Ribera, in Room 18, but there is certainly more emotion, and the painting is richer and more dramatic. Ribera worked in Italy for a considerable time and the strong light and shade

that is usual in his pictures reminds one of Caravaggio. He
seems to have a stronger sense of colour than most of his
contemporaries. Zurbaran's pictures, for instance, are
almost black and white. This is strange, for the pictures of
the fifteenth century were very bright and beautiful in colour,
and there were Titians in abundance to be seen. Possibly
this restraint in the use of colour was owing to the influence
of the gloomy Court by whom the painters of the early
sixteenth century were employed. Again, the political condition of the country would not tend to brightness and gaiety
in the hearts of the painters or of the people. Even Mazo,
the son-in-law of Velasquez, experimented little with colour,
although he was the one artist of this period to paint landscape for its own sake. He did it beautifully and in a spirit
almost modern. His treatment of foliage almost anticipates
Corot.

Valdés (1500–1541), Leal (1630–1691), and Murillo (1617–
1682), who were contemporaries, inspired a little more warmth
and glow into their pictures, and that may account for the
popularity of Murillo. Murillo's pictures have a warmth, a
tenderness, and an intimacy that would be very endearing,
after the aloofness of his immediate predecessors. There is
a sentimentality in his religious pictures that is insipid ; but
we must succumb to the charm of his beggar children, his
smiling boys and girls, and all his renderings of the people
from whom he had sprung. There were other painters
during the seventeenth century, but no one of great importance, and the mass of uninspired religious pictures that were
produced is wearisome.

GENIUS THAT LIT UP A DIM AND STERILE AGE

THE eighteenth century is distinguished by the circumstance
that it produced Goya. Nature is very strange. In a
period of almost complete sterility she suddenly demonstrates that the qualities that go to the making of a great
artist are still in existence. One of the greatest artists of
Spain and one of the rarest in the world, Goya possessed
sufficient inspiration to equip a dozen. He had every necessary quality. A great command of his medium enabled him
to express every conceivable emotion to which humanity is
subject. He was gay and sparkling, dramatic and sordid. He
could render with equal skill and beauty a " fête-champêtre "
or a squalid street scene ; the village fair, or the gloom of a

prison cell. His paintings of *The Maja Nude* and *The Maja Clothed* (Prada gallery, Madrid) are among the most beautiful and famous in the world. His portraits rank very high. Who does not know the type of man that Dr. Peral was? (Room 17, National Gallery.) His colour is light and delicate, as is his quality of paint, and it gives continual delight and pleasure. His etchings of prison scenes and other sordid subjects are very celebrated.

In the nineteenth century interest in Spanish painting was sustained by Fortuny, Madrazo, Pradrilla, but of greater fame and more typically of his country is Ignacio Zuloaga. He has much of the force of El Greco but he lacks the charm which, in the earlier artist, is present even in gruesome subjects.

THE STORY OF PAINTING IN ENGLAND

WHERE does painting in England begin? Probably down the centuries where its architecture began, but one seeks in vain in the galleries for specimens earlier than the sixteenth century. In the Victoria and Albert Museum, London, there is an altar-piece in tempera which is early fourteenth century, and scattered over the country there are the remains of wall paintings in more or less good condition. The one in Canterbury Cathedral in St. Anselm's Chapel, of St. Paul and the Viper, and another in Winchester Cathedral in the Chapel of the Holy Sepulchre, well indicate that Byzantine influence was general in England during the thirteenth century. There was much activity at this time, for Henry III. was interested in the arts. St. Albans was a great centre, and artists went from there to many parts of the country.

One of the most important examples of late thirteenth-century work is on the wall of the Bishop's Chapel at Chichester, a Virgin and Child enclosed in a quatrefoil. The arrangement, drawing, and sentiment are exquisite, and it would be difficult to find greater charm in any work of this period, or of any other for that matter. Coming to the late fourteenth century there is the panel-portrait of Richard II to be seen in Westminster Abbey, and the altarpiece in Norwich Cathedral, about 1400, representing scenes from the Passion of Jesus. This also is a panel painting, and shows that English artists were not much behind their continental brethren.

3

There are not a great many panel-paintings left, and the few that we have must have been used for the decoration of church furniture. In East Anglia there are several rood-screens with paintings in more or less good condition, but they frequently show distinct Flemish influence. One feature that is interesting is the expressiveness of the hands. They are crudely drawn, but very expressive. The most interesting remains of the fifteenth century, however, are the series of wall-paintings in Eton College Chapel, which are supposed to have been executed between 1479–1488. There is a breadth of conception and execution, an understanding of the beauty of mass and of line, which makes them quite the most important examples we have of the capacity of the English artist of the Middle Ages. In the beginning of the sixteenth century there were numerous portraits of kings on panels. The Richard III at Windsor shows the efforts artists were making to get away from the stiffness of previous periods. The king is removing a ring from his finger, and the action is very well rendered.

The destruction that followed the Reformation in 1534, and that later took place during and after the Civil War is very much to be deplored. There is evidence that great numbers of paintings were destroyed—paintings which would have allowed us to form an opinion of native work, which is quite impossible now. From the arrival of Holbein in 1526, foreign influence dominated, at any rate until Hogarth (1697–1764) came upon the scene. Thornhill had considerable talent, and Highmore also, but Hogarth may be said to be the first outstanding genius of the English School.

BEAUTY PRODUCED WITH A MORAL PURPOSE

A GREAT painter, his work adds much to the beauty of life. A large proportion of it, moreover, was produced with a moral purpose. He created numberless engravings and pictures and spread them abroad with the sole desire of doing what he could to arrest the volume of bestiality and corruption that must have been prevalent in his day. The series of pictures at the Tate Gallery entitled *Marriage à la Mode* and those at the Soane Museum, 16 Lincoln's Inn Fields, London, *The Rake's Progress* and *The Election* show his talent as an artist and a satirist. The moral purpose is to be found in them all, but it never detracts from the artistry. In each one, especially in the *Election* series, it is the sparkle of the colour, the light and shade, and the variety of incident and form that attract and holds one's attention. In *The Entertainment*—No. 1 of the *Election* series—the colour is as bright and gay as a bunch of flowers. It is only when we concentrate our attention on the meaning of it that we realise the nastiness of the incidents and the sordidness of the types. It is the same with them all. The paint sparkles, the colour scintillates and the " line " moves. At the Dulwich Gallery there is a picture by him entitled *Fishing* which is full of lightness and charm. At the National Gallery one can also realise his power and individuality as a portraitist. *The Shrimp Girl* is astonishing, for Manet did nothing more modern.

Hogarth could hardly be said to have founded a School. Contemporary with him was a group of painters of distinct individuality, with whose development he had nothing to do, and with whose work he probably had little sympathy. They might perhaps be named landscape-portraitists. Their pictures, full of charm and naïveté, representing the English gentleman in the midst of his rural possessions, and in all his air of self satisfaction, are just beginning to arouse interest. Room 5 at the Tate Gallery now contains many of them. Wootton, Stubbs, Wheatley, are painters of this class ; and perhaps that erratic genius Morland can be placed with them, although his talent was so individual that he cannot be said to belong to a group. Like the others, however, he was typically English. Reynolds, Gainsborough, Raeburn, Romney, Hoppner, Lawrence, are names known to all, and no mention of the English School can be made but visions of pictures by them arise.

GRACEFUL PORTRAITS OF A CULTURED AGE

IN the latter half of the eighteenth century the prosperity of England was rising rapidly. Wit, beauty, wealth, was met everywhere : and learning was abroad in the land. The aristocrat frequently had more than a smattering of culture and the wealthy merchant assumed it. Conscious of, and pleased with themselves, what more natural than that they should wish to perpetuate their appearance ? The painters responded wonderfully to the need. Reynolds rendered all that was solid and substantial : Gainsborough all that was light and full of grace. How they made the canvas live ! Gainsborough, however, was far more than a portraitist. He was a creator, and a new order of beings and a new world arose from the play of his fancy and his brush. A great landscapist also, he added to everything an essence of his own. His women not only suggest the quality of human flowers but one can almost detect the scent they exude. His touches, also, were light as petals ready to be dispersed and scattered by the first breath of wind.

Towards the close of the eighteenth century, there appeared the strange individual William Blake. He might almost be called the Greco of the English School, though he was even more a mystic than was the Spaniard. Poet, prophet, painter, he lived more in the other world than in this. Vividly conscious of its existence and of all its existence signified, he tried by every means at his command to bring home to man his blindness. It is difficult for us to place him artistically, for we have no standard for this type of artist, but there can be no doubt that he had in great volume the rarest and greatest qualities that an artist can possess. Technically his paintings are perfect. His colour is beautiful, and his design expressive. His drawings, which are far the most important of his works, by simple and direct means leave on our spirits just that feeling of concern and apprehension that he was so anxious to convey. We may not like them, but we cannot, if we are observant and thinking beings, pass them by without asking ourselves what a phenomenon like William Blake indicates for us. He died in 1827.

ENGLAND'S BEAUTY IN WATER-COLOUR AND OILS

INCLUDED in one's conception of the English School are the landscapes of this period. Essentially a native growth, they include work by Gainsborough, Wilson, Constable, Turner, and by a School within a School—Crome and Cotman, and one or two others at Norwich. Wilson possessed much that he brought from Italy, but even in the most classical of his compositions there is a freshness and coolness of atmosphere that can belong to nowhere but England. Turner all must know as one of the great geniuses of the world, but the importance and capacity of Constable is not of such general knowledge. One cannot help but think that he was the first to make his studies " right up to nature," to compare them in tone and colour with nature. Previously, the artist had made pencil drawings and colour notes, and the picture was painted in the studio. Constable changed this, as his numerous painted sketches show. A wonderful craftsman, his pictures are so charged with all that is fresh and clean in nature, that in front of them we are almost impelled to take off our hats to let the wind blow in our hair. It was this aspect of them that so impressed and influenced the French painters in Paris in 1824. Bonington also was of great repute in France.

David Cox, who was later, had qualities which were very English. He was essentially what could be called a pastoral-painter. His subjects were almost entirely confined to the most lovable aspect of English and Welsh landscapes—the edge of the forest with lazy cattle ; the wind-swept common, with one or two " battling " figures ; the haymakers ; the cornfield and the gleaners ; and similar subjects. Both in his water colours and oils there is an " airiness " which is pleasant. His touch was light and free and his colour tends to the ochres and delicate blues and greys, with spots of positive colours on the figures. Remove the pleasant memories that his pictures evoke and there is little left, but all the same it is good to have them. He was born at Birmingham and many of his pictures are to be seen in the Art Gallery of that city. *The Vale of Clwyd* is perhaps the best known of his works.

TURNER : A MASTER AT THE AGE OF TWELVE

TURNER, born in 1775, was one of the greatest artists and one of the most precocious. At the age of twelve he could be said to have been almost a master. A discerning and benevolent gentleman by the name of Dr. Munro gave opportunity to several boys of talent to draw at his house two evenings a week from drawings he provided. Turner from the first displayed understanding. There are in existence many of his drawings of this early period, and we can see how, by altering the arrangement, adding something, taking away something, he invariably improved the composition. The variety and number of his works is prodigious. His paintings and drawings are to be found in almost every collection, private and public, in the British Isles. There are sufficient in the National Collection to make a dozen reputations. He must have worked unceasingly from the age of twelve to seventy-five.

Turner's work falls naturally into three periods. In the first, which lasted until about 1802 he painted mainly in water colour and adhered more or less faithfully to the natural appearance of his subjects. At this time he used to tour the country making water-colour drawings of some of England's big estates and selling them to the owners. In this way he not only earned a reasonable living but laid the foundations of his later fame.

In 1799, at the age of 24, he became an Associate of the Royal Academy and by 1803 had painted his first big oil picture. This work *Calais Pier* (in the National Gallery, London) marks the beginning of his second period. The pictures of this time are darker, less delicate and perhaps more vigorous than those of his later life. Outstanding works in this manner are : *Sun rising through Vapour* (1807), *Dido Building Carthage* and *Crossing the Brook*. All three may be seen in the National Gallery, London.

From 1820 until his death in 1851 Turner worked ceaselessly producing pictures which seem to vie with one another in the brilliance with which they depict sunset, storm, evening, morning and nature in all her many aspects. In this period his style reached its full maturity, as may be seen from his *Ulysses Deriding Polyphemus* (1829), his *Fighting Téméraire being Towed to her Last Berth* (1839) and in many other paintings to be found in the National Gallery.

During his lifetime Turner found an enthusiastic admirer and warm advocate in John Ruskin, the critic, and after his death the work he bequeathed to the nation was given to Ruskin to catalogue and arrange.

Turner's memory was amazing and he appears to have been able to " revisualise " everything he had ever seen, even to the smallest detail. He could do anything with his medium, either in oils or water-colours. Some of his larger " subject " pictures are a little like transformation scenes in a pantomime, and they are not in much esteem to-day ; but in his work one can find all the qualities of " vision " and " paint " that are so much appreciated to-day. His later pictures anticipate much that is being done now. They are very definitely " abstract " and with qualities of pigment and colour that are not approached in modern painting. His pencil drawings of architecture, and the small water-colour " notes " done on his travels abroad, are amongst the most interesting of his works. He died in 1851.

Contemporary with Turner was Thomas Girtin. As boys they worked together at Dr. Monro's house and developed along similar lines. Girtin's water-colours of landscape and architectural subjects are perfect in every way, and English art lost much when he died in 1802, aged only twenty-seven years. Turner appreciated his talent so highly he is reported to have said : " If Tom Girtin had lived, I should have starved." There are drawings by him at the Victoria and Albert Museum, at the Tate Gallery, and at the British Museum.

Looking back over the nineteenth century one must conclude that from the beginning of the second third, painting began to decline in England. The rise of the merchant class, its wealth and power and its ignorance in all matters pertaining to art, had a destructive effect ; and all that promise brought over from the eighteenth century was rapidly destroyed.

ART ENGULFED BY A WAVE OF COMMERCIALISM

ROUND about the eighteen-fifties a group of very earnest young men, " The Pre-Raphaelite Brotherhood," consisting of Rossetti, Millais, Ford Madox Brown, Holman Hunt, Burne-Jones and others made a very serious effort to put life into the failing art. But the movement was soon engulfed and absorbed by the wave of commercialism that flowed everywhere. The Brotherhood professed to be inspired by the spirit that produced the works of the painters before Raphael's time, but while there is every evidence of their earnestness, there is very little of any inspiration. The effort to render slavishly the multiplicity of detail in nature (quite impossible anyhow), does not necessarily produce a beautiful result. The work of the Pre-Raphaelites tended to be harsh in tone and crude in colour and one would invariably prefer nature itself. Rossetti was an exception and one can get a great deal of pleasure from his luscious, sensuous colour. He was a great colourist at a time when the colour sense seemed dead. G. F. Watts also held aloof, and did much to create a higher standard among his contemporaries. Certainly there was nothing commercial about him, but his work was so much inspired by the Venetian School that it could hardly be classed as English at all. Madox Brown's pictures entitled *Work* and *The Last of England* have also withstood the test of time and are still within the compass of general appreciation.

WAS WHISTLER OF THE ENGLISH SCHOOL?

THIS is a question one asks about Whistler : " Was he of the English School ? " In spite of his own objection to being considered British, if one can claim him much distinction is added to the English School in the latter half of the nineteenth century. Modified by his appreciation of the decorative aspect of Chinese and Japanese Art, his pictures have a charm and delicacy of colour and a balance of composition that is very rare. He sees everything through a veil of tender haze, and renders it with an enchanted brush. The barge on the river becomes a dragon fly's wing, and the chimney by its side, as he himself said, a campanile In his portraits there is strength and a sympathetic understanding of the character of the sitter, all rendered by the most consummate technical skill. He was also one of the greatest etchers of the world. Perhaps his pictures in the Tate Gallery look a little faded compared with the robust and somewhat harsh painting of to-day, but when one thinks of the period in which they were produced, and of the influences by which he was surrounded, one must admit him to have been a rare artist and a great man.

Mason, Walker, Pinwell, were famous in the 'sixties and 'seventies. Mason, with his gentle poetical rendering of English rural life, will one day receive more acknowledgment as a poet and painter. The reputation of the others will rest with the water-colourists and illustrators.

PAINTERS WHO USURPED THE RÔLE OF THE WRITER

OF the many popular painters of the latter half of the nineteenth century it is difficult to say much. It saddens. There was any amount of talent but it seems all to have been diverted into the wrong channel. The pictures were almost invariably " literary " : that is, the subjects could nearly always have been rendered by words quite as effectively as by paint. The painters of this period encroached upon the domain of the writer. They told a story. There was the sad story of the sick child and the doctor watching by the bedside. There was the lovesick maiden and her departing lover. There was the Lady of Shalot whom Tennyson had already effectively described. There was the picture of the sea—rugged grey rocks and rolling green waves, waves so heavy and ponderous that they looked as if they would " roll " out of the frames and swamp the rooms in which the pictures were placed.

The literary interest dominates all those popular Victorian painters—Landseer, Frith Royston, Leighton, Fildes and the others. A striking exception in this period was Alfred Stevens, who was an accomplished painter and draughtsman. His portrait of Mrs. Collman in the English Room of the National Gallery is second to none. He also produced very successful wall decorations. In this particular branch of the artist's calling, Brangwyn was very successful and his fame spread even to the East. In Japan he is much esteemed. And this brings us to Augustus John, whose large frieze in the Tate Gallery suggests his ability in this direction.

John is the one artist of our time whose genius was of sufficient volume to enable him to rank with the great artists of the world ; but unfortunately he seems much more interested in the talent of others than in developing his own. The War picture for the Canadian Government gave an earnest of his capacity in dealing with a great subject ; but now he appears to be obsessed by the lure of " studies," still-life and portrait heads. He is a great craftsman, a great draughtsman, a great artist ; but one may wish that he would look up for his standard instead of down. There were others of this period, the end of the nineteenth and the early twentieth century, who sustained the credit of English painting : the group that was launched by the New English Art Club —Steer, Sickert, Tonks, and others. Orpen had great qualities but succumbed to success. Innes, that rare phenomenon an innovator, came very near to founding a School, and in spite of an all too brief career, certainly founded an enduring reputation. The Glasgow School did much for English reputation on the Continent.

GERMAN ART PASSES FROM BEAUTY TO BEAUTY

ALL that has been said with reference to the development of painting in Italy up to the fourteenth century applies to Germany also, and during that century a similar development took place. Cologne, the city and home of the great German mystics, became the centre of German painting. The teaching and spirit of St. Francis was carried on and spread by Suso and it affected very much the types portrayed in the pictures. The Madonna, from being a cold and unemotional matron, now became a youthful and gentle Virgin and all her attendants sweet and simple maidens. The apostles and the saints also are benign and good and there is nothing of the hardness and severity that was to be seen earlier, nor the harshness and ugliness that appeared in later pictures.

The actual creator of this style was Herman Wynrich, who worked in Cologne from 1390–1413, and is the so-styled " master of the Altar of Mary," the altar of Mary being in the Cathedral. Picture No. 3662 in Room 19 of the National Gallery, while still displaying Byzantine influence, illustrates very well the beginning of the change of type. No. 705 in the same room, *Three Saints* by Stephen Lockner, shows the influence carried on to a very much later period, 1451. There is a charming Virgin and Child by him at Munich, with the same simple little type for Mary, but there is a great advance in the surroundings; angels play and disport themselves, some in the midst of a border of flowers, and others float in the air behind the Virgin's head. In the upper left hand corner is a very genial God the Father, and opposite, the Holy Ghost in the form of the Dove. Draperies are well cast; Mary wears a very elaborate and bejewelled crown, and the whole is rendered with considerable care and skill.

THE GERMAN PAINTERS' MASTERY OF COLOUR

ANOTHER picture in the National Gallery, No. 252, by the " Master of Werden " is interesting as illustrating the different quality arrived at by the German artist. Compare the landscape background with that of an Italian artist of the same date—Francesca, for example. The latter treats it as part of the whole colour scheme, and as part of the pattern, whereas the German has observed much more closely the tone and colour in nature. His greens approach very nearly the richness and heaviness of early summer, and the stag is far more realistically rendered than the animals in the Francesca *Nativity*.

The German artist of this period is very fond of a rich green and a deep rose, and probably no other artists until the nineteenth century approached the lush colours of nature so closely. In the St. Hubert picture it looks very odd compared with the flat gold sky. In No. 707, by " The Master of St. Bartholomew," in the same room there is evidence that the German painters of this period could paint a sky beautifully. Technically they continued to paint beautifully, marvellously, but there is very little evidence in the later centuries that they either saw or felt beautifully. The elaborate compositions that came later, compositions teeming with figures and incident were remarkable but not exactly lovable. See No. 1049, *The Crucifixion* in Room 19, National Gallery, by "The Master of the Aaden," for instance.

TWO MASTERS WITH WIDELY DIFFERENT QUALITIES

THERE is, however, the great Dürer (1471-1528), and the great Holbein, two of the masters of the world, and one must not forget Grünewald. Dürer, the mystic, the poet, the realist, the visionary, was a great painter and engraver, a great thinker and teacher. As a painter he is not well represented in the National Gallery, but the portrait of his father is well known. There is a very representative collection of his engravings in the British Museum. Holbein, craftsman and realist, saw accurately and recorded beautifully, but his capacity for feeling was very limited. He spent many years in England and about 1536 he was appointed Court Painter to Henry VIII. He recorded king and merchant, priest or fine lady, with equal fidelity and with equal indifference to any emotion within. The little objects with which, in everyday life, his sitters were surrounded, excited his interest and served to display his skill as much as the sitters themselves. He is well represented in the National Gallery at Windsor, and in many English collections.

Grünewald, in spite of his cruel naturalism and his delight in coarse and brutal types and in horrid incident, was a great colourist and painter. He was the first German, perhaps, to use paint as a painter and not as a draughtsman. He thought more in masses of colour and light and shade than in line. His greatest works are to be seen at Colmar.

Working in the sixteenth century were many other rare and gifted artists, Baldung, Lucas Cranach, Burgmair, Amberger, Bruyn, Elshiemer, and Altdorfer. The compositions of Elshiemer and Altdorfer became much more free and fanciful, but the technique, which seems to have remained the same, was entirely unsuitable for expression in a bold and flowing style. Altdorfer is especially interesting, for he seems to have been one of the first artists in Germany or elsewhere to paint landscape for its own sake and not as a background for figure subjects. Elshiemer also painted landscape with much feeling and beauty. With the close of the sixteenth century the influence of Italy, especially of Venice, destroyed the native character of German painting, and as a distinct school it came to an end. Political and religious struggles are not conducive to activity in art, and not until the middle of the nineteenth century did a distinctive character begin to display itself again in German art. Thoma, Klinger, and Stück were names that were well known, and Louis Crointh and Leibl were much esteemed in their own country.

COURAGE AND SINCERITY IN MODERN ART

IT is extremely difficult to decide when what is called modern painting began, but probably one would not be wrong in saying that the moment when Gauguin decided to abandon the stock market was not far from the exact time. Anyhow, the appearance of Gauguin, Van Gogh, Cézanne and Renoir about the same time completely destroyed the power of the old tradition. In landscape the Barbizon School and its followers had lost their freshness, and painters like Harpigny had become stereotyped. The impressionist group which had comprised Manet, Degas, Monet, Berthe Morisot, Sisley and others seemed to have exhausted itself in that great burst of genius. The flood of commercialism which during the latter two-thirds of the nineteenth century had over-whelmed and absorbed nearly everything original in art in England, was not without its effect upon those gifted men in France ; and when the American buyer came upon the scene, Europe seemed to turn itself into a vast picture factory. It is said that more Corots went over to the United States in three years than Corot could have painted in three or four lifetimes. The living painters were in great demand also, and the supply adapted itself.

In a genius of the nature of Gauguin the urge from within was so great that no earthly power could prevent its flow ; but Gauguin was awake to destroying influences around him and in self-preservation he fled to the South Seas and there brought into being some of the most original and inspired works that the world has ever seen.

Van Gogh remaining in France, also, from the peculiarity of his temperament, was able to resist outside influences. Again we have the creation of something original and fresh. —an El Greco in landscape. Cézanne, less violent, was equally in revolt against the debasing of the artist's calling. Seurat was convinced of the possibility of " standardising " the method of producing great pictures and succeeded in doing it. There is a very remarkable picture by him in the Tate Gallery, and pictures by most of the great Frenchmen of the period are to be found there.

THE PLEASURE THAT PATTERNED NATURE CAN GIVE

THEIR pictures show a return to the decorative and emotional aspect of painting as opposed to the representational and sentimental. The pleasure and emotion is given by what is on the canvas; it is generated by the arrangement and pattern, by the beauty of colour, and possibly enhanced by the peculiar application of the pigment. These artists may remind one of nature, but there is no effort to imitate. Take their pictures for what they are, and do not condemn them for the lack of something we think ought to be there. We accept a piece of tapestry or a carpet with no grumble because the figures or flowers are arranged and conventionalised. In music we do not condemn a prelude or a sonata because it does not imitate the sounds of nature, and our attitude should be the same to the picture. The imitation of the cuckoo's note in Beethoven's *Pastoral Symphony* will demonstrate how irritating " naturalism " in music can be.

These four great men, Gauguin, Van Gogh, Cézanne, and Renoir, founded no School, but they started a revolt which has spread over the whole world. They expressed the urge of a new spirit, and by their example gave courage to numberless followers to do the same. As a result, various movements, societies, and groups came into being. Post-Impressionists led to Futurists, Cubists, Fauvists, and a host of other " -ists." It led in France to Matisse, Pissaso, Braque, Derain, Vlaminck, Utrillo, Metzinger, Herbin, and many others. It led in England to Duncan Grant, Vanessa Bell, the brothers Paul and John Nash, and to various groups.

MODERN ART THAT REQUIRES A SIXTH SENSE.

IN recent times there have been further developments and the " Unit-one " Group and the " Seven and Five " Group have appeared. They define their pictures as " Objective Abstractions," as attempts to render " psychological reactions " to nature; as attempts to render " psychological states that cannot be expressed in words." These are complex and difficult themes and it does appear as if it will be necessary to classify the particular " psychological states," and also definitely to fix and classify the symbols used to interpret these " states " and " re-actions." Whether we shall derive any delightful or exciting experience from their pictures when these conditions are clearer remains to be discovered. At present it is difficult for most of us to " pick up " what it is wished to convey. Possibly we have only average intelligence and subnormal spiritual development ; but then these artists can hardly expect a special audience to be provided for them. Meandering lines and wobbly patches, splashes of pigment of no particular form and very poor quality of colour, may convey something to some, especially if they are very young, but most of us have been born lacking the sixth sense, which would enable us to be enthusiastic.

Nevertheless we must feel admiration for the people who produce these pictures. At any rate, they are not commercial. They are courageous. They do seem to be striving for something, and endeavouring to give expression to a new spirit that is burning within. May it soon take form, and may we live to see appear out of all this labour a great spirit who will draw together these scattered parts and lead a movement or found a School which will unmistakably demonstrate to mankind that all art is a manifestation of the existence of what we call God.

PAINTING IN PRACTICE : HOW THE AMATEUR MAY CAPTURE BEAUTY

IT is astonishing how general is the desire to draw and to paint. The number of people that we see carrying a camera is an indication of the interest there is in the pictorial aspect of life. It is not always a desire to record a visit to some place of historic interest, or to bring back memories of some pleasant human intercourse. Just as frequently it is the delight given by some thing of beauty—a group of figures, an open landscape, a group of trees, a flock of sheep, a herd of cows, the ploughman and his team ; or another of the incidents and scenes that go to make up life in town or country. To-day the camera is brought into use, chiefly because it is easier, but there is no doubt that if time and trouble were spent, nearly all who use the camera would be able to produce a drawing or sketch sufficiently good to bring back to them the memories they desire. It would take a little longer, but then the concentrated vision necessary would impress so much more that even the slightest scribble would bring back the memory or sensation desired.

For the amateur it is often difficult to determine what impresses at the time. The landscape, for instance, may appear delightful, but when the sketch is made there is something lacking. It is quite possible in this case that he was influenced by a scent or by an agreeable feeling of warmth rather than by the form, the atmospheric effect, or the colour. Here is a group of trees, with sunlight touching the masses of foliage, dark shadows on the grass and intermingled with the shadow, a flock of panting sheep. It is charming and we make the sketch (the medium does not matter), but when we look at it afterwards it fails to please. Probably we did not definitely decide what we wished to record. If it was the beautiful form of the trees, then we possibly gave too much attention to the sheep. If the sunlight and warmth attracted us then we gave too much to the detail of the trees, and so on.

In a scene like this it would probably be the light and shadow and warmth ; then we should give the utmost attention to the shapes of the lights on the trees and the shadows on the grass. The sheep should only be vaguely " felt " in the shadow, and not over " detailed." A sparkling light playing on the backs of the sheep to enhance the mystery will be useful and must be placed with the greatest care. This will give a lead. We must decide very definitely before we begin what it is that impresses us, and simplify as much as possible.

The medium in which we do the sketch or note must depend upon our own preferences, but probably water-colour is the best. A rapid " splash " in water-colour usually has a charm of its own, even if its representational value is not great ; but a rapid sketch in oils, unless in the hands of a master like Constable, usually results in " slime." Beautiful " quality " in water-colour " happens " from the flow of the wash over the paper, but in oils it has to be made, and that is a process for the studio.

Having decided the medium, whose materials shall we buy ? Here again it is a matter of personal preference, but there is little fault to be found with any of the well-known makers. In oils, brushes are a difficulty because there are so many cheap inferior makes on the market. The only advice one can give here is " Go to a good maker and pay a good price." This applies to sables, as well as to hog-hair, to water-colour brushes as well as to oil.

HOW TO TREAT YOUR BRUSHES

IT is hardly necessary to wash oil brushes in soap and water every day. Once a week is sufficient, but every night after use, rinse them well in paraffin and then lay them in a dipper with *turpentine* covering the bristles. Rinse in paraffin, lay in turpentine. If the former is used to lay them in, any paint left between the bristles tends to harden. For sketching purposes, the wooden boxes with space in the lid for panels are best. They can be obtained with a light tripod on which to fix them. For work in the studio, canvas on stretchers is best, and again let it be good canvas, and not too smooth.

The methods of painting in oils may be brought down to two. In the first, the paints are mixed, either with the palette knife or brush, and applied direct to the canvas, thick or thin as may be preferred, or as may be necessary to render the object. Turpentine may be used as a medium, or a mixture of linseed oil and turpentine in equal parts. Little else is needed. The same method may be used in the studio, but if any approach to the " quality of paint " of the great crafts-men is preferred, then a second method must be employed—one which has fallen almost entirely into disuse since the middle of the nineteenth century. Here the whole subject is " laid in " in monochrome, that is, in various tones of the same colour—black and white, or umber and white, for instance—and any thinning that is necessary can be done with petroleum or turpentine. The composition is settled, and to a certain extent the " impasto "; that is the solidity, thickness or thinness of the paint. When dry, this mono-chrome is changed by glazing over with thin transparent colour, or " scumbling " with opaque.

To " glaze " is to rub over with colour and medium, with no admixture of white. To " scumble " is to use the colour with some white. The result is entirely different. Which treatment shall be employed is a matter of experiment. When the whole picture has been changed by this process, there may be a loss of form, and a lack of definition. It can be built up and corrected again, either by solid painting or by thin. If great strength and brilliance of colour is required, say of red, then the particular object may be " laid in " in tones of red, and another red, preferably transparent, glazed over.

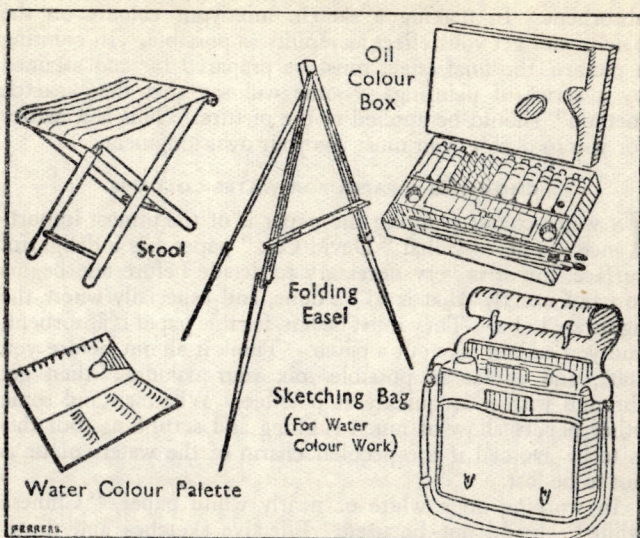

Oil Colour Box

Stool

Folding Easel

Sketching Bag
(For Water Colour Work)

Water Colour Palette

FERRERS.

8. COMPACT EQUIPMENT FOR OUT-OF-DOOR SKETCHING

The equipment must be easy to handle, light in weight, yet strong. Particularly is this so with the stool and easel. The sketching-bag is useful as it is light and compact and will easily carry everything that the artist may need.

This will give much greater brilliance, but considerable judgment must be used. After each stage the canvas must be allowed to dry thoroughly.

Before the next painting, if the whole picture is to be worked on, wash with warm water, and when dry, rub over thinly with linseed oil and turpentine (equal parts). If only a small passage is to be worked on, the necessary condition of the surface may be produced by breathing on it, and then oiling. It is better to arrive at the effect desired as directly as possible, for too many glazings or scumblings may give a soapy or stodgy effect which is not pleasant.

The ground on the canvas is important. The lead ground from the colourman is more frequently used, but it is interesting to experiment with a tempera or plaster ground, which nearly every colourman can supply. It is more or less absorbent. In making a sketch, mix your colours on the palette and get your effect as rapidly as possible. In painting a picture, the final effect must be prepared for and attained by a series of paintings. Some will say that the " sketch method " should be applied to the picture. This is a matter for you to decide, you must use your own judgment.

CHOOSING A PAPER FOR WATER-COLOURS

IN water-colour painting the paper is of the utmost import-ance. The so-called " David Cox " paper has a delightful surface, but it is very necessary to decide before one begins to paint exactly what is to be done, and especially where the lights are to be. They must be left, for this paper is absorbent, and you cannot take out a patch. Think it all out before you start, and as far as possible mix your colours ; then get through with it as quickly as possible. Whatman and some other papers allow of much rubbing and scrubbing, but this is to be avoided if the peculiar charm of the water-colour is not to be lost.

In working on a white or nearly white paper, " Chinese white " should not be used. Effective sketches and draw-ings are made on tinted paper, usually grey, and the colours mixed with white to obtain the lighter tones. This is called " Gouache." The tone of the paper is used and the colour is changed by a wash of colour. Where lights are necessary Chinese white is used thickly or thinly as may be desired. Turner produced some delicious sketches in this method, and later Brabazon excelled. Do not, even here, use too much white, or the effect will be horrid.

For out-of-door sketching the easel is of some importance, for it must be light and easy to unfold and pack up. It would be difficult to find anything better than the " Fred Mayor " easel, invented by the gifted water-colourist of that name. It will not take anything very large, but fourteen inches by ten inches is quite large enough for any water-colour sketch done direct from nature.

Water-colour drawings and sketches should be shown in white or cream mounts, " lined " or not, but the lining does away with a certain baldness in plain mounts. The frame should not be too deep and may be of gold or wood. There is a great variety of coloured woods to-day and they are very effective. The framing of an oil-painting is altogether a matter of experiment and judgment. One can give no rules.

There is a great variety of patterns and colours on the market, and they are to be seen "made up," which is an advantage. There is no doubt that the new colours and methods used in facing the mouldings are to be preferred to the golds and blacks of past times.

PAINTING AS A PROFESSION

IN the days before the War the distinction between the professional and the amateur artist was very clearly defined. There was the professional who, whether he practised painting from the urge that was in him, or merely from a desire for, or an appreciation of beauty, was faced with the necessity for making an income ; and there was the amateur, who practised it for various reasons, possible from talent or genius, from a delight in handling the medium, or from a desire or necessity to fill up time, or to pose as being accomplished.

It was not considered quite " the thing to do " for the amateur to sell. There was still a slight taint of the vagabond attached to the artist's calling unless he was labelled and classed by one of the Societies or Institutions. To-day all this has gone. The rich amateur holds the stage and the time is rapidly approaching when it will be impossible for anybody else to practise painting. He may be talented or not, but the fact is there, that without an income the only place for the painter-artist will be the pavement. Even then it will be uncertain and precarious, for the numbers will be so great that the police will interfere and say, " Move on."

It is interesting, the fascination of painting, and amongst the poor who try to practise it there will be many martyrs. Art is a religious system in which there have always been martyrs. The entrance of the rich amateur also tends to lower prices and put up expenses. The rents of studios and of so-called studios go up, and the prices of pictures go down. The artist without means could not possibly live and pay his expenses on the prices some rich amateurs accept for their work.

Painting is a hazardous occupation, for to-day there is not only competition with the living but with the dead. " Boomed " and exploited by the dealers, the " Old Masters " have diverted into other channels vast sums which ought to have been expended on the encouragement of the living artist. Food is placed by the dead but the living starve. One reveres the works of the great men who have gone, but feels that it would have been better for art if the business activities of the dealers had been confined to other channels.

WHERE THE STUDENT MAY GET HIS TRAINING

IF, however, in spite of all discouragement, the beginner has sufficient urge and talent, and is prepared to take the risks, what is the course to adopt ? Training of any length does not appear to be necessary to-day, but if the student feels that it is better and more interesting to know more than he is called upon to employ, then there are many schools, private and public, where all that is necessary to-day to give him a start may be learnt. At all the large towns there are schools of art where advice may be obtained and a beginning made. If the student is in the provinces and desires to train in London then scholarships may be gained at the Royal College of Art, at the Slade School and at the Royal Academy Schools, but except at the first-named, they are awarded only to students attending the school. There are numerous well-conducted and well-equipped private schools in London, but as the fees are fairly high they are mainly attended by the student and amateur with private means. The Royal College of Art and the Slade School each award a diploma which qualifies the holder to teach.

HOW THE ARTIST MAY HOPE TO SELL HIS WORK

IT is rather a bad time in which to say anything about markets, for, as far as one can ascertain, there appear to be none. In the days before the War Germany was a good market for English pictures. Paris also bought pictures, but mostly the works of her own countrymen. In England there was great activity, but, looking back, it seems that English people bought reputations rather than indulged any love for works of art. Anyhow, pictures sold in considerable numbers and the dealers prospered. There were two ways by which the painter might hope to make an income : one by means of exhibitions at public galleries and at dealers' galleries, the other by personal contact with those who were seriously interested. In those days there were people of culture, leisure, and means to whom a visit to an artist's studio was a pleasant experience. If it happened that the artist had something to show that interested, they did not hesitate to take a risk and buy. If the artist's personality was attractive as well as his work, then other visits and other sales followed.

Nowadays this type of buyer seems practically to have disappeared. He does exist, but in so small a number that he can hardly be relied upon as a source of income. There remains the public exhibition and the dealer. At the former there is some evidence of an increase in the number of sales, but it is all too uncertain, and the competition too great to be relied upon. The same may be said of the dealer. However, if one has talent and work to sell the dealer is the best person to go to. It is necessary to remember that he is not a philanthropist; but he is very human and not a bad fellow at all. He runs his business for profit, has heavy expenses, and so it is not surprising if he needs a somewhat large commission on sales—twenty-five or thirty per cent., and even more.

There may also be a charge for the gallery from fifteen to thirty pounds a week, and possibly more. The better dealers, however, will only give a " show " if they feel that the work has sufficient merit to enable them to make their profits from the commission on sales. The dealer can do much to accelerate the making of a reputation, which is a slow proceeding if the artist relies upon the efforts he makes from his own studio. Here one would like to say that it is a mistake for him to expect to make a large income. If he can obtain sufficient to enable him to live simply, very simply, and to get on with his work, then he should be content.

WHERE THE STORY OF PAINTING IS TOLD

THERE is a vast literature on the subject of painting, and if we have not access to galleries much knowledge and pleasure may be gained from reading. This can be augmented and confirmed when opportunity arises to see the works themselves. Those who wish to go more deeply into the history of painting are recommended to begin with *The Birth of Western Painting*, by R. B. and D. T. Reed, and to follow this with *The History of Modern Painting*, by Professor R. Muther. *Painters and Painting, 1490–1900*, by Sir Frederick Wedmore (Home University Library, Thornton Butterworth Limited), also provides an excellent historical survey of the subject.

When the reader has the outline of the subject clearly in mind he can then choose which period or School interests him most. Attractive and instructive works on particular schools of painting are : *The French Primitives and their Forms*, by A. L. B. and V. de Mazia and A. L. Barnes ; *An Account of French Painting*, by Clive Bell ; *Modern French Painters*, by Ian Gordon ; *Flemish Art*, by Roger Fry ; *Great Masters of Dutch Painting*, by W. Bode ; *The Story of Dutch Painting* and *The Story of Spanish Painting*, by C. H. Caffin ; *English Mediæval Painting*, by J. B. and E. W. Tristram, and *English Painting from the Seventh Century to the Present Day*, by Charles Johnson. The titles of these books sufficiently indicate their scope.

Enjoying Pictures, by Clive Bell, provides an entertaining and helpful reply to the question : " What should one look for in a painting ? " and is illuminating even to those who are sure of their own answer. There are, of course, many books published on the practice of painting, but here it is much better to experiment than to read.

EXPRESSION IN PEN AND PENCIL :
THE DELIGHT OF DRAWING

by J. W. S. FERRERS

IT is a commonplace that children not only desire to draw, but actually do so long before they possess any vocabulary worthy of mention. It is the desire for expression that urges them to draw, and thus they are doing what all artists do, or should do—expressing themselves. They are attempting to give expression to some thought that has been started by the sight of some exciting thing such as a train or motor-bus. At this early stage of life they have a breadth of vision which is slowly lost the older they become, until finally it vanishes completely unless definite steps are taken to revive and train it. By this, an artistic training is meant.

This child vision, this observation which scorns all detail in a truly impressionistic manner and only sees the essentials, is ideal from an artist's point of view. One has only to look at a young child's drawing of, let us say, a motor-bus to realise this breadth of vision. The brilliant red of it, together with the movement of it, are the two points that have impressed themselves upon the child mind. Large, often too large, wheels are the factors which express movement to a child in such things as trains, buses, and carts, so we get the wheels made very important parts of the drawing. Next to this, colour is all important, so vivid daubs of red will indicate the body of a bus. In exactly the same way, a train consists of wheels and furious volumes of smoke.

By citing the child we do not mean to imply that children are all natural artists, needing no training. On the contrary, if this very breadth of vision is not controlled by a more experienced person, it will soon degenerate into an untidy chaotic muddle. The great art in teaching young children is to guide yet in no way to stultify. It is fatally easy for an adult to impose his or her mannerisms upon a child's drawing to the complete nullification of all originality in the child.

To the adult this breadth of vision is very difficult to acquire. The untrained grown-up who attempts to draw is continually embarrassed by a wealth of detail. They cannot see the trees for the wood, and it is quite impossible for them to see

the object looked at in simple shapes. If they try to draw a
person's head—and this is always a favourite task for a
beginner to choose, probably because it is one of the most
difficult to do—they are led astray by minutiæ. The eye-
lashes and individual hairs of the head, the little creases and
lines on the face, captivate them and everything else is forgotten in their pursuit. The fact that the head is an oval of
varying sizes in which all this detail is contained is quite lost
sight of. The child drawing his father first of all draws a
rather lop-sided circle and into this he proceeds to place
smaller circles for eyes and a gash for the mouth, this last
generally rather large, because his attention is frequently
called to it by the sound which issues from it whenever his
father speaks. This child conception may well be crude,
yet it is very much nearer the mark than many attempts of
untrained adults.

THE PEOPLE WHO "CAN'T DRAW A LINE"

ANY one who is connected with teaching will be only too
familiar with the phrase : " I can't draw a line." It
may be delivered with anger or hopelessness, yet whatever
the tone, the meaning is always the same. The drawing is
wrong and the fault cannot be seen. When the mistake is
pointed out, it cannot be put right. The drawing becomes
worse and worse. Who that has attempted to draw has not
experienced this slough of despond ?

There is another type of person who is fond of using this
phrase, but generally embellishes it with the word " straight."
" I can't draw a straight line," you will be told. " Of course
I should love to be able to draw, but there it is, I can't."
There are very few people who will tell you that they cannot
draw, and that they do not want to either. We are, therefore,
justified in assuming that in most people the desire to draw is
present, but the technical ability is absent.

In the face of this we shall now proceed to make a statement
that will be disagreed with as well as disbelieved by many.
Any one who has the desire to draw and is prepared to work
can learn to draw. By this we do not mean that any one can
attain to the genius shown by Holbein or Dürer, for such have
the divine gift from birth ; but without doubt a certain
reasonable standard may be reached by all if they so wish.
The standard attained may not be very high, but as constant
practice plays such an important part in drawing, so much

depends upon the amount of time that can be given to it when trying to assess a possible standard. The cleverest artists become rusty if they do not constantly practise.

The tremendous amount of pleasure that can be derived from even a small ability to draw far outweighs the question of what standard can or cannot be reached. The ability to sit down and sketch some charming old building that delights one's eye on a holiday is worth much hard training, and the result is far more intimate as an aid to memory in after years than any snapshot. The mere fact that one has sat in some quiet corner for a couple of hours while making the sketch tends to have an excellent effect on one's senses. For a short while the busy, rushing, modern world has been put aside, and a space of quiet contemplation of a beautiful thing has taken its place. The very concentration and observation which must go to the making of a successful drawing is bound to impress the beauty seen lastingly upon the mind.

It would, of course, be wrong for the draughtsman in the making not to want to improve. It would be fatal for him to be quite content with a mediocre standard for all time. He must wish to advance, and in order to do this he must train himself in the ability to differentiate between good and bad drawing.

CULTURE THAT BEGINS WITH DRAWING

To the layman the æsthetic value to be gained from a knowledge of both the principles and theory of drawing is great, and it has a tremendous cultural value as well which is bound to affect the whole outlook. In gaining this knowledge he will have trained his powers of observation. He will have learnt to see accurately, and to put down what he has observed concisely and in an ordered way. Through studying many examples of good and beautiful drawings he will have acquired a critical faculty which will train and refine his taste. It will be impossible for him to isolate his study to drawing alone, but he will, under the urge of his broadening knowledge, turn to the study of the other arts which have their basis in drawing. Thus will he acquire an æsthetic culture which will be of ever-growing value so long as he may live.

The recreative value of drawing is much more obvious than the cultural value. Most people like to scribble, and if their efforts can be lifted to something higher than scribbling and become by practice the work of a trained artist, then the pleasure of sketching is enormous. Drawing, after the first difficulties have been overcome, affords a perfect recreation. The ability to sketch, in pencil let us say, the things we see upon our summer holidays is ample recompense for all the patient practice we have put into the initial training.

The practical value of drawing, and by this we mean either financial or definitely helpful to one's work, is much wider than would at first appear. There are a number of professions where a knowledge of drawing is advisable, indeed almost essential. Architecture, branches of engineering, and carpentry, are three that spring to the mind at once, while teaching, and many branches of work in the business world are made very much more efficient if an ability to make quick sketches is present. And the business man well knows that more efficiency means financial gain, which is a very practical value to him.

WHERE LINE TAKES THE PLACE OF COLOUR

IN a painting colour plays such an important part that even the layman can say, " I like that colour " or " That combination of colours is very effective," but in a drawing we are bereft of colour, and our judgment must depend upon line and form alone. This often makes judgment of a drawing very difficult for a layman. We are so used to associating colour with objects or to looking at the monochromatic imitation of the photograph in which the tones are shown and not the line, that a drawing looks quite foreign to our eyes.

We frequently speak of line in drawing and it is of extreme importance, therefore we must consider carefully what this word " line " really means. It does not only mean the actual quality and type of line employed by an artist, for it can equally well refer to the pose of a figure, or the placing of figures and objects in a composition.

In Fig. 4 we have what we may term a diagrammatic drawing of Velasquez' famous Cupid and Venus picture which is in the National Gallery. It is diagrammatic, for in no way but pose does it bear any resemblance to the original. We are not concerned with the lovely colour or with the brilliant rendering of the flesh tints. Neither are we concerned with the subtle modelling of the figure or the composition of the picture. The only thing that we look for in order to illustrate our point is the beautiful sweeping curve of the body. This is what is meant by line in pose.

The human figure can take up an infinite variety of poses

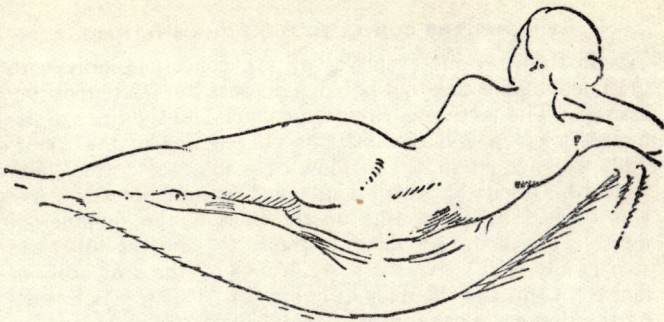

4. THE MEANING OF "LINE" IN DRAWING

In this diagrammatic drawing of Velasquez's famous "Venus,"
"line in pose" is revealed by the upward curve of the body
and the corresponding downward sweep of the couch combining
to form an exquisitely balanced whole.

or positions, each one beautiful, and each one full of individual expression. The indolent grace of the reclining
figure of Venus in this picture by Velasquez is exquisite in
beauty of line. It is this expression in line in the human
figure that the artist continually looks for, and it is more
readily found in the female model than in the male. The
very anatomical make-up of the feminine figure ensures this,
for the muscles are not so large or so developed as in man,
also the distribution of the superficial fat in the female figure
is so ordered that soft, rounded curves occur, causing the
sweeping lines so often seen in the feminine figure, rather than
the angularity associated with man.

In Fig. 5 we have a similar type of diagrammatic
drawing taken from the famous picture of the Holy Family
in the Uffizi Gallery, Florence, by the great Michelangelo.
In this picture we have interwoven in an exquisite rhythmical
pattern, the Virgin and Child with Joseph kneeling upon one
knee behind them helping to support the Infant upon the
raised arms of His mother, who is sitting with her knees
bent and her feet tucked underneath her, looking up in
adoration at her Son. For the purposes of our analysis of
the composition, the three figures, Joseph, the Child, and
Mary (shaded figure), have been lettered (a), (b), (c).

LINKING THE CURVES TO MAKE THE RHYTHM

As in the previous example, we are concerned only with line, but this time not only line in pose but in composition as well. The picture is circular in shape and the lines of the figures take up and continue the curved line of the frame. This we have attempted to show by a series of dotted lines, which, for clarity of description, have been numbered. Curve 1 is formed by connecting up the lines of the shoulder of figure (a) with the shoulders of figure (b) and the up-raised arm of figure (c). Curve 2 is formed by the two arms of figure (c) and the shoulder of figure (a). Curve 3 is formed by the drapery on the raised knee of figure (a) and again on the other side of figure (c). Curve 4 is formed by the drapery of figures (a) and (c). Curve 5 is formed by the foot, drapery, and knee of figure (c). Curve 6 is formed by the bent knees of figure (c).

It will readily be seen that all the curves have a definite relationship with the circumference of the picture and the whole gives a delightful swinging rhythm to the composition, thus creating a perfect example of rhythmic line in the composition or formation of a picture.

If the word line is used to refer to the actual quality of the drawn line, whether charcoal, crayon, or pencil has been used, then it becomes a question of technique. It is not possible to illustrate this, but a study of those lovely drawings by Holbein of the dignitaries of the Court of Henry VIII. will give perfect examples of the quality of line. Later we shall have more to say about this superb draughtsman. Quality of line not only depends upon the medium used, or upon what paper is selected, but practically entirely upon the artist. A line can have almost as much expression as a whole picture. It can be dull, meaningless, clumsy, ragged, wiry, or sensitive and full of life. Whatever quality a line may have, it is safe to say that it should always have a fresh spontaneity about it. It should never look laboured or smudgy. This, unfortunately for the beginner, means the sparse use, if any, of rubber.

DEPTH THAT GIVES LIFE TO AN OBJECT ON PAPER

With the exception of design which generally requires drawing in the flat—that is to say, only showing two dimensions, namely length and breadth—all drawing aims at

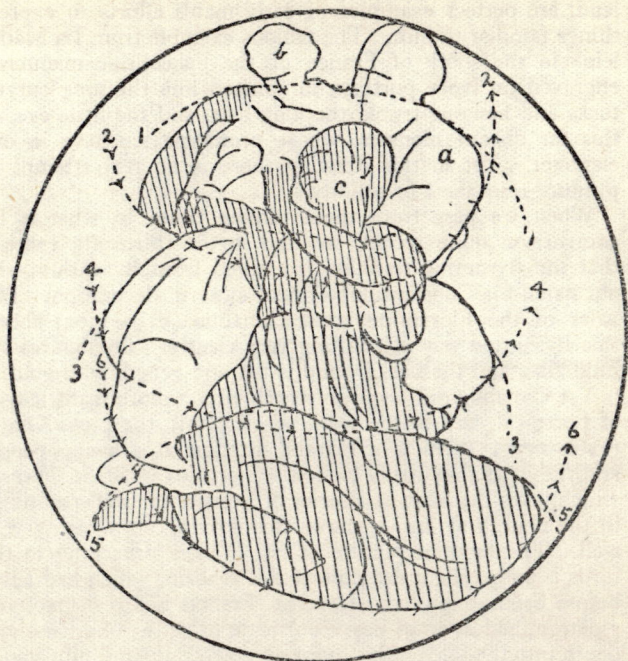

5. RHYTHMICAL PATTERN IN LINE

*How line is used in the composition of a picture is shown in
this diagrammatic drawing of Michelangelo's " Holy Family,"
where the six main curves of the figures a, b, and c take up
and continue the circular line of the frame.*

portraying in as satisfactory and as realistic a manner as
possible the roundness and solidity of an object, or, in other
words, the third dimension—depth.

The artist, no matter of what age or era, has always been
conscious of this third dimension, but he has not always been
very successful in its correct rendering upon a flat surface
such as bone, ivory, slate, cave-walls, parchment, or paper.
The well-known cave drawings in Spain, and the many representations of reindeer, bison, and mammoth engraved upon
bone and ivory that have been found in France and Switzer-

land, are perfect examples of early man's efforts to express things familiar to him. The famous example from La Madeleine in the south of France of the Palæolithic mammoth engraved on ivory portrays in spirited line the long curved tusks and hanging trunk, the long hair, and the little eye, of this far distant monster, whose prototype we have in our elephant. Yet in this drawing there is no real attempt to produce roundness or solidity.

When we pass from these remote times to what is by comparison quite recent, we find in the thirteenth century that the Byzantine tradition (so called from Byzantium, the old name for Constantinople) held sway in decoration. The work of the Florentine artist Cimabue (1240–1302) shows this Byzantine way of painting very clearly. The figures are unlifelike, and the background is flat and generally of gold.

Yet Cimabue did begin to search after a more realistic type of portrayal, and in the work of his pupil, the pious Giotto (1266–1337), there is a marked attempt at drawing people and things as they really looked. Giotto's *Life of St. Francis*, which takes the form of a series of frescoes (or wall-paintings) in the church at Assisi, shows this striving after reality very well. The familiar picture of St. Francis preaching to the birds is an excellent example of this realism, which had never before been attempted. Here St. Francis is a real man, and a determined attempt has been made to get a roundness and depth into the folds of his monkish gown. Behind him stands a follower with hand upraised in amazement at the miracle of the little birds coming down to listen to the words of the great preacher. In this picture the trees are real trees, and the background of pale, misty, blue Italian hills can only be the result of a close study of nature unheard of before this time.

From now onwards we have a complete breaking away from the stiff and formal Byzantine tradition. Now the artist's aim is to portray everything with as much realism and truth to nature as is possible, and this culminates in the researches of the great Leonardo da Vinci. This intellectual giant not only solved for all time difficulties of expressing on the flat the roundness and solidity of an object, but problems of light and shade, and of the diminishing of objects as they recede from the spectator as well. When we pay proper attention to this diminution of distant objects in a drawing we are using what is called perspective.

PERSPECTIVE : "THAT DELIGHTFUL THING"

WE have cited the work of two Italian artists as examples of the search after realism in drawing, and of Leonardo as an instance of the completion of this search. It will, therefore, not be out of place if we name another great Italian artist who was a pioneer in the search after methods of portraying this correct diminution of objects in a picture. This is Paolo Uccello (1397–1475). The artist and famous compiler of the Lives of the Italian Painters, Vasari (1511–1574), says of Uccello that he would work the whole night through, seeking new terms for the expression of his rules in perspective, and when his wife called him to come to bed he would merely reply : " Oh, what a delightful thing is this perspective ! " *The Rout of San Romano* in the National Gallery is an excellent example of this artist's work, and shows to what lengths he would go in the portrayal of the most curious problems in this science he loved so much.

We have called perspective a science and it is so undoubtedly, for it may be worked geometrically and exactly. To the artist the actual mathematics of it is not of the first importance, but the main principles that underlie the science are of the first magnitude to him. It would, therefore, be wrong to leave this matter without going further into the question. Especially is this so, if we wish either to practise drawing or to appreciate it. We have said that when we pay attention to the well-known fact that objects appear smaller as they recede from us, we are using perspective. Why do objects seem smaller at a distance ? It is generally known that our eyes see because they collect rays of light that fall upon the object and in turn are reflected back to the eye. The lens and the retina of the eye enable this to take place. The lens collects the rays of light and these rays are communicated to the retina which lies behind the lens and may be likened to a screen.

In Fig. 6 (1) we have the eye (represented by the shaded portion) shown in a purely diagrammatic form. A post is placed at the points A, B, C, which are at different distances from the eye. The rays of light are shown by the lines (r). It is important that two matters should be made clear here before we go any further. First, it must be understood that the image upon the retina is upside down due to the crossing of the rays of light at the lens. This upside down image is corrected by the eye by means which belong to the realm of the occulist rather than to that of the artist. Secondly, the rays of light emanate from all parts of the object and not from the top and bottom of the post only as shown in the example, but to avoid confusion the lines which should represent the other rays have been eliminated.

HOW AN IMAGE IS CAST ON THE SCREEN OF THE EYE

THE lens and the retina are in fixed positions, and if we study the example we see that the rays of light from the post converge upon the same focal point on the lens no matter what distance the post is from the eye. When the rays are reflected from the post at A, they have only a short distance to travel, so that in order to meet at the lens they have to converge more than is the case when they are reflected from the post at B, which is further from the eye, or at C, which is still further away. This is to say that the further an object is from the spectator the *less convergent* are the rays of light travelling to the lens of the eye.

When the rays of light have met at the lens they cross each other as we said, and continue on behind the lens to be stopped at the retina or screen. On this screen are imaged the things we see. The rays are now going away from the lens so we speak of them as diverging, that is, opening out fan-wise. We now come to the important fact. *The extent to which the rays diverge is exactly proportionate to the extent to which they converge in front of the lens.* Consequently when the rays from the post in position A reach the retina they will have diverged more than the rays from the post in positions B or C. Therefore the image on the retina of the post at A will appear larger than the image of the post at B or C, and thus we see that the further objects are from us the smaller they are bound to appear imaged upon the retina, and consequently they seem smaller to us than do the nearer objects.

A SIMPLE EXPERIMENT WITH PERSPECTIVE

A PRACTICAL experiment will make what we have just explained quite clear. Take a piece of damp chalk or a brush full of black paint and go to a window from which a reasonably distant view may be had. Shut one eye and draw in outline upon the pane the view seen. With one eye shut you will be able to place the chalk or brush quite easily and

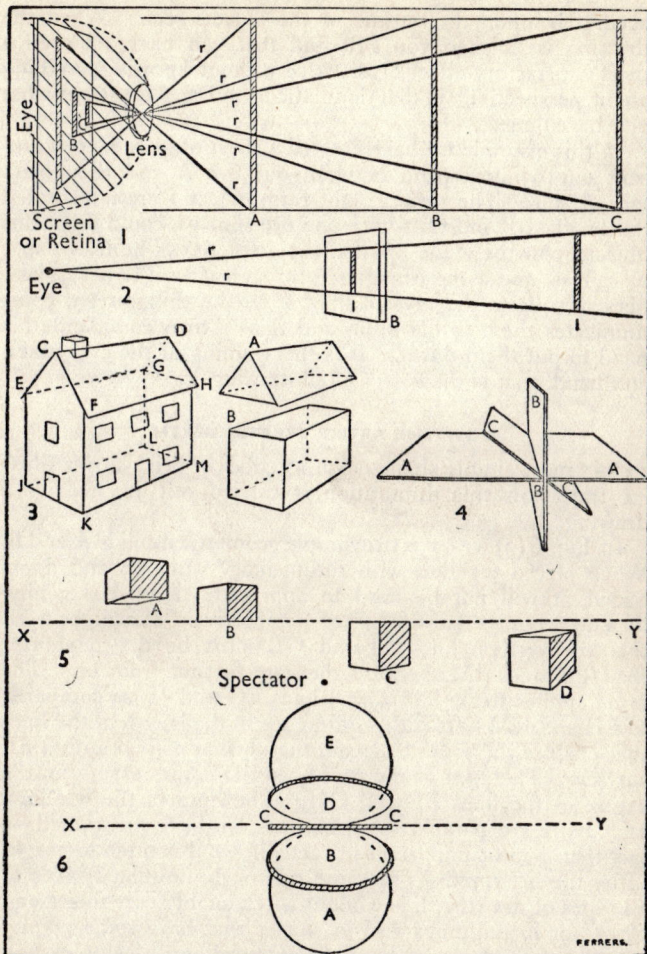

6. "THAT DELIGHTFUL THING PERSPECTIVE"

1. *The apparent diminution of objects as they recede from us ; 2, the experiment of drawing on a sheet of glass ; 3 and 4, the use of simple solids and changes of plane. Diagrams 5 and 6 illustrate the change in appearance of angular or curved objects as the eye level alters.*

4

accurately upon the outline of the objects seen. When the drawing is finished you will find that you have achieved a most satisfactory effect of distance without knowing anything about perspective ; in diagrammatic form Fig. 6 (2) shows what you have done.

In this example we have erected a sheet of glass B to represent our window pane between our eye A and the object looked at 1. The rays of light from object 1 are intercepted by the glass B and thus with one eye shut we could draw this object upon the glass. When the artist draws he uses paper or canvas, and as he cannot see through it as if it were glass, his eye collects the rays of light from the things seen, communicates them to his brain and this in turn commands his hand to put them down. It is this training of the eye, brain, and hand, that is the secret of all drawing.

HOW THE ARTIST CREATES DEPTH

THE most simple shapes such as cubes or brick-forms illustrate how this diminution is carried out in making a drawing.

In Fig. 6 (3) we have two simple geometrical solids A and B. When placed together with rudimentary windows and doors added, it will not be hard to appreciate that all sketching depends upon a knowledge of perspective. It will be seen that the vertical lines EJ and GL must be drawn shorter than FK and HM, because they are further from us. The same applies to the horizontal lines EG and JL as compared to FH and KM. It is this difference in the length of the lines that enables the artist to create the illusion of depth on a flat surface. The apex of the roof C and D comes exactly in the centre of the lines EF and GH. The lines of the windows and doors are parallel to these lines we have mentioned—a fact that is most important in sketching and is often lost sight of by the beginner. The same rule of diminution applies to all types of drawing, but while it is reasonably easy to see and carry out in buildings and in shapes that have some affinity to geometrical form, it becomes extraordinarily complex and subtle in its application when the human figure is attempted.

A PRINCIPLE THAT LIES AT THE ROOT OF ALL DRAWING

As the very substance of drawing both practical and æsthetic lies in the proper understanding of these matters we have had under consideration, no apology need be made if two more important facts in this " delightful thing perspective," as Uccello called it, are dealt with. These are questions of planes, which have a very important bearing on figure drawing, and of the effect upon the appearance of objects when they are below, above, and on the eye level.

In Fig. 6 (4) we have the three planes met with in drawing. There are seven planes in mathematically worked perspective, but these three are really all that concern the artist. They are: AA—Horizontal plane, BB—Vertical plane, CC—Inclined plane. A plane is considered to be an even surface of indefinite area which may be at different angles, and upon which objects may stand or lie. The shapes of objects vary according to the tilt of the plane. A house stands upon a horizontal plane, the earth, the walls are vertical planes, and the roof is an inclined plane.

The tilt of a plane is not the only thing that alters the shape of an object to the eye. The position of the spectator's eye level must also be considered in this respect.

In Fig. 6 (5) the line XY is the spectator's eye level, and four cubes in the same position, standing on a horizontal plane, are placed above, on, and below the eye level. Cubes A and B are to the left of the spectator, while cubes C and D are to the right. Cube A is above the eye level and we only see underneath it. B and C are on the level, but B has its base on it while C its top. In each case the important thing to notice is that the part that is on the eye level appears a straight line. D is below, and consequently we only see on top of it. It will be noticed also that the vertical lines never vary. They remain at right angles to the ground and perpendicular to the spectator. It is only the horizontal lines that alter ; when they are above the eye level they slope down to it, and up to it when they are below. In the diagram of the house, Fig. 6 (3) the eye level is above and we are looking down as if from a hill.

Curved objects behave in the same way as objects bounded by straight lines—a fact which is clearly shown in Fig. 6 (6). The line XY is the eye level and hinged to it is a circle A. This circle goes through three changes. In position B it has been lifted nearer to the eye level, and at once it becomes elliptical. When it is lifted still more and reaches the exact level of the eye it becomes a straight line, CC. The circle moves on, and in D it is above the eye level and we see underneath it. In E we have reached the same view as in A, with the difference, of course, that we are really looking at the underneath of the circle. In A we look immediately down upon it, while in E immediately underneath it. Both views appear as perfect circles.

MODES OF EXPRESSION GREAT ARTISTS HAVE USED

WE have now, as it were, erected a scaffolding upon which all drawing is based, and we are therefore in a position to deal in a reasonably knowledgeable way with different types of drawing as well as with the work of artists both of the past and of the present. First of all let us consider the difference between drawing and painting. The word " drawing " is used by both critic and artist in rather an arbitrary way. For instance, when the critic looks at a painting he often says it has good or bad drawing in it. Here he may be referring to the composition or to the shape of the objects that go to make up the picture. The artist draws just as easily with his brush as with a pencil, and he will use the word " drawing " to express what he is doing with his brush, where the layman would say " painting." Obviously, then, we must clarify the interpretation placed upon the word " drawing."

For the purposes of this section, which deals with drawing as distinct from painting, we shall mean those works of art that have been carried out with pencil, chalks, charcoal, pen and ink, or by the processes of etching or engraving. Sometimes we shall not be able to keep absolutely to this list, for we shall have to include tinted drawings. The early eighteenth century water-colours come under the heading of tinted drawings. These were very careful drawings in line, either in pencil or ink, and were merely faintly tinted with flat washes of transparent colour afterwards. The early work of the famous Turner and of the short-lived Girtin, his friend, come under this type of " stained drawings " as they were called. Indeed these two started their artistic careers apprenticed to " topographers " and spent their time laying flat tints upon architectural drawings.

There are, however, many drawings which, although they are done with a pencil, have no line such as an outline, but are expressed entirely in gradations of tone. The painfully laboured drawings of the nineteenth century such as the work of Sandys are examples of this tone drawing. In complete contra-distinction to these, we have the brilliant drawing of an artist of our own day, Augustus John. Here the drawing is frequently expressed in most sensitive line with very little shading or tone.

THE GOOD ARTIST NEVER COPIES

IT may be asked here, " How does the artist know when to use line or tone and when to combine the two ? " It would be well-nigh impossible for him to say, for it is instinctive with him. What is an outline ? There is no outline in nature really. We only see things because one tone impinges upon another. We may say, then, that an outline is merely a convention used to show the change of one tone to the next, and that tone is used to aid the illusion of solidity and round-ness upon a flat surface. Hence we get both line and tone used in most drawings. In fact the aim of the artist is to put down as truly as possible an impression of what he sees. We have purposely used the word " impression " and not " copy," for the camera may copy but the artist never does. It is the individual touch given by the artist to a picture that gives it its charm.

What particular method the artist employs to get his im-pression depends upon three things, the subject, the medium used, and the individual technique of the draughtsman. One of the worst things an artist can do is to dwell upon the effect he may produce in a drawing. His whole mind should be concentrated upon the portrayal, not upon the method. If the method comes first, then we often get what is called a " mannered " drawing. Certain characteristics in the work of the facile Sir Thomas Lawrence in the eighteenth century are examples of this " mannered " drawing. He was very fond, for instance, of giving his female sitters a long and swan-like neck, quite irrespective of whether they had one or not. The portrait in the National Gallery of Princess Lieven shows very clearly what soon became known as the " Lawrence Line." It would be wrong to confuse an artist's characteristic technique with this mannered effect. One may always tell a Dürer drawing from a Rembrandt by the differ-ence in the handling of line and tone. This is technique, but when truth is sacrificed for effect, as it is in the " Lawrence Line," then the result is a " mannerism."

The artist will instinctively alter his technique according to the medium used and the demands of his subject. Different papers as well as differently graded pencils such as very soft or very hard ones will alter the draughtsman's technique to a certain extent, but although some thought is given to this matter, the artist's concern is mainly with the actual portrayal of his subject, and he will use line and tone combined quite subconsciously to express that which he sees before him. Just as we do not spell out each letter of these words before we read them, but without a conscious effort recognise their significance, so does the artist draw.

In a word, the artist does not ask himself, " What effect will this line give me or this medium ? " Rather does he ask : " What do I see ? " Let us suppose he is drawing from the living model. He sees the line of the pose first of all, and this he must fix upon his paper to the exclusion of all else. This is the action of the figure, and it is *the* important thing, for it is fatally easy to make a beautiful shaded drawing but with as much life in it as a piece of wood. So, keeping the action of the pose ever in his mind, he puts down the lovely shape of the figure, using line and tone combined to get his result, which in the end will be an impression of the model full of life and beauty.

THE ARTIST MAKES HIS OWN CONVENTION

IT should be remembered that in whatever way a drawing may be expressed it must always be to a certain extent a conventional treatment and not a copy. This is a very important point, and therefore we must consider it more fully.

When looking at a pencil portrait of a person, we must not expect to see every hair, every spot, speck, and eyelash ; neither must we expect the rich colour of lip or cheek, for that belongs to the province of paint. We must accept the convention employed by the artist in his effort to put down an impression of the head, and we must also realise that the medium used, such as pencil or charcoal, dictates to a large extent the conventions used by the artist.

The portrait drawings of the great German artist of the sixteenth century—Holbein—are perfect examples of this conventional treatment, and it is very fitting that we should cite him, for between the years 1531 and 1543, the year of his death, his whole time was taken up with portraiture, his sitters being mostly English. Thus he may be termed the father of English portrait painting as we know it to-day. As most of his portraits were paintings, it may be asked here what connection they have with drawings as discussed in the foregoing paragraph. The answer is that in practically every case Holbein made a drawing, generally in chalk, of his sitter, and from this drawing the portrait was painted.

WHAT THE BEGINNER IN DRAWING SHOULD KNOW

PERHAPS one of the greatest faults that a beginner makes is to use a hard, unsympathetic outline, rather as if he were drawing a map, and he forgets completely about what is inside the outline. This can best be understood if we consider the figure. If we attempt to draw the human figure, and here we refer to the figure in the nude, in outline alone, we blazon abroad the fact that we know nothing about the anatomical structure of the body. If we had this structural knowledge we would know at once that some muscles come in front of others, and thus the outline cannot be continuous as it would be in a map.

THE ONE WAY TO LEARN TO DRAW

PEOPLE often ask artists and art teachers what they should do to learn to draw. The answer can never be any different from what it always is : constant practice and continual study of good drawings. The practice may be got in Art Schools, or better still, if you want to do life drawing and have a studio of your own or can borrow one, employ a model. There is no lack of models, and most of them charge about 1s. 6d. to 2s. an hour. If the figure is not wanted, then there is no better thing to do than to go to nature, where if one drew solidly all one's life one would not exhaust an iota of the wealth she has to offer.

Practice, practice, practice, this must be the lay of him who wishes to draw, and never must he allow himself to be cast down by failure. The most skilful of draughtsmen have bad spells, when every line they put down is wrong, and their fingers are like thumbs. It is very often at this depressing time that a step forward is made. It is recorded of Sir William Orpen that in one of his portraits he spent days trying to get the drawing of a foot right, and no one could deny that he was a skilful draughtsman indeed. Drawing can never be a mechanical process which always comes off and is always the same, and we must be thankful that this is so.

We have mentioned the hard, unsympathetic outline of the beginner as one of his chief faults. A contributory cause of this is often the way he holds his pencil. At first glance this may seem a very unimportant point, but it has far-reaching effects upon the freedom with which a drawing may be done. The artist when he draws does not usually hold his pencil as if he were going to write with it. The best method of holding the pencil is arrived at in the following way :

Lay the pencil on the table ; now pick it up in a perfectly natural manner. You will find that it is held between the thumb and first two fingers, and that the hand is curved so that the hollow of it covers the end of the pencil. Next, turn the hand slightly so that when the pencil point rests on the paper, which is pinned to a board that is inclined, the backs of the second, third, and little finger rest on the paper and are used as a steadying support. The particular merit in this method lies in the fact that when the pencil is held thus, the whole arm is used and the line is drawn from the shoulder and not with the fingers from the wrist, as occurs when writing. This means that a far freer and more sensitive line may be executed.

At first this way of holding the pencil seems very awkward, but with practice this soon passes. This method is instinctively used both by the trained and the untrained, if any attempt is made to draw with a very short pencil. There are times, of course, when the artist draws holding the pencil as if he were writing ; it largely depends upon what he is doing. To lay down any fixed rule is the last thing one desires to do in art. The only advice one can really give is that the handling of a pencil, chalk, or what you will, should be as dexterous and skilful as possible, and practice alone will give this facility.

RICH STOREHOUSES OF LOVELY DRAWINGS

Now, where may the student or he who wishes merely to appreciate and not to practise go, in order to see good examples of drawing ? At once names such as the British Museum, the Victoria and Albert Museum, Windsor Castle, and the Tate Gallery spring to the mind, while in the Provinces the cathedral libraries are generally rich store-

houses of early pen drawings and lovely illuminated manuscripts. These libraries are open to visitors, and it has
always been the writer's experience that if interest is shown,
there is never a lack of eager, willing, and well-informed
people, who, because they love their charges, are the very
best guide to them and under the warmth of a stranger's
enthusiasm will expand and become veritable mines of information. No mention of libraries would be complete
unless the famous Bodleian Library at Oxford was added,
and there one may see beautiful line drawings from the
eleventh and twelfth centuries.

FROM MANUSCRIPT TO CARICATURE : GREAT CRAFTSMEN OF EVERY AGE

WE have spoken of illuminated manuscripts first of
all, for they are the natural beginnings of drawing in
England, especially as the English have always excelled in the
portrayal of things in line rather than in tone. We must not
expect to find correct renderings of perspective in these early
drawings, for they were done long before the rules and laws,
some of which we have discussed and illustrated, were discovered, but this does not matter at all, and we only mention
it so that he who is unfamiliar with this early English work
may not approach these delightful drawings in the wrong
frame of mind.

Fig. 7 shows a small part from the 320 ft. long Tapestry
of Bayeux. We are familiar with the story of this amazing
piece of embroidery on linen, and we know that Queen
Matilda and her women are supposed to have worked it. It
illustrates the whole story of the Norman Conquest. The
part which has been selected for our example shows two of
Duke William's cavalry galloping to the summit of a small
hill in order to discover if Harold's army can be seen. It
may be asked here : " What has embroidery got to do with
drawing ? " Quite a lot really, for before any form of needlework can be attempted the subject must be drawn. But apart
from that, we have mentioned the illuminated manuscripts
of the eleventh and twelfth centuries, and the type of drawing
in those old parchments is very similar in treatment and
conception to the example here reproduced from the Bayeux
Tapestry.

Here we see the simplicity and vigour with which the

subject is expressed ; it is this almost naïve treatment which
is so characteristic of this early work, be it English or French.
Particularly do we see this in the rendering of the donkey
eating grass in the border at the bottom. Yet we must not
make the error of thinking that this early work is childish.
We have only to analyse the design of this small example to
realise at once that great artistic ability, far removed from
childhood days, went to the placing and planning of it all.

So, starting from this vigorous early draughtsmanship, and
also bearing in mind such lovely pen drawings as appear in
The Winchester Gospels in the Bodleian, or the intricate
patterns of *The Lindisfarne Gospel* in the British Museum
dating from the eighth century, we may proceed to the
equally beautiful although far more sophisticated drawings of
the artists of the Renaissance.

NAMES THAT SPARKLE IN THE HISTORY OF ITALIAN ART

UNTIL the coming of Holbein to England in the sixteenth
century there was no real draughtsmanship practised in
his manner, so we must leave Britain and turn to the land
that produced so many brilliant artists—Italy. In Italy the
Renaissance occurred much earlier than in England, and the
work of the artist Masaccio (1401–1428), short-lived though
he was, carried drawing in one step from the early attempts
of Giotto to the almost complete realisation of form portrayed
on the flat, and this more than a century before Holbein came
to England. From Masaccio the path of the student of
drawing is made brilliant by the names of the great Italians
such as Botticelli, Lorenzo di Credi, Raphael, and the great
Leonardo. The exquisite drawing of this last-named artist,
or of the fanciful Botticelli cannot be gazed at too long, while
the single study of a baby's arm by di Credi in the British
Museum is the epitome of perfect draughtsmanship, so rounded
and soft is it. In this drawing we have an example *par
excellence* of the combination of line and tone.

We have mentioned but a few great names out of the many
whose work should be studied by the serious searcher in the
realm of drawing. There is no need to keep to the Italian
School. We have already spoken of the work of Holbein,
and no mention of German art of the early sixteenth century
would be complete without the name of the greatest of all
that country's artists—Dürer. Holbein spent so much of
his time in England that we have come to look upon his work

7. HISTORY RECORDED IN EXQUISITE TAPESTRY

In the Bayeux Tapestry the whole story of the Norman Conquest is set down in embroidered drawings which, for all their apparent simplicity, are masterpieces of artistic planning and cleverly contrived, well thought out design.

as something belonging to that country, but Dürer, although he travelled and studied much in Italy, is definitely of the German School. His work is of particular interest to the student of drawing, for apart from his paintings his reputation rests on his wonderful engravings which, of course, are purely line work.

Dürer was first and foremost an artist, and thus upon all his travels, whether in Italy or in his own country, his note-book was as essential a part of his baggage as a toothbrush is to the twentieth century traveller. The lovely little notes of wayside stones and weeds, of bird and animal, that constantly occur in his notebooks are mute witness to his ceaseless sketching. It is said that he invariably arrived late at an appointment, for he would stop and start to draw anything that happened to attract his ever eager fancy. The use to which Dürer put these copious notes can easily be seen in the picture of the Adoration of the Magi, where all manner of grasses and weeds grow between the stonework of the stable, and a butterfly most exquisitely and faithfully rendered rests awhile upon a stone in the foreground.

IGNORANT CRITICISM THAT DIMMED REMBRANDT'S BRILLIANCE

OF artists belonging to the Dutch School, Rembrandt (1606–1666) is perhaps the best to cite in any article on drawing, for his etchings alone demand the attention of a draughtsman. Rembrandt is one of the greatest exponents of light and shade, and indeed it was this very research into the possibilities of chiaroscuro, as it is termed, that was to prove his downfall. This is exemplified in his famous *Night Watch*. Although it is a superb picture, full of mysterious dusk save where light flickers and glimmers upon a moving mass of people, the worthy Dutch patrons for whom the picture was painted disliked it intensely upon the grounds that none of the people who subscribed to have their portraits painted could be recognised because of the shadow effects. Few artists could stand such ignorant criticism, and Rembrandt, already terribly shaken by the death of his wife, certainly could not. For seven years the days were very dark indeed for him. His second marriage brought new happiness and new hope, but his first brilliance had gone never to return, and a year before his death his eyesight began to fail and his drawing became pathetically uncertain.

In this brief survey of the draughtsmen of different countries we may not mention more than one from each School, and to represent Spanish draughtsmanship no better artist can be cited than Lucientes y Goya (1746–1828). The great Velasquez is primarily a painter, but Goya produced many wonderful drawings quite apart from his painting. Moody, temperamental, and often ferociously fiery of temper, Goya was frequently in trouble with the Spanish authorities, so much so that a short sojourn in Rome was indicated. In 1775 he was back in Spain, and his marriage made him more settled. To Goya all form of artistic insincerity was terrible, and in consequence, his drawings and paintings possess a stark realism and literalness which may be seen in their most searing form in his portrayal of the horrors of the French invasion and occupation of Madrid. Fierce and morose of temper, Goya nevertheless had a love and a great attraction for children, and always a warm generousness towards his friends. He died in France at Bordeaux in 1828, and the force and sincere honesty of his work became a model for the French School of Impressionists more than thirty years later.

MASTERLY PORTRAYAL OF A PRETTY AGE

THE Revolution splits French art into two groups. The outstanding artist of pre-Revolution days is Antoine Watteau (1684–1721). This brilliant draughtsman and painter of " Fêtes Galantes " is the perfect recorder of the superficial and insincere age in which he lived. His delightful and sensitive drawings in red chalk give the lie at once to the cricitcism of prettiness sometimes levelled at his work. Watteau portrayed a pretty age, but his work is that of a master to whom the word " pretty " would be an insult, influenced as it was by the work of Titian and Veronese. He died of consumption in 1721, yet before that date he had become the greatest draughtsman of his age.

In 1789 the Bastille fell, a prelude to the Revolution that was to sweep away the world that Watteau's genius has immortalised for us. With the Empire period a revival of the classical tradition in art took place. Later came the triumphant entry of the English and Prussian armies into Paris, and Napoleon's lonely exile began at St. Helena. It is to this period that the work of Ingres belongs, although he was working before the fall of Napoleon, and in fact painted a portrait of the Emperor. The numerous minutely finished pencil drawings of single figures as well as of groups of people are perfect examples of this artist's work, and are of particular interest to the draughtsman. Ingres is the master of pure line and academic correctitude. It seems odd at first glance therefore that the great French Impressionist, Degas (1834–1917), based his studies on the work of this artist. We say " at first glance," for when we come to examine the matter, it is perfectly reasonable that an impressionist should first of all have been academic. Before liberties may be taken, the sound scaffolding must have been laid. So much of the modern work to-day fails because liberties are taken before the necessary background of knowledge has first been acquired. No one can look at the brilliantly drawn *Ballet Dancers* of Degas, mostly in pastel, without realising that he was a draughtsman of the first order.

THE VERSATILE GENIUS OF TURNER

WE have already spoken of the tinted water-colour drawings of the eighteenth century in England, and we
mentioned Turner (1775–1851) in connection with them.   It
would be impossible to write about the English school of
draughtsmanship without some reference to Turner's wonderfully careful architectural drawings.   One of the best places
to see examples of these is the Tate Gallery.   There, in the
Turner Rooms, a whole series of these meticulous drawings
of Gothic ruins may be examined at leisure.   Many of them
are in pen and ink of a sepia tint with slight washes of colour.
An earlier eighteenth-century artist, whose work had a great
influence upon Turner, was Gainsborough, and in the British
Museum one may see a number of delightful landscape
drawings by this artist, who was one of the first to realise
that the English countryside had its own individual beauty.

So important is Turner in English Art that it is impossible
to leave him without making some mention of his other works,
although strictly speaking they do not come under the heading
" Drawings."   *The Garden of the Hesperides* in the Tate
Gallery, London, *Ulysses Deriding Polyphemus*, and *Dido
Building Carthage* both in the National Gallery, are three
perfect examples of the classical type of picture, the fashion
for which was started by the great Richard Wilson, the father
of landscape painting.

Turner was far too brilliant to stop at the classical type of
picture.   All was grist to his mill and whether he expressed
himself by pen or pencil, water-colour or oils, it made no
difference and his subjects were as varied as his mediums.
We have some nineteen thousand water-colour drawings done
both in England and abroad, then great classical pictures and
finally his later more impressionistic work such as—the most
famous of all—*The Fighting Téméraire*, together with *The
Frosty Morning* and *Rain, Steam, and Speed*, a picture of a
train crossing a viaduct.   These three are in the National
Gallery, London.   Here indeed is versatility.   We have a
man who in the same breath as it were, can portray that secret
Garden of the Gods and a train crossing a viaduct.   Surely
no one could ask for more variety.

A contemporary of Turner's was that strange visionary
William Blake (1757–1827).   We do not always think of these
two artists as contemporaries, for Turner died twenty-four

years after Blake. Moreover it is to this later period that Turner's colourful impressionistic work belongs, and it is by this work that the layman remembers him rather than by the earlier, careful, architectural drawings of which we have spoken. Blake's whole training was in the classical tradition, and this is clearly seen in the flowing folds of the draperies in his drawings. While his drawings, which depend practically entirely upon line for their effect, and are sometimes faintly tinted, may seem peculiar in many ways to us, and quite possibly we do not like them, we cannot deny that they show a splendid draughtsmanship and a fine sense of design.

"IT'S CLEVER, BUT IS IT ART ?"

MENTION must be made of the meticulously careful drawings of the late nineteenth century. We have spoken of Sandys, and belonging to the same type one may add the drawings of Millais, Burne-Jones, and Holman Hunt. The unwearying manner in which the drawings of these artists, and a host of other lesser lights too, were shaded, laboured and worked upon, until each hair and crease had been put down is quite incredible. Yet nothing is too small or minute for representation to the type of mind that can, with amazing patience, paint each curled shaving on the floor, as did Holman Hunt in *The Shadow of the Cross*. Now is this slavish imitation in a drawing or a painting good and desirable ? The answer is "No," if we are to stand by our statement that a drawing must be an impression and not a copy.

We have mentioned *The Shadow of the Cross* by Holman Hunt as an example of almost photographic imitation, and although it is a painting and not a drawing, it will serve the purposes of our argument very well. The drawings of these artists were just as minute as their paintings, so either would do to illustrate our meaning. In *The Shadow of the Cross* we see Jesus in the carpenter's shop and all about Him are the implements and the litter of the worker in wood. The Divine Worker has paused to stretch his arms, cramped from the long use of plane and saw, and His upraised arms in conjunction with the tool rack and his body form upon the wall the Shadow of a Cross. Now this picture is meant to awaken in the mind of the beholder an emotion of awe and reverence at this prophetic vision of the sorrow that is to come, and as the chief aim of a drawing or painting is to awaken some emotion this would have been very well. Yet, when we look at this picture, our minds are so bewildered and led astray by the mass of irrelevant detail that anything the artist may have to say to us is stifled at birth. What importance can the appointments of a carpenter's shop have to us when we contemplate the tragedy of Calvary ?

So it is with most of these laboured drawings of the nineteenth century. There is no particular merit in the incredible realism of the marble of Alma-Tadema, and what have we gained by the minutely stippled pencil portraits by Sandys ? We are not concerned with the exact number of hairs on a person's head, but we are very much interested in that person's individuality. We desire above all else in a portrait that the personality and the very soul of the sitter shall be portrayed. The good portrait does this. The likeness is there, but combined with it is the inner self of the sitter.

To copy is definitely artistically bad ; this we may say quite dogmatically. The Pre-Raphaelites desired to portray nature truthfully, but in their absorption in minutiæ they lost the simplicity of rendering that only a broader treatment can give to a work of art. The French Impressionist Degas gives us in his *Ballet Dancers* all the glitter of the footlights, and we can almost hear the applause of the audience as the Dancer floats from the gloom of the wings into the full glare of the limelight. Thus, an emotion has been given to us by this impression which contains no detail, and we are, like Degas, in no way concerned with the fact that the scenery is put together with nails, or that the dancer has curly hair or straight. These facts, however, would have been of the first importance to a Pre-Raphaelite. Yet Degas could be as minutely careful as any Victorian draughtsman and just as academic.

A GREAT VICTORIAN MASTER : ROSSETTI

BEFORE leaving the subject of nineteenth-century art, however, it would not be just or correct to allow an idea to be formed in the reader's mind that all Victorian Art was bad. We have mentioned the meticulous draughtmanship of Sandys, and although technically it was excellent, imaginatively it was not of a high order. On the other hand, the nineteenth-century artist Rossetti produced drawings full of the same meticulous draughtmanship yet at the same time possessing an imaginative quality that at once raises them to a level above the work of Sandys. Rossetti was perhaps the greatest imaginative artist of his period, although his later portrait drawings have not the unique quality of his earlier work.

One of the most familiar of Rossetti's works and one of his earliest—it was painted when he was a boy of twenty—is the *Ecce Ancilla Domini* (The Annunciation) in the National Gallery, London. Again Rossetti's *Head of Christ* must be familiar to many from the numerous reproductions that have been made of it. Not so familiar, yet showing well Rossetti's imaginative qualities together with his sense of design, is the triptych in Llandaff Cathedral, Cardiff. The numerous *Blessed Damozel* pictures of his later days are, of course, well known, but the curious facial characteristics that he gave to his women—the large mouth and rather exaggerated chin —are not now so much appreciated as they once were.

To-day the pendulum seems to have swung in the other direction, and far too many artists practise a loose, formless draughtmanship which, in an endeavour to scamp the difficulties of drawing, becomes consciously peculiar. This, however, does not matter so long as there are leaders of the brilliance of Augustus John, Frank Brangwyn, and many another, to set the pace and standard.

"LIFE" THE GREAT TEST OF THE DRAWING

Now what is a good drawing and what constitutes a bad one? We have laid stress upon the importance of perspective, yet we have seen in the early English manuscript drawings a complete ignorance of this science, and in spite of that they are full of exquisite beauty and life. At the other extreme we have the drawings of the nineteenth century with their perfection of perspective and their realistic rendering, and yet we find them dull, unsatisfying, and dead. By this comparison we see that correct perspective and careful shading is not everything. It is life that really matters in a drawing, and if that vitality is lacking, then no matter how carefully or how technically perfect a drawing may be it will be bad.

This essential feature—life—need not only refer to drawings depicting living things, for it may equally well be present in a sketch of a building or in a still-life group. Here the interpretation placed upon the word "life" refers to the quality of line used. A good drawing must be alive and sparkling, and whether the portrayal is realistic or conventional depends upon the artist. It must always be remembered that a drawing can be realistic without becoming a slavish, uninspired copy.

WHEN THE MAN WITH THE PENCIL LAUGHS

THERE is a branch of art that, standing quite apart as it does, still affords an excellent example of this fact that copying is no good. We refer to caricature.

What do we mean by the word caricature ? A dictionary will tell us that it is the art of applying the grotesque to the purposes of satire. As a matter of fact the meaning that the man in the street attaches to the word is a drawing of some one with whom he is familiar, either personally or through the photographs in the daily papers, made to look funny. This last description is only partly correct, for it covers only one side of the question. Caricature may be placed into three divisions : the political cartoon, the comic drawing, and the caricature of the individual. We shall deal in this order with these divisions.

The great days of the political caricature were the eighteenth century. The political drawings of this period were full of malicious humour, definitely aimed at exciting contempt and hatred against the caricatured. The bitter humour of Hogarth (1697–1764), moralist and social satirist, is an example of this. Hogarth, apart from the distinction of being the first true English artist (for until the eighteenth century art in England had been in the hands of foreigners), stands supreme as the first satirist in art. This cannot be disputed unless we wish, in some pedantic spirit, to go back to the stone carvings of the Middle Ages, such as the heads of gargoyles, in which people have attempted to see some hidden satirical meaning. In the famous series of pictures called *Marriage à la Mode* Hogarth portrayed the licentiousness of his times, and it was this aspect with which he was more concerned than with the political side.

The work of James Gillray (1757–1815) later in the century was mainly political, and in the hands of this artist the art of political caricature attained its highest form. These eighteenth century caricatures, whether social or political, had a far deeper meaning and a wider scope than is attached to such work to-day. They were recognised weapons intended to stir up the hatred and rancour of the mob by grossly exaggerated drawings of the people in power.

A contemporary of Gillray was Thomas Rowlandson (1756–1827) well known for his coloured prints. In Rowlandson we have a happier type of caricaturist, and we see in his drawings that kindlier humour which was to grow out of the eighteenth-century bitterness and which was to culminate in the geniality of *Punch*. If we take two examples of the work of Rowlandson it will be enough to show the type of thing we mean. There are two prints entitled *Filial Affection*. In the first we see an eloping couple making a runaway trip to Gretna Green, their heads sticking out of their respective coach windows looking back at an irate and deserted father. The second print shows the couple married and repentant, seeking the parental forgiveness which is not withheld.

Any time of upheaval brings forth the caricaturist at his bitterest. The French Revolution can show a collection of the most scurrilous drawings depicting the hated aristocrat in every guise of depravity. The World War produced a host of drawings ridiculing the Kaiser and everything German, and, of course, England and the English were equally lampooned and with equal ferocity by the other side.

SATIRE SOFTENS INTO GENIAL HUMOUR

As we have said, gradually the bitterness of the eighteenth-century caricature gave place to more genial humour, and in 1840 *Punch* was founded. We now enter upon the second of our divisions—the comic drawing. The names of Tenniel, Charles Keen, George du Maurier, Phil May, Raven Hill, and Bernard Partridge, to mention but a few, stand out as pioneers of the comic drawing. Their humour is genial and happy, and whether it is the pathetic waifs of the gutter portrayed by Phil May, or the vagaries of the aristocracy in du Maurier's work, no attempt is made at any form of bitter sarcasm. When any political matter is illustrated, as in the famous cartoons of Raven Hill and Bernard Partridge, then the point at issue is dealt with in a sober and ceremonious manner, and if humour is intended, then the wit is in the very best John Bull vein which could not possibly give offence to the most sensitive.

The comic drawing must be looked at as quite distinct from the caricature of the individual, for a comic drawing in most cases illustrates a representative type such as a yokel, a city man, or the housewife. Generally these drawings are mild caricatures, for the artist exaggerates the hall-marks of each type and profession in order to lend point to the joke that he is illustrating. We have in *Punch* excellent examples of this type of drawing. Often the drawing is no caricature at all, but a perfectly straight representation of a particular type with, perhaps, a funny expression upon his face or in the pose.

Every country has its comic papers of varying degrees of importance and standing, and appealing to the types of people to whom the jokes are most suited. But perhaps no country can produce such inimitable comic drawings, as drawings, and requiring no letter-press to point their meaning, as France. The humour may not always be to the Anglo-Saxon palate, yet artistically the drawings are superb. In these modern French drawings we get very much nearer to the caricature, for more exaggeration takes place, and the drawing is self-explanatory. This last point is important, for a caricature should need no explanation. There must be an instant appeal if it is to succeed. The clever drawings by Fougasse approximate most nearly to this requirement.

Strube's little man is another example of a caricature of a type. He immortalises the middle-class office worker, who, forming the backbone of the country as he does, still bears quite meekly the load of taxation and other Govermental vagaries so peculiar to modern civilisation.

Again, Bateman's drawings are generally caricatures of types, such as the Guards Officer, or the choleric gentleman who lives at his club, has a perpetual Anglo-Indian liver, and hates everyone.

CARICATURE IN ITS MOST POPULAR FORM

WE now come to our last division, the caricature of the individual. Perhaps this is the most popular and most well-known type of caricature. It is caricature as understood by the layman—the funnily exaggerated face. The artists who stand out as perfect exponents of this very difficult art are such famous men as Max Beerbohm (" Max "), Leslie Ward (" Spy "), Low, and Dyson, while in the realm of the sporting caricature Tom Webster must stand supreme.

The caricature of Bernard Shaw by " Max " is a perfect example of the popular conception of what a caricature should be. In this drawing we have all the well-known characteristics of the great man exaggerated, and yet an undoubted likeness needing no explanation is immediately apparent to us. The caricatures of Aldous Huxley and James Maxton by Low are brilliantly clever examples of exaggeration and elimination, two of the principal points in all caricature. Not only the face, the long jaw and the lock of hair of James Maxton are there for us to laugh at, but the whole pose of the man as well, as he sits with arm curled round the back of the chair in what is undoubtedly a characteristic attitude.

So we see that it is not enough merely to put down an exaggerated drawing of the outstanding features of a person's face. For it to be a good caricature artistically, the personality of the sitter must be portrayed as well. In fact, those points that we lay down when speaking of portraits, must be present in a caricature too. A mere copy of Lloyd George's moustache, hair, and cape, are not enough. There must be all the dominance and virile energy of the man as well, and it must radiate from the whole drawing as it does from the man himself.

A DANGER FOR THE UNWARY CRITIC

THERE is a grave danger that lies in wait for the unwary critic of caricatures. It is that the true artistic value of the drawing may easily be lost sight of in the interest of its implication. We are apt to laugh or be angry at what we see to the exclusion of all else. It is only human to derive a malicious pleasure from the ridiculous portrayal of some one we know personally or by sight, and in the savouring of this unholy joy we are quite likely to lose sight of the fact that the drawing that pleases us so much is artistically bad. This we must always guard against when criticising a caricature.

We have now said sufficient to make it clear that caricature differs from ordinary drawing inasmuch as it is an exaggerated impression, which an ordinary portrait is not. Yet, before we leave this subject, we would add this. Caricature is by its very nature spectacular, and like all spectacular things it has a large following who all long to be able to " do " it. The question, " How can I learn caricature ? " is frequently asked, and it must be said quite clearly at once that caricature cannot be taught.

We have attempted to point out that this most difficult art depends upon exaggeration, elimination, discrimination, and a remarkable insight on the part of the artist into the very soul of his proposed victim. These qualities are gifts, and may not be acquired. The fact that copying alone is not enough cannot be too much stressed.

BOOKS THAT WILL GUIDE BOTH CRAFTSMAN AND STUDENT

THERE are a number of books which may be read with pleasure and profit by those who desire to go further into the subject of Drawing. An essentially practical book which will afford a comprehensive guide to the student is *The Art of Drawing in Lead Pencil*, by Jasper Salwey (Batsford). *Drawing for Art Students and Illustrators*, by Allen W. Seaby (Batsford) is an immensely helpful book that can be thoroughly recommended. It is written by the Professor of Fine Arts in the University of Reading. A book that is ideal for the layman who desires to improve his sketches without being lost in a maze of scientific fact is *Perspective in Drawing*, by D. D. Sawer (Batsford). The author is not only an expert teacher but a sympathetic guide as well.

The catalogues issued by the British Museum are a good starting-point for those taking up the study of drawings. The *British Museum Catalogue of Drawings by British Artists*, compiled by Laurence Binyon, and the *British Museum Reproductions from Illustrated Manuscripts* both deal with the exhibits in the Museum and form an excellent background for a study in appreciation.

SCULPTURE : THE CARVED WISDOM OF THE AGES

by *ALLAN HOWES, R.B.S.*

SCULPTURE is one of the eternal methods of self-expression and communication, neither superior nor inferior to other methods, only different. It is the art of expressing ideas in a three-dimensional form, usually but by no means necessarily without colour, and relying on light and shade to give meaning and value to the work. A unique method, it forms the only means by which can be expressed certain interesting aspects of many ideas. The first function of a piece of sculpture is to be a finely designed mass, giving mental pleasure; the second is to be an explanation to the onlooker of the idea which the sculptor sought to express in solid form.

From the earliest days man has endeavoured to express his thoughts in some permanent material, often for his own pleasure only and often unconscious of any artistic value in the result. He has retained that desire, even if he only meets it by carving two hearts pierced by an arrow, or some initials on a tree or seat. It is from their expressions of this desire—the desire to create—that we can best learn now the movements, habits, and histories of past races, while, thanks to portraiture, we are aware of the physical appearance of many of the great figures of history, who would otherwise have been to us nothing more than names.

As in all the arts, evolution is a thing of which sculpture knows nothing; some of the finest carvings ever made are the work of palæolithic man. What does really happen is that the level of sculptural achievement rises and falls; a certain school arises, reaches a climax, and then declines, and so on through the ages. To-day we are in a trough of a wave; the finest sculpture has either been produced, or will be produced later, and at the present moment we have at best a vague promise of great future achievement.

THE MISTAKEN DEMAND FOR " A PERFECT COPY "

A MISTAKEN idea of most people is that sculpture should be an exact copy of an object, a perfect or camera copy of, say, a figure. They expect the sculptor to copy exactly every bone and muscle, to include even toe-nails and the hooks and eyes on a costume, and should the model be such a perfect copy, it is, in the estimation of the public, a magnificent piece of work. They do not realise that what they are really asking for is not a piece of sculpture, but a stuffed human being.

The art of sculpture need have no concern with such things. A far more important consideration in the enjoyment of sculpture, especially of sculpture when set in the open, is the kind of silhouette the piece makes. Another point demanding consideration is the question whether the spaces are properly distributed, making a good design. Only when these larger matters have received attention is it suitable to pass judgment on the anatomical and other details. If the work is really well balanced, both in its masses and in its voids, a number of carelessly handled details can be easily pardoned. Sculpture must be judged not by any standard of lifeless exactitude but as a representation of the subject in question made in stone or metal, the treatment throughout being made suitable to the material used.

A practical understanding of these various points can best be obtained by a careful examination of the sculptures in Westminster Abbey. On some of these the greatest wealth of chisel technique has been bestowed, but it is labour wasted because the artists have concentrated on details which are meaningless since they are not related to the design—the shape and balance—of the pieces. There is no sculptor but must view Roubillac's marble skeleton with a lively grief that so superhuman a mastery of marble should have been used to so completely purposeless an end.

A further example can be made of the marble angels and cupids, also to be seen at Westminster Abbey, which are suspended on iron rods some distance from the wall. The man who treats marble in this way commits a crime against the nature of the material in which he is working. Marble is a weighty stone which needs to stand firmly on a steady base. It is as incongruous to make it appear to flutter in the air as it would be for a man dressed in a top hat and tails to ride a bicycle down Piccadilly. One of the first conditions of every art is that the artist should respect and understand the nature and conditions of his medium. A piece of sculpture worth the name will not look as if it wanted you to forget the stone it is made of. Rather it will make you realise the qualities of that stone better than you had done before and those qualities will play an essential part in its design.

THE WRONG WAY OF USING SCULPTURE

THE wrong way of using sculpture in connection with architecture can be seen on many recently erected buildings where carving is applied without the least excuse of a constructional, æsthetic, or functional connection, and appears to be stuck on like a postage stamp. Examples of the right placing of architectural sculpture can best be seen by looking at the doorways of the Gothic cathedrals where, by the way, the figures were placed after they had been carved in the workshop. They were not, as many people imagine, carved on the building.

The fetish should be dispelled at once that it is a question of any real importance whether the sculptures are carved on the building or not. What does really matter is whether the sculpture suits the architecture and the architecture the sculpture. Sculpture and architecture should make a complete whole, unified, so that nothing can be added or taken away, without detriment to the work. No detail should cry out against another; there should be the perfect marriage of sculpture and architecture.

In the case of sculptured groups, one can afford to remember the dictum of Michelangelo, that a sculptured stone group should be sufficiently self-contained to be rolled down a hill without serious damage to it. But, as will be shown later, this test could not be survived by many famous pieces of sculpture to be seen in various Museums and Art Galleries; such vigorous treatment would almost annihilate them as pieces of sculpture, because they were not, in the first case, conceived in terms of stone or some other brittle material, but were created as clay models to be turned into sculpture by means of a pointing machine. Incidentally much of this would-be sculpture is beautifully worked and finished, but it originated not as sculpture but as a sweet or sentimental rendering of a literary idea.

Fortunately there are opportunities to-day for sculpture to be used in a better way. It can be brought into use in everyday things and not allowed to grow as an exotic flower. It is a heritage that must be a part of our life and not a thing abstracted and apart, while the materials used, bronze and various stones, enable it to be the most permanent of all media to express human ideas.

MISREADING THE HISTORY OF SCULPTURE

WE have in our possession masterpieces of sculpture that have been produced both thousands and hundreds of years ago, over widely separated areas, according to conventions radically different one from the other, and as the expression of strangely different purposes. It is largely due to this accident of nature that the principles of sculpture to-day are in so fluid and unfortunate a condition. It might seem that with so broad a historical background the principles of sculpture would be peculiarly stable, but unfortunately this is not the case. Instead, a school of practice and criticism has arisen which has enabled a long series of pastiches of many primitive and powerful types to gain credence as constructive and creative modernisms.

This series has had the unquestionable virtue of giving the lie to the totally opposite vices of Victorian and Edwardian sculpture—the vices of ostentation, sentimentality, bad design, and misuse of materials—and has discredited much of the academic work that is still being produced by a number of highly placed, well patronised technicians. But the fact that some of these " modernisms " are much superior to the production of the academic school is no excuse for the dogma, that is only now being slowly dissolved in the acid of common sense, that if a picture or a piece of sculpture has been produced according to the dictates of certain formulæ, mannerisms, and conventions then it is good art. What is good is good, and for no other reason than that it is good, and artistic virtue is far too subtle and illusive a thing ever to stay " put " within the limits of the most intelligent convention. If the achievement of great sculpture needed nothing more than technical, competent obedience to great forerunners, European sculpture would have little need to-day of new ideas and a modern School.

The only true modern works of art are those which, whether they were an achievement of yesterday, a hundred years, a thousand years, or ten thousand years ago, are able to give one the true æsthetic thrill. Then they are alive. To give a concrete instance, if an Easter Island carving, produced thousands of years ago for a religious purpose the meaning of which we can guess at only, is able to thrill highly civilised

Europeans of the twentieth century to a higher degree than can a piece of sculpture, say, by Brancusi or Picasso, then it is obviously more modern than the productions of these contemporary figures.

SCULPTURE FROM ITS EARLIEST TIMES

SCULPTURE of some kind or other has, in a crude form, been practised since mankind first appeared. The expression was sometimes no more than a number of parallel lines made into a clumsy pattern, but of the work done in these earliest days we have unfortunately little trace, though prehistoric archæology has revealed a certain amount. This era, the last of the completed geological periods, is termed the Quaternary period. In this period France and England were still joined, and Northern Europe with Scotland were covered with ice. Few animals had been domesticated, and man, who had scarcely learned the arts of agriculture or of building, lived in caves and huts made of branches of trees. Notwithstanding this, he had learned how to chip flint axes and make a small number of weapons and implements which frequently possess great beauty of shape, so fulfilling an inborn, though unconscious, desire for expression. With an increase of mastery over the arts of agriculture and building came an increased capacity for self-expression. Man's weapons and tools became more decorated, designs appeared on the walls of his cave dwellings, incised with flints and often coloured. The designs in the cave dwellings are generally of animals ; they still rank as some of the most beautiful drawings ever made and in their own way they have never been surpassed.

ART THE OUTCOME OF COMMUNAL LIFE

FOLLOWING the age of cave dwellings, small settlements of people began to build for themselves, and groups banded together for protection. The formation of collective units naturally favoured the production of art which has as one of its principal requirements the means for quiet thought and meditation. For a variety of reasons art gradually came to be accepted by the general mass of the community who were somewhat losing their fear of the unknown. This is termed the First Stone Age, when all implements were made in stone. Tombs and circles of undressed stone, known as dolmens, cromlechs, and menhirs, were one of the more marked features of this age, and traces of them are found in various parts of Europe. At this period metal was almost unknown, all tools, weapons, and implements being made of polished stone, bone, or horn. With the discovery of metals, however, the whole outlook was changed.

Gold and copper were the first metals to be used, and later tin was discovered which, melted with copper, produces bronze. This discovery gave a great technical impulse to man, opening new horizons. The age of bronze saw further development in the ornamenting and embellishment of man's tools. The work of this age is nearly all ornament and decoration; sculpture in the sense in which we usually think of it to-day was scarcely known then. The patterns and designs were probably done for the sake of personal vanity, for as individuals increase in wealth so they elaborate their belongings.

With this increased vanity also, men now erected tombs to honour their dead; it was out of this that sculpture proper grew. But in practically all cases, animals and foliage alone were represented. Not only were different animals used to symbolise the various attributes of a god, such as the eagle for strength and swiftness and the cow for fertility, but obviously powerful inhibitions stood between the human form and its then sacrilegious use as material and inspiration for the artist. In Western Europe man was not incorporated in the design of sculpture until the invasion of Gaul by Cæsar, though the East was more advanced.

EGYPTIAN SKILL WE CANNOT IMITATE

THE Egyptians early decorated their buildings with sculpture, while the Pyramids they erected to their kings contained chambers full of beautiful carved and cast sculptures. At this time Egypt and Babylon led the world in the art of representation and expression in stone and metal, producing, often by means of slaves, some of the finest sculpture. Methods of casting in metals were also practised which even to-day, with all the aid of science, we cannot equal, while stones were used which we, despite tools of finely tempered steel, find difficult to cut. The Egyptian religion and the extreme slowness of social development had as one of their consequences that all building was of great permanence. For a similar reason, their sculpture expresses what is perhaps the most fundamental of all the qualities of stone or bronze, that of perfect immobility—a quality which was a genuine reflection of the timelessness which belonged to a religion consisting of little more than reverence and ritual for the dead.

About 2000 B.C. a new centre of activity arose in the Greek Archipelago, especially in Crete. The Cretans were possessed of a far more liberal ferment and a quicker rate of development than the Egyptians, but were nevertheless deeply influenced by them, all their work being tight or archiac, that is to say, formalised rather then naturalistic. Greek sculpture was soon firmly started on its way, and Egypt, through various political causes, came to its long period of decadence and foreign conquest, though it still continued to influence the younger art of Greece. In all probability the sculpture of Egypt, expressing the strongly dynastic qualities of its social order, had considerable technical influence on the sculpture of Assyria.

The Assyrians confined themselves generally to reliefs, only a few statues in the round having been found. Their principal subject was the history and activities of their kings and was expressed in large reliefs of muscular men and winged animals. Their sense of design and decoration was undoubtedly very great and was sufficient to make great art out of what were in reality merely chronicles of the times. The influence of Assyrian art spread to Persia and Asia Minor, reaching to the north of Armenia. The sculpture of the Persian Empire which followed the Assyrian was also based on the Assyrian but was marked by greater dignity and freedom, and in turn influenced the course of Greek sculpture.

"THE GLORY THAT WAS GREECE"

IN the dark age which preceded the great days of Greek art, Etruscan sculpture stands out in solitary excellence. Only certain types and shapes were allowed to be used, but, though this limited its range, making for a rather stereotyped convention, Etruscan sculpture was vigorous, bones and muscles being strongly marked. Greek sculpture followed next, with all its brilliance. First came the archaic period, during which it was confined within the styles of Egypt and Assyria, but which saw nevertheless the creation of much magnificent sculpture. This was about the time of the Persian wars.

The next stage was the age of Pheidias and his compères, during which Greece, absorbing the influence of Egypt, evolved a new style all her own, showed the heights of her

powers and achieved the work by which she has since been
able to dominate the world's sculpture on so many occasions.
With the age of Praxiteles, came also the decline of the empire
and with it that of Greek sculpture. Sculptors attempted to
make marble a vehicle for representing actual objects instead
of interpreting them in terms of stone. Thus decay set in.
Greek sculpture never rose again, but it left a lasting effect
on civilisation.

The final blow to Greek sculpture was of a political nature,
in the form of the Roman legionary ; the onset of these well
disciplined products of a great middle-class society brought
the empire of Alexander the Great to an end and with it any
of the remaining creative force animating Greek sculpture.
Just as in our own great middle-class colonising epoch of
the last century, the Romans greatly admired Greek sculpture
and, again, as in the Victorian era, they began a cumulative
process of imitating the worst qualities of the Greeks. With
the decline of the Roman empire, Eastern influences working
on the dregs of the inheritance of Pheidias created the
beautiful but restricted sculpture of Byzantium.

For the next four or five centuries little seems to have been
done in sculpture in the western world. After this long delay,
a mingling of influences resulted in the development of a new
style of scuplture known as Romanesque. This was closely
related to Romanesque architecture and both were restricted
but often very beautiful in design. The new style spread to
the north of Europe and there developed into Norman
Gothic. Its especial quality was that it was very rarely
designed apart from a definite architectural background.
Whether is was used to fill niches on walls, for tombs, or as
gargoyles or water spouts, it belonged entirely to the wonderful
churches and cathedrals that were springing up in France,
England and elsewhere. This Gothic sculpture reached the
height of its perfection in the twelfth and thirteenth centuries,
leaving us a magnificent legacy of beauty.

THE NOON-DAY AND AFTERGLOW OF THE RENAISSANCE

AFTER this period of activity, all art seemed to suffer from
a long blight. Signs of a new growth appeared in the early
fourteenth century in various parts of Europe, notably in
Flanders, where it first came to a fine growth. Later with
the Renaissance, art in Italy and France entered upon a period
of glorious light, illuminating the whole known world with its

brilliance. To the afterglow of this glory a number of old-fashioned sculptors of to-day pay homage. This Renaissance was really a brilliant but somewhat forced rejuvenation in which art was being created not by means of faith and love, as in the Middle Ages, but under a patronage in which the patrons were more concerned with their rivalry of one against the other than with art itself. Nevertheless, we have good reason to be grateful for the light of those past days.

At the decline of the Renaissance all art became more or less academic in treatment, possessing neither life nor inspiration. Among the probable causes of this decay were Italy losing its liberty to Spain and Austria and the Counter Reformation, which brought into prominence a religion whose patronage favoured garish decoration and a sentimentality of the worst type. Students of the sculpture of this period should not long remain in doubt as to what is meant by " the misuse of marble."

Sculpture still largely remains in the doldrums into which it fell three centuries ago. This period of decadence has largely coincided with the increased organisation of society, and there can be no doubt that growing means of transport broke up the collective groups of people under which sculpture flourished formerly. But perhaps the greatest influence making for decadence has been the steady decline of religious strength during the last two and a half centuries. Religion has lost the binding qualities that the faith of the Middle Ages had and has become, in short, respectable, without genuine utility or function.

A PLACE FOR SCULPTURE IN EVERYDAY LIFE

THE present day suffers also from the excessive number of exhibitions showing sculpture that belongs to nowhere. This is not altogether the fault of the sculptor, but as much that of the people who do not know how to use him in the correct way, turning him into little better than a maker of trifles. So perhaps this is the sculpture that we deserve. At the present time the great majority of people regard sculpture as something apart from normal life, a luxury rather than a necessity. They are unable to realise that there is a place for beauty in the environment of every individual, and that every life will become the fuller for an appreciation of the arts. Fortunately, however, there is slowly arising everywhere a genuine appreciation of the beautiful, largely in the teeth, it must be confessed, of the " blah " of the critics, the art dealer, and the middleman and small coteries of neurotics.

THE MODERNS LOSE THEIR SENSE OF VALUES

ART criticism is to a great extent responsible for the present state of things, so few critics being capable of giving a constructional criticism, in place of the mere expression of opinion, which is not true criticism. In the actual practice of the arts, how many artists are there in any medium have not their tongues in their cheeks, taking a pose of naivety, copying Easter Island idols, Romanesque reliefs, and other strange gods, strutting about, declaiming and proclaiming, modestly, of course, but loud enough for all to hear, what truly and genuinely original and wonderful people they are ?

The true artist, whose work alone has any chance of survival, approaches the matter in a spirit of humility, hoping that he will one day produce a thing of beauty. The public and many architects, however, seem to prefer the " blah," and as they know so little about sculpture in general, are enchanted at the sight of so-called modern sculpture. They forget it is the fashion to praise such work ; if they cared to look with their own eyes at the Romanesque reliefs at Chichester or the idols of Malaya at the British Museum they would at once realise that the great mass of this so-called modern sculpture consists of but poor copies of some fine manner originally achieved according to the reasonable demands of some definite utility and full of a genuine though long unrealised beauty which has, however, no place in a twentieth-century pastiche. Too many people seem to think that because all good art is modern in spirit, all modern art is good.

WHERE TO SEE SCULPTURE IN ENGLAND

A FEW examples only of individual sculpture can be enumerated here. Early cave dwelling carvings unfortunately can be seen only on the continent of Europe, at the caves of Combarelles, Dordogne, Fond de Gaume, and elsewhere. Menhirs can be seen in various parts of the world, the example nearest home being at the New Grange, near Dublin.

The earliest examples of stone sculptures can perhaps best be seen at the British Museum. Before entering the building itself, one should pay attention to the stone figures from the Easter Islands standing on each side of the entrance. From among so many masterpieces of sculpture it is somewhat difficult to choose those most deserving of mention, but the following pieces are worth studying : the Assyrian winged Bull and colossal lion, the statue of King Ashur-Nasir-Pal, believed to be the only Assyrian statue in existence, and the numerous Assyrian relief carvings. Mention may be made of the Etruscan Harpy tomb in the Archaic room. The Egyptian Archaic room contains a large number of important pieces of great simplicity and grace, and the gallery displaying the sculptures of the Parthenon will require many visits. The galleries devoted to Egyptian sculptures can be seen several times to advantage.

Upstairs are early bone and horn carvings, decorations of the Bronze Age, beautiful Greek bronzes such as the head of Hypnos and several other small figures. There are many cases of medals and coins that can be studied with advantage, especially those from Syracuse and the medals of Pisanello and Matteo de Pasti. The Maya sculpture of central America should be examined and much can be learnt from the study of pottery.

FINE EARLY CARVINGS IN THE MUSEUMS

EXAMPLES of early bone, horn, and ivory carvings are displayed in many museums in England. The best examples are perhaps at the British and the Victoria and Albert Museums and at the Wallace collection. Special notice should be taken of the following at the British Museum : a Palaeolithic carved tusk ; a figure of an Egyptian king, Abydos 3400 B.C. ; a gaming box, Cyprus, 14–11th century, B.C. ; a Gothic tryptych of the relief of St. Michael ; the crucifixion and the coronation of the Virgin. There are many other examples that will repay study.

At the Victoria and Albert Museum, South Kensington, some more beautiful examples of ivory carvings are available, generally of a later period than those at the British Museum. The following should be studied : a Romanesque walrus tusk relief ; a Virgin and Child, 15th–16th century Gothic ; a box from Moorish Spain, A.D. 969–970 and the early Christian Diptych. Much other sculpture is worth examination, such as the early Gothic carvings, the sculptures of the Renaissance, the bronzes and marbles of Donatello and his school, the coloured English alabaster carvings, and the beautiful lettering on the Trajan column. These masterpieces require long and

5

patient study and too much should not be attempted at once. It is better to look at a few examples only at a time and try to understand them with some thoroughness.

The very beautiful work in the Henry the Seventh chapel at Westminster Abbey should be seen, but care should be taken to avoid the monstrous monuments of the Victorian age, which destroy the spaciousness and proportion of the great church.

A CARVING WHOSE EVERY STAGE MAY BE TRACED

A FINE Michelangelo relief can be inspected in the Diploma Gallery at the Royal Academy. Particular note should be taken of this relief, which is in itself sufficient to form a complete course in the art of carving. All the stages of carving are shown, from the first roughing out of the marble to the final touch of the chisel.

Wells Cathedral contains a great deal of fine Gothic sculpture, though it is only on the Continent that we can see the finest architectural Gothic sculptures, such as those at Reims, Amiens, and Chartres.

When travelling in England, every opportunity possible to visit ancient buildings should be taken, as churches and cathedrals form a store house of sculpture that should on no account be neglected. Mention can be made of the two fine Romanesque reliefs in Chichester Cathedral which have influenced many sculptors of to-day, and of the early work in Ely and Winchester Cathedrals. The carvings of Grinling Gibbons decorate a number of churches in the city of London, while the work of many artists, from Victorian days to the " moderns " of the present time, can be studied at the Tate Gallery. Concerning these artists comment would be invidious.

Always remember when looking at sculpture, or, for that matter, at any works of art, that the greatest pleasure and reward comes from the quiet assimilation of a few pieces at a time. Constant study and observation of sculpture is a necessity for either its practice or enjoyment.

SCULPTORS WHO ARE INFLUENCED BY ANCIENT SCHOOLS

IT may be of interest to the student to note the influences of ancient Schools in the works of the following sculptors ; *The Wellington Memorial*, St Paul's Cathedral, by Alfred Stevens ; *The Eros Fountain*, Piccadilly, by Alfred Gilbert ;

the reliefs of *The Stations of the Cross*, Westminster Cathedral, by Eric Gill ; and *Rima* of the W. H. Hudson Bird Sanctuary, Hyde Park, by Jacob Epstein. The finer work of the last mentioned sculptor can be seen in some of his portraiture, examples of which will be found at the Imperial War Museum, South Kensington.

In addition to these sculptors, the work of the following can be studied with interest : Bourdelle, Brancusi, Gaudier Breszca, Frank Dobson, Reid Dick, Richard Garbe, Alfred Hardiman, Hernandez, Charles Jagger, Gilbert Ledward, Maillol, Paul Manship, Meštrović, William McMillan, Henry Moore, Carl Milles, W. Reynolds Stephens, John Skeaping, Alfred Turner, Charles Wheeler, E. S. Frith, A. J. Oakley, and Zadkine.

HOW THE SCULPTOR LEARNS HIS ART

THE best way to learn to carve is, of course, to be apprenticed to a stone mason or carver, cutting or carving stone in the daytime to gain practical knowledge of various stones, and modelling and drawing in any spare time, preferably from life, at an art school. The continual experience of cutting various stones, such as Portland, Hopton Wood Stone and Marble, is the only way to learn their limits and possibilities.

Sculpture comes from a word meaning to cut or carve, and this must always be understood as the basis from which to obtain a knowledge of or to approach sculpture. Where modelling involves building up piece by piece, the craft of sculpture is to reveal the conceived idea by removing its covering of superfluous matter. This superfluous matter it is the sculptor's business to cut or chip away.

The tools needed are few and simple, consisting of a drill and some bits, a turntable (heavy) for stone, a lighter one for the plaster model (if one is used), a short-handled, steel-faced or iron hammer (about 4 lbs. in weight), steel tools, claw, points, etc., a few old riffles and files, iron compasses, foot rule, plumb line and a piece of York stone for sharpening the tools. All the tools can be obtained at most tool merchants. The steel tools should be of a good length and will have to be tempered according to the material to be cut.

In practice, the hammer is generally held in the right hand and the tool guided by the left. In starting on the stone it should be pitched off, that is, knocked off roughly into shape with a hammer and point. After this rough shaping, the final shape is more and more nearly revealed as the carving proceeds. The best stone for the beginner to choose is perhaps such a stone as Beer Stone, which is soft; then he should pass on to Portland stone and so on to the harder stones such as Hopton Wood Stone, etc.

HOW TO BRING THE MODEL TO SHAPE

THE easiest way to work is first to make a careful model, preferably half size, in clay or wax, of the design required, cast it in plaster and from this plaster model take numerous measurements by means of a pointing machine. All these measurements are transferred to the stone or marble by drilling a hole in each case at the relevant spot to the correct depth, the position being decided by the detail of the model. At this stage, the plaster model will be covered with small crosses, marking the measurements, and the block of stone or marble will be roughly hewn and covered with innumerable holes. The stone or marble is then cut away, so connecting all the holes (depths) and so arriving at the shape of the model. Closer points are then taken and transferred to the stone or marble; they, too, are connected in a like manner until the stone or marble resembles the model in every way.

This method is, of course, most likely to be successful when the desired result is a dead copy of a model rather than the production of a piece of sculpture, owing to the unfortunate fact that modelling is not necessarily sculpture. Different materials require different treatments. Bronze can be freer in movement and treatment than stone because it is self supporting, but the same design carried out in stone would require an attachment to some other part. There are in certain museums works by eminent sculptors who have transgressed sadly in the use of stone and marble, many of their pieces having large supports from limb to limb. Such conventions did not offend the taste of their day but they nevertheless form a direct contradiction of all the laws of sculpture. It is not always realised to-day that these works are mere copies of clay models.

MAKING THE WORK EMERGE FROM THE STONE

PERHAPS the best way to make a piece of sculpture is first to have a clear conception of what one wishes to do, then to

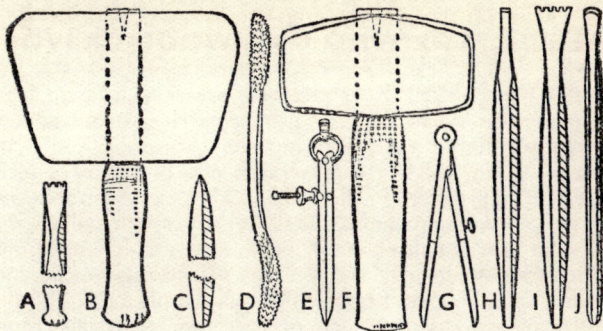

8. SOME OF THE TOOLS USED IN STONE-CARVING

The equipment of every stone-carver should contain a selection of mallet-headed tools (A), for soft stones, a mallet (B), punches (C), a few riffles of the type shown at D, dividers (E), an iron hammer (F), compasses (G), with three cup-headed chisels, claws, etc. (H, I, J), for harder stones.

make the necessary drawings, covering all the more important aspects of the work proposed, and also to make a small model in clay or wax, of the main masses and lines. This will help to keep the idea fresh. When the size of the stone has been determined and a satisfactory piece secured, it must be mounted firmly on a banker or turntable. A start can now be made pitching off the stone until it begins to resemble the shape of the idea. The cutting continues until the shape and mass desired is arrived at. This is a longer method than that of the pointing machine, but on the whole it is more satisfactory to the sculptor; while to be able to watch the emergence of the work from out of the stone is a thing of the utmost fascination.

A work can be taken to any degree of finish, the use of materials such as carborundum, emery, etc., enabling one to achieve a fine polished surface. This is also a great asset for work that is to be fixed out of doors, as the polishing of the stone will help to fill the pores and prevent the wet and frost from entering and bringing about early corruption. As in everything else, continual practice is necessary; even to cut a straight line in stone is not so easy as it appears. But it is amazing after how short a practice at cutting or carving stone the feel of it comes.

THE SCULPTOR WHO USES WOOD OR IVORY

THE tools required in woodcarving are very different from those required in stone or marble carving, because wood is a totally different material from stone. It is more easily cut, but has a grain which naturally raises new problems of technique and expression. The tools, which can be purchased at any good tool merchant's, should consist of two mallets, one large and one small (box or beech), several iron clamps, one or two wood hand-vices, compasses (iron and pencil), foot rule and steel gouges, firmers, fluters, parting tools (about a score is sufficient with which to start), some turkish stones to fit these tools to sharpen them and finally, a stout bench or table on which to cramp the work. All these tools can be augmented as the knowledge of how to cut the wood progresses. All tools should be kept very sharp, the final edge being gained by stropping them up on a prepared leather. Care should also be taken to avoid cutting against the grain of the wood as much as possible, although at times it cannot be avoided.

HOW THE WOOD-CARVER MAY BEGIN

IT is perhaps best to begin by copying models of some kind until one has become sufficiently used to the tools and the wood to be able to proceed to more ambitious things. When figures are carved it is often best to carve them upright. This is done by clamping the wood to be carved on a post which in turn is firmly fixed to the floor and ceiling or joist. All wood to be carved must be held rigid. The actual procedure of carving is very similar to that of cutting stone, only there is a greater freedom in the use of wood. This can be seen in the work of Grinling Gibbons, which was not cut from the solid but was added, piece by piece, as the carving was finished ; the drawback to this method was that it failed to bring out the genuine sculptural qualities of its material ; it was a trick method, and as such should not be copied.

In carving various woods, it will be found that grains differ greatly, and the best way to suit one's design to a particular wood can only be learned through practice. Should one desire to carve a figure in the round and of some size, one should be careful to have the piece built up, that is, to have it composed of a number of pieces glued together.

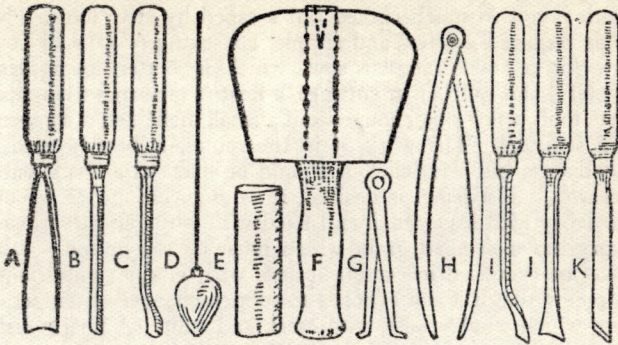

9. TOOLS THE WOOD-CARVER WILL REQUIRE

In addition to the usual equipment of bench, pencils, and footrule, the wood-carver will require a variety of gouges (A, B, and C), a plumb line (D), a Turkish stone for sharpening his tools (E), a mallet (F), callipers (G and H), and a selection of other tools of the type shown at I, J, and K.

This will prevent the wood from splitting and opening as it might do if it were in a single block. Should a single block of wood be used, be sure that a large hole is drilled the length of the work. This will do much to allow the wood to dry evenly all through and help to prevent opening, but it is not as satisfactory as a block made of many pieces and glued together.

IVORY : A FAVOURED MEDIUM OF THE ANCIENTS

IVORY is the modified tooth substance of a certain group of animals such as the elephant, the hippopotamus, the rhinoceros and the extinct mammoth and throughout history it has been a material of high value. Carved ivory objects have been found on the supposed site of Troy and also in the ruins of the temple of Minerva, dating about 900 B.C. The Greek sculptors Pheidias and others used ivory in their statues ; the famous statue of Zeus by Pheidias, for instance, was faced with ivory. The finest quality of ivory is the African ; it has a close grain and its colour remains purer than that of other types.

In carving ivory one is limited by the shape, size and curve of the tusk. This should be borne in mind and proper advantage taken of the frequently delightful curve. Ivory in truth is not so much carved but scraped by steel tools. The tools required are few and simple, consisting of a small bow saw (or a small circular saw, which is better, being less wasteful and quicker in cutting), a float (a tapering, triangular steel tool), a few small gouges and a small mallet, steel scrapers and scorpers. The work, if in the round, is best held in a wood vice, but if a relief, it should be fixed to a board with beeswax. If a panel is desired, the design can be drawn on the ivory with lead pencil and fixed with white spirit varnish. Ivory has a decided grain which must be recognised ; care must be exercised in cutting it and, what is more important, in seeing that it is not exposed to sudden changes of temperature which would cause it to crack and split. A final polish can be obtained by rubbing the ivory with pumice powder on a damp cloth.

THE ESSENCE OF THE MODELLER'S ART

IF possible, one should learn to model by working in a sculptor's studio, if only for one or two days a week. In this way practical experience can be gained which is otherwise unobtainable. The remaining time should be spent at an art school, studying drawing and modelling, preferably from the life. Especial attention should be paid to drawing, since all sculpture is but drawing plus a specialised technical knowledge, while with drawing also comes increased powers of observation.

The materials required for modelling are a turntable, an easel, a plumbline, wood and wire tools, callipers and compasses, and clay or wax. All of these can be purchased from an artists' colourman. A start should be made by copying simple plaster casts, which can be obtained either from an artists' colourman or from the cast department at the Victoria and Albert Museum, South Kensington. After copying a number of simple casts, the novice can begin modelling a head from life.

The first thing to do is to prepare the armature or support to hold the clay. First procure a board about one foot six inches square, with battens or cross pieces to prevent the damp clay from warping the board. To the centre of this board fix firmly an upright post, about three inches square, and a foot or eighteen inches high. At about six inches from the top of this post, nail on opposite sides some lead or compo

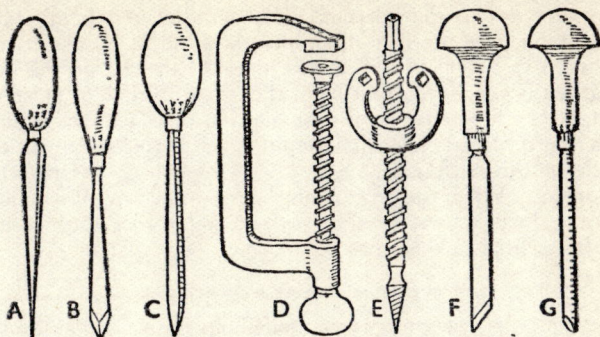

10. PART OF THE IVORY-CARVER'S EQUIPMENT

*In addition to one or more small saws and a small mallet,
the ivory-carver will require some steel scrapers and scorpers
as shown at A, B, C, F, and G, the two clamps illustrated at
D and E are for wood-carving.*

piping (about five-eighths of an inch thick) so as to make a
loop which will be, at its highest, some nine inches above the
top of the post. That done, all is ready for the clay which
should be kept soft and of an even consistency—so that it can
be easily worked. On to this armature the clay must be built
to form an oval the size of an average head.

The following measurements which must be taken very
carefully with the callipers, are essential. It is a good plan to
keep a record of them permanently on paper as they are
marked off, so saving much time and much annoyance to the
sitter. The principal measurements required are : from the
chin to the bottom of the orifice of the ear, the chin to the root
of the nose, the width of the eyes from outer corner to outer
corner, the width of the face at the ears. These measurements
are usually marked in the clay head with dead match sticks—
the phosphorus in the live ones would discolour the clay. The
sticks are pressed into the clay until they tally with the
measurements taken from the sitter, and must remain as
fixed points from which all other measurements are taken.
Useful minor measurements are the length of the nose, the
size of the ear, the eye and the mouth, and the total height of
the head from the chin.

When these measurements have been marked in the clay,
the next step is to draw the profile. This provides a firm basis

for the rest of the portrait. When the clay is being added piece by piece until it resembles the head of the sitter, care should be taken to keep the head well balanced on the neck, as this is very important from the point of view of poise and dignity. The sitter should be allowed to talk or move about so that the artist may catch the sitter's characteristic qualities—one of the most valuable things in modelling a satisfactory portrait. When the head is not being worked on, it should be covered either by a wet cloth or by a waterproof cage because it is essential to keep the clay moist.

WHAT IS MEANT BY "RELIEF"

RELIEF is the process of modelling against a background and is of three kinds; low or basso, medium or mezzo, and high or alto. The method of working is the same for each kind, the difference between the three being, as their names imply, only of degree. The necessities are a thick battened board with two rasied wooden edges (called *runners*) firmly fixed on opposite sides, the usual tools, and an easel on which to stand the board. The relief can be made in either of two ways; it can be cut out of a slab of clay that has been laid on the board, or it can be built up on the board, piece by piece. A third method consists of a combination of part cutting away, part building up.

In the method of building up on a clay slab, the slab is prepared by knocking a few copper tacks or galvanised brads into the cross battened board at intervals of three or four inches, in order to keep the clay on the board when it is raised to an upright position while the clay is being modelled. When the clay has been added, the slab should be smoothed with a straight edge drawn across the clay on the wood guides or runners mentioned above. When the slab is smooth, the background can be defined and the design put in with clay which is not too wet. The design can then be steadily built up with small pieces until the desired effect is obtained. Much interesting work can be done in relief, which has the great advantage that it lends itself readily to plaster casting.

THE FIGURE ARTIST MUST UNDERSTAND ANATOMY

FOR figure work a turntable is required in addition to the tools mentioned above. A knowledge of anatomy is needed for this work and can be learned from various books on the subject. A knowledge of the skeleton is absolutely

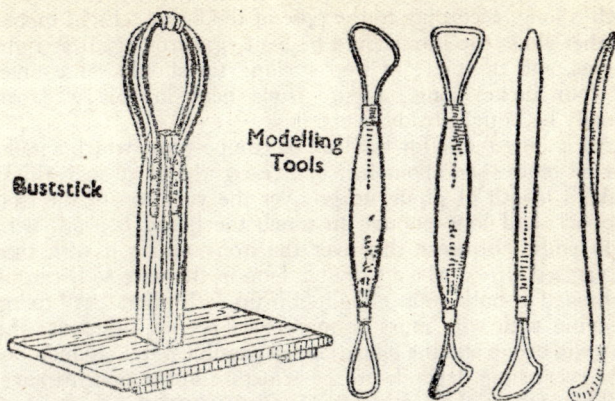

Buststick

Modelling
Tools

11. APPARATUS FOR MODELLING A PORTRAIT BUST

Before setting to work with the clay, the modeller must first prepare a support (known as a head armature or buststick), consisting of lead piping securely fastened on to a wooden base. Modelling tools vary widely in size, but are essentially of two kinds, wooden ones for building up the clay and wire-ended ones for removing it when too much has been added.

essential. It is advisable also to practice drawing from the life at the same time as one is modelling a figure, A model is required and it is perhaps best to work from a male model, as the bones and muscles are more clearly defined on the male body than on the female.

When the pose of the figure to be modelled (from drawing or sketch model) has been decided, an armature must be provided as when modelling a portrait bust. This is built as follows. A battened board about two inches thick and about one foot six inches square is procured and on this, at an equal distance from each side and at about one-third from the back of the board, is erected a bent iron standard, the iron being about three-quarters of an inch square in thickness. This is suitable for a half life-size figure. The iron should be split or splayed at its base into three feet, bent at right angles to the upright. Each foot should be drilled in two places and then screwed on to the board, thus making a firm support for the lead armature. About sixteen inches up the iron should be bent forward at right angles, the bent piece being six to twelve inches long, according to the pose of the figure. Eight inches further along the iron should be bent upwards again at right angles, and the piece of iron sticking up should, of course, be four inches long. Figure irons bent in this way can usually be bought ready made.

All is now ready for the lead or compo pipe, which should not be more than about half or five-eighths of an inch thick. Take a length of piping to go over the very top of the iron support, and long enough to touch the board beneath with both ends. Squeeze this over the iron and tie it with thin galvanised wire. Make a double loop in the wire so it can be tightened at both ends. Tighten it up with pliers. All fixing or tying with wire must be made very secure, otherwise the clay will droop and the figure lose all possible pose. Remember that everything depends on the armature in the first instance.

Then take a shorter length of pipe and tie this to the iron in an upright position, making it in the form of a loop above the top of the bent iron. The height of this, which will form the support for the body, depends on the height of figure decided upon. Then take a single piece of piping and fix this to the upright bend of the iron, and to the piping covering the iron, looping the end. This will support the head and should be fixed where it passes the loop for the torso and fastened firmly to the other piping. The height of this single piece of piping will decide the height of the figure, the centre of such a figure being at about the bottom of the bend of the support iron. For the arms, take two single pieces of piping and lay them on the loop arranged for the body and fasten together by wire. The armature for the fingers can be made by inserting five lead wires into the open ends of the piping for about one inch ; then squeeze the pipe together, thus fixing everything firmly.

CREATING MUSCLES AND BONES IN CLAY

THE piping can now be bent roughly into the pose decided upon, care being taken to bend the pipe in gentle curves, to prevent it from kinking and eventually breaking. The best way to lay on the clay is to follow, as nearly as possible, the shapes of the muscles, bones, and general form. It is best to start modelling everything meagrely, gradually thickening up by completing the form. Do not think about the surface of the clay, as this will gradually come into being as the form is completed. Measurements are very essential, the principal

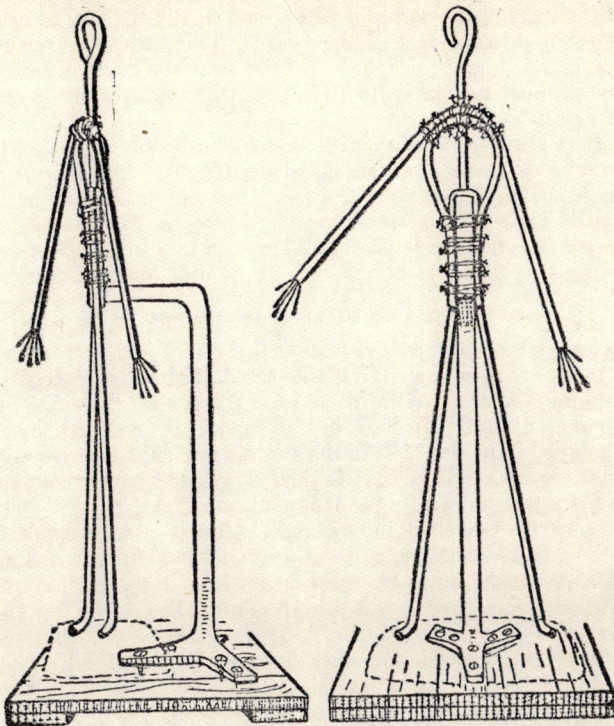

12. THE FOUNDATION OF ALL FIGURE MODELS

The clay used in modelling a figure must be supported by an armature which consists of lead piping fastened with wire loops on to a " figure iron " secured to a wooden base. " Figure irons " can be bought ready prepared, but the artist must arrange the piping himself.

being the height of the figure from the ground (for which a reducing scale must be made when the size of the figure has been decided upon), the height from the ground to the pit of the neck, from the ground to the knee (patella), from the knee to the crest of the hip bone (ilium), from the ground to the centre of the figure (pubic arch), from the pit of the neck to the end of the clavicle or collar bone, from the collar bone to the elbow, the elbow to the wrist, from the wrist to the end of the fingers, the width of pelvis, and finally the size of head in relation to the rest of the figure. This last measurement is important in the proportion of the figure. These measurements must be marked with dead match sticks as in the case of a portrait bust.

It is always necessary to be careful to balance the figure ; nothing is worse than an unbalanced figure, unbalanced in distribution of masses and pose. For animal modelling, a special armature is necessary and requires to be discussed at greater length than is possible here. As in all matters of art, continual practice is necessary for any hope of excellence.

THE PROBLEMS OF SCALE IN MODELLING MEDALS

A MEDAL or coin is always modelled on a much larger scale than that intended for the actual finished piece. Six inches in diameter would be an ordinary size for the subtleties demanded, and afterwards the model is reduced by a machine on the principle of the pantograph. When the design has been decided upon, it is then modelled according to the principles described for modelling in relief. Medals and coins are usually modelled in low relief because it is difficult to force metal into the steel die if the relief is high. In making such designs, plaster casts are made from time to time and worked upon, reverse and obverse, until the modelling and design is deemed satisfactory. The medals of Pisanello and others can be seen and should be studied carefully at the British Museum, which issues an excellent series of photographs of medals in postcard form.

HOW THE PLASTER CAST IS MADE

A VARIETY of ways exist of casting in plaster, of which the most usual are waste moulding, piece moulding, gelatine moulding and wax moulding. Other methods exist, but these will be sufficient for the student. In the general way it is best to make a waste mould, which is used once only. For practice it is wisest to start with a small relief, so that the mould need consist of one piece only. The modelled relief is placed on a board and around it is erected a small wall of clay about an inch and a half in height. This is to retain the liquid plaster until it sets or hardens.

The seemingly simple job of mixing plaster requires in fact a good deal of skill and is a very important process in the business of plaster casting. Take a bowl about two-thirds full of water, and sift dry plaster (Dental or Cafferata, both of which can be purchased at the oil shop) through the fingers until it can be seen just below the surface of the water. Then stir the mixture briskly, below the surface, with a spoon, until it is smooth like cream. As this is to be the first coat of the waste mould, the plaster must be tinted by adding some earth colour, such as yellow ochre, to the water before mixing the plaster. The reason for this will be given later. The plaster when mixed should be a deep cream in colour. Plaster should be neither too thick nor too thin. To test for the right thickness, dip in a finger. If the plaster sticks to it, the consistency is correct. Quickness in handling is necessary as plaster sets hard in about ten minutes.

CLOTHING THE MODEL OF CLAY WITH PLASTER

SPLASH the plaster on to the clay model with the fingers and distribute it as evenly as possible, until it is about a quarter of an inch thick. Do not attempt to smooth the surface, but let it remain lumpy as thrown on. This will form a key for the thick casing of plaster which has to be placed over the thin colour coat. When this coloured coat has set, brush here and there with clay water, that is, clay made into a thin mixture with water. The value of this is that, when the outer white mould is cut off, the coloured part of the mould, which serves to give warning of the nearness of the plaster cast inside the mould, is revealed more easily.

Now thicken up this first coat to about three-quarters of an inch, with plaster mixed in clean water, and strengthen up the mould with iron rods, three-eighths of an inch in thickness if the mould is a small one. The size of the iron should be proportionately larger according to the size of the mould made. When the plaster has set, the next step is to take it off the model. This can be done by letting water run between the model and the board, then, with the help of a blunt chisel wedge the mould off the board. When this has been done, the mould can easily be lifted off. When the mould is off, pick out the clay with a modelling tool and wash the mould out with a brush and water, or, better still, use a syringe which will force out the remaining clay without harm to the mould. When the mould is clean, it must be allowed to dry for an hour or so.

The next step is to make a saturated solution of soft soap

(Green) which must be well brushed into the open mould with a soft brush. After it has been well frothed, it must be thoroughly removed, leaving the mould again clean. A little olive oil is next lightly brushed, and then the mould is made thoroughly wet, in order to prevent suction or air bubbles, which would occur with a dry mould. All is now ready to make the final cast.

The mould is laid on its back, with the opening of it ready to receive the plaster. Mix an amount of plaster sufficient to fill the mould and then brush or pour it in, remembering to shake the mould about to prevent air-locks. When the plaster is sufficiently thick and set, the mould should be turned over and the outer casing cut off by using a blunt chisel and hitting it with a wooden mallet. Chip off the mould until the coloured coat is revealed, the coat which gives warning that you are getting near the cast. Greater care is now needed. A smaller chisel is now used to reach the white surface of the cast inside. All that remains to be done is to pick out of the cast the remaining pieces of the coloured mould.

MOULDS THAT MUST BE MADE IN PIECES

To take a cast of a model in the round the same process is used as for a relief, but the mould has to be made in two or more pieces. A head is usually cast in two pieces, a figure in three. A plaster cast of a figure must have iron supports inside the plaster in the arms, legs, body and head, since otherwise the cast would break to pieces when the mould was removed.

Piece moulds are more difficult to make than waste moulds and should not be attempted until proficiency is attained in making the latter. The advantage of a piece mould is that the pieces can be arranged in such a way that the cast can be lifted out without damaging the mould. Consequently almost any number of casts can be taken from one mould.

There is another type of plaster casting in which the mould is made of gelatine instead of plaster. This method is useful because it allows a mould in one piece to be taken from a model containing undercutting (see Fig. 13). When the mould for a model of this kind is made of plaster, it has to be a piece mould. The use of gelatine, as will be seen later, allows the mould to be made in one piece.

A further advantage of using a gelatine mould is that the cast can easily be lifted from the mould without damage to either mould or cast. The mould can therefore be used many times over instead of just once, as in the case of a waste mould. The process is rather difficult at first, but as in everything else, experience is a good teacher.

Shellac (french polish) must first be brushed over the model that is to be cast, sufficient to make the surface shine (it is assumed that a relief is being cast). When dry, the model must next be covered with tissue paper, after which clay is placed over it to about an inch thick. The purpose of the tissue paper is to prevent the clay sticking to the model. Care must be taken to follow the form the model takes, and this is done by gently pressing the clay evenly all over. When

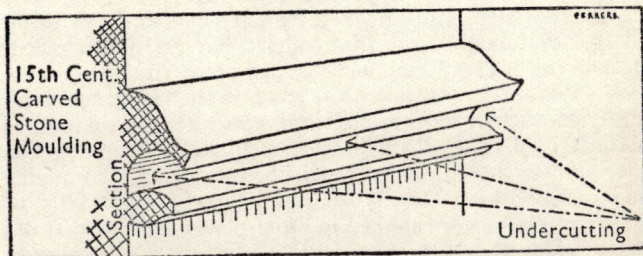

13. AN EXAMPLE OF UNDERCUTTING

Unless a gelatine mould is used, undercutting on a model involves difficulty in casting, because the mould must then be made in more than one piece.

the surface is smooth, cover with about an inch of plaster, strengthened with irons. This is termed the box.

When the plaster has set, it must be taken off and shellaced on the inside until it also shines. Next take the clay and tissue paper off the model and then grease both the inside of the box and the model with olive oil, taking care that no parts of either are left without a covering of oil. Then cut three holes through the plaster box, two to serve as air vents and one for pouring in the melted gelatine. The plaster forming the holes must be shellaced and oiled. Meanwhile the gelatine should have been on the fire, in a double boiler, for several hours previously and should now have the consistency of thick glue. The gelatine should be warm, not hot, when it is poured into the box.

Before the gelatine is poured in, the box is placed in position over the model by fitting it into certain keys or guides to which it is securely fastened. There should be at least two of these guides, but too many are only confusing. On the largest hole of the three place an oiled flower-pot or wide funnel, and fill up all intervening crevices between the funnel and the plaster box with soft clay. Over the other two holes build up chimneys of clay, which are to act as air vents. As the gelatine fills up the box it will push the air out through these chimneys. When the gelatine has reached the top of the chimneys all the air will have been forced out of the box. When the gelatine has been poured in and the chimneys filled, the tops of the chimneys are squeezed together and then the whole is left to cool for a few hours.

The next step is to lift off the plaster box and then to lift the gelatine mould from the model. The gelatine is placed back in the box, and the mould is then prepared to receive the cast. French chalk is first brushed on to the mould to absorb any grease left from the model, and after that, a solution of alum is used to toughen the surface of the gelatine. When the alum has dried the mould must be brushed out thoroughly and then, with another brush, a mixture of Russian tallow and olive oil must be applied in order that the plaster may not stick. The mould is now ready to be filled with plaster, which is mixed in the same manner as that described for waste moulding. When the plaster is just set the plaster box should be lifted off and the gelatine bent away from the finished cast. After the plaster cast has been taken out, be careful to replace the gelatine mould in the plaster box and cover all with a cloth to keep out the air as much as possible.

THE PURPOSE SERVED BY THE MODEL IN WAX

To take a cast of a sketch model it is sometimes useful to make a wax mould. The procedure is to melt the wax (beeswax or paraffin wax) in a saucepan, then to brush the hot wax over the clay model and when the wax is about one-eighth of an inch thick, cover it up with plaster, thus making a case for the wax. Open the mould and pick the clay out with a modelling tool and finally wash the mould out with water and a brush. The mould is then filled with plaster and allowed to set. After this, the outer casing of plaster is chipped off, leaving only the wax covering to the plaster cast, which is melted off by immersion in hot water. This method is limited to use with small clay or wax models.

Plaster models can be treated with stearine or wax, which, if applied hot to heated plaster, penetrates into the surface of the plaster for a considerable depth. The best results are obtained by immersing the plaster model in the melted stearine or wax. Plaster should not be exposed to the weather, unless protected by lead paint and even then it will disentegrate with the elements. Moreover, painted plaster never looks well. Apart from reproduction in plaster it is possible to cast a model in many other mediums, such as bronze, terra-cotta, pottery, artificial stone, and cement. As with plaster reproduction there are a variety of casting processes, some of them very complicated. Reproduction in these mediums, however, needs furnaces and machinery, so that it is rarely, if ever, carried out in the studio. The usual procedure is to entrust the work to a firm which deals in such things.

HOW THE SCULPTOR MAY SELL AND EXHIBIT HIS WORK

ALL work intended to be shown or sold should be made or executed in some permanent material, such as stone, bronze, or pottery. Works in plaster are apt to get broken, and a mutilated work in plaster will never look well. It is almost impossible to sell a plaster model, because its usefulness is limited, but such models can often be shown at exhibitions and if afterwards commissioned, can be executed in whatever material the patron demands.

There are a large number of exhibitions held in London and in the provinces, particulars of which can be found in such publications as *The Year's Art*. Work of varying degrees of merit can be shown at these exhibitions, and in most, though by no means in all cases, only a very small percentage of all sales is charged. Exhibitions afford a good way both of showing and of selling work, as practically all the money paid for the work goes to the artist.

When a dealer sells the work he takes from a quarter to a third of the value of it, thus leaving little for the sculptor. That is why " one man shows " are, from the dealer's point of view, so useful, since he generally looks at art only as a means of making money. The possibilities of selling sculpture are at first very limited indeed, but as the reputation or notoriety, as the case may be, of the artist increases, so the sales increase.

WHAT TO READ ABOUT SCULPTURE

For those interested in reading about sculpture and model-ling, the illustrated catalogues and booklets issued by the British Museum and by the Victoria and Albert Museum pro-vide an invaluable guide and introduction. The prices vary from sixpence to eighteen pence. An excellent, well-illustrated account of sculpture in the modern civilised world is provided by Kineton Parkes' *Sculpture of To-day*, 2 vols. (Chapman & Hall).

Readers who want to know more of sculpture in the past are recommended to consult the following books, according to which period appeals to them most : *Celtic Art*, by J. Romilly Allen (Methuen); *Egyptian Sculpture*, by Maspero (Heinemann); *A Handbook of Greek Sculpture*, by E. Gardner (Macmillan); *Greek and Roman Sculpture*, by A. Furtwangler (Dent); *The Sculptures of the Parthenon*, by A. Murray (Murray); and *Florentine Sculptors of the Renaissance*, by W. Bode (Methuen).

ARCHITECTURE : THE ART OF NOBLE BUILDING

by REGINALD TURNOR, B.A., A.R.I.B.A., A.A. Dipl.

IN the first consideration of the real essence of architecture, it is tempting to define it once and for all as good
building.

At first sight, too, this definition seems sound, for at least
it does not imply that building, to be architecture, must
conform to any particular style, nor that it must be dressed up
in ornament, or be confined to Temples, Cathedrals, and
Town Halls. But when the definition is considered more
deeply, it becomes clear that although good building is always
architecture, architecture is by no means always good
building.

There is such a thing as bad architecture, indeed there is
more bad than good, nor can it be held that because a building
is bad it is therefore not architecture. The South Kensington
Museums are architecture ; so are the Albert Memorial,
Keble College, Oxford, the Prudential Building in Holborn,
the Law Courts, the new Regent Street, and hundreds of
other buildings both Victorian and Neo-Georgian. No one
can deny this, but there will be many to deny that these
buildings are good.

Architecture may be best described as building that is
consciously designed both in its practical and in its aesthetic
aspect. It is designed to fulfil a purpose and at the same time
to create an effect. A man who builds a house with no end
in view other than that of keeping out the weather is not an
architect ; nor is one who paints beautiful façades on stage
back-cloths. Each of these men is only interested in one of
the two essential aspects of architecture.

This may seem too obvious to be worth mentioning, but it
should nevertheless be borne in mind by those who are
beginning to approach the study of architecture. Otherwise
they are in danger of being led astray by so-called Functionalists, who would have them believe that efficiency is always
beautiful, or by Romanticists whose architecture consists in
the dressing-up of buildings in pretty ornament.

Having assumed, therefore, that architecture is simply the

conscious design of building, the blending of the practical with the beautiful in one harmonious whole, we can safely make some apparent concessions to the efficiency school.

WHY THE FALSE DESIGN IS UGLY

IN Greek Architecture it was impossible to span great lengths with stone slabs. For this reason the trained eye rejects as ugly a slab which is apparently made of stone but is in reality formed by a steel beam covered with stone, spanning twenty feet. That may be seen in badly designed pseudo-classic work of the twentieth century and is always ugly, for it is false and proclaims its falsity. If, on the other hand, the same distance or a greater were spanned by a reinforced concrete beam supported on piers, the effect might be beautiful. The beam would be doing work for which it was well fitted and would even appear absurd if it were placed over an army of closely-spaced supports.

Again, the standard brick size has been arrived at not because it was thought to be attractive to look at, but because it was the most economic and easiest to handle. The eye has become accustomed to it and would be profoundly shocked at the sight of bricks three feet long and two feet wide. The very real connection between Truth and Beauty is clear.

ARCHITECTS WHO "BUILDED BETTER THAN THEY KNEW"

IN an un-selfconscious age it was possible for pleasing buildings to be built without conscious designing. There are great numbers of cottages and farmhouses of the fifteenth and sixteenth centuries that show no evidence of good planning, design of elevations, or orientation, yet are pleasant to look at on account of the good craftsmanship, good materials, and complete sincerity which went to their making. They are buildings which seem to have happened rather than to have been designed, and a trained eye can appreciate them, admiring them for their trueness, their honest expression of the spirit of those who built them.

But it must be realised once and for all that any attempt to copy these buildings in an age that is foreign to their spirit involves an artistic lie of the greatest magnitude. No building must be allowed to "happen." Every part must be planned to work in relationship with every other part, so as to form one coherent design. We live in a self-conscious age, and although it may perhaps be difficult to be sincere in a period of quickly changing ideas, it would certainly be fatal to try to revert to unselfconsciousness.

Architects are at least tied down to sincerity in planning, for they must make their buildings work, and as soon as the new tradition is firmly established, complete sincerity will be as easy for the many as it now is for the few.

Architecture embraces all the departments of living and demands an intensive research into every activity of the civilised man. It finds out what is most important in the life of a community and stresses it, relating it to what is less important but essential to the proper working of that life. If architecture of late years has been in a state of some chaos, it is because values have become obscured. There remain people who believe that the Church is still the centre of the life of a community ; others give pride of place to the Law and Government; while many regard the gaining of money through commerce as man's greatest goal. Hence, it is difficult to achieve a proper relationship between Civic, Ecclesiastical, and Commercial design.

The writer is of opinion that this age should and could be one in which education and housing formed the main ideal of the community. The schools and housing schemes of Holland, Austria, and Republican Germany point the way towards the realisation of a great social and architectural ideal.

ARCHITECTURAL IDEALISM THAT WOULD BANISH SLUMS

Now real ideals are always closely connected with practical problems, and there is no essential incompatibility between idealism and common sense. The idealism that we want to give spirit to our architecture is a worldly idealism. It could find its expression in a great co-ordinated plan for slum-clearance and re-housing, if ever the opportunity were offered. That is the biggest thing that could fall to the lot of architects to plan, and they could see to it that the greatest need of our country was satisfied in a complete and comely manner, never forgetting the essential part that must be played by education in any attempt at a civilised standard of living.

Since architecture is largely a profession of planning, starting from the small units of the essential needs of living and building up round them, it is clear that architects should be consulted about any and every scheme of planning, whether it be a question of housing or of bridges and transport. Architects are the only people who are trained to plan, and they will criticise pillar boxes, knives and forks, and inkpots as keenly as cathedrals, or discuss the proportions of a beer bottle, convinced that these things are, or should be, their business.

WHY MACHINERY BROUGHT UGLINESS

UGLINESS in building comes from ugliness of the mind. Before the Industrial Revolution there were plenty of badly planned buildings, many that were incoherent in design, but no ugly buildings. Such trivialities as Horace Walpole's Gothic villa, Strawberry Hill; Fonthill, various ruins and other follies rightly belong to the period of revivals and are in this respect ahead of their time. They are no more a part of Georgian building than the new City Banks are of modern.

Now it is essential to understand why ugliness only came into existence after the introduction of machinery, not only because it is a topic of general interest, but also because in this problem lie the seeds of good architectural theory. Ugliness of mind was not the prerogative of Victorians. There was plenty of that before their time, and there is plenty to-day. What then caused this sudden outburst of ugliness?

It is clear that when machinery was first introduced, nobody had any very definite idea of the extent to which it would be developed, or the uses to which it would ultimately be put. There were those, very probably, who thought and hoped that machinery was a craze that could be laughed or disapproved out of existence. There are some who still regard modern architecture in that light. When the first motor-cars were built, it was the intention of their designers to make them look as much like carriages or dog-carts as possible. They took it for granted that they could not make them look like motor-cars because nobody knew what motor-cars did look like. We know that the results were far from beautiful, but now that cars have ceased to try to look like anything that went before them, they have achieved beauty.

It seems, then, that ugliness really arises from unsuitability; a car made in the image of a coach is ugly; a cathedral designed in the twentieth century in the Gothic manner, built in hard stone and covered with machine-made detail is ugly; a cinema in a half-timbered outfit is ugly. And these things are so, apparently, because coaches did not have engines, Gothic cathedrals were built by craftsmen, and there were no cinemas in Tudor times. But because unsuitability is ugly, it does not follow that suitability is necessarily beautiful.

Modern architects are trying, and surely they are succeeding in the attempt, to build a Tradition that will be real, a tradition of building sincerely, sanely, and in the manner best adapted to the problems in question, making the best and most beautiful use of the materials most suited to their various purposes. They want no striving after styles ancient or modern, but if they are sincere in their working for practical and beautiful solutions to modern problems, they will achieve an architecture as fine as any that flourished in the past. They have enormous scope for design, perhaps more than architects in the past ever had, and unless any economic or political upheaval throws us back into barbarism, they will improve and add to their new tradition as the years pass.

HOW TO LOOK AT ARCHITECTURE

A SOUND understanding of the main principles of architecture gives additional interest to travelling either abroad, in the traveller's own country, or even to a walk in one's own village. Many people look at buildings every day of their lives without having their consciousnesses affected either by pleasure or dislike. At the most, they get a confused impression of the town in which they live or work.

Now there is no doubt that although everybody does not want to be an architect, everybody can derive much pleasure or much stimulating annoyance from the observation of architecture. Nor is it essential to make any special pilgrimage to do so. In fact it seems that sight-seeing, looked upon by so many people as a duty, tends to diminish the pleasure that is to be had from observation. There are, however, those who, when confronted by a building, form very definite impressions of it which they are unable and perhaps unwilling to analyse. If the emotions are really stirred, as they too seldom are, it is natural to be content with the sensation without asking what it is that causes it. But if the observer is at all of an analytical nature, he will want to know just why the buildings he sees are good, bad, or indifferent. He looks at a building and finds it dull and drab. It depresses him and makes him feel convinced that it is the work of a pompous devitalized architect; it must be deadening to live or work in, and is only fit to be got away from. Why?

THE FAULTS THAT LIE BEHIND UGLY BUILDINGS

THE first and most obvious question to ask is : is it built of materials sufficiently unattractive to kill even a good design? Is it built of hard shiny yellow or red bricks, or faced with dingy grey stucco? No, the material is good Portland Stone and we know there is nothing wrong with that.

Perhaps it is covered with unpleasant and unnecessary decoration that obscures the composition. That would give it an appearance of drabness because it will seem to be trying to cover up its poverty of design. Or perhaps it is simply and fundamentally a bad composition, its parts lacking any real relationship, without any dominating feature to attract the eye or having a feature that is too dominating and so overwhelms the rest of the design.

There may be a monotony in the relationship of window space to solid wall. If wall and window take up about the same amount of space, the result is usually dull. A building divided horizontally into two equal parts by a string or heavy moulding is dull, giving the impression of being two buildings, one on top of the other, rather than one coherent design.

A symmetrical composition needs to have a void in the centre. A Greek temple with a column in the centre, of the entrance façade would (if there were such a thing) obviously be a bad piece of design. The natural place to enter a building of symmetrical design is in the centre, because that point is more strongly stressed than any other point. But if there is a column there, those entering must either walk round and behind it, in which case the entrance is partially obscured, or else enter through a doorway that is not in the centre.

This very obvious example is taken in order to show that there are such things as rules of composition, and that architects do well to follow many of them, whether they can find a practical reason for them or not. If a certain arrangement of parts is irritating to the eye, that should be a sufficient reason for avoiding it. If the architect likes to do some research into the practical reasons why the eye is irritated, he is at liberty to do so, but he need not. He can safely rely on certain very well defined rules.

THE IMPORTANCE OF SCALE

ONE of these is called Scale, which means, broadly speaking, that it should be possible to tell the size of a building from the design. A door, which is based on the height of a human being, is said to give scale to a building. If a building had a door twenty feet high and ten feet wide, the door would tend to throw it out of scale. Small buildings treated in an elaborate classic columnar style are absurd, because the column and entablature have been generally applied in the past to large buildings such as Temples, Town Halls, and Museums, and the human eye's idea of a column is of something tall, massive, and grand.

Some modern architects think that it is ridiculous to acknowledge any particular laws of composition that are to be everlasting in their bearing on architecture. There can be no doubt, of course, that a rigid adherence to any set of rules is unlikely to produce great architecture ; it is also true that new forms may need new compositions ; but it is difficult to invent proportions and abstract relationships to fit the new way of designing, and many of the elementary rules of composition that are taught in the first year of the school courses apply just as much to modern as to traditional architecture. Unless you have some rough rules which your eye tells you are often reliable, it is difficult to know why a building is good, and therefore, unless you are a genius, difficult to design well.

NOTHING NEED EVER BE UGLY

ANYONE can become architecturally minded when once it is realised that everything that is made falls within the architect's province, and that there is never any need for any thing to be ugly. This attitude of mind is rather a question of preferring planning to muddling than of having any great knowledge of the various styles of building.

There are still many people who take it for granted that industrial buildings, factories, power-stations, boiler houses, goods yards, and mining works must inevitably be ugly and at best can only be tolerated because they are necessary to our civilisation. It is true that nearly all existing buildings of this kind are ugly, but there is no reason whatever why they should be so. The Battersea Power Station is one of the best buildings in London, and the Boiler House of the Vereinigte Stahlwerke's coal mine at Geselkirchen is an extremely fine composition, beautiful both on account of its fitness and its consciously achieved effect.

The much discussed electricity pylons have a certain dignity when they are suitably placed ; telephone boxes, newspaper kiosks, public lavatories, letter boxes, tram standards and lampposts can all be well designed, indeed they must be if they are not to spoil the effect of a well-designed street.

THE ECONOMY OF PAYING FOR GOOD DESIGN

GOOD design is no more expensive than bad design ; it may even be cheaper on account of avoidance of waste both of space and unnecessary trappings. A good designer can adjust his design to the amount of money that he knows is available for the job, in other words he will take the best possible advantage of the resources that are at his disposal.

On the other hand it is an expense that nobody can afford to allow buildings to be built by people who are not trained to design, and many badly-planned schemes are the work o the so-called practical man. Architects, be it said, are for the most part more inclined to concentrate on efficiency of planning than on achieving schemes which they find amusing or exciting to themselves. Indeed, there are very few of those dreaming, artistic, unpractical and misleading architects of whom clients are so much afraid.

It is the untrained enthusiast for building who usually indulges in quantities of expensive detail, and great sums of money must have been spent and wasted on putting Gothic capitals on the cast iron posts of railway-stations.

BEAUTY MISSED IN THE CULT OF STYLE

IN order to have a true appreciation of architecture, it is essential to realise that no style, as such, is superior to any other ; that the cult of styles has done architecture a great deal of harm, and that there are good and bad buildings of all periods.

Enthusiasm for the antique and the archæological methods of approach towards architecture has been carried to such extremes that many people now adopt a compensating attitude of contempt for what is old, and are fond of pointing out how much better we can build now than our predecessors in the past. Such people in their exclusive enthusiasm for

modern building tend to miss the true significance of architecture as a living art.

I suppose it would be true to say that we could, if we so
wished, design technically better Georgian houses than the
Georgians did. We could see to it that the rooms all faced
the right way instead of placing all main rooms behind the
main façade no matter what its aspect might be. We could make
all four elevations work, instead of giving the entrance front
a magnificence and refinement in sad contrast with the back
and sides. We could do these things, but our Georgian houses
would be dead, devoid of sincerity, and without the charm
of old buildings or of new.

Why should this be so ? Why is the Parthenon beautiful,
while the exact reproduction of it in Tenessee is not ? Is
it because one is old and mellow and the other not old enough
to have acquired texture ? It cannot be that, for if it were so,
we should have to admit that it is age and texture that makes
a building beautiful, and we know that is not true.

The answer to the problem is that copying is not creative
and can hardly be sincere. We are not Georgians or ancient
Greeks but members of a twentieth century industrial
civilisation. We do not feel as the builders of the past felt ;
we have different needs from theirs. If we copy their buildings
we are lying.

The first question, therefore, for an observer of a building
to ask is : Is it good of its kind and time ? To apply twentieth
century standards to sixteenth century buildings is clearly
absurd, and the man who cannot appreciate the best both in
English Renaissance and modern German has not succeeded
in grasping the meaning of architecture.

THE ARCHITECTURE OF THE PAST

JUST as it is difficult to say exactly what architecture is,
so is it extremely hard to give any date at which it may be
said to have begun. Prehistoric building is too fragmentary
to give any definite clue as to the purpose for which it was
constructed, or the effect it was intended to create ; otherwise it would not be prehistoric. The earliest buildings in the
Historic Tradition, those of Egypt, are the work of an already
advanced civilisation, and so cannot be supposed to have
sprung suddenly from the imaginations of the first real
architects.

Yet Egypt must be taken as the land where historic architecture has its roots—that architecture which has spread in all its later phases throughout the world of Western civilisation. It will be necessary to outline this process of growth in order to demonstrate how tradition was broken after the Industrial Revolution and explain why it cannot now be revived.

The broad characteristics of Egyptian architecture are the use of the column and beam, entrance pylons (or gateway with towers on either side of it), the battered or sloping wall surface, and the capital of vegetable or flower form. Egyptian architecture has a spirit which suggests it was built for eternity and this is not surprising when we realise that the purpose of the tomb was to preserve the body for thousands of years till the return of the soul.

One of the most famous of Egyptian temples is the Great Temple of Ammon at Karnak which was begun by Amenemhat about 2466 B.C. It is not the result of a complete plan, but was added to by the command of numerous kings from the Twelfth Dynasty until the period of the Ptolemys. The massive stone roof is supported by 134 columns in 16 rows and the central avenues are about 80 feet high.

Of the many other temples of Egypt, it would be well to mention that of Edfu (237 B.C.) which belongs to the Ptolemaic period. Here there is an excellent example of the massive pylon or entrance wall that is such a notable feature of Egyptian architecture. Through this entrance, decorated with reliefs and inscriptions, access is obtained to the great Court round which a colonnade runs. Beyond this is the great hall, and behind this were the various smaller rooms, last being the sanctuary.

The walls of Egyptian temples were extremely thick and made usually of sandstone or limestone, often sloping inwards towards the top so as to give an appearance of immense strength. Openings, colonnades, and doorways were usually square-headed, spanned by heavy beams, and roofs were composed of slabs of stone supported on outer walls and internal columns.

THE LINK BETWEEN EGYPT AND GREECE

THE architecture of Greece, like that of Egypt from which it was partly derived, was an architecture of post and beam. The same structural principles underlay the two kinds of architecture, though the forms taken by the Greek column, post and roof, were different from those of Egypt.

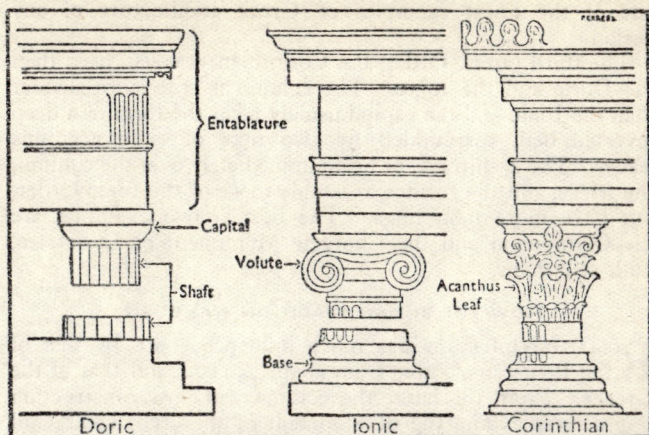

14. THE THREE ORDERS OF GREEK ARCHITECTURE

The finest example of the earliest order, Doric, in which the columns were stout and comparatively plain, is the Parthenon. The second order, Ionic, with its voluted capital, becomes more decorative, while the Corinthian style in which the Olympieion of Athens was built may be recognised by its still more slender column and its foliated capital.

Of the three styles of Greek architecture—usually called Orders—Doric, the earliest and stoutest, forms the most obvious link between Egypt and Greece. It is the simplest of the Orders in form and can best be seen in the Parthenon and in the Theseion at Athens, and in the Temple of Poseidon at Paestum in Sicily.

The second of the great Orders, the Ionic, is most easily distinguished by the capital, or head of the column. This takes the form of a volute or scroll, possibly derived from the nautilus shell or the ram's horns. The Ionic column is more slender in comparison with its height than the Doric, and the frieze is far more ornamental, often bearing a continuous band of sculpture.

The best known Ionic Temples are the Erechtheion and the small temple of Niké Apteros in Athens. The Great Temple of Artemis at Ephesus can now only be judged by reconstruction and restoration drawings and fragments in the British Museum, but there can be no doubt that it was one of the finest examples of Greek architecture of any period.

The third Greek Order, the Corinthian, was less used than the Doric and the Ionic. The column is still more slender than the Ionic and the capital usually takes the form of a deep inverted bell, surrounded by two tiers of eight acanthus leaves. The architrave, or beam immediately over the column, the frieze, and the cornice, resemble those of the Ionic Order, but have more mouldings. The best known examples are the Olympieion and the Choragic Monument of Lysicrates, both at Athens.

HOW THE ROMAN TRADITION WAS BORN

ROMAN architecture was much influenced both by that of the Etruscans, dating from about 750 B.C., and that of the Greeks. From the latter the column and post construction was derived, while the development of the arch, vault, and dome was owed to the former.

The keynote of the earlier style of Roman architecture is the combined use of column, beam, and arch. Thus the Romans used as decorative features motives that in Greek architecture performed essentially constructive functions. This may be seen where piers supporting an arch are used together with half columns that are not necessary to carry the weight.

The Romans added two more Orders, the Tuscan and the Composite, to the original three used by the Greeks, the Tuscan being a simplified form of the Doric and the Composite a combination of the Ionic and the Corinthian.

Whereas temples were the most important buildings of the Greeks, Roman civilisation produced a need for more diversified building necessitating the use of several storeys. Baths, theatres, aqueducts and bridges all gave immense scope for the great constructive ability of the Romans, whose architecture was thus naturally spread over a wider field than that of the Greeks. The main characteristics of Roman architecture are the great use of the vault and arch derived from the Etruscans and the extension and adaptation of the Orders of Architecture of Greece.

CONCRETE MAKES ITS APPEARANCE IN ROME

WHILE the Romans at first used large blocks of stone without mortar for the building of their walls, they eventually hit upon the more economic method of using concrete, composed of small pieces of stone, tufa, marble, or broken bricks, mixed with lime. Concrete vaults were built that have been equalled in size only by those that have been constructed since the introduction of steel.

The Romans, by means of their management of vaulting, found themselves in a position to use the dome as an architectural feature. In all these ambitious constructive forms, concrete was the important factor, making it possible for vaults and domes to be cast in one solid piece.

It is now clear how Roman architecture developed out of Greek and Etruscan and found new solutions to new problems. Tradition was not broken, even when architecture was needed to serve purposes that were unknown to the Greeks.

"THE GRANDEUR THAT WAS ROME"

THE buildings of Ancient Rome are so numerous that it will be impossible to mention more than a very few of them, but it may be said that the following are among the most important :—

THE PANTHEON is in a state of remarkably good preservation and provides a most excellent example of the ability of the Romans to use the dome.

THE COLOSSEUM, the great amphitheatre begun by Vespasian and completed by Domitian, is elliptical in plan, having an arena 287 feet by 180 feet surrounded by a wall 15 feet high. A great knowledge of engineering was needed for the construction of such a building.

THE ARCH OF SEPTIMIUS SEVERUS is a white marble triumphal arch, dedicated to the Emperor and his two sons to commemorate their victories over the Parthians.

THE BATHS OF DIOCLETIAN were built to accommodate three thousand bathers, and of these and of the smaller Baths of Caracalla enough remains to fix the positions of the various rooms, tepidarium, calidarium, frigidarium, and so forth.

There are many temples, some in a fair state of preservation, but the best preserved Roman temple is at Nîmes in South France, and is known as the Maison Carrée. Others that may be mentioned are the Temple of Fortuna Virilis, the Temple of Castor and Pollux, and the Temple of Saturn, in Rome ; and the Great Temple and the Temple of Jupiter at Baalbek in Syria.

6

THE EARLY CHRISTIAN ARCHITECTS

THE next great period in the historic tradition of Architecture was the Early Christian, which lasted from the fourth to the tenth century A.D. It was a period of the natural development of architecture from the Roman methods of building, but it cannot be said that any new constructive problems were solved in this age. The Early Christians, for financial reasons, used as far as possible the materials that were at hand in the many Roman temples and buildings that could no longer be used for their original purposes. Early Christian churches were modelled on the lines of Roman Basilicas, and old Roman columns were altered and adapted for their new positions.

This period of architecture, however, is extremely interesting in that it forms a link between the great Roman period and the growing up of the Romanesque style in Europe. It thus connects the Classic with the Gothic that developed from the Romanesque. The chief characteristic of Early Christian churches is their great length, considered in relation to their height. The rows of colums running from back to front of the churches combine with the comparative lowness of the roofs to create a very impressive effect.

Examples of Early Christian or Basilican churches are; S. Clemente, S. Maria Maggiore, S. Paolo fuori le Mura, and S. Sabina, in Rome; and the Church of S. Apollinare in Classe, in Ravenna.

A LINK BETWEEN EAST AND WEST

BYZANTINE architecture may be said to date from the fourth century A.D. and thus had its beginnings at about the same time as Early Christian Architecture. The broad difference between the two is that whereas the Basilican type of building, with its great length and pitched roof is typical of Early Christian work, the chief characteristic of Byzantine architecture is the use of the dome. Thus in the former character was derived from Ancient Rome and in the latter from the East.

Nevertheless, Byzantine architecture forms a part of the tradition of historic Western architecture, and the system of building in concrete and brick, introduced by the Romans, was adopted by the builders of Byzantium.

Byzantine architecture is thus a link between East and West in its use of the traditional oriental motive of the dome together with the classic column. The Byzantines placed domes over square compartments, whereas under the Romans they had only been used to cover circular or polygonal spaces.

The most famous example of Byzantine architecture is S. Sophia in Constantinople, though S. Mark's in Venice is probably almost as well known. Other examples are : S. Front, Périgueux, S. S. Sergius and Bacchus, Constantinople, and the Little Metropole Cathedral in Athens, which is the smallest cathedral in the world, measuring about 38 feet by 25 feet with a dome only 9 feet in diameter.

ARCHITECTURE AFTER THE FALL OF ROME

AFTER the decline of the Roman Empire, those countries which had been under its dominion evolved a style that combined many of the features of Roman architecture with those of Byzantine, consolidating the main influences at work in the historic style to produce Romanesque. The natural growth of tradition is clear up till now and it may be said that, allowing for differences in national technique, architecture developed smoothly and naturally until the Renaissance.

Romanesque architecture survived until the end of the twelfth century when, with the introduction of a more complex system of vaulting and the pointed arch, it gradually developed into the Early Gothic style. Romanesque builders used the round-headed arch, but they were the first to attempt to apply the principle of equilibrium to building, instead of being content with the simple inert stability of Roman work.

It was in this way that the idea of elasticity and equilibrium, which resulted in the complex magnificence of Gothic building, was first introduced. Romanesque architects thus produced the quadripartite or four-part vault, which was to give place in its turn to the various systems of vaulting which are the real essence of Gothic building.

Examples of Romanesque architecture are : Pisa Cathedral, S. Michele, Pavia, and S. Zeno Maggiore, Verona, in Italy ; S. Madeleine, Vézelay, Notre Dame la Grande, Poitiers, and the Abbaye-aux-Dames and the Abbaye-aux-Hommes, Caen, in France ; the Church of the Apostles, Cologne, and Worms Cathedral in Germany.

Romanesque architecture in England will be dealt with in the outline of English architecture that follows. It is clear that the architecture of all countries of the historic tradition grew gradually out of the great building traditions of Egypt, Greece, and Rome.

ENGLAND LEARNS ARCHITECTURE FROM HER INVADERS

THE English are commonly supposed to have a genius for deriving what is best from the culture of other nations and incorporating it in their own. This has certainly been true of their architecture in the past, for nearly the whole of the historic buildings of the past grew out of the influence of those nations or tribes that at one time or other conquered the island.

There is little evidence of architecture in England before the Roman occupation and most of our knowledge of the building of that period is based upon theoretical reconstructions. Indeed it is difficult to think of English architecture as being clearly defined until Anglo-Saxon times, and it will therefore be simplest to begin at that period, just as we took Egypt as being the civilisation that saw the first clear beginnings of the historic architecture of the world.

The earliest architectural period that can be called specifically English is the Anglo-Saxon, but although this name is given to a period lasting from the fifth to the eleventh century A.D., there is not a great deal of evidence to be drawn upon in order to give a conclusive estimate of the architectural character of the time.

It may be assumed that timber was extensively used for construction, and that is why little remains of the buildings. Many buildings, too, were built up of fragments of Roman work as was the case with Early Christian buildings on the Continent, and rough copies were also made. There is a theory that the form taken by stonework in some of the early churches was caused by the influence of timber construction, as in the "long and short work" (Fig. 15) at Earls' Barton tower, the stone strips at Sompting and Bradford-on-Avon churches, and the triangular-headed windows at Deerhurst in Gloucestershire.

The main characteristics of the architecture of this period may be said to be the rough round-headed window openings supported on heavy stone supports, often to be seen in couples, and the " long and short work " already mentioned, the latter consisting of blocks of stone placed alternately in a vertical and a horizontal position at the angles of the walls. The walls themselves were usually of rough rubble, the stone

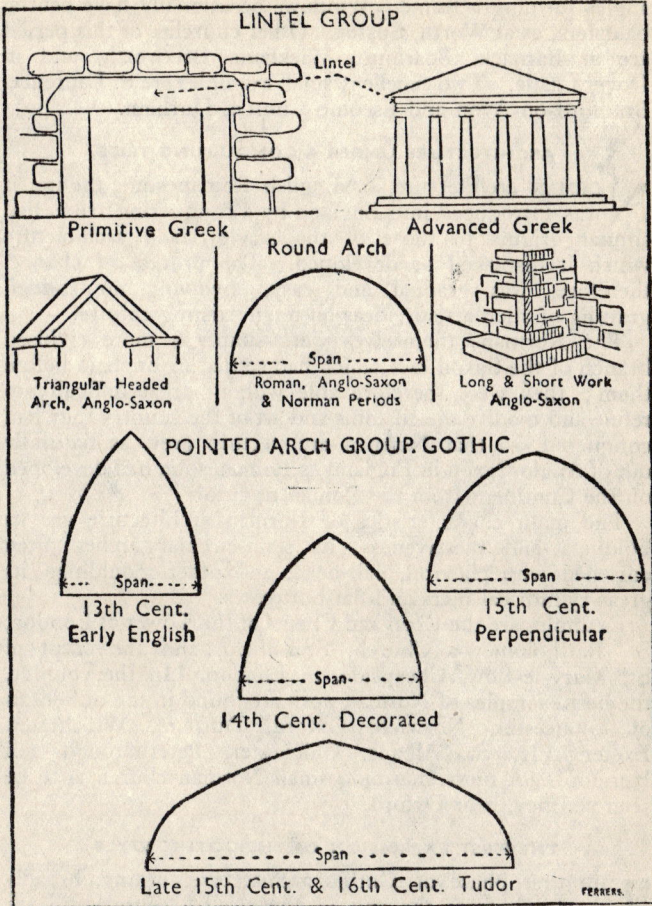

LINTEL GROUP

Lintel

Primitive Greek   Advanced Greek

Round Arch

Triangular Headed   Roman, Anglo-Saxon   Long & Short Work
Arch, Anglo-Saxon   & Norman Periods   Anglo-Saxon

Span

POINTED ARCH GROUP. GOTHIC

Span

13th Cent.   15th Cent.
Early English   Perpendicular

Span

Span

14th Cent. Decorated

Span

Late 15th Cent. & 16th Cent. Tudor

FERRERS.

15. ARCHITECTURAL FEATURES TYPICAL OF THEIR AGE

The shape of the arch is one of the clearest indications of period change in building. Lintel construction is characteristic of Greek architecture. The round arch introduced by the Romans, and extensively used by the Anglo-Saxons and Normans, later gave place to the pointed Gothic arch in all its phases, from the Early English to Tudor.

angles forming a frame. Windows occasionally have central
balusters, as at Worth, Sussex. Other churches of this period
are at Barnack, Boarhunt, Wickham, Brixworth, and in
Dover Castle. Two excellent small examples are S. Laurence,
Bradford-on-Avon and Escomb Church, Durham.

ARCHITECTURE UNDER A CONQUERING TRIBE

NORMAN architecture, or English Romanesque, though it
was introduced into England by a conquering tribe, had
similar origins to those of the Anglo-Saxon architecture
which it displaced or developed. The process of change,
therefore, was gradual and easy, involving no sudden
grafting of alien artistic ideas on to an existing culture.

The Normans themselves were simply a more civilised
branch of the Saxon race which had settled in England before
them ; they were therefore able without great difficulty to
refine and modify the customs and art of the country they had
conquered, so that Norman architecture grew as naturally
out of Anglo-Saxon in England as Romanesque had developed
on the Continent from the Roman tradition.

The main characteristics of Norman architecture are its
boldness and massiveness, its semi-circular arches often
enriched with chevron, nail-head, and other mouldings, its
great cylindrical piers and flat buttresses.

Examples are the Keep and Chapel of the Tower of London,
St. Bartholomew's Church, Smithfield, and the crypt of
St. Mary-le-Bow, Cheapside, in London. In the country,
the best examples of Norman work are found in the cathedrals
of Gloucester, Norwich, Oxford, Durham, Winchester,
Exeter, Ely, St. Albans, Chichester, Peterborough and
Hereford. A most charming small Norman church is to be
seen at Iffley, near Oxford.

THE FIRST EXPRESSION OF THE GOTHIC STYLE

THE first phase of Gothic architecture, lasting, broadly
speaking, from the end of the twelfth century till the
beginning of the fourteenth, is known as Early English. It
is distinguished by its simplicity of decoration, projecting
buttresses, steep pitched roofs, pinnacles, and the long
narrow pointed or lancet windows which were the first
expression of the Gothic arch.

The heavy Norman piers gave place to groups of tall thin
shafts connected to slighter piers. The deep mouldings of

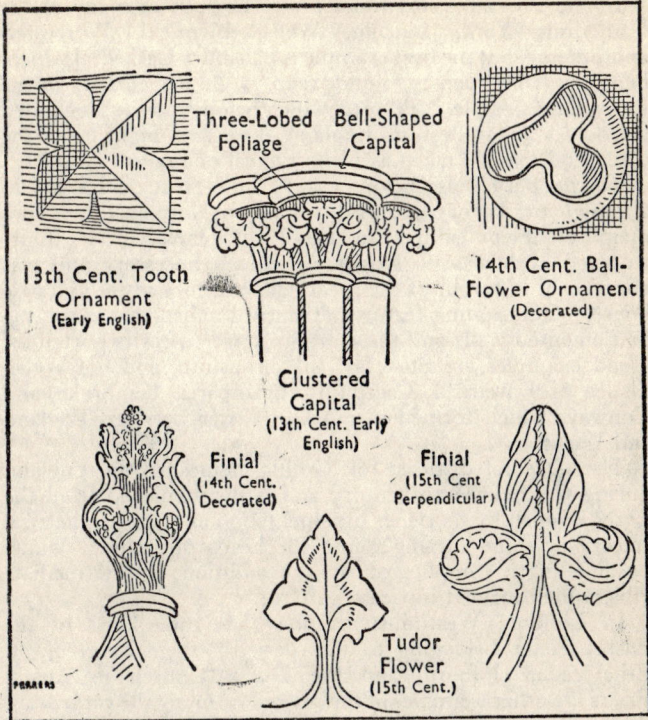

Three-Lobed Foliage

Bell-Shaped Capital

13th Cent. Tooth Ornament (Early English)

14th Cent. Ball-Flower Ornament (Decorated)

Clustered Capital (13th Cent. Early English)

Finial (14th Cent. Decorated)

Finial (15th Cent Perpendicular)

Tudor Flower (15th Cent.)

16. FROM EARLY TO LATE IN GOTHIC ORNAMENT

*The four phases in Gothic architecture are represented here—
Early English, Decorated, Perpendicular, and Tudor. The
type of ornament used on a building is one of the most reliable
indications of its date and style.*

arches are often enriched with dog-tooth ornament, and the
capitals of columns take a foliated form. Vaults are of the rib
and panel pointed kind, such as can be seen at Westminster
and Lincoln. Other Early English work is found in the Eastern
arm, transepts and Chapterhouse of Westminster Abbey,
as well as in five of the bays of the Nave and part of the
Cloisters; in the Chapel of Lambeth Palace, and in parts of
Southwark Cathedral.

In the Provinces, examples are to be seen in many of the Cathedrals—York, Lincoln, Wells, Lichfield, Worcester, and others—but the best example is Salisbury Cathedral which, being built between 1220 and 1260, is almost entirely in the Early English style. Its spire, which belongs to the Decorated period, is the tallest in England (404 feet high), and the Cathedral may be taken as being typical of English Gothic.

To this period also belong many of the great castles which, although the keeps were mostly built in Norman times, owe many of their features to the Plantagenets. The four-storeyed keep was no longer considered necessary and was abandoned in favour of the great hall, entrance tower and gate house. Outstanding features of Early English castles are the battlemented walls and the entrance tower with its portcullis. Good examples are Stokesay, in Shropshire, and the Welsh castles of Edward I, Caerphilly, Beaumaris, Pembroke, and Conway, which formed a military barrier between England and Wales.

The Decorated phase of Gothic flourished in England during the fourteenth century and is distinguished from the Early English by its richer ornamentation and the geometrical tracery or stone carving round the heads of arches. Vaults became more complicated by the addition of intermediate ribs, which formed intricate patterns.

In London, Westminster Abbey has three bays of the East Cloister belonging to this period ; the Chapel of St. Etheldreda, Holborn, and the Dutch Church in Austin Friars are other examples of the period. Among the cathedrals, decorated work can be seen at Ely, York, St. Albans, Lichfield, and Exeter, and in the chapterhouses of Wells, Southwell, and Salisbury. Of the great castles, parts of Kenilworth, Raby, Broughton, Haworth, and Ludlow belong to this period.

WHAT IS MEANT BY PERPENDICULAR GOTHIC

FROM the end of the fourteenth century until its decline and disappearance, Gothic architecture in England is known as Perpendicular, the name being derived from the upright lines of window tracery and panelling. Windows were extremely large and had to be strengthened by horizontal members, or transoms, and vertical mullions. Arches tended to be much flatter in design than in the early periods, though the pointed arch was still in general use.

Fan-Vaulting belongs to this period, and many will find

this type of vaulting, with its numerous panels, ribs, and pendants, the most fascinating of all. It may be seen at its best in the chapel of Henry VII in Westminster Abbey, and there is a very fine example over the staircase at Christ Church, Oxford, though the latter, oddly enough, was not built till 1630.

Examples of Perpendicular Gothic in London are the South and West Cloisters of Westminster Abbey, St. Margaret's Church, Westminster, Savoy Chapel, and Westminster Hall. Fine examples in the country are the west fronts of Winchester and Gloucester cathedrals, St. Georges' Chapel Windsor, the Chapel of King's College, Cambridge, Sherborne Minster, parts of the cathedrals of Canterbury and York and many colleges at Oxford and Cambridge. Perpendicular work can be seen at the castles of Warwick, Warkworth, Bodiam, and Hurstmonceaux.

THE RISE OF A GREAT DOMESTIC ARCHITECTURE

ALTHOUGH the influence of the Renaissance was first felt in England at the beginning of the sixteenth century, Tudor architecture nevertheless belongs in reality to the late Gothic or Perpendicular period. Owing to the waning of the power of the Church, the Tudor period was one of great domestic architecture, and the deeply religious spirit that had underlain the Gothic methods of building, and had caused the conception of the spire as a symbol of religious aspiration, was in abeyance.

Gothic architecture with its intensely subtle and mystic design, its spires, its lofty piers and intricate system of window and arch construction, its gargoyles or grotesque water-spouts, its bosses and foliated carvings, was essentially an architecture of religion. There is always something more than the simple desire to build behind great architecture. Thus we find, underlying the magnificence of domestic work in Tudor times, a sense of throwing aside the too stern dominion of the Church and a realisation that fortification against enemies was no longer necessary. There is also a strong feeling that the age is one of kingly splendour and that its architecture, therefore, should glorify the idea of King and State.

Now although Tudor building, as has been said, belongs in essence to the late Perpendicular period of Gothic, it was, on account of its domestic character, well suited to the gradual application of Renaissance details and refinements.

Examples of Tudor work may be seen all over England, but notable ones are parts of Hampton Court Palace; Compton Wynyates, Warwickshire; Layer Marney, Essex; and Sutton Place, Guildford.

THE ARCHITECT SEEKS INSPIRATION FROM THE PAST

THE Renaissance, which had its beginnings in early fifteenth-century Italy, forms a break in tradition in that it derived its culture and inspiration from the past. This is not to say that it was a period of copyism, for Renaissance architecture was one of essential vitality until its decline, but it was nevertheless due to an enormously increased interest in the buildings of Greece and Ancient Rome. Gothic architecture had never taken a very firm root in Italy, which was still very much influenced by its own ancient traditons, so that the seeds of the new Renaissance style were sown in a fruitful soil.

Over the rest of Europe on the other hand, Renaissance architecture, while being in a sense an inspiration from the past, also evolved gradually out of existing Gothic tradition, the new method being applied first to details and finally to planning. On this account, it cannot be said that the Renaissance constituted a violent break in tradition over Europe. Moreover, it was found that classic planning and design were more in keeping with the new demands of a domestic and civic culture than the Gothic methods of the preceding period. The fear of God and of earthly opponents was no longer so insistent as it had been in the Middle Ages, and was beginning to give place to a desire to glorify the achievements of this world.

Gothic and Tudor methods of building lingered on in England for a century or more after the first impact of the Renaissance, but in spite of traditional work that was still being widely done in small buildings, the classic method was firmly established by the time that Wren (1632–1723) was giving proof of his genius. The Renaissance, though a break in the continuity of tradition was, then, essentially a progressive and not a retrogressive movement.

The main characteristics of Elizabethan architecture are towers, gables, parapets, balustrades, decorative chimney stacks, mullioned windows, oriels and bays. There was as yet no conception of classic planning, the Great Hall was still the main feature of a house, and rooms were still planned round courts. Examples of Elizabethan architecture are

Kirby Hall, Northamptonshire; Montacute, Somerset; Wollaton, Nottinghamshire; Sizergh Castle, Westmoreland; Castle Ashby, Northamptonshire; and Hardwick Hall, Derby. In Jacobean architecture, classic detail and motives became increasingly common until the appearance of the first completely classical buildings of Inigo Jones. Amongst great Jacobean houses are Hatfield House, Herts; Holland House, Kensington; Bramshill, Hampshire; Blickling, Norfolk; Audley End, Essex; and Knole, Kent.

ENGLISH RENAISSANCE IN ITS FULL DEVELOPMENT

THE term Anglo-Classic may be used to describe the architecture of England that followed upon the transitional Elizabethan and Jacobean. Renaissance architecture all over Europe was proving itself to be a style providing almost unlimited scope for design, and although it made its appearance later in England than on the Continent, it was used with great success by Inigo Jones as early as 1619 when his Banqueting House in Whitehall was begun. Here is seen the first example of a completely classic building in England. There is no longer any compromise with Gothic forms either in planning or in detail. Jones had studied extensively in Italy and therefore spent less time than other architects of his period in throwing aside traditional ideas. Other buildings designed by Inigo Jones are St. Paul's Church, Covent Garden, Greenwich Hospital, York Water Gate, London; and a number of country houses among which are Raynham Hall, Norfolk, Chevening Place, Kent, and parts of Wilton House and Kirby Hall.

The buildings of Wren are so numerous and show such extreme diversity of design that it is natural to regard him as the major figure of the English Renaissance. His genius enabled him to make of Renaissance architecture an immensely adaptable, elastic method of building. He used the Classic Orders, motives, and details in such a way as to give expression to his own personality, and never in order to attempt to copy the buildings of the past. Wren had opportunites of designing buildings of almost every kind, for the Great Fire of London gave rise to an enormous demand for new churches after a long period during which few had been built. St. Paul's Cathedral and the City churches are evidence of how well he used the English classic style for ecclesiastical building. His Domestic work includes Hampton Court Palace, two

blocks of Greenwich Hospital, Chelsea Hospital, Temple
Bar, the Orangery at Kensington Palace, the Temple, Win-
chester Palace, Morden College, Blackheath ; Abingdon,
Guildford and Windsor Town Halls. Among the country
Houses he designed are Belton House, Lincolnshire ; Groom-
bridge Place, Kent; and probably Honington Hall, Warwick-
shire ; Melton Constable, Norfolk, and the House in West
Street, Chichester.

LITTLE DIFFERENCES THAT MARKED A GRADUAL CHANGE

THE evolution of English Renaissance architecture from
its early beginnings in Elizabethan times to its finish after
the Industrial Revolution was a gradual process of change in
detail rather than in spirit, similar to the evolution of Gothic
from Norman times down to the Renaissance. The period
of Wren and the architects of the William and Mary and
Queen Anne periods was one of free designing in classic
motives allowing great liberty to individual architects. The
Georgian period saw the gradual emergence of a stricter,
more scholarly architecture, possibly more refined and
certainly less exuberant than that which preceded it, but
never so tyrannically narrow in conception as the architecture
of Palladio in Italy. The Baroque style, therefore, which
was largely the expression of a protest against too much
discipline in design, was never so popular in England as in
Italy, and was chiefly used for details and decorative features
such as altars, fonts, monuments and tablets. The porch of
St. Mary's church, Oxford, is, however, an interesting
example of English Baroque.

In Georgian buildings, sash windows have narrower
frames and glazing bars than those of the Queen Anne period,
and the latter may be distinguished by the broad painted
sash boxes forming bold frames for the windows. Georgian
windows are usually set in deep reveals on the inner face of
the wall. Among famous Georgian architects are Vanbrugh,
the designer of Blenheim ; Nicholas Hawksmoor, James
Gibbs, William Kent, George Dance, John Wood who with
his son re-planned the city of Bath and designed its Crescent
and Circus ; Chambers, and the Brothers Adam.

THE END OF TRADITIONAL ARCHITECTURE

THE architecture of the early nineteenth century, which
followed upon the work of the Georgian period, is distin-

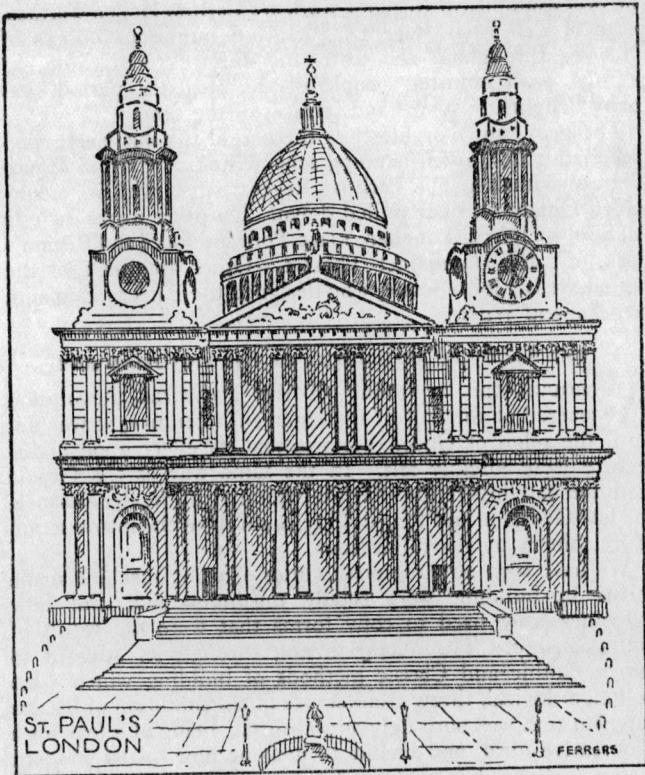

ST. PAUL'S
LONDON

FERRERS

17. WREN'S MOST FAMOUS CHURCH

The Grecian columns and round Roman dome shown in this drawing of the façade of St. Paul's reveal how England's greatest Renaissance architect contrived to embody features of the Classic style in buildings which are essentially expressions of his own very English genius.

guished by its heavier design, which inclines towards pomposity, and by the general use of painted stucco for wall facings. It may be that Classic architecture had by this time reached a stage of inevitable decline, but the buildings of this period have a charming simplicity even though they cannot be compared with Georgian buildings for refinement of detail. In London the best examples of Regency work are Carlton House Terrace, parts of Pall Mall, Regent's Park, and numerous houses of all sizes throughout the town and suburbs. Brighton, so popular with cultured people of the Regency period, has many delightful squares and terraces of the time.

The best known architect of the period is John Nash, who designed a fine town-planning scheme linking Carlton House Terrace with Regent's Park by Regent Street with its colonnaded Quadrant, since pulled down. His other works include All Soul's Church, Langham Place, Portland Place and Regent's Park, and the Haymarket Theatre. Other architects of the period are Sir John Soane, who designed the Bank of England, Smirke, and Wilkins.

THE ILLOGICAL ABSURDITIES OF THE VICTORIAN AGE

ALTHOUGH the beginning of the Industrial Revolution occurred at the end of the eighteenth century, it was not until the reign of Queen Victoria that its effect upon architecture were forcibly felt. In the same way as the Gothic tradition had lingered on after the beginning of the Renaissance, the late Georgian and Regency styles survived the introduction of machinery by several decades.

We have seen how the possibilities of using machine-made forms in building were totally misunderstood, and how machines were used to copy forms that were the result of craftsmanship. The Victorian era, through its attempt to revive Gothic and Classic methods of building which were no longer logical, threw architecture into a condition of lifeless copyism that was both ugly and absurd. Being at a loss for a progressive ideal, and unable to imagine how to use modern materials to evolve modern design, Victorian architects fell back on the dead tradition of the past, denying the advantages that science had given them. The smaller domestic work of the period was even worse than the larger examples of Classic and Gothic Revivalism, for in this there was no understanding even of accurate copyism.

Though the essence of the break was the misuse of machinery, it must be that there were other forces, moral and social, at work to produce so much ugliness, and these have already been lightly touched upon.

Architecture, except for a very few isolated buildings, was a dead art in the Victorian Age, and the unconscious dissatisfaction of architects may perhaps have been demonstrated in their several attempts to revive past styles. In a great majority of cases, Victorian architects failed even to copy accurately, succeeding only in falsifying and insulting the buildings of the past. There are many buildings of this period that can boast of fine planning, a fact which serves to show that a great deal more than planning is needed to produce good architecture.

Towards the end of the last century, Norman Shaw and Philip Webb did something to rescue architecture from an untimely end, and Lutyens did much to give it back its self-respect. Modern architecture is now working out its own salvation and its own tradition.

ARCHITECTURE OF OUR OWN AGE

IN a great majority of architectural text-books of the first quarter of the twentieth century, there is no mention of what is now termed modern architecture. The phrase was used to describe the architecture of Revival or adaptation of traditional forms and expressions. In these books modern architects are, broadly speaking, divided into Classicists and Gothicists. It was naturally admitted that these two great schools were capable of modifying their styles and adapting them as far as possible to modern needs, but there was no conception of designing without reference to the historic styles.

So little was modern architecture taken seriously, that the student who read learned books on the art was generally left in complete ignorance of the existence of such pioneers as Mackintosh in Scotland, Otto Wagner and Adolf Loos in Austria, Berlage in Holland, and Frank Lloyd Wright in America. It is only now, when modern architecture is at last being taken seriously, that the importance of the work of these men becomes clear. Just as Richard Wagner in the world of music and Cézanne and the post-Impressionists in painting, were thought in their own time to be pernicious charlatans, so were the founders of modern architecture derided and disapproved by the orthodox before their movement gained general recognition.

MODERNISM THAT WAS CONSIDERED A CRAZE

IT cannot be said that there was such a thing as a sound modern movement in architecture, apart from the work of isolated architects, until after the World War. Even for some years after the War, the Architectural schools of England regarded any break away from Traditionalism with no more than tolerant good-humour. Modernism was thought to be a mere craze, a sign of the general disillusionment that prevailed after the War. This phase would pass, the traditionalists thought, as soon as they had been able to put everything back where it was. There cannot be many people who still hold to this view of the situation.

Modern architecture has come to stay and will progress as long as modern civilisation survives. Now this modern architecture, which consists of designing in modern materials for modern needs, acknowledging new forms, flourished exceedingly in Germany after the setting up of the Weimar Republic in 1918.

In the light of after events, there are those who see in this plain stark building the evidence of defeatism and disgust with the past natural in a nation that had been humbled and penalised by the rest of Europe. It seems far more probable, however, that Republican German architecture was a healthy expression of a wish to have done with the old traditions that had caused the horror and misery of war and the unspeakable suffering that was the aftermath. The bad old days were over; let there be a new unstained architecture to give expression to the better times that were to come.

It may be that modernism in Germany had no deeper roots in the country than the Social Democracy that bred it, but even if that was so, it is not condemned, any more than the pioneers of modern architecture are condemned by their rejection for a quarter of a century or more.

Modern architecture is an architecture of idealism, crude and imperfect though it often is, giving expression to the idea that civilisation's only hope of survival lies in the abandonment of nationalism, militarism, and sentimentalism.

ARCHITECTURE THE COMMON INTEREST OF NATIONS

Now in referring to the internationality of modern architecture it is necessary to point out that architects would not wish to abolish national character altogether, even if they could. It is the fear of a cold drab standardisation that naturally repels traditionalists from a serious study of the aims of modern architecture. Modern architecture is international in the sense that it uses to a large extent international materials such as steel and reinforced concrete; it is an expression of the fact that civilised human beings have the same interests at heart whether they live in England, France, Germany, or anywhere else.

Modern designers are usually men who believe that international co-operation is essential for the survival of civilisation, and they naturally like to express their convictions in their art. Nevertheless the best modern architecture still retains a national flavour. Amsterdam and Hilversum have not in the slightest degree lost their Dutchness even though they possess some of the finest modern buildings in the world.

Holland, it is true, is wonderfully fortunate not only in having a long tradition of peace, but also in having produced Berlage and W. M. Dudok, the latter one of the greatest architects of to-day. In the same sense, the work of Erich Mendelsohn, the best known and most dynamic of modern German architects, is pronouncedly German, just as Asplund's and Tengbom's work in Sweden is essentially Scandinavian, and Tait's in England English. Yet there is a strong bond of community of aims linking the work of different nations together.

WHY THE SHAKESPEARE MEMORIAL THEATRE IS IMPORTANT

WE have seen how modernism in architecture was until lately regarded as a craze. It appeared likely, even, that many young enthusiasts took to it because it was easier to design and draw, thus appealing to a generation that was doubtful if anything were worth an effort and had thrown aside the ideals and beliefs of yesterday. It appeared to be concerned with shock tactics, with attempting to be original and startling by reason of its difference from the design of the old schools. The first-fruits of modernism in England after the War may have been startling but they were extraordinarily bad.

It was not until Betty Scott won the competition for the new Shakespeare Memorial Theatre at Stratford-on-Avon that the public realised, to its horror, that modern architecture was going to be taken seriously. The public's opinion of this very building is enlightening in that it shows the result of surprise and of the muddled thinking of conservative minds.

The Shakespeare theatre still looks, to many members of the public, like a jam factory or a power station. It is definitely not the public's idea of a theatre. The reason for this is clear :

the building does not look like a theatre to the public, because it is the only theatre the public has ever seen that does look like a theatre.

The conservative conception of theatre architecture is an ornamental façade, highly decorated, that might just as well mask a restaurant or a skating-rink as a theatre. Public opinion is therefore profoundly shocked by the sight of a theatre in which each part and feature is clearly expressed; the stage with its great height for storage of scenery; the fan-shaped auditorium; the foyer and bar treated domestically, and the octagonal staircase. All these parts are formed into one harmonious design which could never be anything but a theatre. But public opinion is too greatly surprised.

THE DESIRE TO STARTLE IS OVERCOME

THOUGH at the time the Shakespeare competition was held there was hardly any architecture in England that could be called modern, there are now other buildings of equal quality and goodness, among which the most noteworthy are those of T. S. Tait. Modern architects have got over their early desire to shock or be different for difference's sake and have settled down to work in an already established tradition. They will not, however, attempt to set up any unchanging laws of design or construction, for the keynote of modern architecture is its realisation of the fact that change is inevitable and ever more rapid. But though change may be rapid, it is still true that one idea or invention grows out of another and real tradition need not be broken.

Modern architecture is improving at a most encouraging rate. Perhaps another era is at hand when architects will be able to write an intelligible history of their time and place.

A REVULSION AGAINST OVER-DECORATION

SOME critics see a poverty of inventiveness in the new lack of detail. While not suggesting that we should apply traditional detail to our buildings, they do think that we should design our own. At present, they say, we make a virtue of not thinking of anything more intricate than bare white walls and built-in furniture.

There may be something in this view; it may be that when modern architecture is regarded as the only sane way of building, we shall evolve detail that will fit in perfectly with our buildings. At present there is a strong revulsion of feeling against the over-decorated architecture of the last century, though this is no reason, the critics will say, for going to the other extreme. And yet extremes usually lead to other extremes. Men feel that what went before was so bad that it is best to get as far away from it as possible and build up from the bottom again.

Moreover, many modern designers now design without detail because they prefer not to have it. They are no longer, consciously at any rate, protesting against over-elaboration. They prefer to get their desired effect out of shapes, materials, and lighting arrangements, with an occasional picture or piece of sculpture forming part of the scheme.

Most modern detail is still uncertain and bad and, that being the case, we are better without it. A piece of sculpture in an important position against a bare expanse of brick wall is at least as effective as a general treatment of mouldings, medallions, and nîches. It will not be surprising, however, if good detail is soon evolved out of new architectural forms.

ARCHITECTS WHO ARE LEADING THE WAY IN ENGLAND

IF in England there are at present few buildings from which the layman can gain much insight into modern architecture, there can be no doubt that there are more to come. Competitions are being won by modern architects, and that is a healthy sign.

We have now the Shakespeare Memorial Theatre by Betty Scott ; the Battersea Power Station, the elevations of which were designed by Sir Giles Scott ; the Masonic Hospital at Ravenscourt Park, Curzon Cinema, and Oxford Street flats, by Tait ; the Head Office of the Underground in Westminster and a number of charming Underground Stations by Adams, Holden, and Pearson ; several fine modern churches by Welch, Cachemaille-Day, and Lander, the best of which is probably St. Saviour's, Eltham ; there are small houses by Wells Coats, Connell, Ward, and Lucas, and others of the more extreme modern school, and many, owing more to tradition, by C. H. James, Louis de Soissons, Oliver Hill, and P. D. Hepworth. There can be no doubt that a true English tradition is being built up.

The leading exponent of modern architecture in England is T. S. Tait, and the best examples of his work are the Masonic

Hospital at Ravenscourt Park, the Curzon Cinema, and the large block of flats at Marble Arch (Mount Royal).

He was one of the first English architects to use the flat roof for small domestic building, notably in his houses at Silver End. In the use of brickwork and massing of the component parts of a building, Tait's work bears a likeness to that of the Dutch master, Dudok. There is a similar solidity, so pleasing in an age when materials tend towards a certain thinness suggesting that many modern buildings are only temporary. Tait's buildings are also like Dudok's in that they have charm, that delightful quality that is too often missing from the architecture of efficiency. He makes of the new civilisation that seems implied in modernism something bright, clean, and joyous, instead of the drab, hard, machine civilisation so much feared by upholders of Tradition.

It is interesting to compare Tait's Adelaide House at London Bridge with his later work which it only antedates by a few years. The amazing rate of improvement in modern architecture then becomes clear. Adelaide House is a modern building and owes little to conventional traditions, but it has not the sureness of design that is seen in the Masonic Hospital, which is one of the finest buildings of any period in England. The solidity of Adelaide House is heavy; it has little charm, whereas the hospital has succeeded in charming even opponents of the modern tradition.

For it is true to say that Tait and his followers are building up a new modern tradition in English architecture, and we must be grateful to him for this as we are to Sir Edwin Lutyens for having revived the almost dead body of architecture in England at the end of the last century. Each has played an important part in the history of the country, and will not be forgotten.

DUDOK : PERHAPS THE GREATEST OF MODERN ARCHITECTS

THE work of W. M. Dudok, the great Dutch architect, whom the writer would venture to call the greatest architect of to-day, is comparable with that of Tait on account of that solidity, massing, and charm that are to be found in both. Each seems to favour brickwork, though in Dudok's case this is probably because Holland is a country whose traditional building was done almost entirely in brick. Each could, no doubt, design successfully in reinforced concrete and glass, but their work is evidence of a preference for solidity.

Dudok had wonderful opportunities of displaying his genius in Hilversum, a town in Holland which has greatly increased in importance since the War, and in the building of which he has been the moving spirit. He has built housing schemes, many schools, public baths, abattoirs, shops, and the Town Hall, so that he has a great experience of every type of building. Perhaps his schools are the most charming of all his works.

Dudok is no slave to style or convention and is not afraid of using the pitched roof, a feature over which controversy now rages as it once did over the classic Orders. He realises the importance of the rules of composition, so often rashly thrown aside by architects of revolutionary tendencies, and attaches major importance to composition of mass. It is through the influence of Berlage and Dudok that Holland has now a fine, real, architectural tradition.

AN ARCHITECT FASCINATED BY MACHINES

IF Dudok is the moving spirit in the modern architecture of Holland, Erich Mendelsohn played a similar part in the German Republic that was established after the War. His work is less easily appreciated than that of the Dutchman, and the layman may at first be repelled by its apparent harshness. Mendelsohn is the high priest of steel, concrete, and glass, and for this reason many people have thought of him as an architect who believed that beauty was a necessary result of efficiency.

Actually he is first and foremost a designer, and if traditionalists think that his buildings partake more of engineering than of architecture, that is because their ideas of architecture are not his.

Mendelsohn is a designer who is fascinated by machine forms, those forms that have arisen from the use of new materials. He designs in such a manner as to utilise modern materials to the most complete advantage, and also, I would even say especially, in order to create an effect.

His effect is almost always dramatic rather than charming or cultured. Unfortunately, Mendelsohn's best known building, the Potsdam Tower, happens to be one of his least successful, and although its dramatic effect is striking, it is crude and more likely to repel than to convert the opponents of modernism. His Schocken Stores and the Universum Cinema in Berlin are typical examples of his best dynamic buildings, while his own house shows that he can design with charm.

Mendelsohn thinks that England is very backward in architecture, but is an admirer of the Crystal Palace, a building which, if shorn of its detail, would greatly resemble some projects of his own.

SOME PIONEERS OF MODERN ARCHITECTURE

WALTER GROPIUS was one of the pioneers of modern architecture in Germany. Like Mendelsohn, he delights in the use of great expanses of glass rather than in the solidity of wall surface favoured by Dudok and Tait, and it may be broadly stated that this is a characteristic of German and French building, the English, Dutch and Scandinavian tending more often towards the solid. Gropius' most famous building is the Bauhaus, at Dessau.

In Hamburg, where there has always been a tradition of brick building, the German architect Höger has designed some extremely fine shops, offices, churches, and other buildings. He is fond of hard clinker brickwork of a pleasing brown or purple colour, with the horizontal joints raked out. Höger's work approaches more nearly towards that of Dudok and the Dutch than towards Mendelsohn and the dynamic school.

In France, and to a great extent all over Europe, le Corbusier has achieved a certain fame as the oracle of modernism. He was responsible for the saying : " A house is a machine to live in," which has become a kind of battle cry for Functionalists. Le Corbusier has designed schemes for the city of the future and there is no doubt that he has a vital and original mentality, but his own work too often shows signs of the forcing of forms which play no essential part in the main design.

THE ARCHITECT IN TRAINING AND PRACTICE

THERE are two choices open to a man or woman wishing to become an architect : to enter the office of an established architect as a pupil, or to take a course at one of the architectural schools. The former method was the more favoured of the two until well on into this century, but since the war there has been a great increase in the number of students at the schools. There are, however, still a number of people who prefer the old system. A pupil generally pays the architect in whose office he works a premium for the benefit of his knowledge and instruction and for the use of his office. The pupil will at first be expected to do the less skilled work of the office, such as the tracing of full sized details and the setting out of the simpler drawings. Gradually he will come to understand the more complicated parts of the office work and may sometimes be allowed to contribute his ideas on design.

The chief advantage of the pupilage system is that the pupil is in constant touch with the practical side of his profession and learns something of office routine, how to deal with clients, builders, sub-contractors, and so forth. He will, however, have to produce drawings, done largely in his spare time, in order to be able to sit for his examinations, since most architects will wish to qualify for membership of the Royal Institute of British Architects (R.I.B.A.), which is the most important official architectural body in England.

The chief disadvantage of the pupilage system is that the student has an insight into the work and design of one man or firm only, and does not have the benefit of hearing conflicting arguments on design. He may tend to copy the work of the office in which he is a pupil, or at least to become unduly biassed in one direction or another. His grasp of architecture as a living art is likely to be more limited than that of a student who works in a school where there is great diversity of design and talent. He will probably not save any time by becoming a pupil in an architect's office, even though the period of training at the school may at first sight appear to be unduly long.

A pupil is unlikely to be capable of passing the R.I.B.A. intermediate examination after less than three years' work, even if he can find time for study out of office hours ; while the passing of the Final involves a good deal of reading, drawing and taking notes which, in a school, would form part of the curriculum.

The full school course, which qualifies a student, after a year's office experience, as an Associate of the Royal Institute of British Architects (A.R.I.B.A.), lasts for five years. If the student satisfies the school authorities in his studio work, and passes all the school examination papers, he is exempted from the R.I.B.A. examinations. The school intermediate takes place at the end of the third year, and the final at the end of the fifth. It is necessary to have done a year's work in an office, but this may be done either before or after completing the school course. Students are also called upon to pass an examination in Professional Practice and Procedure at the R.I.B.A.

WHAT THE SCHOOL WILL TEACH THE STUDENT

THE first year course at the school consists of studies in geometrical drawing, free-hand drawing, elementary design, composition and construction, together with lectures on the history of architecture, building construction, composition and colour. All the students in the year do the same subjects, which range from twelve-hour sketches to design or construction subjects for which a month or five weeks may be allowed.

In the studios, the masters and their assistants go the round of the students, helping and making suggestions. The masters naturally have their own ideas of design and construction, and the student, though possibly bewildered at first, soon realises that the only way to acquire a full understanding of architecture is to know something of the views of men of all schools of thought.

When a studio subject is finished, the drawings are hung up in a lecture room and marked, and a criticism of each student's work is given by one of the masters, after he and others have made their awards on a jury. There is much to be learned from these criticisms, since the drawings are all on the same subject. Thus each student has an opportunity of judging perhaps fifty or sixty solutions of the same problem. A general review of the programme and the best ways of meeting it is also given.

In the later years, the work naturally becomes more advanced ; a study is made of larger designs, of the elements of steel and reinforced concrete construction, of building materials, drainage, decoration, drawing from life, and, in the final year, of Town Planning and professional practice. The studio work progresses from the design and construction of summer houses to that of Town Halls and Exhibitions.

Sometimes special criticisms or lectures are given by outside members of the profession, often distinguished foreign architects ; visits to buildings in course of construction are arranged, and enthusiastic students may join holiday tours abroad.

PRACTICAL PROBLEMS THAT ARE OVERLOOKED

IF there is a disadvantage to the school system, it is that students tend to be out of touch with the economic side of the profession. Not much attention is paid to the probable cost of the buildings designed, and indeed it would be extremely difficult to achieve any great degree of accuracy in the matter. Nevertheless, there is a temptation to indulge in exciting design that might in reality prove unpractical on account of the cost, and it is easy, when designing an Embassy or a Mediterranean villa for a millionaire to forget the innumerable difficulties that confront the architect who is lucky enough to be given such a commission.

School programmes usually introduce a few restrictions as to cost, site, and the requirements of the imaginary client, but these are often evaded. If a design shows unusual ability and imagination, the judges at the school are not unnaturally impressed, however unlikely it may be that the design would ever be allowed to be built.

The writer would, however, unhesitatingly advise any young man or woman wanting to become an architect to go to one of the schools rather than to enter an office as a pupil. The best known of the schools are the Architectural Association, in Bedford Square, London ; the Liverpool School of Architecture ; and the Bartlett School at London University. There are also schools attached to most of the universities throughout the country.

By going to one of these schools, the student will learn much, not only about style, but of what architecture really is. He will find, moreover, that his more revolutionary tendencies will not be condemned, as they would be in a great many offices, but rather tempered and encouraged to emerge into an ability to design with enthusiasm, vitality, and sanity.

GREAT ABILITY IN DRAWING IS NOT ESSENTIAL

People often think that in order to become an architect it is necessary to be good at drawing, and young men and women have been prevented from joining the profession on this account. It should be understood that it is perfectly possible to be a good architect and a bad draughtsman. It is, obviously, a great advantage to be good at drawing, but if a student can design, it does not matter much if he is not a draughtsman, provided that he makes his intentions clear on his drawings. It is not essential for an architect to be either a draughtsman or a mathematician, but he must be a designer.

The cost of a course at an architectural school is generally at the rate of £25 a term. Over and above this, there is the cost of instruments, books, paper, paints, and pencils.

INITIAL OPENINGS IN THE PROFESSION

HAVING completed the school course of five years or passed the final examination of the R.I.B.A., the young architect should be able to find employment in the office of a practising architect at a salary of from £3 to £5 a week. Posts are found either by the school at which the student was trained, or by the R.I.B.A., or privately. The work of an assistant comprises the general work of the office, drawing of all kinds, surveying and measuring, detailing, the writing of specifications, and in some cases the carrying out of entire jobs from start to finish.

Some architects who are more essentially draughtsmen than designers may spend many years as assistants in the hope of rising eventually to be partners in the firms for which they work, but most assistants, particularly those who are school-trained, are always hopeful of being offered jobs of their own and setting up in private practice. It is useless to pretend that there can be as much satisfaction in working out and drawing the designs of other people as in designing and carrying out one's own work.

Opportunities occasionally occur of buying a partnership with an architect who has much work but little money with which to pay his office staff, but there are obviously not many young architects who are in a position to avail themselves of such offers.

THE ARCHITECT GOES INTO PRACTICE

LET us consider the position of a young architect who is offered a job by a friend or relative, for that is how most architects get their first chances. If he is working in another architect's office, he will not have time to do jobs of his own, and must either give the job over to the office or start a private practice.

In the case of the small, worrying, alteration job that is the usual first commission of the young architect, it can hardly be worth his while to leave his post as assistant, take an office, and set up on his own. The work will not last long and there is little money in it. In this case, he would do well to induce the office to take it on, if he can.

If, on the other hand, he is asked to build a fair sized house, village hall, or other building that will help to make him known, he would be wise to start his own practice, in the hopes of obtaining fresh introductions from his client or from his friends. In any case, he may well find another position as assistant after his own job is finished. There is nothing against changing offices fairly frequently ; in fact it might well be argued that change brings diversity of experience.

It cannot be said that the early years of private practice are anything but precarious. Clients may appear, but they are as a rule unlikely to want the services of an architect more than once. For those who prefer safety and a small salary to risk and better possibilities, there is the chance of steady rising in assistantship.

THE ARCHITECT'S RESPONSIBILITY

THE architect acts, generally speaking, as the agent of his client, and his work extends far beyond the pleasant stages of design and drawing. It is his responsibility to see that the work is carried out in fairness both to client and contractor ; for although he is primarily the agent of the client, he must always be prepared to say when he thinks the builder has right on his side in any difference of opinion. Being a professional man, he should be bound by the rules of his profession. Thus, he is clearly bound to consider his client's wishes first of all, even though in the matter of design this may not always be easy. If he thinks that no good design will satisfy his client, he can refuse to take on the job. On the financial side, he must guard carefully against being led by enthusiasm into building more expensively than his client can afford. A conscientious architect will find as much satisfaction in discovering ways of saving money as an unscrupulous one would in running up other people's bills.

An architect who is a member of the R.I.B.A. may not advertise, or encourage clients in the use of materials in which he is himself financially interested, without giving notice of the fact. Any sharing in commissions with builders or sub-contractors is strongly condemned.

WHAT THE ARCHITECT IS ASKED TO DO

THE architect's work consists in designing or altering buildings according to the needs of his client ; preparing drawings and specifications ; seeing that these are passed by local authorities ; obtaining tenders for the carrying out of the work and making a contract with the winning contractor, who is usually the one who sends in the lowest tender.

After these preliminaries, the architect must supervise the work in progress, preparing detail drawings as they are wanted, issuing certificates for the client to pay to the builder for as much money as he thinks the work done is worth.

The architect's fees, according to the scale drawn up by the R.I.B.A., are ten per cent. of the cost of the work on jobs costing £500 or less, or for alterations, graduated down to six per cent. for work costing £2000 or more. There are special reduced fees for housing and repetition work. These fees are payable as the work proceeds, at the same time as the contractor's certificates are paid.

COMPETITIONS THAT MAY LEAD TO FAME

ARCHITECTS who are not so busy as they would like to be, and others who are well established and employ large staffs make competition work a part of their practice.

It is announced that a competition will be held for designs for a town hall, a hospital, a sea-side lay-out, or whatever it may be, and architects are asked to submit designs either in limited or in open competition. There are usually three prizes, the winner also drawing his usual percentage for the carrying out of the work.

Many young architects dream of leaping to fame by winning an important competition at the beginning of their careers; some, indeed, have succeeded in doing so, but as a rule it is the experienced architects who win, not necessarily because they are the best designers, but because they thoroughly understand programmes and know the kind of building the promoters want through experience of other competitions. Some firms of architects have carried off so many prizes that competitions form a large and fairly safe part of their practices; but, on the other hand, an enormous amount of work is done on competitions, for which there is nothing to show but the drawings.

Young architects gain experience in planning through entering a few of the smaller or less specialised competitions, but for them to enter for those that are held for such buildings as hospitals, cinemas, and factories, is largely a waste of time. There are firms of architects who have in the course of time acquired a vast experience of the planning of certain types of buildings, and the young and inexperienced architect cannot hope to compete with them.

If he works simply for the pleasure of designing and drawing, and is not disappointed at failure, there is, of course, no harm in his entering for any competition he likes.

READING FURTHER ABOUT ARCHITECTURE

ANYONE beginning to make a study of architecture obviously needs to have a book of reference dealing with the architecture of all countries and periods. Such books of reference are: *A Short Critical History of Architecture*, by H. H. Statham (Batsford), and *Architecture*, by Professor W. R. Lethaby (Home University Library, Thornton Butterworth Limited). For those who are interested in the theories of architectural composition and the growth of the modern movement, two good books are *Architectural Composition* and *Modern Architectural Design*, both by Howard Robertson, published by the Architectural Press. A most delightful book for recreative reading is *The Pleasures of Architecture*, by Clough Williams-Ellis (Jonathan Cape), while a book on the theoretical side that some may enjoy is *Architecture in the Balance*, by Frederick Towndrow (Chatto and Windus). The latter is perhaps too difficult for beginners, but makes stimulating reading.

A very short outline of English architecture for those who want to identify buildings of the various periods is *English Architecture : An Outline*, by M. S. Briggs (Winsor and Newton). The great periods of historic building are treated in separate volumes of *The Historical Architecture Library* (Batsford). Those wanting to read more of Greek, Roman, or Renaissance architecture will find these books very interesting and well illustrated with photographs. An excellent book on that most vital subject, town planning, is *Town Planning in Practice* by Sir Raymond Unwin (Benn). All students of architecture should have a fair knowledge of this essential branch of the art.

DESIGN : THE ART OF BEAUTIFYING EVERYDAY LIFE

by J. W. S. FERRERS

"You do ill if you praise, but worse if you censure, what you do not rightly understand." Such was the considered opinion of Leonardo da Vinci, no mean authority. There are undoubtedly many people who desire to practise things artistic. There are also many who merely wish to know something about artistic matters generally. To these too much stress cannot be laid upon the erroneous idea, which is unfortunately held by so many people, that an appreciation of things artistic may only be exercised by an isolated and select few, who have been chosen for this enviable position by some deity unapproachable by ordinary mortals. On the contrary, the beautiful and lovely things of the past are a heritage in which all may share, and so too, all that is good and beautiful in the present should be our peculiar pleasure and delight.

The diffidence with which so many people approach anything that they term " artistic " can only be due to an inferiority complex engendered in them by a feeling of ignorance, which is probably exaggerated, and a wholly false idea of the difficulties of the subject. The obvious care and thought that is expended by so many women over the choice of material, pattern, and colour of a dress presupposes at once a natural and very practical knowledge of design and colour harmony. It is immaterial that they would be unable to give reasons for their choice or why one colour blends so well with another or not. It is often quite impossible for a trained artist to give a reason for the use of a particular colour or for the hundred and one things he likes or dislikes. It is purely instinctive with him, as it is with a woman choosing a dress material, and so long as the final result is pleasing what matter the why and wherefore ? When all is said and done the artistic instinct must be felt and not subjected to an examination.

PLEASURES AWAITING THOSE UNTRAINED IN ART

IF people who have not received a training in art would only exercise their natural judgment fearlessly and more often and in a wider field, a new and fresh vista would be opened to them which would bring colour and happiness into their lives undreamt of by them. It is not meant by this that there is nothing to learn in appreciation of artistic things. Undoubtedly a knowledge of how an object is made is a great help to its understanding, and this knowledge, provided one does not desire to be an expert, is not hard of attainment.

In this section the principles that underlie applied design will be pointed out, and visits to the numerous museums, not only in London but in the provinces as well, will do more than all the text books upon design. It is a curious fact that a good piece of work, be it in pottery or metal, textile or wood, can be and frequently is instinctively appreciated by people with no artistic training. There is an appeal in a good and true shape that requires no advertisement or pre-knowledge.

Again, it is not necessary to go to a museum in order to see beautiful things. They are all around us in the towns and in the countryside. Nature is the inexhaustible storehouse from which inspiration may be drawn. The houses and churches, large and small, are full of beauty to the discerning eye. True there is much that is bad and ugly, but life indeed would be utopian if this were not so. Then there are the hundred things which go to furnish our houses; furniture, ornaments, china, cutlery, curtains and the like. There is beauty of design often to be found in the humblest of objects.

Do not let us imagine that beauty may only be found in what are called " museum pieces." Chippendale chairs are beautiful things, yet we cannot all have them, and there is no reason why a perfectly ordinary chair may not have equal beauty. Again, do not let us make the appalling and too frequent error of thinking that all that has antiquity must necessarily be good and beautiful. By the same token, if one believes in progress as the word is ordinarily understood, all that is ultra-modern must be delightful. It cannot be gainsaid that age often gives a dignity and atmosphere to an object. The lovely patina to be found on much old furniture is due to many years of dusting, polishing, and rubbing caused by people using it. This delightful colour and sheen cannot be counterfeited, yet it is not the only thing. We shall see how important is correct proportion, and good and honest craftsmanship is an essential. These may be present irrespective of age.

THE COLD ALOOFNESS OF STEEL FURNITURE

THE modern steel furniture not only intended for office use but for the home as well, can never have, no matter how old it may become, this patina. As it is to-day so will it be a hundred years hence, acquiring no dignity or sympathy from use but remaining cold and aloof always. The very simplicity and severity of line which governs the design of much of this steel furniture is against what we may term the homeliness of wood, and unless the surroundings are equally modern this type of furniture cannot satisfactorily be used. We would not, however, imply by this criticism complete condemnation of steel furniture. Often the simple, severe line of its design is artistically good, and if this type of furniture is used discriminatingly, and amidst suitable surroundings, the effect can be quite pleasing.

This brings us to the consideration of what is meant by "the machine-made age." This expression is constantly in use in print as well as in speech, and generally an accent of scorn informs the manner or tone in which it is written and said. Unhappily this disapprobation is too often justified. The manufacturer does sometimes exploit the credulity of the public; he does not always produce that which the public demands but, on the contrary, he sometimes makes and puts upon the market things that the public have to buy because there is nothing else at the price to take their place. Much good work is turned out by the machine, but too often it is obtainable only by the limited few who have the money to purchase. This state of affairs is obviously wrong. It should be quite possible to produce objects for every day use by machine beautiful in design and proportion that are within reach of the most slender purse.

The designer, William Morris, wanted to produce good designs for all, and found that it could not be done. Since his day the machine has become all important. What is required to make the machine produce beautiful work? The answer is obvious. The artist and the manufacturer must come together. This simple fact is being recognised to-day. Never has there been a time so fitting for this amalgamation as now, and happily it is being brought about by exhibitions of Industrial Art, where the manufacturer can exhibit his productions, and where the artist designer who is outside the trade is invited to submit his work, and by bodies such as the

Courtauld Institute where the public may attend lectures
given by authorities upon matters artistic. In this way the
public's taste is developed and guided, and the manufacturer
has for the first time been brought into contact with the
artist.

It is not too optimistic to envisage a time not so far distant
when the term " mass production " will cease to be a stigma.
It is both stupid and quite fruitless to kick against the pricks
of a machine age. It is always impossible, and undesirable
as well, to go back. We must go forward, and it must be our
duty to see that the objects of daily use as well as of decoration
yet unborn shall be beautiful.

Many people think that the machine is either exercising an
ascendency over man, or worse still, has already conquered.
In an age of machinery such as this there must always be such
a danger, yet to be forewarned is to be forearmed, and no
one who reads can honestly say that warning has not been
given in plenty. We must face facts as they are and not as
we would wish them to be. The machine is here and it has
come to stay, therefore, we must control it lest it controls us.

THE MANUFACTURER'S NEED OF THE ARTIST

A MACHINE will only produce that which it has been designed
to produce. If it is worked incorrectly the production
will be poor, so the craftsman is still required. A design for
metal-work, a book-cover, or a table cloth may be good or bad,
and the machine may be made to copy it. It is therefore,
important that the design should always be good. Here we
have the constant need of the manufacturer for the artist. If
this happy state can be brought about then there will be a
blessing in mass production, for there cannot be too many
good and beautiful things in the world and the public may
have, no matter how slender their purse, an ample supply of
well made and decorative things, for the public do desire good
things. They are slowly, very slowly, beginning to realise
that beautiful things are not only for the chosen few, but that
they are everyone's property and care. When this is still
more widely realised we shall be living in a very much happier
world.

This realisation that the humblest things repay a care and
attention in their making is beginning to find expression in
such objects as street name-plates and the colour schemes in
the Underground trains. The bad and clumsy name-plates

of the past are being replaced by well proportioned Roman lettering, and after two thousand years this lettering is still the most beautiful and dignified that we have. There can be no logical reason advanced as to why our eyes should be met by horrors in lettering every time we wish to find out a street name.

Again, there can be no reason why we should not sit surrounded by pleasant colour harmonies and upholstery in trains, even if we only travel in them between the City and our homes during the rush hours. Happily this is being brought about on the Underground. Posters, like machinery, have come to stay : very well then, they must be pleasant to look at. This pleasantness can be combined with a selling capacity, as witness McKnight Kauffer's designs. In these we have delightful drawing, colour, and perfect balance between text and subject. If this artist's work was more often emulated, our eyes would not be blinded, and our countryside made hideous, by the appalling abortions of glaring reds and blues that too frequently appear on the hoardings. Good lettering is of the utmost importance in the design of a poster, and Eric Gill's sans-serif letters are a perfect example of well-proportioned block letters, eminently suitable for posters and public notices.

THE WANING SYMPATHY BETWEEN ART AND CRAFT

To those who love beauty it is inconceivable that there can be any who do not, but although there is a movement towards better things in life, there are still too many who do not care, and we have a long way to go before ugliness and meanness in everyday things are banished. Perhaps the greatest fact that militates against the bringing about of this desirable state are the distinctions that have arisen between what is termed " fine " art and Industrial art. No such distinction existed in the past—that past which produced the beautiful things in our Museums to-day. The lovely objects in metal, pottery, and wood were made by men who did not consider it a degradation to work amongst the smoke and noise of the forge, or the shavings of the carpenter's shop. These were the true craftsman designers.

To-day we too readily dabble in art. We make patterns upon paper, and then leave them for someone else to carry out who is not in the true sense of the word an artist. Of course it is quite possible for an artist to produce, let us say, a design for a book-cover, which he has not the skill to carry out, and the actual execution of his design is done by a bookbinder. The result will not, however, be successful unless the binder is an artist as well. Much good work is done like this by private presses in different parts of England, and here we have the perfect combination of two artists, the one knowing exactly the requirements and limitations of the medium for which he is designing, and the other in full sympathy with the creation of the first.

This amalgamation is not too much to ask, for although the principles of one branch of art are not always applicable to another, there are, as we shall try to point out, underlying principles and laws that can be applied to all branches. We shall see that this is very true in proportion, and the same laws govern designing for furniture, dresses, and architecture. It is these laws that not only all artists must understand if there is going to be harmonious collaboration between the various branches, but the manufacturer and the public as well, if they are going to appreciate and value what is produced. This appreciation and understanding upon the part of the public must have far reaching effects upon more than art.

Beauty has no nationality, it is universal, and it requires no linguistic abilities in order that it may be understood. The stoneware of Germany or the brocades of Italy may just as well be appreciated by an Englishman as Elizabethan architecture or a Cotman water-colour, (typically English) by a German or an Italian. Here we have a bond of unity and understanding that would require a bold man to belittle. It is a true internationalism as valuable as it is far reaching in its effects of bringing countries spiritually closer together.

APPRECIATION THAT STIMULATES THE ARTIST

ART whether it is applied to painting or design in all its branches is a living thing, not dead, and it must not be forgotten that although the artist creates, the public plays just as important a part as appreciator. What Englishman worthy of the name is not proud of his country's past history? With just pride he points to majestic cathedrals and to grey-stone houses of the Cotswolds or to the lovely half timbered cottages of Shropshire. He glories in his country's past artistic achievements, but is quite mute, often counting it as a pose, about the art of his own time. He never realises that he is witnessing what will one day be of the past again,

and most important of all, never realises that he can, if he so
wishes, mould this present day art by his very interest and
enthusiasm in it. Never let him offer as excuse for his lack
of interest in the art of his own day, that he is a business man,
and therefore possesses no time for such luxuries. Let him
remember that if he is an East Anglian, for instance, he will
be very proud of his churches, magnificent in size and architecture, and these were the products of business men's affluence,
for it was the wealth of the wool traders that built them. So
too was it with the Cotswold manor houses, beautiful in
design and proportion.

Finally, let him remember that although the foreigner in
the past was pre-eminent in art, the Englishman when he
turns his hand to really utilitarian artistic objects, produces
examples just as perfect as the foreigner's. As a witness to
this typically English practicality the wrought iron work of
Sussex stands supreme.

So let us begin this practical study of Design in the spirit
that created Emerson's words : " Though we travel the world
over to find the beautiful, we must carry it in our hearts or
we find it not."

ORDER AND RHYTHM : THE BASIS OF DESIGN

ORDER and rhythm may be regarded as the fundamental
laws governing all types of design. The importance of
the application of these two in any form of design must be
obvious to all. Poetry, prose, music, architecture, all these
must possess an ordered rhythm if they are to succeed. Life
is a pattern just as much as any decoration in the rooms in
which we live, and if the pattern of life is not ordered, then
sooner or later chaos will ensue.

The squares which form a chessboard are an excellent
example of an ordered pattern. It is simple, yet we have a
certain rhythm in the alternating black and white of the
squares. Tiny children will recognise the same simple kind
of rhythm in their first attempts at pattern making at school.
With only the barest suggestion of a lead from the teacher,
they will quite naturally employ this first great principle of
ordered rhythm in simple patterns. However advanced and
complicated a design may be, this first simple law of order
and rhythm must govern it.

There are other principles of ornament as important as

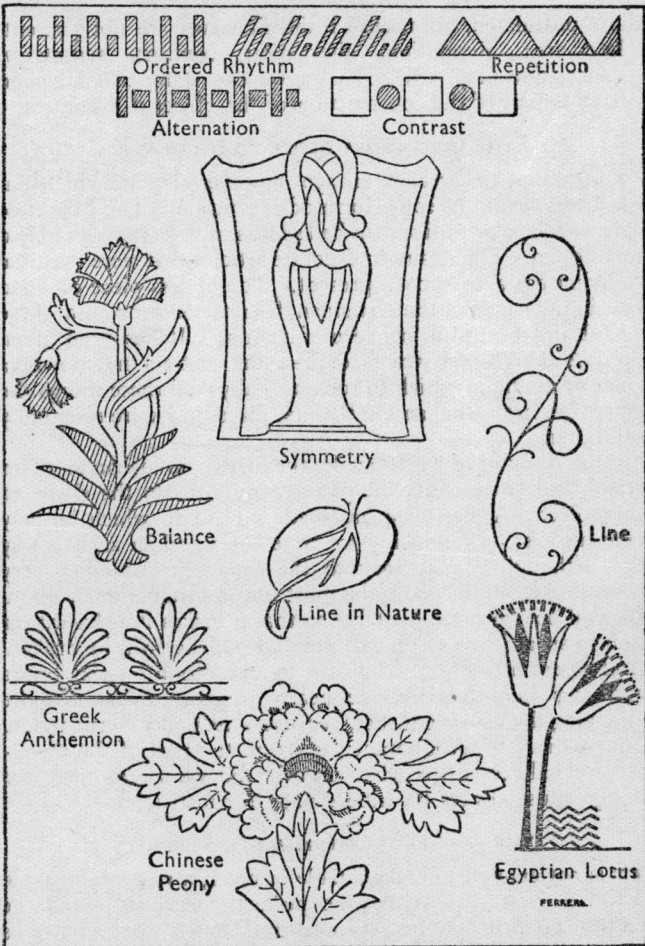

Ordered Rhythm — Repetition — Alternation — Contrast — Symmetry — Balance — Line — Line in Nature — Greek Anthemion — Chinese Peony — Egyptian Lotus

18. APPLYING THE PRINCIPLES OF PATTERN

All good design, with its myriad variations in pattern, rests on certain of the principles illustrated here—rhythm, repetition, alternation, contrast, balance, symmetry, and " line." How the different principles have been used in three designs of ancient origin is shown in the Greek Anthemion, the Chinese Peony, and in the Egyptian Lotus.

those postulated, but useless if the first two are not present. They are: Repetition, alternation, contrast, symmetry, balance, line (Fig. 18). Finally, we can state, that all good design is part of the construction of the object it decorates.

THE INSTINCTIVE DESIRE TO DECORATE

THERE has never been an age, however remote, which has been devoid of some form of decoration. The first rude clay vessels of primitive man had some simple pattern scratched upon them. The desire to decorate articles that were essential to living has always been present. The lifeless piece of wood has, in the hands of the craftsman, been transformed into some useful and beautiful article of furniture. It has been given life. A table upon which to place the platters and bowls, a chair or cradle in which to rock his baby—all these things the craftsman has made, and in the first place they were essentially utilitarian.

After they have been made, the desire to decorate them arises, and of necessity the pattern conforms to the shape of the object. A man who has made a chair in which he may take his rest, is not going to carve the wood in such a way that although it may look to the superficial observer very charming it will in reality be most uncomfortable to sit upon. He will not decorate his table so that it makes it awkward for him to sit at it, or so that corners jut out that will be broken. And again, he will not so distort by decoration his clay bowls and jugs that they become nearly useless. What is more annoying than a tea-pot that, because of its faulty construction, due possibly to an ignorant vagary on the part of the manufacturer, always drips when used ? So we see at once that design must always be subordinate to construction.

THE PART PROPORTION PLAYS IN BEAUTY

IT is not enough to make a table or chair, a vase or a tea-pot and decorate it. It may be perfectly serviceable and the pattern upon it may be very beautiful, but if the proportions are wrong then all the work expended upon it has been wasted. Let us take for example two chairs. Both are well made from the point of view of strength, both are well upholstered in the same material and they are reasonably like each other, yet we like one better than the other. Why ? If we analyse our reaction to each chair we shall discover that the back of the one we like less seems just a little too high as compared to the length and width of the seat. Its front legs are ever so slightly too short compared to the back ones, which gives it a curious tilt that makes us feel vaguely uneasy about sitting on it. The arms also are just not quite in the right place when we sit down.

It will be observed how necessary it is continually to say, " compared to " some part or other. Correct proportion or size is always a matter of comparison. Not only must we consider the proportion of one part of an object to another part, but we must consider the proportion of the object as a whole. It is not enough when looking at a pattern upon a cretonne for us to think only of the proportion of one unit (*i.e.* one flower, fruit, leaf, bird or whatever the design is based upon) to another unit. We must also look at the complete pattern and ask ourselves if it will be in proportion compared to the chair it has to cover and the size of the room in which it will go.

The placing of flowers in a bowl or vase is not only a matter of arrangement. It is, or should be, a matter of proportion as well ; the width and height of the receptacle compared to the height and size of the flowers that will be placed in it. The question of proportion is constantly exercising our minds and is not confined to the artist alone. A woman trying on a hat, a couple furnishing a room, a person playing a game, all are constantly using this faculty for judging shapes, sizes, or distances, all of which are questions of proportion. The only difference is that some folk, and artists in particular because of their training, have this judgment very finely developed, in exactly the same way as a musician's ear is trained to distinguish subtle variations of tone that to the layman are not noticeable.

HARMONY BETWEEN MATERIAL AND DESIGN

WHEN an artist uses the word " medium " he is referring either to the material he is using, such as stone, wood, clay, metal, paint, or to the oil, turpentine, water that he mixes with his paint. When he tells you that the design is not suitable for this or that medium, he means that the particular pattern in question would look all wrong and would probably be impossible to carry out in, let us say, stone or wood.

A pattern that would be ideal for needlework would obviously be ridiculous if an attempt was made to carry it out in copper. In order to be able to design a suitable decoration for any object, be it stone or any other medium, it is essential that some knowledge should be possessed of the technique required to carve in stone or work in metal. Without this knowledge on the part of the designer, especially if the design is going to be carried out by someone else, the final result is almost inevitably a failure.

All mediums have their characteristics and their limitations in very much the same way as human beings, and if these qualities are changed or overstepped the results will be bad artistically. What can look worse than stone that has been carved and twisted until it looks like anything but stone, or needlework that has been shaded by the introduction of numerous tints so that from a distance it looks like a painting ? All mediums possess their own dignity, and so soon as they look unlike themselves they lose their beauty and become undignified and mean-looking.

Certain mediums such as stone or wood by their very nature call for a simple and austere treatment. The precious metals such as gold and silver lend themselves by their richness to a rich treatment. So we can make this our guide, not in any hard and fast way, for no art can progress and expand if it is tied down by inflexible rules, but rather as a guide when in doubt. A rich medium such as gold, silver, ivory, velvet, or silk may have a rich and lavish treatment if desired. It must always be borne in mind, however, that sometimes the medium itself without any decoration at all is preferable. A plain and simple medium such as some types of stone (especially granite), iron, linen, wool, may have a simple treatment. We do not place diamonds upon tweeds or woollen jumpers, yet they look very well upon the richness of velvet or silk. We do not carry out embroidery in wool upon silk, and the richness and delicacy of gold and silver work would look peculiar if attempted in iron.

In the past when so much craftwork was carried out by the carpenter or blacksmith—and very beautiful much of this work was too—the dignity and individual characteristics of the mediums used were well understood and accepted. But in this age of machine-made goods much that was impossible to the craftsman can be carried out by the cunning of the machine, and mediums that are beautiful in themselves are often twisted and tortured out of all recognition in the effort to make tin look like silver or deal look like oak.

There is a simple beauty in pine-wood, and an object made

of this may very often look far more delightful than pseudo oak three-ply. The lovely wheelback chairs of the past were made of simple English woods, and their beauty lies not in elaborate decoration, of which they have none, but in the excellent and fitting proportions and honest workmanship. Decoration does not only lie in putting a pattern upon an object. An object may be most beautifully decorated merely by using the right medium, the right proportions, and finally placing it in the right position.

NATURE : THE ARTIST'S ETERNAL INSPIRATION

IT has been recognised since the first revolutionary masterpieces of the great Italian painter Giotto that nature is not only the store-house of beauty, but the eternal inspiration for artists as well.

> " The painter will produce pictures of little merit if he takes the works of others as his standard ; but if he will apply himself to learn from the objects of nature he will produce good results."

So wrote Leonardo da Vinci four hundred years ago, and it is as true to-day as it was then. The famous Chippendale drew an inexhaustible inspiration from nature. Look at the back of a Chippendale chair, and the exquisite foliated carving almost as delicate as nature's own truimphs will be apparent.

Not only the loveliness of plant-form, but the play of light and shade upon the grass, upon the mellow warmth of old stone or brickwork, is an inspiration to the designer. The wonderful tracery of shadow cast by the gently swaying branches of a tree suggest a thousand patterns. The possibilities in the dappled, ever-moving river are limitless.

The great designers of the past have left us a heritage which, perhaps, is not too well valued by enough people to-day. If you go for a walk along some English country lane with eyes that not only look but also see, and then go into the little old church so characteristic of our villages, you will at once recognise much that you have seen on your walk in the carvings on pew-end and capital. The leaves and berries, animals and birds which form the units for so much of the glorious wood and stone carving in our ancient churches, are a clear indication as to where the designers of the past turned for their inspiration.

Let us by all means become familiar with all that is good in

design of the past, but let us beware how we imitate. Soon
imitation becomes a stereotyped and mannered copy, bereft
of all life. The work is dead, and when an artist's work is
that, he might just as well die also.

So, with a knowledge of all that is good from the past
forming a theoretical background, the designer to-day must
go to nature for his inspiration, as did the glorious Benvenuto
and all great designers before and after him.

THE RIGHT WAY OF USING COLOUR

CONSIDER what your life would be like without colour.
When the full horror of this has come upon you, consider
what it would be like if, instead of being colourless, we had all
the colour to which we are used, but out of place. For example,
red grass instead of the varied hues and tints that delight and
soothe our eyes. We have seen that order must govern the
placing of shapes so that we may have a design. In exactly
the same way, order must govern the use and placing of
colour.

It is perfectly possible to have a very lovely and fitting
design without the use of any colour, yet colour plays a
tremendous part in our lives and decoration. It must, however,
be clearly understood that colour alone will not make a bad
design good. If the first conception is bad, then the most
beautiful colour in the world is useless. If the forms employed
are mean and poor, if rhythm is lacking and proportion is
wrong, colour will not help.

If from the point of view of form we must go to nature,
a thousand times more must we do so for our colour harmonies.
And do not let us think only of the rare orchid or the highly
cultivated types of flower. Look at a humble forget-me-not,
look carefully into the little, delicate flower, and see with
what exquisite beauty you are confronted.

The science of colour is a very complicated and difficult
subject. In Professor Wilhelm Ostwald's *Theory of Colour
and Colour Standardisation*,[1] the whole question is brilliantly
and scientifically dealt with. For our present purpose we
shall content ourselves with considering what is really essential
for a colour appreciation.

It is quite a common thing to find people whose colour
sense reaches no further than red, blue and yellow. The

[1] Translated from the German and published by Winsor and
Newton.

many variations of hue to be obtained from these colours
do not occur to them. Many teachers have found that
children are much more sensitive to colour harmonies than
adults. This is probably due to self-conscious inhibitions
that arise in the grown-up.

Colours may be divided into two groups. Those that are
cool and those that are warm. Greens, greys, blues are
examples of the former, and browns, yellows, reds are
examples of the latter. It is often a good plan in a decoration
to place a cool colour against a warm one. A rather unpleasant hot effect is avoided in this way. It is frequently
said that a colour sense cannot be taught, yet experience shows
that much may be done by careful study of good examples of
colour harmony. To look at the collections of china, pottery,
embroidery in our museums is an education in colour which
must, to the serious student, have a lasting effect upon his
colour sense, however dead it might have been.

THE EFFECT OF COLOUR ON THE MIND

THOSE who have lived in cheap lodgings will fully appreciate
the deadening influence of the drab and dingy, so frequently to be found in the houses of the Victorian era. Those
who have walked in a park in the Spring will fully appreciate
the joy of fresh colour visible upon all hands. So, in decoration, colour gives a marked stimulus to the mind.

The reaction of the designer to colour is different from that
of the painter. The latter is more concerned with the play
of light and shade, of texture and atmosphere, than the
former. The designer thinks more in what may be described
as flat tints. When we deal with the application of design to
different types of work this question of colour will be more
fully gone into.

A life without colour is too terrible to contemplate, yet
colour misused can be as painful to the eye and mind as a
discord in music. True, we do not always want the sweet
and sugary in music or colour. We do not want our colours
always to be obvious. A discord at times may be good. It
will wake us up and stimulate our minds, thus preventing
them from becoming cloyed. But the use of discords, like
the tremolo in a singer's voice, must be controlled, as it
always is in the hands of a master. Discord must at no time
be used merely for effect. Rather must it be used, as the
accent in music is used, in order that one clear note may

stand out from the rest, lifting all from what would otherwise
have been greyness.

Colour also is often an indication to us of the origin of some
type of ornament. For instance, a particular tint of green,
blue, purple, and red immediately suggests the paintings upon
Persian and Turkish pottery. In the same way, if we think
of the rich embossed velvets of sixteenth-century Italy, we
at once visualise the characteristic crimson and gold of that
famous weave. It would not be too much to say that every
country has its distinctive colour combinations. We have
mentioned two, and many others readily occur to the mind.
The lovely Delft blue or the rich red lustre of Hispano-
Moresque ware are two more outstanding examples of this
distinctive colouring.

THE PATTERN UNIT : A GUIDE TO ORIGIN

THE shape of the units employed in the pattern far transcends
characteristic colouring as a guide to the place of origin of
an object. Each country employs certain shapes which they
repeatedly use in their decorations. The Lotus plant of
ancient Egypt, the key-patterns, Egg and Dart, and Anthemion
ornament of the Greeks (Fig. 18), are familiar to us all,
especially as they have been so frequently, and sometimes
most unwisely, used in the colossal cinemas of to-day.

The Egyptians used the conventional treatment of the
Lotus—symbol of fertility—again and again, upon papyrus,
temple and urn. In the same way the Greeks used in a thousand
different ways, and upon a thousand different objects, the
Anthemion, which sometimes is called the Honeysuckle
ornament. We know that in our own churches the ornament
upon capital and arch varies, and we probably have been
told that this difference is one of the many ways of determining
the period of construction. For example, the familiar Ball-
flower is a product of the fourteenth century, just as the three-
lobed leaf is of the thirteenth century. So, in exactly the same
way, must we approach examples of ornament of other
countries. It would be impossible to give here examples of
all types, yet the four that have been selected are very typical
and constantly appear in ornament. They are, too, the most
familiar types, which is one reason for their selection.

It would be wrong to say that in all Persian or Turkish
ornament the example given (Fig. 19) always occurs, yet this

conventional representation of the Pink is very characteristic and is found with remarkable frequency upon pottery. The hyacinth was also a favourite unit, and an example of the rendering of this plant is also illustrated (Fig. 19). These two plants were used upon wall tiles, and the blues, browns, and turquoise colours, with their glowing lustre, are very typical. Animals and even the human figure were often used in conjunction with these floral patterns, and the rugs and carpets of Persia show this very well.

Just as the Persian Pink is not always employed, the Indian Pine ornament does not occur in all Indian design, yet it appears sufficiently frequently for it to be looked upon as very characteristic. The example (Fig. 19) is the unit that is so familiar to us upon Cashmere scarves and the printed cottons.

The Chinese Peony (Fig. 18) is as frequently met with as the conventional chrysanthemum, and we constantly come across it among the birds and dragons which form the decoration upon the rich silks and embroideries of this amazing country; a country where the very colours used in the patterns have a religious significance which must be adhered to. And what lovely colours these are. The hue of the kingfisher's wings gives the colour to a silk robe, upon which embroidery glowing with golds, greens, and reds delight our eyes. The elaboration of the designs and the amazing perfection of its execution is typical of the East.

Our last example of the Rose (Fig. 19) is met with continually in all forms of decoration which were carried out during the Tudor period. This conventional representation of the rose may be found carved in stone and wood, worked in wrought iron, or embroidered upon Elizabethan bedspreads. It is, perhaps, familiar to all English people.

WHAT IS MEANT BY "CONVENTION" IN DESIGN

WE have now dealt with some of the principles of ornament and some of the laws that govern the making of a pattern. Also, we have become familiar with a few types of units that have been employed by different countries. Once or twice we have used the word "conventional" when speaking of ornament. For instance we spoke of the "conventional representation of the Pink" in Persian decoration. Let us consider what is meant in design by this word.

Design may be placed in three divisions: Naturalistic Design; Conventional Design; and Abstract Design.

The type of naturalistic ornament shown in Fig. 19 is based upon forms taken from nature, and although the design keeps as near the natural as the pattern will allow, it always falls short of an exact copy. This spray of Lilies of the Valley is taken from a dress of the late eighteenth century in the Victoria and Albert Museum, London. The dress is made of cotton and the spray is printed upon it in natural colours. The pattern is formed by placing the spray in a " drop " manner all over the fabric. The material has become a little yellowed by passing years, yet the effect is still quite charming and delicate.

For an example of our second type of pattern, namely conventional, we cannot do better than to look at Fig. 19. The way the Pink has been treated and simplified is an excellent instance of the meaning of conventional ornament. Here the designer goes to nature for his inspiration, and then subjects the plant he has selected to some form of artistic treatment ; it may be quite unlike nature in the end. The pattern is the important thing. Yet in this type of pattern there is always, however remote, some indication of the design having been based upon natural forms.

The third type of pattern is abstract ornament. This kind of design is not based upon nature at all. If the first idea of the designer was started by a natural form, then it was subconscious, an unsought memory out of the past. He neither goes to nature for his inspiration nor does the finished design resemble it. Much of the modern design falls into this division, and the upholstery in the Underground trains, or the tapestry-covered furniture in the home, together with curtains, carpets, and wall-papers, often have types of abstract pattern.

It will be obvious that a pattern first of all must be worked out on paper before it can be applied to fabric, vase, or metal. Also, it will be realised that the designer cannot aimlessly wander over the paper, drawing units at random and hoping for the best. On the contrary, the utmost attention must be given to the planning of the pattern. There are many well-recognised systems of placing units, and two of the most usual are given in Fig. 19.

A PATTERN FOR WALL-PAPER OR FABRICS

THE first is an arrangement which is perhaps one of the most common in use to-day both in wall-papers and textiles. This is the all-over drop or sprig pattern referred

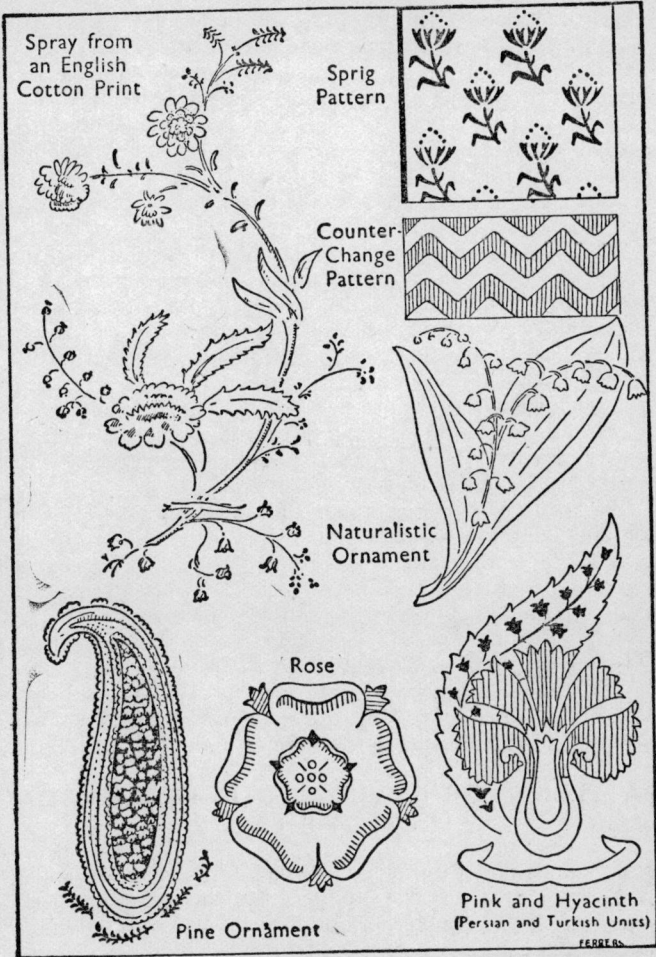

Spray from
an English
Cotton Print

Sprig
Pattern

Counter-
Change
Pattern

Naturalistic
Ornament

Rose

Pine Ornament

Pink and Hyacinth
(Persian and Turkish Units)

FERRERS

19. NATURAL FORMS IN THE DESIGNER'S HANDS

*In all but one of these patterns the artist has gone to Nature
for inspiration, but the difference between naturalistic treatment (in the Spray and the Lily of the Valley) and conventional treatment (of the rose, pink, hyacinth, sprig,
and pine ornament) may be clearly seen.*

to when we dealt with the Lily of the Valley naturalistic design. In patterns such as these everything depends upon the right size of the unit employed and also the correct placing of it, so that not too much space is left empty.

This sprig pattern is perhaps the most frequently used system to-day in printed dress fabrics. When a sprig pattern is printed from a wood-block by hand, the sprig is repeated a number of times on the block so that one printing covers a fairly wide area.

The simplicity of treatment of all hand-printed designs of any period, when we compare them to the rather dull and awful precision of the mechanically produced patterns of to-day is charming. We have become so used to this machine-like perfection that any deviation from it is a shock to us, and we should do well to guard against it unless we desire to lose altogether our appreciation of hand-made things.

Our second example is an excellent method of getting variety into a very simple pattern. This is by means of what is called " counter-change."

The pattern merely consists of a zigzag line, but it is so repeated that the background that is left unprinted is exactly the same width as the printed pattern. This, after a repeat or two has been accomplished, makes the pattern look as if two colours have been used. Elaborations of this principle are numerous and many are extraordinarily ingenious.

In Fig. 19 we have a typical example of the delicate spray patterns of the eighteenth century in England and France. These naturalistic sprays were printed on cotton, and the effect is of studied carelessness as the sprays wander over the fabric.

PATTERNS FOR FABRICS : OUR INSPIRATION FROM THE EAST

WE must now turn our knowledge of design to the application of it to fabrics, pottery and the like. The word textile is used to denote all fabrics made on a loom. These fall into three divisions : pattern fabrics, plain fabrics, printed fabrics. The herring-bone pattern on many tweeds is an example of the first, linen of the second, and any pattern printed from a wood-block or roller of the last.

The Eastern peoples have always exercised an influence over the type of pattern used in weaving and printing, and this may be traced through many centuries all over Europe. The influence India has had upon the carpet industry is very apparent. The old designs are still copied, not only in England, but in India too, and wonderful patterns are produced in the hill districts upon looms of the most primitive kind. Names such as Baghdad, Damascus, and Ispahan call up to the mind's eye the rich fabrics of the East. It is not surprising that these peoples have exercised such an influence over the West when one considers that even their writing is a pattern in itself.

Italy in the sixteenth century was famous for its velvets. Examples of lovely " cut " velvet of this period are in the Victoria and Albert Museum. The large units which form the pattern are based on the artichoke plant, sometimes called the pineapple plant, because of its similarity to that fruit. This large conventional ornament was used for the velvets of Genoa and Florence. These velvets have the pile raised so that the pattern stands out in relief. Often gold or silver is introduced into the background. Typical colouring is crimson velvet upon a cream ground which is enriched with silver or gold thread. The patterns are generally ordered in much the same way, the stalks form the characteristic " ogee " shape and the areas formed by this shape are filled with the artichoke plant. There is marked Persian influence in many of the examples, and the Persian Pink (Fig. 19) is frequently met with. This is an example of the Eastern influence in Europe of which we have spoken.

One of the most important things to be noted in these types of pattern is the perfect proportion of one unit to the next, and not only that, but to the space that they fill as well. They are splendid examples of a most important rule in design, namely, that the background is as important as the pattern. Not one leaf or petal may be added or subtracted from these designs. In a word, they are " right "—a perfectly balanced and proportioned pattern, which delights the eye.

PRINTING THE PATTERN ON THE CLOTH

IF a pattern is not woven into the fabric the design may be carried out by the use of wood-blocks or rollers which have the pattern engraved upon them. This last is the method most used to-day. The printing from wood-blocks is not really practical as a homecraft because so much apparatus is required. But another method of placing a pattern on fabric is Batik work, and is quite feasible for home production.

Batik work consists of forming a pattern in wax on the fabric and then steeping in a dye-bath. The wax does not allow the dye to stain the fabric and thus, when the wax has been removed, an uncoloured pattern appears. This system of producing patterns has been practised in the East from the earliest times, and is particularly centred in Java. The Javanese first roughly indicate the pattern upon the fabric, generally imported cotton, with charcoal. When they have melted their wax, they use a copper instrument rather the shape of a clay pipe with the mouthpiece slightly bent. The liquid wax is poured into the bowl of the pipe and then the charcoal lines of the design are followed out with the wax, the wax being poured through the mouthpiece, as it were.

If this method is not used, then wooden blocks are made having the pattern formed with copper wire upon them. The wax is placed on the block, and then pressed on the fabric, thus leaving a wax impression. Whichever method is used, both sides of the fabric must be treated in the same way. The wax hardens quite quickly and the fabric is then placed in a dye-bath. It is left there until the dye has thoroughly impregnated the cloth. It is taken out and placed in warm water which is brought to the boil, when the wax melts and floats to the top. The cloth is then finished by being dried in the sun.

The same effect is also produced commercially by machine in Europe. The usual colours of the native Javanese work are blue, a rather rusty black, and a dull red, upon a white ground. The most characteristic feature, however, of Batik work is the " marbling " effect due to the wax cracking and the dye sinking through.

POTTERY : A FASCINATING PAGEANTRY OF COLOUR AND SHAPE

UNTIL now we have dealt with the application of a pattern to a fabric, yet no discourse on design would be complete unless mention were made of Pottery design. If textiles are necessary to us, keeping us warm and decorating our homes as they do, the same may be said of pottery. Our lives would indeed be difficult if it were not for the clays which make our china, and not only that, but a thousand and one other objects as well, down to the humble insulators on the telegraph posts and the very bricks of our homes.

How important and how vital a part pottery played in the

20. AGE-OLD BEAUTY FASHIONED FROM CLAY

A German tankard with pewter lid (a), Jasper ware (b), a Greek vase (c), and wine-cup (e), a Chinese jar (d), Red Samian ware (f), Hispano-Moresque vase of Moorish shape (g), Persian bowl (h), and a plate of Italian Majolica ware (i).

lives of the ancients can be seen at once in our museums. There we find all kinds and types of vases and bowls. We may see the red Samian ware of Rome, some of which was made in Britain, or we may turn to the wonder of the Grecian period, where beauty of line is carried to perfection. If we wish, we may brush the years aside, and pass from one century to another, and as we go our eyes will become weary and our minds dazed with the ever changing types, yet go on we must, for it is a fascinating pageantry of colour and history in clay that forbids us to tire. We see the lovely blues and greens of China, and we are delighted with the characteristic " plum blossom " motif which is still produced to-day upon the jars in which we buy ginger at Christmas time. The turquoise, yellow and blue of the Persian ware or the Moorish shapes of the Hispano-Moresque vases equally please us.

The homeliness of the Dutch tiles with the gentle Delft

blue, or the rather prosaic heaviness of the German stoneware with its important heraldic emblems is a happy contrast to the exotic East that we have just left, yet each have their own beauty. The blue and orange of the Majolica ware, and especially the rich gold and red lustre upon the Italian Majolica, as well as the patterns, are an inspiration to any designer.

When we come to England we are met by names that have become familiar to us down the years—Worcester, Chelsea, and Spode. We see the rich gold and crimson of the Coalport, and the many varieties of the famous Wedgwood, the sombre, funereal black basalt or the classical Jasper ware of blue, lilac, and black with its white raised figures. It is a life study, endless and enthralling.

LOVELINESS MOULDED FROM COMMON CLAY

IT is curious to contemplate the almost priceless value attaching to many wares when we consider how plentiful and valueless is the raw material—clay. The beauty that can be made out of this clay is due to its plastic nature and its readiness to take a very high glaze. It is this glaze that is so attractive to us when handling pottery, quite apart from the colour and pattern. When this glaze is not present, as in the case of the red earthenware jugs with the cream rims one buys in Devonshire, the beauty of line is ample recompense. The Greeks were the perfect exponents of this beauty of line in clay and the lovely Kylix or wine-cup shape is an excellent example of this purity of line and proportion.

So perfect are the numerous Grecian shapes, that ever since they have been copied by man. In the eighteenth century in England the famous Josiah Wedgwood introduced his equally famous Jasper ware. This is a pure Greek revival and the ware is still produced to-day. We are all familiar with the blue variety with its white raised figures, which in the originals were designed by the artist Flaxman. Another example of this Greek revival is Wedgwood's Black Basalt ware. Here the only relief from the dull black, for this ware does not have a glaze, is the gilt upon handles or lid.

THE THREE KINDS OF POTTERY

POTTERY is divided into three sections : (1) earthenware, (2) stoneware, (3) porcelain. Under earthenware are grouped the largest number of pottery objects. The difference between the three lies not only in the look but in the composition of the clay. Earthenware is made up of natural clays which when fired are dull and opaque. This dullness is counter-acted by glazing. The Roman Samian ware is an example of earthenware and is a fine red colour with patterns moulded upon it. So is the Delft ware, and most English pottery.

Stoneware differs from earthenware in that it has a large amount of burnt, crushed flint mixed with the clay, and it is fired at a greater temperature. The glaze is obtained by throwing salt upon the fires at a certain heat, when a thin glass or glaze is formed on the ware. This stoneware was perfected in Germany in the sixteenth century. The tall tankards with their pewter lids are typical examples. They generally have coats of arms, together with scroll patterns stamped upon them. Blue, a soft grey, and brown are the colours employed. It was introduced into England by the brothers Elers, who came from Bavaria.

Porcelain, the finest of the three, is composed of a special clay called China Clay which is found in Cornwall, plus bone ash. This bone ash gives to the china a wonderful whiteness. It has a hard white brilliant glaze which is very well shown in the white Meissen porcelain. This was made in Saxony, and it is in imitation of the famous Ming porcelain of China. It was also the forerunner of the Dresden porcelain. The manufacture of porcelain in England commenced in the eighteenth century. The wonderful and exquisite Bow and Chelsea figures belong to this period, and the " Music Lesson " in the Victoria and Albert Museum is a remarkable example of this work. The perfect miniature-like painting together with the delicate modelling of the figures and the bower of white blossom behind them is very lovely. Figures were not the only objects made in this ware, and the naturalistic flowers, birds, and butterflies painted on the famous Welsh porcelain of Nantgarw are a witness to this.

HOW THE PATTERN IS PLACED ON THE WARE

DESIGNING for pottery is a specialised art. The patterns do not have to conform to such an extent to the limitations of the material as is the case in textile designing. What may be carried out on paper with brush and colour may be as readily done on the pottery. It may be painted by hand or the pattern may be engraved on copper plates, from which a transfer is made, which in turn is pressed upon the ware. The pattern may be put on before or after the ware is fired.

Each type has a name with which we are familiar, " Under-glaze " and " Overglaze."

The colours used for painting upon pottery are all metallic in origin, that is to say, they are derived from oxides of metal. To the amateur they are most disconcerting, for the hues change to quite different colours after the ware has been fired. This means that the pottery designer must not be content with the look of his first design only, but he must think ahead and know what the fired article will look like.

Unlike textile patterns where an all-over design based upon some system of placing the units is frequently employed, the designs for pottery generally take the form of naturalistic or conventional sprays, sprigs, and birds. Very often, and especially in modern ware, abstract patterns are used, and border designs are much in use. The shapes and patterns in china have not altered greatly, and the modern ware is very similar to that of the past. Nevertheless, a change is notice-able, and a simplicity is aimed at which is all to the good. It is possibly due to a reaction against the complexity of modern life.

This modern trend towards simplicity is clearly shown in the breakfast and supper services designed for use upon rather rough, coloured linen cloths. The china is plain with austere line borders in a tint to harmonise with their surroundings. We see, therefore, that a design must not only conform to the shape and use of the article, but to its environment as well.

RICH DESIGNS THAT CAN BE WROUGHT IN METAL

PERHAPS the best examples of the adaptation of the design to the medium are to be found in decorative metal-work. If the medium is gold or silver there is scarcely any limit to the richness and wealth of detail that may be indulged in. These metals, apart from their natural beauty of colour, are reasonably soft and therefore readily worked. They may have the pattern beaten upon them as in repoussé work, or some form of pierced or chased work can enrich them. If additional colour is required, then enamels are used, and the famous and well-known gold jewel of King Alfred, familiar to us from illustrations in the history books of our school-days, is an excellent example.

One of the greatest chances for the gold and silversmith

occurred in England during the Middle Ages, when the demands of the Church for all manner of ecclesiastical plate were very numerous. The wealth of the Church made certain that an ample supply should follow this demand, and the abundant examples of chalices, censers, crosiers, and altar-frontals are mute witness to the splendour of the mediæval Church. When looking at these lovely examples of the goldsmith's art in our museums to-day, it is not difficult to picture them again in their proper places, fulfilling their appointed tasks, and glowing and glinting in the golden light of ecclesiastical candle, with the sombre gloom of a cathedral for their setting.

Precious stones and ivory were also used in conjunction with enamels and delicate repoussé work. This Church metal-work was carried out during the Gothic period in England, and consequently the characteristic Gothic decoration is to be found enriching chalice and pyx. The three-lobed leaf of the thirteenth century and the more elaborate and natural foliage of the Decorated Gothic, together with the trefoil and quatrefoil shapes, form the basis of many patterns.

During the sixteenth century this Gothic tradition disappears and its place is taken by Renaissance work. The great Italian goldsmith Benvenuto Cellini produced amazingly lovely work in his own country, while in England this rebirth of art was felt during the reigns of Henry VII. and Henry VIII., and some very beautiful goldsmith's work belongs to this period. The Gothic designs give place to typical Italian influences such as natural fruits, flowers, and foliage banded together with ribbons. Scrollwork and beautifully modelled angels and cherubs are also a characteristic of this period. Towards the end of the sixteenth century the Roman acanthus foliage, carried out in delicate repoussé work and chasing, is a feature of gold and silver work.

It would be wrong to limit work in precious metal to Church plate only. Many lovely articles of domestic use were produced as well, and we have amazing silver salt-cellars designed to look like miniature castles, or bowls, cups and plates. During the seventeenth and eighteenth centuries the diversity of the objects increases, and we have many-branched candelabra, punchbowls, and ceremonial covered cups, generally to be found in the keeping of Corporations to-day. Of the smaller articles spoons are the most common.

BRONZE : A FAVOURITE IN ANCIENT TIMES

MUCH important decorative work has been carried out in the lesser metals, and although intrinsically bronze, brass, and iron are of less importance, they have equal beauty and value artistically. Bronze, which is an alloy of copper and tin, has been used from the earliest times. The Phoenicians were famous for their works in bronze, and they voyaged far, even to the shores of Britain, for the necessary tin with which to make their alloy.

Bronze is particularly suitable for casting, and the Italians of the Renaissance were most skilful at this work. The Perseus by Cellini is an example of this. In Westminster Abbey we may find this Italian skill in bronze work exemplified in the effigies by Torregiano, the Florentine, of Henry VII. and his Queen. Perhaps one of the most attractive things about works in bronze is the lovely patina or colour which it possesses.

If decorative work in gold and silver and bronze is beautiful, there is something peculiarly satisfying to the cultured Englishman in wrought-iron work. Perhaps its simplicity and honesty of purpose appeal more strongly to an Anglo-Saxon mind than does the rich sumptuousness of decoration in the precious metals. Again, wrought-iron is the natural accompaniment of what we may term Britain's national wood—oak. The old oak chests and doors were adorned with hinges, locks, and latches of wrought-iron, perfect in their fitness and design, and what dignity they possess when compared with many of the stupid attempts of to-day, where the door is of oak and the fittings are of chromium plate ! English iron-work was highly esteemed, and especially the Sussex work. The Hammerponds, still sheets of water with a background of beech trees glorious in autumn, that are scattered about the peaceful Sussex county are the only evidence to-day of a one-time busyness.

ART IN IRON THAT BEGAN WITH THE BLACKSMITH

THE village blacksmith was the craftsman responsible for many of the objects in iron, such as fire-irons, knockers, keys, locks, hinges and many other things, and one only has to look at some of them and notice their perfect proportions and workmanship to realise that the man who carried out the work was more than a shoer of horses. He was an artist, a designer of great natural ability, skill, and discernment. Alas, he is almost extinct, save for isolated instances where a smith still carries on the noble traditions of the past. Large objects such as gates, grills, and altar-screens, the last named reaching gigantic proportions in the " Rejas " of Spain with their vertical bars of turned iron, were not the only concern of the smith.

The small catches on lattice windows or cottage doors are frequently very beautiful and worthy of attention. Often they take the form of some conventional bird or animal, or some simple floral motif is used. These are very different from the modern mass productions, and when one contemplates many of the poor and wrong efforts on present-day furniture in the shape of unsuitable handles and lock-plates, one realises what a gulf lies between the old and the new.

One constantly meets with delightful examples of this honest and beautiful wrought-iron work in the towns and villages of England, and often in unexpected places. The old and neglected strong box in the office of a country solicitor may show, upon the rusty lid being turned back, a charming pierced iron lock-case. Conventional flowers and leaves may form the pattern, and undoubtedly the local smith in some dim past had been responsible for the making and decoration of this receptacle of legal secrets, which to-day our modern safes have ousted. The large and unwieldy church keys are very often beautiful in design, and sometimes one finds initials cunningly interwoven into the pattern at the bow.

Fire-irons were very beautiful, and what can look better and more fitting against the brick fireplace which is being built in so many new houses than a wrought-iron poker, tongs, and shovel ? Just as the glow of brass against dark oak is delightful, so too is a well made wrought-iron knocker upon a simple oak front door an object of constant joy each time we enter our home. It is this bringing of the good and beautiful into our everyday lives that is so necessary in this machine-made age. Many of these old knockers must have given the smith much amusement and his fancy must have been allowed free rein ; often one finds the head of some curious and fabulous monster, and issuing from its fiercely grim mouth a ring with which the actual blow may be struck upon the oak.

A MASTERPIECE OF DESIGN IN IRON

THERE are many lovely examples of wrought-iron work in our museums, and quite one of the most delightful is an eighteenth-century French door in the Victoria and Albert Museum. The actual framework of the door is surrounded by a border of eight S-shaped scrolls which terminate in simple flower forms. There are two keyhole plates top and bottom on the left, and the centre is filled with beautifully shaped leaves and flowers that grow upon stalks, which in turn spring from a central stalk that emanates from behind a flat piece of metal cut in the shape of a vase. The simplicity of treatment and the perfect proportion of all the units is a masterpiece of designing. The effect is not of iron but of charming grace and lightness.

Beauty and purity of line must be the first consideration in judging wrought-iron work, just as it must be the first thought of the designer. The early twelfth and thirteenth century hinges upon the doors of churches are excellent examples of this statement. If we consider the well-known twelfth century wrought-iron hinges upon a door that was formerly in St. Albans Abbey and is now in the Victoria and Albert Museum, we shall clearly see what is meant by beauty of line. From a central bar or strap spring lovely spirals slightly decreasing in dimensions, and very simply enriched by chisel marks in a series of zig-zags. In this example we are made aware of another important fact, namely, that the craftsman has been quite content to allow his tools to produce their natural effects, and in no way has he forced them to perform the impossible. The marks and shapes that a tool produces in the hands of a craftsman is good design.

LOVELY GATEWAYS TO ENGLAND'S STATELY HOMES

FROM the twelfth-century simplicity we may turn to the far more sophisticated beauty of the seventeenth- and eighteenth-century park gates, balconies, and fanlights. There are few sights more delightful than good wrought-iron gates at the entrance to some estate. The weathered grey of the stone pillars which support the gates tones wonderfully well with the black of the iron, and the lovely lines of the pattern with their wealth of symmetrical spirals and curves enclosing a noble coat of arms has a fitting background of green lawn and ancient trees to set them off. The eighteenth-century balconies and fanlights are a positive joy, so delicate are the lines, yet many were destroyed by the ridiculous and ignorant demolition of houses during the Victorian period. Happily some were saved from the housebreaker's hammer.

Perhaps the work of the French smith Jean Tijou during the early part of the eighteenth century may be instanced as an example of what rich and foliated effects could be produced in iron by the use of variations of the the acanthus leaf. The wrought-iron work upon the gates in St. Paul's Cathedral are by this craftsman, and there is some more of his work at Hampton Court. Its characteristic features are the fern-like leaves which twist and turn in all manner of graceful curves and spirals.

There is still good wrought-iron work produced to-day, but the demand is confined to the comparatively few who appreciate it. There is ample scope here for the would-be worker in metal, and there is a noble heritage for his guidance and inspiration.

THE FEMININE ASPECT : FASHION DESIGN

WE now come to a subject which has a peculiar interest for women, namely, Fashion Designing. The art of fashion drawing does not, strictly speaking, come within the scope of the Applied Arts, yet so much design to-day, particularly for textiles, is produced for the making of women's dresses that it seems fitting that the art of fashion drawing and designing should not be disregarded.

But the fashion artist is generally concerned with the drawing of clothes that have already been designed. The people who actually create the dress are very gods indeed, and there is no golden road or easy training that can be laid down to guide the steps of aspirants. No man can say what goes to make a brilliant creative artist. Some have the " divine " gift, while others, possibly very able artists, never attain to so dizzy a pinnacle.

Why France should always give the lead in matters of dress has never been satisfactorily answered, but undoubtedly the great French houses do exercise an enormous influence upon dress fashions. These creators of dresses are not concerned so much with how to draw them, rather do they deal with rhythm and line in fabrics. Here we have the difference between fashion drawing and fashion designing. The designer knows to a nicety how to produce a fussiness or a sweeping dignity. The soft, graceful folds of some fabrics and the rather hard glitter of others are completely understood, and materials are used by the designer much in the

same way as an artist uses his pigments. The designer of
dresses must have a knowledge of the laws that govern applied
design, some of which we have indicated and discussed. He
must know to the full the meaning of rhythm in line, and his
sense of proportion must be acute indeed. Three simple
examples will express very clearly the significance of this
last statement (see Fig. 21).

In these three examples we have the same pose and the

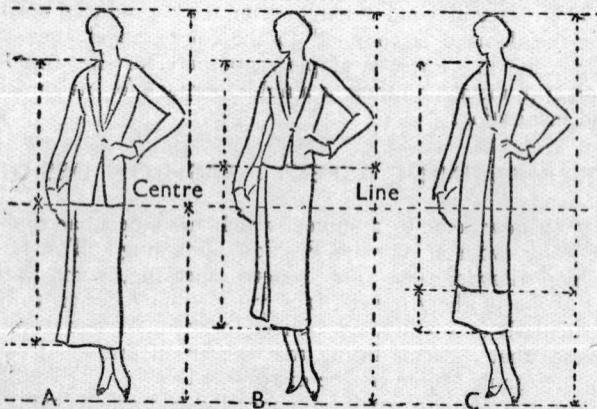

**21. HOW THE FASHION-DESIGNER ADDS INTEREST
TO HIS MODELS**

*In fashion designing, balance based on a sense of proportion
gives a more subtle effect than exact symmetrical division.
Compare the equal proportions of A with the unequal and
more interesting ones of B and C.*

same figure, yet very different effects are produced. The
dotted lines indicate the proportions. In figure A the proportions are exactly equal. The coat is the same length as
the dress, and the end of the coat is exactly in the centre of
the entire height of the figure. The result of all this geometrical exactitude is an appearance of dull dowdiness. The
interest is not awakened, and one does not even ask oneself
whether the length of the coat or skirt is equal or not. One
just dully accepts the fact. It is quite safe to say that in dress
the divisions should never be equal, and in any other type of

design the desirability of equal spacing should be very carefully considered.

In figures B and C we have the unequal division above or below the centre line, and at once the difference for the better is obvious. The short coat of B compared with the long line of the skirt is at once interesting and smart as well as artistically good. With C the long coat line ending far below the centre is very pleasing and graceful. The dress designer must bear this fact that we have just illustrated as well as many another continually in his mind.

WIDE SCOPE FOR THE FASHION DRAUGHTSMAN

WE have dealt briefly with the creator of dresses, and now we must turn to the far wider scope of the fashion draughtsman. When one contemplates on the book-stalls all over the country the colossal number of magazines which have fashion drawings as their chief feature, it is not surprising to know that the demand for this type of drawing far exceeds the number of artists capable of doing the work. This fact should be of a cheering nature to those desirous of taking up fashion work as a profession, yet here we must echo the repeated warning that the way to success is hard and long—an unpalatable commonplace, which will in no way deter the really sincere aspirant.

Fashion drawing, like all the arts, requires a specialised training. There is a curious and erroneous idea held by a number of people that fashion drawing requires no ability in draughtsmanship. Nothing could be farther from the truth. To bolster up this statement, one is told to look at some particular fashion drawing in some leading journal. " Look at that," they say, " why, it doesn't look like a real figure at all. Any one could draw like that." True, this type of criticism is often heard from the lips of very young art students, who know just enough about drawing to know nothing about it. They never realise that this very unreality to the human figure is the product of conventions and liberties that only an experienced figure draughtsman would employ or take.

The paradoxical fact that arises out of this statement is that the would-be fashion artist must first of all be able to draw the human figure before making any attempt at fashion drawing proper. This means that a carefully organised course at an Art School must be undertaken. Most Art Schools to-day are only too willing to guide the student, and lay down the most suitable course to meet his or her requirements. Generally it is a girl who wants to take up fashion work, for by the very nature of the work women are attracted to it more readily than men.

WHAT THE STUDENT LEARNS FIRST

THE most important subject in the Art School for a fashion artist will be the life class, but the student must not expect to commence this work at once. Many schools wisely insist on the beginner first of all drawing from what is called the Antique. This is drawing from plaster reproductions of classical statues. In this way the student is made familiar with the human figure without the added difficulty of movement that is always present with the living model. Anatomy of the human figure must also be studied. This does not mean any real medical knowledge, for the artist is only concerned with the skeleton and the superficial muscles in so much as they affect the outward shape. This study will run concurrently with the rest of the course so that the practical relationship will always be present.

Another subject will be the history of costume, for the statement that one learns the history of the past in order to understand the present is never more true and applicable than when it is applied to modern fashion drawing and design. It requires very little knowledge of costume of the past to see the similarity to it in fashion to-day. With certain exaggerations of style eliminated, the tight bodice and full flared skirt of to-day is quite similar to the fifteenth-century style of woman's dress. Again, sleeves that are tight and moulded to the arm and suddenly widen at the wrist, or the variety that are puffed at the shoulders, together with gauntlet gloves, not only of kid but of velvet particularly, are all products of the past. It is true that fashion is ever changing, yet the really expert fashion artist senses the change even before it takes place.

HOW MANY HEADS TO A BODY?

NOW as to the difference in the figure when used for fashion drawing. While it is almost impossible, and not very desirable either, to make any hard and fast rule for proportions in the human figure, many drawing books give the proportion of seven and a half heads. This means that taking the measurement from the top of the head to the bottom of the chin, it will go into the body six and a half times. No artist uses this when he draws from life, and as each model varies—and it is this very variation that is so charming—this rule is of little use. In fashion drawing, however, a very definite convention is adhered to. Most figures for these purposes are eight and a half to nine heads in height, hence the rather attentuated aspect of many fashion plates. This convention is adopted because it displays the frock to the best advantage.

It must never be lost sight of that a fashion drawing is first and foremost an advertisement designed to sell the dress. In order to do this the whole effect must look smart, the *dernier cri* of the French well expresses it. To get this ultra-smart effect any convention is legitimate, and a careful study of fashion books will readily show this treatment in its most brilliant form.

THE ART SCHOOL : AN ESSENTIAL BEGINNING

IT is impossible to lay too much stress upon the necessity for an Art School training. No study of books can take the place of the training obtainable at a school, and a three years' course at a good school is essential. The career of a doctor or a lawyer would not be contemplated by a person unable to give the necessary time to the training for these professions, and it is quite wrong to think that an artistic career, whether it be for fashion work or any other branch of art, can be jumped into without any preparatory training. In fact we may say that in the applied arts such as metal-work and pottery an Art School training is absolutely essential, for, with craftwork, actually seeing how a thing should be done and then putting it into practice is the only way of learning.

There are some 118 principal Art Schools in London and the Provinces, and these are situated in most of the big towns. Certain schools specialise in types of work, such as the various schools in Birmingham, including the Vittoria Street School for Jewellers and Silversmiths, which is for evening-school work, and the School of Dress Design. We have the same thing in Pottery in the schools at Stoke-on-Trent, and for Weaving and Textiles in the Lancashire schools. Although the student should, if possible, exercise discrimination in the choice of schools, so that his particular requirements may be more readily catered for, this does not mean to say that other schools do not train students in metal-work or pottery.

On the contrary, most of the schools offer a very varied set of courses, and quite the best thing to do is for the student to make an appointment with the head of the school selected, and place his or her case before him. It is very necessary to have a definite aim in view, and this will be welcomed by a principal. It is fatally easy to waste time in an Art School, and there is no blame attaching to the school—it is always the student's fault. Again, be guided by the principal's advice, remember he has a wide experience in art training, and if he wants you to take certain subjects that you consider quite unrelated to your proposed profession, follow out his advice with a good grace. You will find later on in your course that these subjects are very much related and necessary.

Most schools have day and evening classes and Saturday morning classes too. It will depend upon the time that the student can give to his training what course he takes. Much may be done by evening work, generally from 7 p.m. to 9 p.m., but it goes without saying that if the whole day can be given, and best of all a full three years' course embarked upon, it is the most satisfactory to all concerned. Fees vary in different schools and with different courses, and these are arranged with the principal after the course has been decided upon.

WHEN THE TRAINING IS COMPLETE

LET us suppose that the course at an Art School is finished. What is the prospective fashion draughtsman to do next? There are numerous avenues open to him or her. Free-lance work may be undertaken or a position in a Studio or large shop that keeps a staff of artists can be sought for. The most usual and the wisest course to adopt is to enter a Studio. These Studios are firms that definitely specialise in commercial work of all kinds, and there are many, both in London and the Provinces. The applicant must be prepared to take a humble post at first, with probably no more than a £1 per week as commencing salary. The experience gained will be beyond price. Perhaps one of the most important things to bear in mind when applying for such a post is that the employer will not want to examine Art School work as specimens of what the applicant can do. He will, however, very much want to see examples of promising fashion drawings.

If "free-lance" work is decided upon, then the artist

must be prepared to hawk his wares round the market. This requires, apart from artistic ability, a keen business sense coupled with a boldness to face the possible buyer, who is generally entrenched behind a perfect barrage of office boys, clerks, and secretaries. This type of boldness is seldom found in people of artistic attributes. Whatever method may be decided upon, hard work and a certain amount of disappointment is bound to be faced.

Fees always depend upon the reputation of the artist, the quality of the work, and the firm buying it. A drawing may be sold for a guinea or for fifty guineas. This last sum, large though it may appear to the layman, is quite frequently paid for a drawing by an artist in the front rank of his profession. This only applies to " free-lance " work, and if the drawing is sold through an agent, then his percentage must be reckoned with. If the artist belongs to a Studio, a fixed salary is paid which may start at £1 per week and eventually rise to £500 a year.

SOME HELPFUL BOOKS ON DESIGN

EXPLORATION along the various fascinating paths opened up by an interest in the subject of Design may be pursued by means of the many excellent books which have been written on its different aspects. Those who are anxious to learn the principal facts about design in any particular country and their application will find *Historic Ornament*, by Richard Glazier (Batsford), an excellent book. The photographs and line drawings it contains are very helpful from every point of view. *Principles of Decoration*, by R. G. Hatton (Chapman and Hall), is written particularly for students and will afford a good guide to those desiring practical help. The title of *The Meaning of Art*, by Herbert Read (Faber and Faber), is self-explanatory. The book is simply written and inexpensive and offers an excellent guide to those wishing to widen their æsthetic appreciation. *English Pottery and Porcelain*, by W. B. Honey (Black), is a reliable book on the subject and contains a number of excellent photographs.

The whole scope of batik dyeing and pattern making is covered in *Batik and Other Pattern Dyeing*, by W. D. and I. D. Baker (Batsford). A rather more expensive book, but one well worth securing by those who are interested in the history of fashion, is *Historic Costume*, by Francis M. Kelly and Randolph Schwab (Batsford). This is an authoritative

8

survey of the period of fashion between 1490 and 1790 and is beautifully illustrated. *Figures, Faces, and Folds,* by Adolphe Braun (Batsford), and *Fashion Drawing and Dress Design,* by Mabel L. Hall (Pitman), are two excellent books for the student of fashion drawing. Besides giving much valuable information on the subject, they include drawing for reproduction. An aid to the appreciation of the collection of ironwork in the Victoria and Albert Museum will be found in *Ironwork,* compiled by J. Starkie-Gardner and published by the Museum. Those who wish to be kept informed of the modern trend in industrial design will find *Design for To-day : A Monthly Journal for Industrial Art,* an excellent periodical.

THE ART OF THE ILLUSTRATOR

by C. H. LAY

ONCE upon a time ! It is appropriate that an article on illustration should be compelled to start with these words, for they convey vivid recollections of our first books and their illustrations—books that were almost part of ourselves ; illustrations that made the words of those books real for us; illustrations to fairy tales read in childhood. I have said " compelled to start," because the disputes of the archæ-ologists about the dates of Palæolithic periods have prevented me from giving a nice comfortable date for the first known illustration by primitive man.

Once upon a time then, or in the Aurignacian period, whichever way you prefer to think of it, one of our early ancestors made some very beautiful polychrome drawings of himself or his brethren hunting bison and other animals. These drawings are in a cave at Altamira in Spain. They are the best of the earliest illustrations that have been dis-covered ; and if we understand why they are illustrations, though they are rarely if ever described as such, we shall have understood the vital principle of illustration and what it really is.

The opinion has been held that a new art will sometimes throw up its best exponents in the early stages of its career. This is almost certainly true of the exponent who drew those remarkable illustrations on the cave walls so many years ago ; for as illustrations they take their place with the very best, though strangely enough we do not know what they illus-trated. But what has all this to do with book illustration ? It goes to the heart of illustration, for if we can see that the cave drawings at Altamira are incomplete without the un-written book[1] that accompanied them, we shall have grasped the essentials of good illustration. Good illustration has an artistic signification of its own, and one that is not dependent on the words it illustrates ; but the spiritual and emotional signification of good illustration *is* derived from the words the illustrator desires to expound to the mind by the eye, and cannot be divorced from those words.

[1] It may have been a chant, or a prayer.

The cave drawings at Altamira can give complete æsthetic satisfaction, but they cannot give spiritual and emotional satisfaction. They are as a beautiful door to which the key has been lost. Illustration needs a key !

There are a great number of pictures, some of them very celebrated from a popular point of view, that are really nothing but illustrations, and there are many illustrations that are really pictures. All these are the products of minds that are artistically impure. Let us try and see what an illustration is or is not through an artistically pure mind—through Rembrandt's. A portrait or landscape by Rembrandt is a completely satisfying work of art without its title, and without the association of any words. That is obvious, but suppose we consider one of Rembrandt's Biblical pictures or etchings; one of those superb works of art by his hand that tell some tale from the Old Testament. Is that an illustration ? The answer is important to our purpose, and the answer is " No ! "

We can be quite sure we are right about this because Rembrandt, although he re-tells the Bible tale in pictorial form, does not re-tell it in the spirit of or from the point of view of the illustrator. He uses it as a base for expressing the universal appeal of his own feelings and art. The work of the illustrator is mentally interwoven in the work he illustrates. Rembrandt's Biblical pictures can stand alone, and if you enjoy them for the tale they tell, you are not enjoying them for the right thing.

Art is one thing, and a tale is another thing. An illustration is something fresh, made up of the two. Rembrandt, had he wished, might have done illustrations, and his art would not have been degraded by doing them ; but he did not do them, and that is sufficient for our purpose.

HOW TO UNDERSTAND ILLUSTRATION

IT is necessary to take a wide vision of illustration before coming to its modern application to the printed book, for if first principles are understood the mind will be prepared to appreciate illustrations of every kind wherever they occur.

We have seen that an illustration is a work of art that cannot be properly understood when severed from the literature to which it belongs, and there need be little else in the qualities of an illustration to distinguish it from any other work of art of a similar nature. That is the main point, though there are many minor, and also technical, difficulties that the illustrator has to overcome which are unknown, or can be disregarded by artists whose work is intended for the walls or the portfolio. Each art has its peculiar difficulties that are found to grow into wings, or become open gates, when they have been mastered.

The illustrator should never fear or shirk the limitations imposed on him by the literature he illustrates : the subject, the size of the page, the space allowed, the method of reproduction required, and so on. He should take these to himself and use them to help rather than hinder his own purpose.

The foregoing remark is one that might be repeated to the would-be illustrator any number of times without fear of harming him, because so many so-called illustrations are not illustrations at all, but rather separate and somewhat doubtful works of art that have somehow strayed on to the printed page. Let it be said emphatically that a reproduction of a drawing by Titian printed beside a poem about Titian would not be an illustration of that poem. Neither would a photograph of a Japanese scene beside a Japanese fairy tale be an illustration of the tale. Both of these might or might not be decorations, but the worst possible drawing or painting that was based on the spiritual meaning of the poem, or the emotional thread of the tale, would be better there as an illustration than the noblest of Titian's drawings, or the most artful of photographs.

THE BEGINNING OF BOOK ILLUSTRATION

IT is necessary to think here of the early illustrations in books so that we may see the influence of the past on present-day illustration, and how this is still somewhat governed by traditions derived from the days when books were written and illustrated entirely by hand.

When motor-cars were first made, they were made to resemble horse-drawn carriages, and so it was with books when they were first printed : the printed books were made to look very much like the older manuscripts that were in use before the fifteenth century in Europe.[1]

Traditions take a long time in dying, and the modern book has traces of the old manuscripts in and about it. These are easily detected. If a reasonably well-printed book is taken

[1] Printing was practised in China before this date.

and first of all opened at the title-page, it will be seen that the position of the title is always at the top of the page and the author's name not quite half-way down. This unequal division of the space is dictated by good proportion just as it was in the old books, unequal divisions of a space always being artistically better and more interesting than equal divisions. Again, the placing of the printed text conforms to the illuminated manuscript of the Middle Ages in that the margins are more or less in the same proportions as in the old books, particularly the bottom margin which is one and a half or even double the width of the side and top margins. This in the hand-written books was intended to keep the fingers used for turning over the page away from the written words, thus keeping the text clean—a very important consideration when one remembers the scarcity and preciousness of the hand-written book.

That the pre-fifteenth century book was very beautiful is agreed upon by everyone, and its illustrations, being by the same hand (or a similar one) that took such loving care over the lettering, were exactly adapted to that lettering, and therefore conformed to one of the important technical rules of book illustration.

In the modern book it is not possible to rival the ideal of the old illuminated manuscript on its own ground, and it is not possible or desirable to copy it by mechanical methods, so a different ideal has been sought, or perhaps it would be better to say has been evolved.

The ancient illustrated manuscripts were produced by one agency—the human hand. Illustrated books after the introduction of printing were produced by the marriage of two arts—the art of typography, and the art of the engraver and woodcutter. When printed words and the prints from a design cut in wood or metal were put together on one page the modern illustrated book was born.

THE WOODCUT : FATHER OF PROCESSES

THE wood-block after it has been cut to design for use in printing, and the illustrations themselves taken from it, have what one might almost call a Chaucerian look about them, they look fatherly : for as Chaucer was the father of English poetry so is the wood-block the father of English illustration. There is a pleasure in thinking of this, but one does not want to suggest that the modern book should tend to imitate books of the past in its illustrations ; it should be in touch with contemporary movements and use the new methods.

How to make woodcuts will be described later. We are considering the woodcut now as the father of modern methods of reproducing illustrations, and as such it is of great importance. The woodcut and early engraving on metal set free another hand to work in another medium of the printed page which before in the manuscript and missal had been worked upon by only one hand [1] in one medium. Since then the number of hands has steadily increased, so that to-day the artist illustrator may be quite competent at his job, and yet scarcely know what happens to his illustration after it leaves his hand until it appears on the page of a book, magazine, or newspaper. Yet it is best for him to know something about processes, since his work may be unsatisfactory or unsuitable through not knowing.

A block for reproducing line illustrations can be thought of as glorified type, and it is useful to think of it in that way, for then it is more likely to conform in some way with type as good illustration should do.

RESTRICTIONS THAT HELP THE ARTIST

THE arrival of modern methods and processes at one and the same time gave greater freedom to the illustrator, and also restricted him. They gave him greater freedom because they allowed him to work in a variety of media, and they restricted him by that same variety. This may sound paradoxical, but that it is true any craftsman or designer knows well enough. The craftsman and designer welcome conditions and restrictions when they are practical and sensible conditions, and an illustrator is both a craftsman and a designer ; he must have the feeling of the craftsman in his bones even if he is not actually a craftsman in the modern meaning of the word, and that he is a designer need not be stated.

The artist who put the lettering and the decorations in the ancient manuscript books was restricted in all sorts of ways. He was restricted by the materials he worked in, and sometimes, when they were precious materials such as gold and the colour blue, even by the amount of them that he might use ; also there were religious and many other restrictions ;

[1] If two or three artists worked on the same manuscript, the point made is the same.

yet he made a unity, and a very beautiful one, of each page he undertook. Restrictions helped rather than hindered him. In the manuscript book the decorations and illuminations are something growing from the lettering. The lettering looks as though it had burst into flower where the illuminations occur. Illumination is really nothing but a form of illustration. In the modern book the illustrations too often look like artificial flowers stuck on to the wrong branch or twig, and perhaps that is the worst artistic fault in books as we know them.

Perhaps it would be as well to say here that decoration must not be confused with illustration, though decoration may occur in an illustrated book. Decoration of books is the art of making books beautiful, and it need not have any special reference to the text. Illustration may, and does decorate a book, but its special purpose has reference to the text that it illustrates. Decoration merely pleases the eye. Illustration pleases the eye, and expounds the text, and because it expounds the text there are some who do not like illustrations of any sort. They are justified in their dislike in special cases.

Our search amongst illustrations so far has been confined to pure illustration, the real thing, but what about that mass of photographs, line drawings, wash drawings, maps, and so on, that " illustrate " the pages of newspapers, magazines, advertisements, novels, technical books, and other printed productions ? There is really very little to be said about all these. They are for the most part raw materials badly used in an artistic sense, though there are many notable exceptions. By raw materials badly used is not meant that the workmanship of these illustrations is bad or that the printing of them is bad. They are raw materials as illustrations because they bear a crude rather than a sympathetic reference to the text that employs them. To sort out the good from the bad in all this confusion of thousands would be almost impossible even if it were worth while.

The artistically inexperienced reader, and the reader who is going to be an illustrator, should look at works of art by great masters, either in the originals or else in the reproductions that are available to everybody now.

Try this test of good work. Cut out from some magazine that illustration you admire so much if you have bad taste and are honest enough to own that you have it ; that one (any good artist will tell you which it is) of " him looking into her eyes," and pin it upon your walls. Pin beside it a reproduction of one of Albert Dürer's woodcuts. You will find that the false glory that you saw in the former reproduction will slowly fade, and the real glory of the Dürer will rise. When the vulgar illustration looks vulgar to you and you can bear it on your wall no longer, you will know then that you have good taste.

WHAT IS AN ILLUSTRATION?

THE word illustration can have such a wide range of application that it is not easy to set a limit to that application in a short section ; but the discerning reader will make a definition of illustration for himself, one suited to his own activities or that part of illustration with which he is concerned.

A Gothic minster is by some definitions of the word illustration : an illustration of the Bible in stone, wood, glass, and other materials. A drawing of a glass of beer above the words " Buy Blogg's Beer " would by another definition be an illustration too. Then there are fashion-plates to think of, newspapers with photographs in them, catalogues, and so on. What I want to point out here is that illustration, in the sense in which it is generally used, has a vague meaning, and if you are going to be an illustrator you must decide what you mean yourself by illustration, and what you are going to illustrate.

WHAT HAS BEEN DONE IN ILLUSTRATION

WE have seen where illustration began, and a brief outline has been given of its evolution through the process of woodcutting up to the present day. In the next few paragraphs the names of some illustrators of outstanding merit will be mentioned, and though the names of all the great illustrators are not included, yet the task of making a list of them would not be a difficult one if it included only those who were employed on the modern English book. For great illustrators are rare, and the modern illustrated English book did not begin its career until the last quarter of the eighteenth century.

We have spoken of the cave drawings in Spain as the first promptings of a very natural desire upon the part of early man to portray or illustrate his thoughts, experiences, or religious exercises. This desire to express pictorially is common to the smallest child whose queer and conventional representations of mother, father, or objects seen, such as trains and animals, are familiar to all of us. The urge is seen to the very best advantage in the old illuminated manuscript of which we spoke in an earlier part of this article.

The illuminations of the Middle Ages are full of exquisite thumb-nail drawings, sometimes bearing little relation to the text, but done because the monkish artist was in love with the life around him, and had to put down with tender care the flowers and fruits, the birds and beasts, with which his countryside abounded, and which did so much to comfort the long periods of silent meditation that his Order demanded. When the illumination was definitely an illustration to the text it carried out what we have already stipulated as the essence of all good illustration : it expounded the spirit of the written matter. It is this fact that makes the manuscripts of the Middle Ages so artistically good.

Printing by movable types was first used in Mayence, or Mainz as it is now called, in Germany. It was brought to this country by Caxton in 1475, and the same characters that were used in hand-written manuscripts—Gothic characters —were imitated in type. In 1518 the Roman characters took the place of the Gothic. Naturally the presses were crude affairs, and they remained so until the beginning of the nineteenth century. In this article we are not further concerned than this with the printing press. What we are concerned with, however, is the effect upon illustration of the introduction of the printing press.

EARLY MASTERS OF THE WOODCUT

THE method used to illustrate a book at that time and for centuries afterwards was by woodcuts. The first woodcuts were simple compared with the later engraved blocks, about which we shall have more to say presently. These early cuts closely resembled the ink drawings from which they were made, as can be seen in the *Winchester Gospels* of the eleventh century in the Bodleian Library at Oxford. The line used is crisp and of varying thicknesses in order to differentiate between the fold of a gown or the soft wings of an angel, and the whole drawing is kept open and free from large black masses which would have a tendency to smudge when printing. Much the same limitation is imposed on the modern artist when drawing for reproduction. Here the line is generally kept open and crisp or the same reason.

It must not be thought, however, that these early woodcuts were set up with the type as a modern line block is to-day. The page was printed and then the woodcut was inked up and pressed on to the page by hand.

The great artists of the Renaissance in Italy such as Botticelli who illustrated Dante's *The Divine Comedy*, used woodcuts as well as engraving on metal to express themselves, and Dürer and Holbein in Germany were great exponents of the woodcut.

We must now leave the woodcut as a means of reproducing an illustration for a time, although we shall have to return

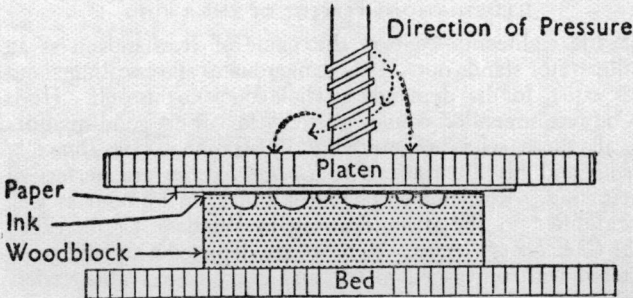

22. TAKING AN IMPRESSION FROM A WOODCUT

The diagram shows a print from a woodcut being made in a hand press. This is printing in " relief," as the portions which make the print are raised from the general surface of the block by cutting away the parts not desired.

to it later. During the sixteenth century engraving on metal became much used. Engraving, that is the incising of lines, either by the use of a chisel or by the acid bath, on copper or steel, was brilliantly carried out by many great artists. Rembrandt was a master of etching ; the delicate coloured engravings of the French artist Watteau are famous, and among British artists, the great Bartolozzi of the eighteenth century achieved engravings which are prized by collectors to-day.

The eighteenth century was also the age of the mezzotint, that delightful tinted print so different from the harder effect of the engraving. Mezzotinting was carried out on a copper plate. The surface was first burnished smooth and then a

" rocker " was used. This was an instrument that gave to the whole plate a roughened surface of an equal uniformity. In this state, if the plate had been inked up, it would have printed a deep, velvety black all over. Certain parts, however, were scraped away so that varying tones were created when printing took place, depending on how much and how deeply the surface was scraped. The final result was a tone drawing and not a line drawing as is the case in an etching or engraving. The process dates from the seventeenth century, and the name of Prince Rupert, nephew of Charles I., is connected with its introduction into England.

ILLUSTRATIONS PERFECT OF THEIR KIND

IN the eighteenth century the name of Rowlandson as an illustrator stands out. It is dangerous to start writing about this artist, for he demands a whole book to himself. He is to be recommended whole-heartedly for all his good qualities to all those who are studying illustration. His *Dance of Death* and his illustrations to *Doctor Syntax* are perfect of their kind. Rowlandson's cynical and grim humour is well exemplified in the wash drawing in Windsor Castle called *The Chamber of Genius*. Here we see depicted a squalid room littered with unwashed plates, and every conceivable variety of lumber. A clothes-line is stretched across a corner of the room with the usual accompaniment of socks together with other articles of apparel, and underneath this lies a fat and blowzy woman. It goes without saying that numerous children and a dog are included to complete a picture of slovenly squalor. In the midst of all sits an artist at his easel, working furiously and quite unconcerned by the babel and muddle around him.

Hogarth the painter was another satirist in line and colour. In his earlier work such as the illustrations to *Hudibras* he is seen more as an illustrator, but in his later and better-known works he is definitely a painter, and one is forced to realise that he had not really the view-point of the true illustrator.

William Blake is one of the outstanding illustrators of the late eighteenth and very early nineteenth century, and his illustrations to the *Book of Job*, for instance, are typical of his mystical style. Much unconsidered rubbish has been written about Blake's work. His technical method of reproducing his illustrations (he claimed that it had been taught him by Heaven) was unique in his day. His metal plates when ready for printing looked very like a modern metal line block, in that the part that gave the imprint was raised above the general surface of the plate. In the plates of Rowlandson and Hogarth, however, " the line " is sunk below the general surface of the plate.

THE GLORY OF THE " 'SIXTIES "

WITH the nineteenth century we arrive at one of the greatest periods of book illustration, and it culminates in a blaze of well-known artists. This period is known as the " 'sixties," and, for convenience, we may consider it to cover the years 1855–1870. It was a period of the " Annuals " so beloved by the Victorians—*The Leisure Hour, Once a Week, The Quiver, Sunday at Home,* and *The Churchman's Family Magazine.* The very names bring back to us a smell of lavender and the sound of horse-drawn carriages of the days that are no more. It was a period when the illustrated weekly papers appeared—*The Illustrated London News, The Graphic,* and *Punch*—although some of these date back before 1855. It was a period that saw the Pre-Raphaelite movement which came to be characterised by that perfect Victorian word " intense." And lastly, it was the period that saw the end of engraving as a means of reproduction. The closing years of the century saw the modern line block of zinc in full use.

With the coming of the Annuals and Weekly papers a demand arose for some means of rapid reproduction. This was met by the artist actually drawing on the wood block instead of on paper, the drawing afterwards being transferred to the block by the engraver. We said in an earlier part of this section that we should have to come back to the woodcut. We have now reached that time. From 1875 to 1885 nearly all reproduction was done by means of the wood block, although from about 1876 line block and half-tone processes were also being used to some extent.

Before the Pre-Raphaelite movement began, such names as John Tenniel, the immortal illustrator of the two " Alices "— *Alice in Wonderland* and *Alice Through the Looking-Glass*—and Birkett Foster come to the mind. Never before was there such a happy conjunction of events as the collaboration of Tenniel and Lewis Carroll. With the Pre-Raphaelite movement one must think at once of Sandys, whose amazingly careful drawings must always be a constant source of wonder to us, who belong to an age where loose and flashy black and white technique is frequently seen. Nevertheless, unlike the work of Rossetti, for instance, Sandys' drawings were not character-ised by very great imagination. Rossetti, Millais, and the rest of the Pre-Raphaelite group were also illustrators, and their work may be found scattered through all the Annuals of the day.

With the names of Charles Keene, great draughtsman and great *Punch* artist, Fred Walker, whose work is so essentially full of Victorian sentimentality, and George du Maurier, famous father of a famous actor son, whose early drawings were so charming and whose later *Punch* drawings were so popular—more popular even than Keene's—we have put on record names that were famous in the " 'sixties " and that will never be forgotten.

METHODS USED AT THE END OF THE CENTURY

BUT these are not all who must be mentioned in any article on illustration. Although they are not so famous as the foregoing, the brothers Dalziel and Arthur Boyd Houghton bring to mind the lovely illustrations in the *Arabian Nights*. Practically all the work of these artists was engraved on wood or metal, and the Dalziel firm were famous for this kind of work. Many of the artists of this period had an extraordinary facility for drawing rapidly on the actual wood block, and stories are told of messengers from the papers waiting while the drawings were dashed off. The blocks were then rushed to the engraver to be cut. The actual cutting of the blocks was amazing in its skill, the very line of the artist's pen being faithfully rendered.

Apart from the illustrated weekly, there were the drawings of Kate Greenaway. In an admirable book called *English Poetry for Children*, by R. L. Mégroz, the author states that:

" Leaving out rare and great genius like Blake's, good poetry for children is mainly due to fortunate employment of writers who can be truly themselves without leaving or suppressing the bounds of childish appreciation."

That remark applies equally to books illustrated for children. A torrent of illustrated books for children now pours from the press each year, but whether children appreciate even a small percentage of such work is difficult to ascertain. Much of it is badly or indifferently illustrated. It would be difficult amongst modern books for children to find anything at all comparable to the fragrancy of Kate Greenaway's delightful work in *Under the Window*. Many must be familiar with the mob caps or poke bonnets and long skirts of her figures, all of them most delicately drawn and tinted.

Again, what modern book for the young can give us such happy fun as do the illustrations in Randolph Caldecott's *Jovial Huntsman?* Caldecott was perhaps the first illustrator to portray that most English of all sports—fox hunting—and his fat, jolly, red-coated followers to hounds, together with his renderings of the hazards of the field, leave us chuckling.

With the general use of the line block of to-day, we have at the tail end of the nineteenth century the familiar name of Aubrey Beardsley, whose decorative black and white work owes so much to the influence of Japan. He gathered round him a host of followers most of whom merely succeeded in imitating his faults. Harry Furness is a master of the pen in quite a different manner from Beardsley, and Phil May, with his economy of line and tone, is in the opposite camp to Furness, whose work is most carefully shaded.

In 1891 there was a movement set on foot by William Morris, artist, designer, writer, and social reformer, against the encroachment of the cheap process reproduction which was flooding the market with inferior artistic work. In protest, Morris founded the *Kelmscott Press*, and from this Press there came a number of books well printed, well bound, and well illustrated, frequently by woodcuts in the old manner. But the flood of cheap work went on, and this praiseworthy effort slowly died out.

Before leaving the nineteenth century mention must be made of two engravers, the first, famous for his wood engravings, and the other, for his steel engravings. These are Thomas Bewick and George Cruickshank. Bewick died in 1828, and it is for his minute wood engravings illustrating *History of British Quadrupeds*, *History of British Birds*, and *Æsop's Fables*, that his name comes down to us. Bewick was a master of wood cutting, to which he gave a new technique. Fortunate is the collector of illustrations that can find any of these volumes, for they are greatly valued by the connoisseur.

Cruickshank, who died in 1878, was the first of the modern humorous illustrators. He excelled in delineating the moralist's point of view, but rarely failed to be humorous at the same time. He was employed on only two of Dickens' books— *Sketches by Boz*, and the better known *Oliver Twist*. Towards

240

the end of his life he became a staunch supporter of the temperance movement, and there are engravings of a very large size depicting the shocking things that happen in the life of a drunkard.

WHERE MODERN ILLUSTRATORS EXCEL

OF the modern illustrator much could be written. If there were a host of illustrators in the " 'sixties," their number to-day is as of the sands of the sea. Good, bad, and indifferent, the work from their pens, pencils, and brushes pours out, and it is not for us here to number them. Rather let us take one or two names, not because they are the only ones, but because they certainly are in the forefront of their profession. We have spoken of Rowlandson, so let us begin with H. M. Bateman, who is the nearest approach to a Rowlandson of our day. Bateman is known to everybody, for his output of work is astonishing. When William Caine and Bateman went into partnership they never failed to make us laugh. The story-teller played into the hands of the illustrator, and the illustrator exactly suited the story-teller. The combination was the happiest possible.

Henry Ospovat as an illustrator of poems stands well to the forefront in this kind of work. He died when he was a young man, but had he lived he would probably have developed into a first-class portrait painter. As it is, his reputation stands on his caricatures, and his illustrations to *The Song of Solomon*, and some illustrations to Matthew Arnold's poetry. He did other illustrations, but those to the books mentioned show his work in its best phase. As good illustrations to poems are extremely rare, Ospovat merits our closest attention. He was poetically minded, and his *Scholar Gypsy* illustration shows how well a poetically minded illustrator can tackle a difficult subject.

Other modern illustrations that come to the mind are Edmund Dulac's coloured fantasies, Arthur Rackham's drawings for fairy stories such as *Peter Pan*, and the work of Heath Robinson. G. K. Chesterton and Hilaire Belloc have both illustrated their own books with great skill and success. H. G. Wells makes most amusing drawings, and one wishes that he had illustrated his *Mr. Polly*. Illustrations to most modern novels seem to have worked their way outwards and become dust covers, but too frequently the illustration on a dust cover bears little relation to the work inside.

SOME MODERN MISTAKES IN ILLUSTRATION

ILLUSTRATION in England has little to learn from either the Continent or the United States, but there is much in the work from both that is best avoided. There is, for instance, the fashion for illustrators to effect a past style of illustration, and simper in lines that do not belong to this age. Before the writer lie three copies of Edward FitzGerald's *Omar Khayyám* One is illustrated with photographs of Persia, another by blocks made by modern methods from woodcuts that abuse the art of wood-cutting by being composed of large masses of unbroken blacks and whites ; the third is illustrated in the Gothic or mediæval manner—its illustrations look almost like rubbings from church brasses.

> " Awake ! for morning in the Bowl of Night
> Has flung the stone that put the Stars to flight."

The illustrations would put everybody to flight eventually. The photographs are, of course, far too literal for illustrations. The woodcuts (pseudo) too heavy and clumsy for a poem, and the Gothic illustrations ridiculous by their style and their lack of appropriateness.

Whether such a work as FitzGerald's *Omar Khayyám* can be properly illustrated is a highly controversial point. Perhaps the right man could do it if the right man came along. But the example of FitzGerald's poem does raise in our minds visions of all those books that ought not to have been illustrated at all, those books that have had their beauty smirched by vulgar and incompetent illustrators, those books that we illustrated mentally and satisfactorily for ourselves without any help from another mind.

ARCHAIC METHODS FOR MODERN BOOKS

CONCERNING book illustration, the modern world has decided that old wine can be put into new bottles so long as the wine is of good quality. Some tastes may find it rather sour, and the writer has made a wry face many a time when looking at modern books illustrated in ancient styles. To be more explicit, when wood-cutting, wood engraving and engraving of metals were first employed for book illustration, and also later when other means were not available, the block or plate used in the actual printing was the one prepared by the illustrator. There is a fashion to-day for employing these and other archaic methods as a start, so that the technique of the old method may influence the style of the illustration, though the block actually used for printing is prepared by photo-mechanical means.

Thus in the sixteenth-century illustrations by wood, the actual wood with its charge of ink was pressed on the paper of the book. To-day a wood-block is cut by the illustrator, an impression is taken from it, and from the impression a block is made by mechanical means. There is a difference of quality in the impression from a wood-block and that from one made by mechanical means to resemble it. The beginner in wood-engraving will be well advised to save himself much bother and avoidable trouble by having a few lessons from some one who understands the art.

Wood-engraving really consists of putting a pattern on a smooth block of wood and then cutting away that part which is to be white on the finished print. Illustrations in rare books and in limited editions are to-day still sometimes printed from wood-blocks, but usually when a wood-block technique is used, the block is made by one of the mechanical processes.

THE ANCIENT ART OF ETCHING

THE excavation or incising of metal for the purpose of forming a pattern or design upon it is a very ancient art, and probably the art of illustrating books by the aid of metal plates evolved from it. Anyway, the craft of printing from metal plates that have been worked upon by the artist is to-day in much the same position as that of wood-engraving : the use of a mechanically-made block that gives a reproduction of a print from the plate made by the illustrator is considered, for rapid production, preferable to the use of the plate itself.

There are various reasons for this. The most important is that an etched plate, being of soft metal such as copper, will not, unless nickel-faced, give more than a very limited number of prints before it begins to wear, losing its detail and sharpness. Nevertheless, real etching is still used for illustration, in both pure and mechanically-adapted forms.

The process of making etchings is simple enough to describe, but in execution it is extremely difficult and it needs a very high degree of skill to get the required result. There are two methods of excavating or incising metal. One by simply cutting or scratching it; the other by eating it away with some corrosive acid. Etching by " dry point " and simple engraving do not employ acids for corroding away that portion of a plate (the " line ") required to hold ink, but etching proper, and in some cases engraving too, requires the use of a corrosive acid.

The plates from which etchings are made are of copper or zinc, the choice of metal depending upon the type of print required. The use of zinc gives a soft and rather blurred line in comparison with the firm sharp line given by copper. The difference is due to the softer qualities of zinc and its consequently greater sensitivity to the acid bath. For a fuller understanding of this last statement the actual process of making an etching must be explained.

FOUR STEPS IN THE PROCESS

LET us take the process in four steps : (1) The making of the drawing, and transference to the plate. (2) The preparation of the plate, and the drawing upon it. (3) The actual biting or etching in the acid bath. (4) The printing.

(1) Individual artists vary in their preparation of the drawing. Some do a very elaborate drawing, then make a tracing of the main lines and transfer that to the plate either by the use of carbon paper or by damping the tracing paper, placing it face down on the prepared plate and passing the two through the press. (The press is on exactly the same principle as the mangle, except that the two rollers are of steel and a steel plate called the bed passes between them. On this bed is placed the prepared plate.) Other artists draw straight away on to the plate as if it were paper.

(2) Take a copper plate of the required size. Burnish it until the surface is mirror-like. Take a bottle of liquid etching ground (white wax dissolved in ether or chloroform and coloured brown with bitumen). Tilting the plate, pour this ground quickly over it. The ether will evaporate at once and the plate is left covered with a thin coating of wax, which will be enough to prevent the acid biting into the plate. The old etchers used a solid ground made of wax. This cake was dabbed on the plate after it had been warmed.

(3) The plate is now drawn on. The etcher calls it " needling " the plate, as a needle is used. Excellent results can be got from a gramophone needle stuck in a wooden penholder. The drawing with the needle is done much as if

a pen were being used, but the needle is held more upright. Everywhere the needle touches the plate the wax is broken and the copper is exposed. When the drawing is finished the plate is placed in the acid bath. There are many baths, but two types will suffice. The first consists of nitric acid and water to certain proportions ; the second is hydrochloric acid, potassium chlorate and water. The varying proportions of these chemicals give a slow or quick acting bath. Variation of tone of line is obtained by taking the plate out of the bath

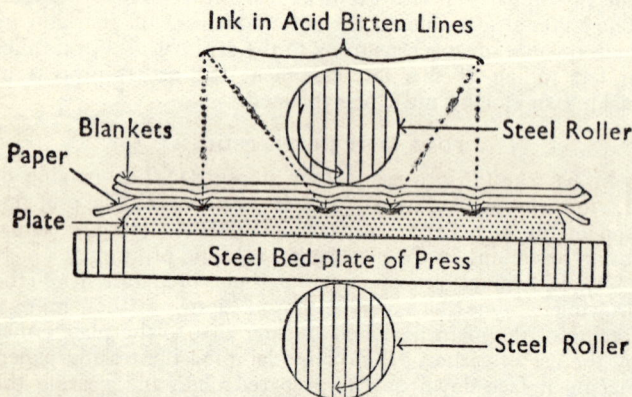

23. TAKING A PRINT OF AN ETCHING

In this diagram a print from an etched plate is being made. This is printing in " intaglio " as the lines that form the print are sunk below the general surface of the plate by the action of the acid. The depth of the ink is here exaggerated.

at intervals and " stopping out " with an acid - resisting varnish. This gives a different depth of line to different parts of the plate and consequently a blacker and thicker, or lighter and thinner, line is obtained when printing.

(4) The plate is cleaned of all wax by the use of benzene. It is then kept warm by placing it on a metal plate over a gas ring. This makes the ink used soft and sticky. The ink is dabbed into the lines bitten into the plate and the surplus ink is then wiped off with soft muslin, leaving the ink, of course, in the bitten lines. Damp paper is placed over the plate which is now put on the bed of the press, covered with several thicknesses of blanket to protect it from the full force of the

steel rollers, and passed through the press. The paper is forced into the etched lines and a print or proof is the result.

Engraving, simply described, is the excavation of a design in metal without the aid of an acid ; the remainder of the process is much the same as etching. Scratch any piece of copper with a pocket knife, rub some soot into the scratch, then press a piece of paper hard against the scratch until the mark of it is transferred to the paper. That is engraving in its simplest form.

LITHOGRAPHY IS INVENTED BY ACCIDENT

A MUSICAL comedy might be written around Alois Senefelder's discovery of lithography at end of the eighteenth century. Senefelder, the son of a performer at the Theatre Royal, Munich, was a student of law at the University of Ingolstadt, and after his father's death tried to be an actor, but without success. He then became an author, but being too poor to pay for the publication of his work, tried various methods of writing on metal, in order that he might then print it himself. He soon found that a composition of lampblack, soap, and wax formed a suitable material for writing, capable when dry of resisting hydrochloric acid. To obtain facility in writing in reverse, as copper was too expensive, he procured some pieces of calcarious stone (lithographic stone) which, when polished, served him to practise upon. His mother having one day desired him to make an account of some linen she was sending to be washed, he wrote it on a piece of this stone with his composition of soap, etc.

It occurred to him afterwards that by corroding the surface with acid the letters would stand out in relief, and admit of impressions being taken from them. He tried the experiment and succeeded, and soon found that it was not necessary to lower the surface of the stone, but that simply wetting it was enough to prevent the printing ink from sticking to any parts except those marked with the composition. Such was the invention of lithography.

The chemical action that occurs in lithography is based on facts that should be familiar to campers, and all who have done any " washing up," and that is the lack of affinity between fat and water. When a lithographic stone on which an image (*i.e.* illustration) has been drawn in greasy ink is moistened with a thin film of water, the image, because it is greasy, repels the water, and thus the moist places are those that are not included in the design. Now when printing ink is supplied to the stone by a roller, it will not adhere to the moist places but it will adhere to the greasy ones, and the design is in this way coated with ink while the remaining surface is not. When paper is brought into close contact with the lithographic stone after it has been blotted with cloth and then inked, the paper will take an impression of the design drawn on the stone.

This is lithography in its simplest form. It is not much

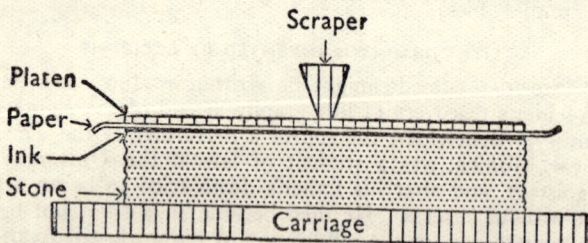

24. HOW A LITHOGRAPH IS PRINTED

This diagram illustrates how a print from a lithographic stone is taken. This is " planographic " printing, as the lines and masses forming the print are on the surface of the stone, and the pressure necessary for making the print is supplied either by passing the stone through rollers or by using the scraper as shown in the diagram.

used in that manner now, as the modern lithographic method almost invariably uses aluminium or zinc instead of lithographic stone. If the cutting of wood blocks and the engraving of metal ones are considered as the father and mother of modern processes of reproducing illustrations, then lithography might well be called the hereditary link connecting the old family with the new. Wood-cutting, engraving, lithography—these three methods are the bases of all methods of reproducing illustrations.

WHY THE LINE DRAWING IS SO OFTEN NEGLECTED

PLACE a sheet of any unillustrated newspaper upon a table and then throw on it at random a small photograph, a black-and-white drawing by pen and a water-colour, all of similar size, and there will at once be evident to you about this loose collection a family likeness between two of the objects, and a lack of it between the others. The pen and ink drawing will be in accord with the typography of the sheet ; the photograph and the water-colour will not. This fact is of great importance to the illustrator, for it shows that line is still the most satisfactory medium for making an illustration.

Why then are the half-tone block (equivalent to the photograph) and the colour block (equivalent to the water-colour) so popular and so universal for illustration ? They are so because in the papers, books, and magazines it buys the public demands not so much an illustration in the proper meaning of the term, as a reproduction of things with which it is familiar through a medium with which it is also familiar. Art speaks in a language that has to be learned ; the photograph and the realistic colour print that is like a photograph with the addition of colour, speak in a closely limited language that is already known.

Referring again to our collection on the printed sheet, it will be seen that the photograph appears as a hole in the sheet, and the water-colour as something that projects from it, and both are for these reasons æsthetically disturbing. But the pen-and-ink drawing is not, for it forms with the printed words a part of the sheet. Now the metal line block can reproduce a pen-and-ink drawing in facsimile ; it does what one may suspect the first woodcuts attempted to do, with this difference, that the woodcut in attempting facsimile reproduction of black and white drawings could not disguise the beautiful qualities inherent in its own technique and material, whereas the metal line-block has no qualities of its own : it just reproduces what has been done in another medium.

The metal line-block or " zinco " is a block usually of zinc resembling a wood-block prepared for use in printing ; it is the past expressed in modern and metallic terms. It is a wood-cut reborn as metal, and reborn dumb. It is the dumb link between the older and the new methods, and because it is dumb it gives the black-and-white artist illustrator complete freedom to express what he has to express by pen and ink.

HOW A LINE BLOCK IS MADE

THE line or zinc block is easily understood now that we know the principle of etching, because in both there is an acid resisting ground on the plate. The artist makes his drawing in black ink. The drawing is then sent to the printers who photograph it to the size required—generally it is reduced, the original being made twice the size required. The drawing is transferred on to a sensitised zinc plate. Wherever the artist has made a black line with ink the camera of the printer repeats it in a greasy substance (bichromate of potash and gelatine).

The plate is then immersed in a bath of nitric acid and ether which eats away all the parts which the artist left white in his drawing. Some of the larger areas of white are cut away with a drill so that there shall be no fear of them becoming smeared with printing ink when printing takes place. The action of the acid leaves the lines of the drawing in relief. Thus the lines are turned into metal in a few hours. The plate is then mounted on a wood block to the height of the type in the printing press and it is ready for use. It will be observed that the line block prints from a *raised* line, and the etching from a *sunk* line.

SCRAPER-BOARD : A MODERN METHOD WHICH APPROACHES THE RESULT OF A WOODCUT

DRAWINGS for line blocks may be done by means of Scraper-Board, and the method is remarkable for its convenience. Scraper-Board has not yet developed a technique of its own, and at present, the general effect of this work is a pseudo-woodcut one.

Plain Scraper-Board is a board covered with a mixture of size and china clay laid on thickly, and there is also an em-bossed Scraper-Board which may be obtained with embossings, or with black lines and dots all over it as well as the embossings. Scraper-Board is easy to draw on with Indian ink, and the ink can be knifed away after application where required. Embossed Scraper-Board can have its texture added to or taken away by scraping. Its full possibilities, which may prove to be considerable, can only be found out by experiment on boards of various kinds.

A CLOSE-UP VIEW OF ILLUSTRATION

NOW that we have taken a general view of illustration, it may be as well to come closer and see the processes by which illustrations have been produced in the past and the processes by which they are produced under modern mechanical methods.

Illustrations made on paper may be classed under three headings : those produced by the hand of the artist ; those produced by non-mechanical processes, or more exactly, from blocks that are not mechanically made ; those produced from blocks mechanically made.

Those produced by the hand of the artist were the manuscripts of pre-fifteenth century date, and were then done on parchment (the skins of sheep). They were superseded by illustrations done from wood-blocks and engraved metal plates (blocks and plates being made by hand, though printed through the agency of a simple machine—the press), and these in turn were superseded by the mechanically-made block mechanically used.

There are, of course, a great many ways of printing, but they can all be classed under one of the three headings.

RELIEF PRINTING as in the wood block (ancient) or line block (modern), where the surface that prints, that is, the part that takes the ink, is raised *above* the general surface of the plate or block.

INTAGLIO PRINTING as in engraving (ancient) or heliogravure (modern), where the surface that prints is sunk *below* the general surface of the block.

PLANOGRAPHIC PRINTING as in the lithograph (ancient) or collotype (modern), where the surface that prints is *level* with the general surface of the block.

THREE WAYS OF MAKING PLATES BY HAND

BESIDES those already given, there were three methods of making plates by hand which should be mentioned now, because each of these methods might be called a machine-made block anticipated and made by hand. These three methods were called mezzotint, aquatint, and soft ground etching. Each was made for the purpose of giving tone to a print or illustration. Engraving and wood-block cutting illustrated by line, and gave tone only by a number of lines. The three methods mentioned above sought to give tone in a reproduction just as it is given in a wash-drawing or water-colour, that is to say not by line alone.

Mezzotint, aquatint, and soft ground etching were all methods that gave very beautiful results, but the results were limited in quantity, and had to be governed in the making by the skilled hand of the artist. They are important to those investigating modern machine methods, for modern methods do what they did, only they do it mechanically and in unlimited quantities.

It is by tone that modern mechanical methods of reproducing illustrations distinguish themselves from their elder brethren. The power to reproduce tone on a printed sheet was a great achievement in reproductive methods, but it was not one that gave a great deal of help to the illustrator who was artistic enough to see that all high-class illustration must be in accord with type : tone and type do not lie together comfortably on the same page.

HOW THE BLOCKS ACHIEVE LIGHT AND SHADE

THE line-block, whether of wood or metal, had the disadvantage considered as a medium of reproduction (though not necessarily as a medium for illustration) that it would not reproduce those gradations of tone such as are seen in a sepia-wash or a photograph. Half-tone blocks remove the disadvantage, for they can reproduce any gradation of tone. Half-tone blocks accomplish this by means of dots, by dots innumerable large and small.

The half-tone block is dots all over, big dots for the dark portions of an illustration, and small dots for the light portions. All these dots are made by what is called the " screen." This is a plate of glass placed inside the camera of the process engraver and ruled with a network of black lines. These screens are made with great care. When placed inside the camera that is to take the photograph of the object to be reproduced, they split up the light at the time of exposure as it passes the camera's lens into small units or windows that reach the sensitised plate. This then takes the image in that condition.

Where the object photographed is light, plenty of light will pass to the plate, and where it is dark, little light will pass. The consequence of this is that the sensitised plate is covered with dots of different sizes that, seen altogether after being developed, give the effect of tone and thus are for practical purposes a reproduction in reverse of the toned object or illustration that was placed before the eye of the camera.

The dots from the glass plate are transferred to a metal plate (preferably copper) by a further photographic process, and then the metal block is corroded with acid in much the same way as an etched block until the dots left as ink holders are so small that they can scarcely be seen by the naked eye— so small that they give the effect of tone. A half-tone block feels almost smooth to the touch. It is very much like our old friend, the mezzotint plate.

NEWTON'S DISCOVERY THAT RESULTED IN COLOUR PRINTING

BEFORE the introduction of mechanical methods, the means whereby a coloured illustration could be made were very limited. There was the coloured aquatint, the chromo-lithograph, and the coloured wood-block. All of these had their own charm but they could not reproduce a picture such as an oil painting so that the reproduction would bear an almost exact resemblance to the original. Mechanical colour printing alone made that possible. Newton might readily be called the inventor of colour printing, for it was through his discovery in 1700 that the colour of an object depends on the light by which we see that object that colour reproduction was made possible.

Photo-mechanically-made colour blocks are an extremely clever invention, and the making of them requires great skill. They are, broadly speaking, half-tone blocks that will print one on the top of another, and as each plate in printing is charged with one of the primary colours, namely, red, yellow, and blue, that colour when applied upon other primary colours will give the colouring of the original it is intended to reproduce.

THE TWO CLASSES OF REPRODUCTION

METHODS of reproduction may be divided into non-mechanical and mechanical processes in the following manner :

NON-MECHANICAL PROCESSES.	MECHANICAL PROCESSES.
Lithography	Line Block (zinco)
Colour Lithography	Four-Colour Process
Soft Ground Etching	Three-Colour Process
Woodcut	Duplex Half-Tone
Wood Engraving	Pantone Process
Stencil	Double Tone
Metal Engraving	Heliogravure
Dry Point	Photogravure
Mezzotint	Rotary Photogravure
Aquatint	Collotype
Etching	Photo Litho Offset
Stipple	Photo Lithography

Illustrations reproduced by the various non-mechanical processes will usually bear sufficient evidence of the method of their manufacture about them to enable the amateur to identify and classify them under different headings such as woodcuts, etchings, lithographs and so on : but illustrations produced by mechanical processes do not make their origin so patent. The reason for this difference is that the non-mechanical processes are essentially artistic or autographic processes, and are governed by an artist's hand controlled by a mind thinking in terms sympathetic to the reproductive process, whereas the mechanical processes not being governed in the same way attempt, and in most cases attain, a quite different ideal.

The ideal of the non-mechanical process might be said to be that of showing the individuality of the reproductive medium, and that of the mechanical the disguising of it. Thus in wood-cutting the technique proper to the cutting of a wood-block by the knife is manifest in the print from that block, but a modern collotype reproduction of the same print is very nearly a facsimile of that print, and tells us nothing about collotype.

IDENTIFYING THE PROCESS BY THE RESULT

PRINTS from most of the autographic methods of repro-duction may be distinguished by the marks of the principal tools used by the artist making them, or by some characteristic of the materials worked upon. The following table indicates briefly how the process by which an illustration has been reproduced may be identified :

Process.	Tool used by the Artist.	Characteristic of the Print.
Wood-Cut.	The Knife.	Grain of the wood can be seen in the blacks if the wood-cut is pre-pared from the " plank." Few lines cross, owing to the labour in-volved in cutting angles with a knife.
Wood-Engraving.	The Burin (a V-shaped tool).	Precise white line on black or *vice versa*.

Process.	Tool used by the Artist.	Characteristic of the Print.
Metal Engraving.	The Burin. ▼ Section of Burin.	Little variation in the thickness of the line. It is a ploughed line.
Drypoint.	The Needle.	Sensitive line with a " burr " to it. (" Burr " is the rough edge.)
Soft Ground Etching.	Pencil or Point, followed by acid.	Resembles a chalk drawing. The grain of the paper placed above the soft ground for the artist to work on can be detected.
Mezzotint.	The Scraper.	Velvety appearance. The zig-zag marks of the rocker with which the plate is roughened can be detected.
Lithograph.	Crayon or Ink. If ink, a knife too.	Resembles a drawing done with a crayon.
Aquatint.	The Needle, followed by acid.	The grain of the resin dust with which the plate is treated can be seen under a microscope.
Etching.	The Needle, followed by acid.	Great variation in the blackness of the line.
Stipple.	The Mattoir, followed by acid.	Dots all over to give tones.

ADVICE FOR THE FUTURE ILLUSTRATOR

THERE are three valuable words that would-be illustrators should keep in mind as guide-posts. They are: *observation, instruction, intuition*. Let us take the second word first. If you would become a professional illustrator get all the instruction you can, and get it wherever possible. Get it as soon as possible, for one is never too young to learn. If you did not learn anything about how to illustrate at school, then make amends by going to a School of Art as soon as you leave. If you cannot go to a School of Art by day, then go to evening classes. If you can work under the instruction of a good illustrator that will do as well as the School of Art, but if you are an only pupil you will miss the competition of the other students, and that competition will be good for you. If you live in the country and are unable to attend a School of Art or get personal instruction of any sort, then take one of the much advertised postal courses, for some of them are very good and well considered. Nevertheless, in this case, discretion should be used. Get instruction of some sort and save yourself endless trials and avoidable troubles.

Now for our first word, *observation*. Use your powers of observation to the full. You may think you have seen this and that; but you have not really seen this and that until you can draw them. Draw from memory. Start now! Draw a motor-car with people in it, then have a look at a real one, and you will find out where you had observed incorrectly, or how little you had observed. Do the same with anything wherever and whenever you can.

Now for the third word, *intuition*. To have intuition you must, as Oscar Wilde said in another connection, be careful in " your choice of parents." Your intuition will tell you whether you should " take up " illustration, and there is nothing more to be said about it.

REWARDS THE ILLUSTRATOR MAY EXPECT

HOW long you take to become proficient will depend on your natural ability and on how you apply yourself to your work. If you have great natural ability you may start earning money by your illustrations almost at once; if you have not, you had better anticipate several years of unrewarded labour.

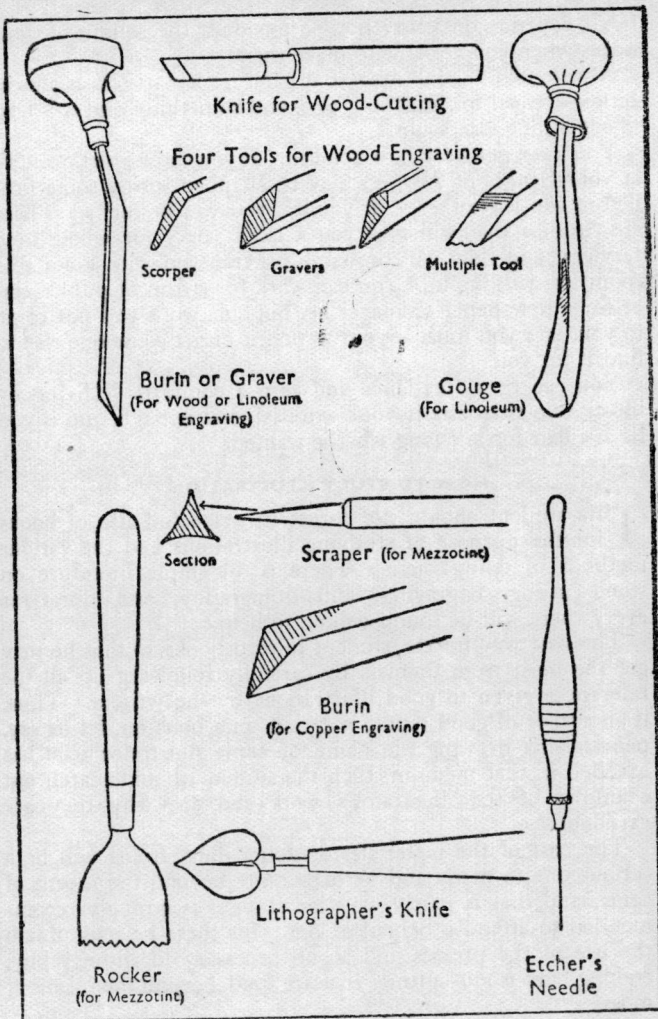

25. TOOLS FOR THE GRAVER IN WOOD AND METAL

At the top are examples of the gouges and gravers a well-equipped wood-engraver should possess, while at the bottom are some of the various implements of the worker in metal.

It all depends on yourself. So too does the selling of your wares when you are able to make them.

Always take the job nearest at hand for a start. It is almost certain to lead to something else, and something else will lead to something else again.

You must get work how you can. If you show great promise at your School of Art you may be snapped up by some firm before you leave there ; if you do, you will be lucky. There are Studios that will give you a fixed salary for whole time services, and they will probably provide you with a suitable room for working in. You can work for a firm of publishers, or for a newspaper or magazine, but this work will not come to you, and you must set out to find it or get some one else to find it for you.

You can be a free-lance and earn a comfortable living by illustration that way if your work is good enough, and if you have a flair for knowing what is wanted.

HOW TO STUDY ILLUSTRATION

THE student should not forget to make full use of books for the purpose of studying illustrations and the various methods of doing them. There is an ample literature on wood-cutting, engraving, and lithography, and librarians everywhere will be found willing to help.

The best way for the student to read books so that he may get the most from them is by carefully following up all the references given to good illustrations by the writers. Thus, if an author of good repute mentions in a book on, let us say, pen-and-ink drawing the name of some illustrator who has excelled in that medium, then the student should search out examples of the illustrator's work and see why they are excellent.

The cost of the materials for doing illustrations will be a serious one to many and perhaps quite beyond the means of some, and that is partly why the student is strongly recommended to attend a School of Art ; for there he may obtain the use of the presses and so on necessary for lithography, etching, and wood-cutting, that are quite beyond the means of most.

The cheapest methods of doing illustrations are by pencil and pen. Good books on the use of both these media have been written by Borough Johnson and G. M. Ellwood, and there are many others. Two other interesting books which may be recommended are *Illustrations of the 'Sixties* by Forrest Reid (Faber and Groyer) and a German book, *Das Ständebuch*, published by Insel-Bucherei of Leipzig. The latter contains reproductions of 114 wood-cuts by Jost Ammanns (1568), and it is not necessary to understand German to appreciate their beauty.

As a cheap means of doing illustrations the stencil should not be forgotten. The art of stencil cutting is a fascinating one that has never been properly developed in England, though in Japan it has been used with astonishing subtlety and skill. By stencil an artist can illustrate the whole of a strictly limited edition of a book entirely by his own hand—an achievement to be proud of.

9

THE ARTS RELATING TO ADVERTISEMENT

by WALTER R. H. JOHNSON

WHO has not been impressed at some time or another by the innumerable advertisements and posters that meet the eye in the newspapers and magazines, on the hoardings and in the shops ? Some attract by their beauty, some stimulate our possessive instincts, whilst others perhaps repel. We read of the advantages of using branded foods; we are told how and when to buy our clothes, how best to spend our holidays, and which route to travel by. We even learn how best to provide for our old age. We read and react. Advertising is, therefore, an important factor in modern life.

HOW ART MAY SERVE THE ENDS OF BUSINESS

THE qualities needed to produce an advertisement satisfactory from the artistic and from the commercial point of view are :

Taste in the choosing of those essentials which are necessary in the advertisement. In a recent press campaign for a certain photographic film, for instance, photographs were obviously desirable, and considerable taste was used in the choice of those which, while being excellent photographs from the artistic point of view, yet preserved an unstudied, almost accidental look.

Inventiveness and *psychological insight* from the appeal point of view. A message must be driven home, and considerable ingenuity is needed to do this in the most vital way.

Design considered as a method of relating essentials. Great variety of effect may be obtained in arranging these, as will be seen later.

Colour where possible, as an emotional stimulant. The use of reds, yellows, and warm browns is definitely stimulating, while blues, greens, mauves, and greys achieve a calm reflective effect. Black, except when used as a contrast to some bright colour, can be very depressing.

Advertising also allows great scope for all manner of technical innovations, especially in the designing of cartons, cut-out showcards, etc., and for good draughtsmanship. It is with the artist and his problems that we shall deal in the following pages.

CATERING FOR THE WOMAN READER

DAILY newspapers are roughly divided into two groups : the national dailies and the various local papers. These, along with the Sunday newspapers, carry the great mass of general advertising. The host of weekly periodicals and monthly magazines, each one of them appealing to a definite section of the community, offer great possibilities for a more specific method of advertising. Almost all the insertions in the women's magazines, for instance, contain what is termed " women's appeal." Advertisements of fashionable wear and furniture, food, and beauty preparations, vie with each other. In the popular illustrated publications, particularly the weeklies, advertisements of motor-cars, tobacco, tailoring, and whisky are found ; a more masculine type of appeal is here observed, while the many trade papers contain announcements of technical interest to their readers. About seventy per cent. of all advertising is addressed to women.

The large hoardings offer scope for a more permanent but simpler form of advertisement. You may read the press insertion at your leisure, should it gain your attention ; but the message of the poster must be brief and to the point. The smallish posters to be seen on many railway station platforms are more akin to press advertisements. Because of the time that can be given to their perusal these posters usually contain more type-matter than the larger kind.

THE GROWTH OF ADVERTISEMENT

FROM small type-insertions in the few newspapers that existed in the latter part of the eighteenth century, modern press advertising has developed to a degree undreamed of by our grandfathers. From the gently worded invitation to attend the sale of the Hull of a Good Ship, set shyly and in an unconspicuous position on a page, we have the full-page illustrated advertisement couched in alluring phrases and telling us of the advantages both mental and physical that attend a cruise in the Mediterranean.

The public demand for news was stimulated by the growth of the reading public made possible by compulsory education, which dates no further back than 1880. Hence the growth of the cheap newspaper. Because newspapers reached a wide

public, results from press advertisements became quickly
apparent. More and more space was bought for publicity
purposes. It is obvious to the least discerning that a modern
newspaper without its advertising revenue could not exist
for a day. The cost of paper alone for one of the American
Sunday papers is more than the amount realised from the
actual sale of the newpaper.

Very soon advertisers found themselves confronted by a
multitude of problems. While it was desirable to reach the
greatest number of people, it was vital to impress the potential
consumers of their goods. Some newspapers "pulled"
better for certain articles than others. It was necessary to
find out what value a newspaper with a large circulation in a
small area had over another which covered a greater area
with perhaps a smaller sale ; what advantage was derived
from advertising in local papers as against the national
dailies ; how to use the weekly journals and monthly magazines, and so on. For the proper solving of all these problems
an expert became absolutely necessary, and therefore the
advertising agent came into being. He made it his business
to answer these problems, and also to offer sound advice about
the type of advertising appeal best calculated to bring the
desired results. It might be better, for instance, to advertise
a certain commodity on a Monday than on a Friday. With
this knowledge of the pulling power of the Press came ideas
about the proper use of posters, and it was but a step to
carry this knowledge into the sphere of booklets which are
used to supplement information already available.

THE APPEAL ON THE HOARDING

WE have seen that the poster offers a more permanent
but simpler form of advertisement than that which
appears in the press. It must attract immediate attention and
must deliver a message which can be read by all. As its appeal
is to that sense which is most readily attracted—the sight,
so its work is better performed by suggestion than by
argument.

The poster may be whimsical, grotesque, beautiful or good-
humoured, but above all it must be vivacious and bold. To
that end colour may be used in one or two ways. When
the design is free and full of movement—that is dynamic—
the colour-scheme may be of the contrasting, vivid order.
When the design must impress by its dignity and charm,

then, however simple the colour scheme may be, it will attract the lazy eye by its harmony and good taste. Even when the poster contains almost photographic likenesses of people or still-life objects, these should be simply drawn and the colour should be dramatic. Nothing looks worse than insignificant colour and indeterminate or scrappy forms in the poster. This leads us to consideration of the illustrated pun and slogan.

To be successful the pun should be a slogan also, for the pun itself is so essentially a literary form of humour that any illustration of it is rather superfluous. The mere statement of a good pun should be sufficient. The slogan is used for two purposes. Firstly, it draws attention to, and may perhaps help to explain, the drawing, and, secondly, it conveys its message to the mind in words which cannot easily be forgotten.

As a general rule the lettering on the poster should be arranged horizontally, though designers of the calibre of McKnight Kauffer and Cassandre sometimes place lettering in a vertical position with great effect. Jean Carlu, a French poster artist of exceptional ability, often achieves an effect of movement and gaiety by placing lettering on a slant. Only in rare instances should lettering be superimposed upon parts of the pictorial matter, and conversely lettering should never be obscured by the picture, especially if this be of the naturalistic life-like order. One of the excellent German italic types is advisable, if a free type of letter is necessary.

Life-like objects should not be placed on a flat decorative area. Nothing looks more incongruous than a well-modelled bottle of beer seemingly poised in mid-air. If a decorative background must be used in this instance, it should look as if it had depth and solidity. When enlarged photographs are used in the poster it is best that they should be rectangular in shape. When for some reason the photographic silhouette or other irregular shape is used it is desirable that the shape should be simple and should not be displayed along with other drawn elements. The irregular shape is always more effective when it occupies an isolated position.

THE LAY-OUT IS MEANT TO BE READ

SPEAKING generally, there are four main elements that go to the making of the lay-out : the caption ; the drawing ;

the main body of the text, and the name-block. Sometimes other standardised copy of a technical or descriptive nature must appear in each insertion. This copy is usually termed " standing details," and may with advantage be presented within a cartouche or simple border.

A caption should be so worded that its meaning is obvious at first glance. If for any reason words need emphasising for their better understanding, then they should be displayed either in italics or in capital letters.

In the successful lay-out, one or other of the elements mentioned above should predominate. Usually this will be the drawing, though nearly always it is the caption that is seen first, and this in spite of the fact that the name block is generally displayed quite large. The reason is that the reader reacts more readily to a clever caption than to a mere name, but the name should nevertheless be such as to draw its due share of attention.

Only in rare instances, and then only when the name-block is displayed prominently, has it been intended that the lay-out should present merely a decorative effect. The well-known Oil and Petrol advertisements are good examples of this method : a humorous drawing, a line or two of copy, and the name-block. This method of appeal is only possible where the commodity, through previous advertising, is well in the public eye.

SUITABILITY THE REAL TEST

THE irrelevancy of the remark that a certain drawing is too good for a certain purpose should be self-evident, yet one hears it very often. A drawing is either suitable or not suitable. The advertisement drawing may be enclosed within a rectangle, or it may be of irregular shape, that is, vignetted. It can have that strong character usually associated with the woodcut and bold brush drawing, or the more detailed quality of the wood-engraving or pen-drawing. It may be in wash or line. Speaking generally, whatever the character of the drawing, it is usually simple in workmanship, conventional in form, and as self-explanatory as possible. Sometimes its purpose is to serve as a provocation or inducement to read the copy. More often nowadays it occupies the most prominent position in the advertisement.

When two or more drawings of a dissimilar character appear in the same advertisement, care should be taken that they

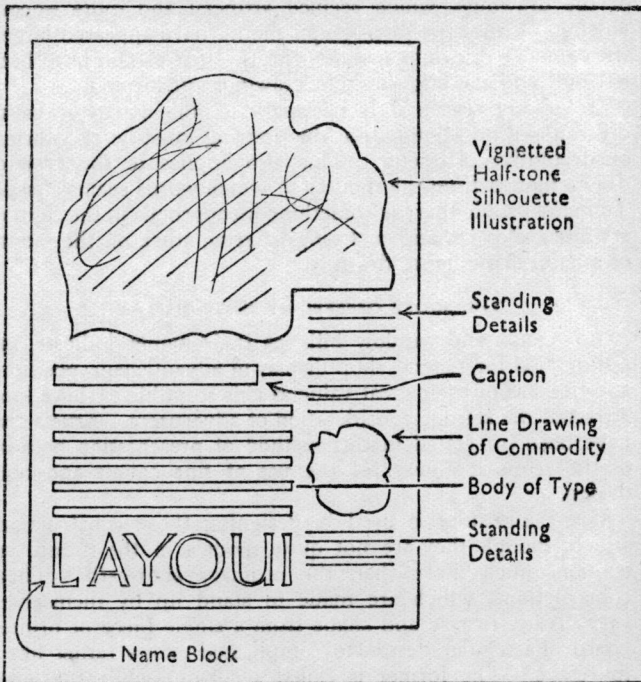

26. A PRESS ADVERTISEMENT ANALYSED

The analysis of a formal type of press advertisement designed for a space about 11 by 6¾ inches, showing the elements which should be considered in a lay-out. In many modern advertisements some of these elements—especially the " standing details "—are either omitted or cleverly disguised to form an integral part of the artist's idea.

do not contain the same amount of interest. One drawing should predominate. An instance of divided interest was given by a certain fashion advertisement. An excellent photograph within a quarter circle was set at the top of a full-length half-page, and below it were five elegantly drawn naturalistic fashion drawings, each as large as the photographic figure. The result was incongruous. One quite naturally compared the drawings with the photograph, to the detriment

of the drawings, which seemed artificial and quite uncon-
vincing. Either the photograph should have appeared larger,
with smaller drawings in line beneath, or it should have been
left out, and the large fashion drawings substituted.

If for any reason it is necessary to link a pen or brush
drawing with a photograph, the drawing must be of a formal
or decorative character. This also applies to the type of
drawn figures from the mouths of which words seem to issue.
To many people there is something incongruous in the sight of
a white balloon shape enclosing lettering stuck on the mouth
of a naturalistic figure drawing.

THE SCOPE OFFERED BY SHOP DISPLAY

SHOWCARDS and window bills, as their names indicate, are
intended for general shop display in advantageous positions
and because of their great value as aids to publicity have long
attracted the serious consideration of advertisers. Artists also
have been interested in this method of presentation because
of the scope it allows for the use of fine colour and bold
design.

Great ingenuity is used in designing those constructions
which, though they are not quite models in the round, yet
contain much more than the ordinary showcard. These
constructions, which are made to stand up by themselves,
vary greatly in size and shape from a single piece of printed
board of irregular design to complicated affairs rather like a
toy stage. The former is called a cut-out while the latter
comes under the heading of window display. Many attractive
results can be obtained by the use of thin metals of various
colours, glass, and cellophane, and of course, the humble
three-ply board.

Lettering and copy (which is usually brief), must as a rule
be displayed as high as the exigencies of the design will allow,
to ensure that it is not hidden by articles placed on the shop
counter or in the window. Where lettering is used alone it is
well that the showcard should be of some simple rectilinear
shape. Ovals should be avoided. What has been said
regarding the poster applies equally well here. Lettering
should never be obscured, however slightly. An uneasy
feeling and lack of solidity is engendered by lettering which
passes immediately behind a well-modelled element in the
design. When a free type of letter is considered necessary
a good italic type should be taken as a model. If imitation

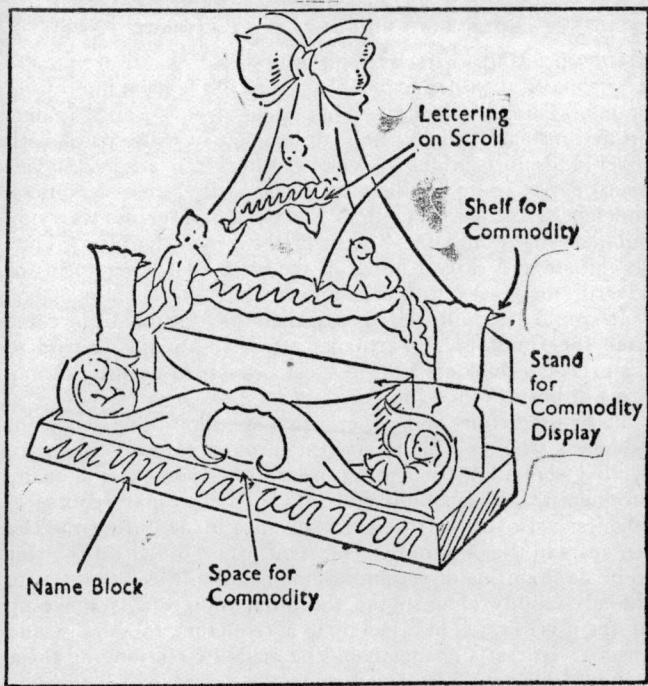

27. A TYPICAL CUT-OUT FOR WINDOW DISPLAY

A " cut-out " is a showcard for the display of goods in a shop window. It may be more or less elaborate, will stand by itself, and can support one or two samples of the article it advertises. It can be made of various materials. The one here analysed is typical in construction and lay-out.

handwriting must be used it should be of the most formal kind.

Very rarely do showcards of the merely lifelike or naturalistic order pull their full weight in the fight for recognition. If for some reason the artist is obliged to depict a commodity in this manner then it should be shown in what might be called " splendid isolation," perhaps upon a simple one-colour background.

BOOKLETS AND BOXES MUST ATTRACT

FINE printing, attractive make-up, and good design are regularly absorbed by booklets—one of the most interesting branches of advertising. The range, from simple folders printed in black or one colour to booklets of many pages with cover and illustrations in colour, offers the artist designer many entertaining problems. Along with boxes, wrappers, and labels, the booklet offers great possibilities for carrying publicity right into the homes of the buying public. They accentuate and extend much of the work that other forms of advertisement set out to accomplish.

It would be quite fair to say that the best booklets come from the Continent. Particular attention should be paid to the excellent booklets and prospectuses issued by the clothing firms of both France and America.

Packs or cartons and paper wrappers allow wide scope for designers who are able to suggest through pattern, colour, or symbol something of the nature and purpose of the many products that are bought and sold in the ordinary course of business. In spite of the great advance made during the last ten years in the designing of pleasant packs, much yet remains to be done in this direction. Some firms still feel doubt as to the advisability of changing the often frankly ugly make-up of their wares. They feel that a reduction in sales would ensue. At least a change could be made by rearranging those standard elements displayed upon the carton which through long use have become familiar to the buying public.

FROM IDEA TO EXECUTION

FROM small beginnings the advertising agency has risen to undreamed-of importance during the last fifty years or so. Its remuneration is provided by special discounts allowed by newspapers, periodicals, and magazines on the price of advertising space used, usually ten per cent. or according to value. In other words, the client pays a certain sum of money to the newspapers for the space which is occupied by his advertisement. Ten per cent. of that sum is allowed by the newspapers to the advertising agent for his services. Usually the only charge made by the agency to the client is the cost of finished art work, the copy and service being free.

No particular advantage is to be derived by firms contracting direct with the newspapers ; they would still have to pay the full amount for space used and also pay for art work and copy, unless the latter was written by their own advertising manager. Agencies usually obtain profits upon the production of printed material and blocks. Where work is not covered by such commission it is usual for the agencies to charge a small fee. The agency is an organisation of experts in particular spheres of advertising ; the justification of agencies is that they place at the disposal of advertisers the services of several experts, whereas few advertisers could themselves afford to employ more than one or two.

Speaking generally, there are two kinds of advertising agency, each of which has many points to recommend it. The first has as its centre the advertising expert whose word, by virtue of knowledge and experience, is law. He is assisted by experts in the various branches of advertising practice. The other kind of agency is usually much larger, and consists, on the creative side, of groups composed of artists and copy-writers under the guidance of a group manager.

The organisation of any one agency differs very little from another. There are two distinct sections : the mechanical side, which concerns itself with the collection of valuable data, buying of space, ordering of printed material and blocks ; and the creative side, which provides advertising schemes, ideas, and copy. It is on the creative side that some agencies are superior to others. Important agencies are usually divided into departments, such as advertisement production or planning, art department, accounts, space buying, voucher, and copy detail.

HOW THE SCHEME DEVELOPS

WE will assume that contact has been made with the advertisers either through the presentation of an un-deniably good scheme which, in the first instance, has been more or less speculative (a rare occurrence nowadays), or, as more often happens, an account or campaign has been placed with the agency because of its high reputation and standard of production. In either instance a scheme or campaign is presented to the client, usually with the idea of covering a run of six months or so.

It is the business of the advertisement-planning department, through careful analysis of their client's previous campaigns and by their own experience, to calculate exactly what type of appeal will obtain the best possible results and to decide what proportion of space-appropriation will be made in specific daily, weekly, and monthly papers and magazines, how much should be expended on posters, showcards, booklets, etc., always with due regard to the initial amount of money at their disposal.

The art director, if it is a small agency, or studio manager if it is a more important agency, after consultation with his director or contact man and copy chief, will apportion jobs to the various artists under his direction, while copy writers will concern themselves with problems set by the copy chief.

The method of appeal may take one of many forms, though there are about half a dozen which through experience have been found to possess great selling possibilities, and have therefore become more or less standardised. We easily recognise these when we see them. Hygiene and health, the economic and good-value-for-money, the social and snobbish, the fashion and travel, the humorous and provocative, are some of the more obvious appeals. Great variety may be obtained by a judicious combination of two and in rare instances three of these methods. For instance, the health appeal may be coupled with the travel, the social with the economic.

Perhaps the reader may remember the campaign of a certain brand of cigarettes in which nearly half of every insertion was occupied by a large hand, the first and second fingers of which were stained with tobacco tar. The caption ran : " Look at your fingers and think of your throat." Quite obviously the appeal was on the grounds of health and, secondarily, value for money. A stocking campaign may be remembered for its smart sophisticated presentation and copy, with a caption, in one instance at least, which stressed the economic factor, " 'Ware wear—wear ——."

Once the appeal has been settled the problem of the layout artist is to present it in the best possible manner. He may do it in one of many ways. He may choose to present the health and travel appeal in a smart social manner. Or if the appeal is of the social with economy type then he may use an extremely dignified kind of presentation.

Whether the advertisement will have a well-balanced, dignified effect or will be full of movement and life largely depends on the type of commodity and appeal. A smart hotel, for instance, would never be advertised in other than a reliable, dignified manner which might be coupled with either a smart social or economic appeal. Conversely, the latest toy novelty would demand a jolly, flippant type of advertising.

It is in the solving of these problems no less than in the statement of them that the expert lay-out man reveals his worth. Often it is he who determines whether the drawing shall be in line or wash; at this stage he may also suggest the particular artist best fitted to execute the finished drawings. He will decide upon the type best suited to the lay-out, and perhaps make suggestions regarding showcards and packs, should they be necessary.

MAKING THE ELEMENTS FIT THE SPACE

WE have seen that the Press advertisement consists of four or five main elements : caption, drawing, body of text, name-block, and often subsidiary matter. For obvious reasons the space-appropriations vary greatly in size and shape, and ultimately considerable ingenuity is required to fit the elements into the space allowed : ultimately, because as a rule the scheme is presented to the client as a series of hypothetical insertions, of about 11 by $6\frac{3}{4}$ inches.

Many space appropriations are much smaller than this. When this is so and the drawing is bold in treatment it is usually sufficient if it is reproduced smaller. When the drawing will not stand a smaller reproduction it is sometimes possible to mask various portions of it, thereby achieving a smaller drawing which, compared with the actual size, looks bolder in treatment. If this is not possible, a new drawing must be made for the smaller space. Copy is often re-written and subsidiary matter cut to the minimum.

Under the heading of standing details comes the coupon. When used, it should be placed across the bottom of the lay-out and must be seen clearly. It may with advantage be placed within a simple border. Care must be taken in the use of white space, which in the lay-out seems to emphasise the tastefulness of the drawing and type, but which in the newspaper, because of the printed matter on the reverse side, is apt to appear blotchy and uninteresting. This, of course, does not apply so much to magazine insertions.

Borders may either be drawn, or designed and made up from standard units supplied by all good printing houses.

It used to be sufficient for the client that he received rough pencil indications of the proposed campaign, but nowadays advertising agencies go to great lengths to present roughs which appear very like actual press advertisements, with the possible exception of the area devoted to type matter. Here lines of appropriate thickness are ruled to represent lines of type, the actual copy being placed on the opposite page of the folder containing the lay-outs. Even here instances have been known where type has been specially set up, and pulls from it pasted upon the lay-out.

It sometimes happens that the drawing will occupy so important a position in the eventual insertion that a very definite idea of the ultimate appearance must be given. In this case the chosen artist is commissioned to execute one or two drawings, which are photographed to the requisite size and pasted upon the lay-out. Otherwise a rough indication in line or wash will suffice.

We shall not go into all that is discussed between the client and the contact chief. For the purposes of this section we shall assume that the scheme has been passed, and it is time for the more mechanical side of the agency to come into operation.

WHAT KIND OF DRAWING SHALL WE USE ?

HERE we shall deal more particularly with the free-lance artist who is commissioned to execute finished drawings. He may have prepared roughs for the client's consideration in the first place, but if not, then he must be guided by the views of the art manager and be prepared to work from roughs which were executed by the agency lay-out man. It is not always sufficient that he merely copies these roughs. Often departures necessitated by the client's views must be made. Sometimes he will be required to continue a series of drawings on a given theme. If the drawings are to be in line he must decide if they should be pen drawings, scraper-board drawings, or wood-engravings ; if in half-tone, whether they should be in chalk or body colour.

The artist must know whether the drawings are intended for reproduction in the dailies or in the better printed weeklies and monthlies. Above all, he must get the views of the art manager correctly and know what time he has at his disposal.

The line [1] drawing may present many different qualities.

[1] For a more detailed account of the processes of illustration and reproduction, see pp. 227-257.

There is the pen drawing, usually light in tone, which ranges from the highly conventional or stylised to the free naturalistic. Wood-engravings and more rarely woodcuts have a charm and distinction peculiarly their own, and for that very reason their sphere of usefulness is limited.

Along with the wood-engraving we may place the plain scraper-board drawing. Objection is sometimes made on the score that the scraper-board drawing sets out to imitate a wood-engraving. This should never be so. Used in the best way the two techniques present very different appearances. At its best the scraper-board technique consists of a bold brush drawing qualified by white lines which are parallel or cross-hatched, while the wood engraving usually appears much darker, with greater areas of black.

There is also the grained scraper-board, which may be drawn upon in the usual way. A variety of grain can be obtained by lightly scraping the surface. White is got by scraping the grain away altogether. This method is admirably suited to still-life subjects and conventional drawings, and when used correctly resembles a coarse half-tone block.

Another method which achieves a resemblance to a half-tone is that in which a drawing is made in chalk upon a canvas grained paper. The chalk is carried on the top of the grain, the interstices of which remain clear.

Specific areas in a block made from a simple line drawing may be covered with a line or stipple tint at the choice of the artist. These patent mechanical tints are called Ben Day Mediums, and the screens for them are manufactured by one company. They are designated by standard numbers and are obtainable from most block makers.

A bold, free technique can be achieved by brush drawings made upon coarse paper. Those areas which become grey and are therefore incapable of being reproduced in line may be retouched with flake white.

THE WIDER RANGE OF TONE-DRAWINGS

Drawings which will be reproduced in tone are not nearly so restricted in technique as those in line, though it is well to bear in mind that unless the block has been made through a fine screen [1] and is intended for printing upon paper of good quality, the drawing must be exaggerated in its tone-values. In other words, the blacks must be made blacker

[1] See p. 250.

than is necessary, and the whites kept clean. It must be re-membered that unless the block-maker has instructions to clean out certain white areas they will be covered with an almost imperceptible dot pattern and the blacks will print slightly lighter owing to the interposition of the screens.

Drawings in tone are generally carried out in mixtures of lamp-black and flake-white water-colour paint (body colour), which may be made to retain its workableness by the addition of egg tempera or ox-gall. Diluted Chinese ink may be used with advantage in instances where fine work is necessary.

For figure work of a realistic kind there is nothing quite so pleasant to use as oil paint, the only drawback being that it takes at least five or six hours to dry properly, even when a quick-drying oil is used. Black chalk is another pleasant medium in which one may achieve a variety of texture according to whether the surface of the paper used is rough or smooth, though great care must be taken to see that the chalk is fixed properly by a mixture of shellac and methylated spirits.

Decorative drawings of great charm may be made with the air-brush, an instrument like a fountain-pen, which is attached by a tube to a cylinder of compressed air. The water-colour paint is applied as a fine spray through a small nozzle at the end of the instrument, and is regulated by finger pressure. The air-brush has made possible colour effects which would be almost impossible to obtain by any other method of colour application.

THE RICH RANGE FOR THE WORKER IN COLOUR

POSTER art in England is equal to that of any other country, though where the illustrated magazines are concerned we still lag behind in the production of advertisements in colour. Perusal of the better class type of American magazine will prove this.

Colour can be used as flat decorative pattern or it may be used to achieve a lifelike appearance, that is, naturalistically. There are practically no restrictions as to its use. Some few colours are more expensive to produce than others—emerald green, for instance, though its use is a matter for the client to decide rather than the artist. Gold and silver may be included in the colour range as they can now be printed as easily as any other colours.

Oil paint is certainly the best medium in which to execute naturalistic works, particularly if they are figure subjects.

Otherwise the most useful medium is body colour, that is, water-colour containing a certain percentage of flake white. The lighter the colour the more white it contains. This body colour or gouache method is by far the best medium in which to carry out flat decorative designs or works which, while not being merely decorative, yet rely for their effective appeal on the use of certain flat areas.

SYMPATHY AND INSIGHT THAT HELP THE DESIGNER

IT is perhaps only during the last sixteen years that the full importance of the artist designer to publicity has been realised. With the appreciation of ordered presentation, judicious emphasis, and good taste in illustration, and the fact that these elements must make a harmonious whole, came the demand for the specialised designer. From experience it has been found that the temperament best suited to this kind of work is one possessing a strong social sense (that is, sympathy with " the man in the street ") combined with a good psychological insight (ability to analyse the reactions of the man in the street).

A derivative artist of the highest order seems to succeed much better than a highly creative artist. The main concern of the highly creative artist is with the adequate expression of his ego in artistic terms, whereas the artist in advertising is more concerned with the tasteful application of current styles in art, typography, and advertising appeal.

INSIDE THE ADVERTISING AGENCY

THE days have almost passed when an artist could call himself an all-round publicity designer. True, he must know all about advertising practice, and must have a thorough knowledge of the various technical styles and methods of reproduction, but the standard of technical excellence in the various artistic branches has become so high that it is absolutely necessary for him to specialise early.

Within the agencies the artists are roughly divided into three categories : the visualisers or lay-out men, artists for pictorial roughs and sometimes for finished work, and lettering experts. The first deal with the general appearance of the advertising " scheme," as a series of insertions in the press is called. They decide upon the subject and type of drawing ; what space shall be given to the written matter or " copy " ; and what the relative importance of the slogan and name-block to the whole will be. Sometimes the lay-out man himself finishes the scheme sufficiently for it to be shown to the client, but more often the collaboration of the artist who specialises in pictorial roughs, and of the lettering expert, is sought.

It is necessary for the artist who does pictorial roughs to draw the figure well, and to be able, within the limitations of the pictorial subject, to display it in a forceful or subtle manner. It often happens that the studio manager or art director has in mind a particular artist who will be asked to execute the finished drawings. Sometimes he is even called in at this stage, his advice is sought regarding treatment, and he may perhaps work on the actual lay-outs before they are shown to the client. Or he may be commissioned to do one or two drawings which are photographed to the necessary size, prints of these being then pasted upon the lay-out.

The third man is an expert in all forms of drawn letter, and in many instances has a good knowledge of type-faces and their use.

THE OUTSIDE MEN

COMMERCIAL studios exist to supply finished art work to advertising agencies and printers. It is by no means unusual nowadays for an agency to run a studio of its own as a separate concern, making the studio pay for itself by taking work from the agency which would otherwise be given out to some other studio. Very often these agency studios execute finished drawings for other agencies than their own.

The commercial design studios, usually composed of a number of specialist artists working together, generally specialise in straightforward still-life subjects, showcards, cut-outs, and lettering. Sometimes a figure artist is included, but more often than not he is a free-lance working on his own account. There are, of course, one or two notable exceptions to this rule—studios whose output is composed almost entirely of fashion and naturalistic figure drawings. These studios employ representatives whose business it is to see that efficient contact takes place between studio and agency, and to interview prospective clients.

The free-lance artist is always a specialist, and is usually a graduate from one or other of the studios, more rarely from the advertising agency. His specialisation is the outcome of some years spent with either of these firms, during which he has acquired knowledge and experience which cannot be otherwise attained. It is unlikely that an artist can begin his career as a free-lance and make it a paying proposition from the start ; his work will have to be of very outstanding quality to bring in orders right away. Often the free-lance is represented by an art agent—one who is acquainted with the appropriate sources of demand for the work of his clients. Such agents, acting between customer and artist, save the time of the latter in soliciting work, and when they are efficient and businesslike, are well worth the twenty or twenty-five per cent. they charge for their services.

THE ARTIST IN TRAINING

MENTION has been made of the necessity for early specialisation. This applies to the artist who is already connected with publicity in some way, but not so much to the young student. Primarily it is the student's business to become a good draughtsman and to develop his sense of design. He must be able to work in the various media, and be acquainted with lettering, costume, architecture, and methods of reproduction. Later perhaps an aptitude for a certain line of development will become apparent. Although many people do not approve of the art school system, it still remains the best in spite of the fact that important printing firms and studios of commercial art take apprentices. Even then it is absolutely necessary that these apprentices should attend an art school.

Day and evening instruction may be obtained at the various schools of art throughout the country. Classes are held in preliminary and advanced drawing and painting, general design, and lettering. The best of these schools include classes and lectures on process reproduction, costume, and architecture, as well as special classes for trade apprentices.

Perhaps the most difficult time of all for the young commercial artist is that which occurs between the time of finishing his student days and the money-earning period. His problem is to adapt himself to the commercial world. Now, perhaps, more than at any other time must he make himself familiar with the work of the best publicity artists at home and abroad. There are a number of admirable journals which contain current examples of the best of this work, chief among them being *Gebrauchsgraphik*, a German monthly, *The American Annual of Advertising Art*, which is well worth the price that is charged, and at home Studio Publications Ltd. publish, besides *Commercial Art*, an annual in which are reproduced examples of the best work in Germany, France, America, and England.

The most obvious and perhaps the best way in which the prospective commercial artist may start his career is through the advertising agency. Another is by way of the commercial studio. In either instance he may be lucky enough to obtain a position by answering one of the advertisements which appear from time to time in the various magazines devoted to advertising and advertising art, or by writing the kind of letter which obtains an interview and perhaps a position. These letters should contain a brief account of his studies and the sort of work in which he is proficient. They should state also that the desire in the first instance is to obtain an interview, during which the aim of the applicant will be more fully stated.

The young commercial artist should continue drawing practice in the evenings, either at an art school or at private sittings. Too often he fails to reach a high standard of production merely because his draughtsmanship is mediocre.

WHERE THE ARTIST GETS HIS " RAW MATERIAL "

ONE of the most important considerations of the publicity artist is the employment of labour-saving methods. Often it is necessary for him to work far into the night on a drawing which must be delivered the next day. The reader can see the necessity for the drawing being done " out of the artist's head " or by the aid of reference. Publicity artists of experience keep properly indexed files of press cuttings, photographs, and reproductions which are likely to be helpful to them. These must be constantly supervised, the useless cuttings eliminated and more up-to-date examples added. The value of such reference cannot be over-estimated, for it is impossible for the artist to remember the hundred-and-one details of everyday life which he may be called upon to depict at a given moment.

Good costume models are used when the drawing demands a realistic treatment or when the reference becomes inadequate for the job. It is possible for the artist to pose for himself with the help of a large mirror (which no studio should be without) and a little ingenuity. He may even make use of his friends for such a purpose, though care should be taken that they do not pose for longer than ten minutes or so !

The nearest public library may be explored with advantage, while references such as photographs of celebrities, the beach at Brighton, or the Grand National steeplechase may be obtained from the various press photographic agencies on payment of a small fee.

Remember, as the aspect of publicity art constantly changes, so are there exceptions to all advertising rules. The demand for a new style of drawing is continuous. Fashions in typography come and go. It is the duty of the publicity artist not merely to become conversant with the work of his contemporaries, but also to make use of the latest innovations in design of the more experimental modern artists. It is hardly necessary to remind the reader of the great use to which some aspects of the cubist movement have been put.

To be successful the practice of publicity art must be a full-time job. Magazine illustrators may be called upon to draw for advertisements, but rarely is the advertising artist commissioned to execute drawings for illustration—that is to say, that while the advertisement may make use of illustration for the achievement of its aim, rarely does illustration make use of the art of advertising.

To conclude, the artist in publicity need not have much business ability, but it is imperative that he cultivate the business virtues of punctuality, reliability, and diplomacy.

WHAT TO READ NEXT ABOUT THE ART OF ADVERTISING

MANY excellent books dealing with the various aspects of publicity art exist for the edification of the student and commercial artist, and some are deserving of particular mention.

A very comprehensive and copiously illustrated volume is that published by B. T. Batsford Limited, *The Art of Pen Drawing*, a manual for students, illustrators, and commercial artists. An intimate little book well worth studying is that by Ashley, entitled *Line Drawing*, published by The Studio Limited. *Processes of Graphic Reproduction in Printing*, by Harold Curwen (Faber and Faber), is a more comprehensive work for the advanced student, as well as a book on modern illustration by Stephen Spurrier, published by Pitman.

Modern Fashion Drawing (Chapman and Hall), is an excellent study of its subject. For the lay-out man particularly, two books which will be very helpful are : *The Typography of Newspaper Advertisements*, by Francis Meynell (Ernest Benn Limited), which contains a selection of fine type faces, and *The Art of the Printer*, which has 250 Titles and Text pages selected from books composed in the Roman letter printed from 1500 to 1900 (Ernest Benn Limited). The whole range of advertising is discussed in Sir Charles Higham's excellent little book, *Advertising* (Home University Library, Thornton Butterworth Limited).

The annual publications of The Studio Limited are the only volumes of their kind published in England, and therefore should not be overlooked. They are *Modern Publicity*, *Decorative Art* (Studio Year Book), *Modern Photography*. Four periodicals reproducing examples of the best current advertising and illustrative art are : *Commercial Art*, published monthly by The Studio Limited, *Gebrauchsgraphik*, published by International Advertising Art monthly, and *Arts et Métiers Graphiques*, published every two months.

LETTERING AND TYPOGRAPHY

by EASTLAND FORTEY

"TAKING things for granted" is a phrase which slips easily off our tongues, and the habit is an easy one to acquire. But let us for a moment stop to consider what it really means. In its best sense it should stand for an easy acquaintance with those everyday things which we use without needing to understand them too deeply. But to alert minds there are few things that fail to yield interest to any attempt to understand their working, and an enquiring habit of mind leads to a fuller and richer life.

So it is with the subject of this section. At first glance you may ask why Lettering and Typography should be included under the name of Art. The alphabet is our useful friend, but can there be an art in the making of such apparently simple things as letters? The answer is that many men give their lives to the study of the alphabet and find in it a fascinating pursuit. Our object here is to interest you in the shapes of letters so that you will be able to judge for yourself whether those you see about you every day are good or not, and why. You may already have noticed that some letters are pleasant to the eye and others are ugly, without knowing why this is so. Once you understand the basis of good letter forms you will be able to help in the growing movement to use only lettering which is good to look upon. Beautiful characters are just as simple and easy to make as ugly ones, sometimes very much easier ; it is only necessary to know why certain shapes are better for this purpose than others.

Everybody makes use of letters, if only for their handwriting, but some of us have occasion to make some bolder and more easily read notices. Times when it is uneconomical to use the services of the expert artist, such as Dances, Whist Drives, and other forms of social activities, need posters. If we own a business we sometimes like to make our own tickets and showcards. In the lay-out of these, and in designing printed bills and cards a knowledge of good lettering is a very useful thing to possess.

KNOWLEDGE THAT MUST BE GAINED IN PRACTICE

IT might be thought that this knowledge could very easily be obtained merely by examining the very many examples we see about us. The eminent sculptor Eric Gill, who is also a great authority on lettering, once wrote : " The copy-book of to-day is the printed page." But he meant this as a warning rather than a precept. At the present time we are overwhelmed by a flood of printed matter such as the world has never before seen. The popular daily newspaper with its regular series of advertisements forcing clothes, food, petrol, and films upon our attention, and the posters that struggle for our notice on every hoarding, may delude us into thinking here is all we need in the way of example close at hand. But any amount of looking at the outside of a car will not teach us how to drive it ; so with lettering, some study of the construction of its forms is necessary before we can expect to produce letters which will do their work well.

The leading architects, artists, and designers of to-day are combined in a magnificent effort to bring back the essential virtue of simplicity into our everyday life. It also happens to be the most important factor in beautiful lettering ; in the alphabet simplicity and legibility are synonymous, but in the latter half of the last century this quality of simplicity was conspicuously neglected in lettering as in many other spheres of design. The evil legacy of grotesque and distorted forms has not yet been exhausted and one frequently sees lettering in advertisements so tortured into " artiness " as to be difficult to read, thereby completely defeating its own purpose.

A little enthusiasm in research will soon convince the reader that the alphabet will repay respect with a great deal of pleasure. Once he has learnt to construct his letters properly he will realise that each character has life and a vital quality of its own. The good shapes look good and happy, and if tricks are played upon them their expression does really change, usually for the worse. Most of us are aware of the humorous effect of extremely fat letters, and conversely the mean and miserable look that very thin upright characters have. Between these two extremes is the normal standard, and this can best be found by studying the finest historical examples.

PRINTING AND LETTERING ARE NOT THE SAME

IT will be useful here to deal with a popular confusion of the words " Lettering " and " Print." Briefly, the first includes all letters which are not printed from metal types in a printing machine. That is, " Lettering " means words made with the brush, pencil, pen, or carved with the chisel. If reproductions of these are made through the medium of the Press it does not alter the fact that they were originally made with the tools mentioned. Printed lettering from metal types is another matter, since the shapes are determined by the processes of cutting the " punches," and we shall deal with this further on. For the moment it is only necessary to point out that it is incorrect to call any hand-drawn or written letters " Print."

The making of written and carved records has always been a highly specialised craft during the peak periods of civilisation, and provides an interesting index to the artistic and intellectual culture of an age. One may safely make the generalisation that fluent and generous characters go hand in hand with an alert interest in things of the spirit. We find that degenerate ages and periods of purely material prosperity have usually expressed themselves in cramped and distorted forms.

We are primarily interested here in the alphabet of Western Europe, that is, in the letters we ourselves use as opposed to the group which includes Greek and the various Eastern characters. We still call ours " Roman " letters after the people who brought them to the shapes we recognise to-day. If an educated Roman citizen of two thousand years ago could revisit us now, he would have no difficulty in reading any of the Latin inscriptions we carve on our public buildings. Experts agree that the letters of the inscription carved on the Trajan Column which was erected in Rome in A.D. 114 remain to-day the standard from which little variation need be made for our normal letter forms.

In ninety per cent. of the cases where words are used, the most important consideration is that they should be quickly and easily read. This legibility is largely a matter of simple construction and comparative proportion. It will be seen from the illustration [1] that the Trajan letters fall roughly into two groups, wide letters and narrow ones, and since these are

[1] Page 283.

the normal proportions of the type we are most accustomed to, it follows that any radical departure from these standards will result in a loss of clarity. Letters are pre-eminently symbols, and a symbol must be consistent in form to have any value at all, particularly such an abstract set of symbols as letters are.

In addition to their comparative proportions one with another, letters have other important characteristics such as vertical stems, crossbars, bowls, and tails, and the positions of these are bound up with the width of the letter. These are the real features of the letter, and should be studied with care. Usually the first thing to strike the amateur is that certain parts are thin and others thick, but the easiest style to use for studying proportion is the letter of equal thickness, such as the " Gill " letter used for the headings in this book. This is called a " sans serif " or block letter, because letters of equal thickness never have serifs, the name given to the usual termination to the thick and thin letter. It is not caprice which determines whether a letter should be of the same thickness all over or not, and some consideration of the tools used for writing and lettering will make this clear.

LETTERS FOUND IN EGYPTIAN TOMBS

PROFESSOR LETHABY wrote : " Of all the arts, writing shows most clearly the formative influence of the tools used." He was referring to formal writing, but the remark applies equally to letters produced by other means. We do not know how or by whom the first written letter was made. Excavation and research by scientists have brought to light very early forms which are more or less pictorial representations of objects and people, which we call picture writing. Only the simplest messages could be conveyed by such means ; the power to indicate more abstract meanings came later with the use of groups of symbols. The pictorial element was soon conventionalised into more abstract forms which were more rapidly and more easily drawn, showing increasingly the characteristics of the tool with which they were made. Usually this was a reed pen such as designers use to-day, and the material on which the symbols were written was the papyrus which the Egyptians have rendered familiar to us, and from which we get our word " paper."

The Sumerians of seven thousand years ago used clay

ABCDE
FGHIJK
LMNOP
QURST
VWXYZ

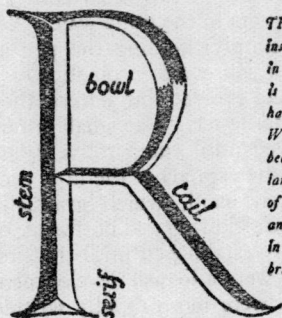

stem *bowl* *R* *tail* *serifs*

THIS alphabet is taken from a photograph of the inscription carved on the Trajan Column, erected in Rome in 114 A.D. by the Emperor Trajan. It is the basic type on which our best capital letters have been modelled ever since. The letters HJKU WYZ are missing from the inscription and have been designed to harmonize with the others. The larger outline letter R shows the actual appearance of these chiselled letters and how the play of light and shade makes the V-section visible. Inscriptions in this incised form of letter were usually painted in bright colours. Compare it with the modern Gill Sans.

(This note is set in Caslon Old Face Italics.)

tablets on which they impressed their characters with a square-ended stick or " stylus." This gave the wedge-shaped characters which we call "Cuneiform" writing. The free-flowing pen of the Egyptians tended to preserve the original shape of the character or picture, while the Sumerian method more quickly developed conventional symbols. The alphabets we know are descended from a combination of both these types of writing, influenced from time to time by the particular tool employed. In much later times the Romans used the pen and the brush, but they also excelled in the use of the chisel to give permanent form to the inscriptions recording on their triumphal arches the conquests of their legions and the growing frontiers of their empire.

WRITING LETTERS ON STONE

IN a carved letter, the V-shaped section was the natural one for the chisel to make, and the thin, pointed, and slightly curved serifs the natural termination to such a section for the stems and crossbars. A brush will give similar serifs, and probably these inscriptions were painted or rather written on the stone with a brush before the chisel fixed them. The disposition of the thicks and thins suggests the flat brush.

Although our most perfect capital letter forms have come down to us through the medium of the chisel, the pen was responsible for the general shapes. A broad-nibbed pen will give a wide, thick line downwards and a thin one across. If it is held slightly on the slope with the end of the penholder pointing over the right shoulder, it will give us the thicks and thins in their correct order. One of the most common faults of the uninformed person is to put the thick line of the capital A on the left-hand side, or to give the N two thick verticals and a thin oblique line. S also suffers in the same way. Yet if one makes these letters quite simply, holding the pen as described above, the correct forms will come automatically.

When the early pictorial signs had evolved into letters, they first of all developed into the capital letter. The small letters as we know them were not evolved until comparatively late in the history of writing. The rustic capitals of the fifth century were followed by the uncial hand, which gradually became more cursive, that is, more flowing. The forms of the small letters were not generally established until the first thousand years of this era. They were a logical development of the capitals, for as the capitals were more rapidly written certain forms were altered and the modifications gradually produced a distinctive set of forms.

By the time printing was introduced into Europe, that is, in the fifteenth century, the manufacture and copying of books and other documents by the professional scribes had grown to immense proportions, and each country had its own characteristic form of writing. Generally this had developed until it was possible to write at a rapid speed, which made for uniformity of the letters and a pleasant, even filling of the page. The margins of the page were often covered with delicate ornament in colours and important letters such as headings and initials were frequently gilt. Minutely painted miniatures illustrated the work and provide the historian of to-day with valuable insight into the lives of the people, since the scribes in common with the painters of the time copied the costume and customs they saw around them. Examples of these beautiful Books of Hours, Psalters, and other devotional works, as well as romances, can often be found in museums and may be studied with great profit.

So exquisitely stylised had the letter forms become by this time that the first printers simply borrowed them without alteration for their wooden types. There was another good reason why they did this. Encouraged by the natural opposition of the scribes, who could not have been expected to acclaim this menace to their profession, the superstitious common people looked askance at printing as an invention of the Devil, and the printers accordingly tried to pass off their mechanically produced books as genuinely hand-written. Sometimes they even went to the length of adding hand-painted ornament and illumination after the body of the book was printed.

The printing press rapidly gained recognition, however, and was soon able to put off these pretences. Books could then be speedily produced and multiplied, and so the scribes found this side of their occupation gone. From that time onwards their influence was confined to the teaching of handwriting as such. Many interesting copybooks were issued through the medium of their vanquisher, the press, but the virtue of simplicity which had been developed under the stress of speedy working was now no longer of paramount importance, and the various hands show a distinct leaning towards involved flourishes. The form of writing which we still call " copper plate " was the final gesture before the invention of the typewriter further assisted in the decay of handwriting, resulting in the untidy scrawls we see to-day. However, various efforts are now being made to revive the use of a formal hand, and in many schools children are once more being taught the use of " script writing."

THE PRINTER TAKES OVER THE ART OF LETTERING

THE development of letter designing now passed over to the printers and certain modifications in shape and finish at once occurred, dictated by the processes of cutting the punches, casting the type, and the need to obtain a clear impression on the rough surface of the hand-made paper of the time. This paper was made from rags and was extremely durable. Nowadays this is too costly a method, except for the most expensive works, and the paper we use for books is made either from grass or from wood fibre and perishes rapidly. It is highly unlikely that any of the thousands of novels and the millions of newspapers now existing will endure for a century, yet the fifteenth and sixteenth century books treasured in the libraries will probably remain unchanged for a further thousand years if they escape the menace of fire and flood.

The first types were cut on wood and the shapes were practically unchanged from the handwritten letter. When the invention of cast metal type came into use, the thin lines the pen made easily were thickened to withstand the wear and tear of printing, while the broad thicks were slightly reduced. In consequence, the general appearance of the printed page became much greyer.

Immediately before the invention of the press, when the profession of the scribe was at its zenith, there were two main forms of letter in use. Northern Europe favoured a rather narrow angular hand which we still remember as " Black Letter " or " Old English." A development of this continues in Germany at the present time, while some newspapers still use it for their titles. In the south, particularly in Italy, the shapes were much rounder and more elegant. This is the " Humanistic " hand and is sometimes sloped. The sloping form is familiar to us in the type we call " Italic " and is used to give emphasis to words, owing to its difference from the usual upright or " Roman " letter. Both the

" Italic " and the " Roman " have their capitals and their small or " lower case " letters and figures.

The printed book quickly reached a very high standard of beauty in typography, presswork, and in its general shape, its margins and its lay-out. From the sixteenth to the eighteenth centuries some of the most beautiful printed matter the world has yet seen was produced, and though printing suffered a temporary setback in the nineteenth century, in common with most other arts at a time when material prosperity was the first criterion, the past fifty years have seen a notable revival. It is significant that during the last few years the Monotype Corporation, which produces a good deal of the type in use to-day, has re-cut and issued many of the " type faces " designed by the great Italian and French printers who flourished during the best periods of the past.

A GREAT STEP FORWARD IN PRINTING

MENTION of the Monotype reminds us that here is another revolutionary influence in the printing world. From the beginning of printing in the fifteenth century until about the last third of the nineteenth century all letters were cast upon separate pieces of metal, and the hundreds of pieces which made up a complete page had all to be assembled by hand and fastened tightly together in a frame before printing. This method of hand composition is still used by many printers, but for certain classes of work it is now possible to save much time and tedious labour by using machine composition. In principle it works like this. The operator has a machine with a bank of keys rather like a typewriter, on which he types the matter to be set. In the Monotype machine this makes perforations on a roll of paper like a player-piano roll. This is put into a second machine which translates the perforations into newly cast separate type in the correct order. Another composing machine called the Linotype gives very much the same result, but in one operation and in solid lines of type, hence the name.

Such machines are very largely used in newspaper offices and large works where speed of operation is essential. One immense advantage they possess over hand composition in addition to their speed is that the type is always new. It therefore prints clearly and does not get broken or mutilated like hand-set type which has to be used over and over again. The machine-set type is usually re-melted after use.

SOME ODDMENTS FROM THE PRINTER'S STOCK

So far we have only discussed letters. Numerals have had a rather simpler development. During the periods mentioned there have been only two distinct forms of the symbols man has used to denote numbers. The first is the Roman numeral, still used to-day in civic inscriptions and on the familiar clock face, but rarely used for high numbers on account of its cumbersome form. The second, a later and much more widely used system, is the Arabic, which came into use in Europe during the early Middle Ages. Arabic figures are both upright and sloped to go with the Italic letter.

The rest of the printer's stock includes the sign called the " Amperzand " (&) which stands for " and." He also uses straight and curved strips of metal called " rules " which make borders, and ornaments which he calls " flowers," though they do not usually in the least resemble flowers. Here are a few

They are used for ornamental borders, and to separate lines in titles and other places. They should only be employed very sparingly, as otherwise they detract attention from the letters, which after all are more important. There are also various signs such as the asterisk (*), the dagger (†), and the paragraph mark (¶) to call attention to footnotes, paragraphs, and so on.

STRANGE TRICKS OF THE TYPE FOUNDERS

WE have mentioned the temporary eclipse which affected good taste in printing during the nineteenth century. The quality of the paper, the presswork, and the general lay-out of the printed page all suffered, as well as the forms of the letters themselves. Type founders began to play tricks with their shapes, producing distortions which had little relation either with tradition or usage, and worse still, the " condensed " letter came into being. This is a type where all letters are of the same width—the narrowest being taken as standard. Newspapers were the greatest offenders owing to their habit of spreading long titles in one line at the head of a single column. To-day we are so used to seeing a heading spread over several columns or even across a page that a newspaper of twenty years ago looks very severe indeed. In the new style of popular journalism the printer uses letters of normal width, and the condensed letter has almost disappeared.

Some of the types which the nineteenth century invented, such as the " fat " type of Robert Thorne, a printer who worked round about 1820, were developed from shapes popular in the latter end of the preceding century, and were favoured by signwriters and advertisers. Very similar fat letters are still being used to-day, and in some circumstances there is something to be said for them.

FANTASTIC DESIGNS THAT CONFUSE THE READER

PRIOR to the nineteenth century the use of printing was mostly confined to books, and later on, to newspapers. The advance of the industrial era saw a great increase in the use of the press for advertising purposes. Letter forms accordingly took on certain changes to meet the demand. A book, while it is being read, has no other distractions to fear, and is so arranged that it can be read easily without either strain to the eyes or waste of space. The free flow of the narrative is not interrupted to emphasise any particular point ; that is the author's business. On the other hand, an advertisement is always straining to catch your attention, to outdo the many others that are competing for your interest.

The necessity of attracting attention led at once to the use of larger and blacker, that is, thicker, types than were necessary for book printing. Not only size and weight, but also variety began to be sought, and still is to this day. Every year sees the outpouring of new type faces, each a slight variation on standard forms, and often in merely fantastic guise, just for the sake of novelty. The net result of all this is simply to make confusion worse confounded. A glance at a daily newspaper carrying a large number of advertisements makes this obvious at once ; nothing can stand out from that welter where all shout at once. Eric Gill has said that the " typography of industrialism should be free from exuberance," and it is a fact that people who are sensitive to well-designed things do shudder at certain advertisements in the daily press.

The rise of the poster as an advertising medium has helped to establish the " Sans serif " letter as a particularly useful form for this purpose. It is of uniform thickness throughout, and has no serifs to hinder its easy visibility from a distance.

10

The good modern poster is an affair of simple areas of flat colour, for ease in reproduction and printing. Its shapes are often square and geometrical, and the traditional thick and thin letter with its subtle curves seldom goes well with such a design. So the designer employs a bold character of considerable weight and strikes his curves with a compass. It is important to appreciate that in this case the lettering cannot be judged apart from the rest of the design, and must in fact be part of a well-knit whole.

HOW TO MAKE LETTERS

DRAWN letters are made with the pen, pencil, and brush. Of these the pen is the simplest for the beginner to handle, as it makes the correct forms with each stroke, while the pencil and brush are used for built-up characters. Almost any smooth paper is suitable to begin with, and it should be secured to the drawing board with drawing pins. The board itself must be sloped at a comfortable angle so that the artist is not cramped. A tee-square and a celluloid set-square are necessary for ruling writing lines and margins. These are best done lightly with an HB pencil.

The mediæval scribe used turkey and goose wing feather quills. These together with reed pens can be obtained from any good artists' colourman, and are the best tools for this purpose when the artist has learnt to cut them himself and to keep them in order. The beginner will find a square-ended steel nib, such as those made specially for formal writing, will give quite good results, though they lack the sensitive response of the older tools. They are quite good enough to practise with until the shapes have been learnt. Whichever the artist chooses, he will need a bottle of unfixed black Indian Ink with a quill filler fixed in the cork. If this filler cannot be obtained, a small cheap brush must be used to fill the nib with ink. On no account should the nib be dipped into the bottle, as the ink must only be held on one side of the nib; to have ink on both sides will prevent the nib from giving a thin sharp line. To begin with select a nib about one-eighth of an inch wide, as it is easier to make the forms on a large scale at first.

EXERCISES WITH A PEN

HOLD the pen slightly on the slope with the penholder pointing over the right shoulder. Left-handed people cannot hold the pen correctly in their left hand and must use the right for this purpose, if in any way possible. Test the line made by the nib without trying to force the split ends apart. The nib should be used firmly but lightly.

Make an X, the thick stroke downwards towards you and the thin one down from right to left. You should never push the nib upwards; if you do, you will soon find that it only ploughs up the paper and scatters ink in a series of blots. The height of capitals should be about seven times the nib width, and of lower case letters four to five times the nib width for the body of the letter, with rather less for the ascending and descending limbs and tails. So with a nib about one-eighth of an inch wide you will rule your guide lines in this order, starting with room for the ascenders—three-eighths, nine-sixteenths, three-eighths, nine-sixteenths, and so on. Do not attempt to form the whole letter without lifting the pen from the paper. Each letter is made up of two or more strokes, each neatly joining with the others.

The written alphabet given here (Fig. 29) is a good standard hand. Slight variations are possible in forming certain letters, and will occur naturally as speed comes with practice. But these shapes must be followed exactly at first, until you have mastered the basic forms. Be very sparing with your flourishes or you will soon vulgarise your letters.

Copy out these capitals and lower case letters as many times as may be necessary until ease in handling the pen is obtained and you know the forms by heart; then start to write out a page of prose—any quotation will serve for this purpose. Begin with a large initial letter, or write the first line or two lines in capitals. Whichever way you choose, here is an excellent opportunity for introducing a second colour, preferably red or blue, using black for the body of the text. The left-hand margin is easily kept as a straight edge, but do not at first try to force the right-hand edge to be a straight one. Let the words terminate naturally, as they would if you were using a typewriter. Any attempt to squeeze or lengthen the last word to fill the space exactly will spoil the “ colour ” of the page. You will find later on, with practice, that a reasonably regular right-hand margin can be kept by adjusting your letters throughout the whole line. It is far more important to form each letter roundly and to keep them nicely massed together into words, each letter neatly joined on to its neighbour. A common fault with beginners is to make narrow letters too widely spaced, so that all the faults in workmanship are glaringly apparent.

At the end of paragraphs where a line finishes short it can be filled in with some pen-made ornament. There is an inexhaustible variety of these and many are extremely interesting, but they should be kept very simple. They are made of the same kind of stroke as is used in forming the letters themselves. An amperzand and alternative forms of an f, g, and q are also given (Fig. 29).

These are only the elements of formal writing. If the reader would like to learn more about its practice, its history, and possibilities, how to use and care for quills, and the secrets of gilding and illumination, he will find it fully treated in Edward Johnston's justly famous book, *Writing, Illumination, and Lettering*, which has been the standard textbook on the craft for over twenty years.

THE USE AND QUALITIES OF THE BRUSH

FAMILIARITY with this written alphabet will provide a sound basis for constructing the corresponding letters with the brush. The Trajan alphabet[1] should be copied out to a larger scale, about two and a half inches high, certainly not less, and larger if you prefer. The letters should be lightly pencilled in first and then filled in with a nicely pointed brush and indian ink. A No. 3 sable brush is recommended for this work. Cheap brushes are worse than useless and are a false economy. Buy a few good ones and keep them in good order, washing them well after use, and never letting them stand in the ink or water jar. Cheap brushes have neither spring nor point, and are only of use as pen fillers.

As in the written letters, your aim should be to form the letters directly with as few strokes of the brush as possible. The curves should be swept as rapidly as you can with one movement from the wrist. It is a good thing to watch sign-writers at work. They form their letters with the minimum number of strokes, and it is a fascinating sight to see them sweep an O in two halves.

Do not worry if at first your edges are not very neat. Practice will overcome this particular trouble, but pay great attention to the proportions of each letter and to the serifs, which must not be too thin and hair-like, nor must they be clumsy and obtrusive. Work with the whole length of the

[1] See page 283.

ABCDEFGH

Capitals seven pen widths in height

IJKLMNOP

QRSTUVW

XYZ.& *Angle of pen* R I *& order of strokes*

1234567890

abcdefghijkl

lower case 4½ to 5 pen widths high

mnopqrstuv

wxyz & ßfgq;

29. A GOOD STANDARD HAND-WRITTEN ALPHABET

brush, lifting it slightly at the end for the point to form the
serifs naturally. Each stem should be made with two strokes,
one for each side and one little touch to join the serifs
together.

After you have succeeded in making the Roman capitals
correctly, tackle the lower case letters and the italics. The
latter must all slope the same amount, and it is a good practice
to rule parallel lines as guides. Notice how certain letters,
such as the a, f, g, differ in italics from the upright Roman
forms.

When combining the brushed letters into words, the spacing
must be carefully watched. There is no set rule here to guide
you. It is no use thinking you can measure the letters apart
mathematically. An eye for proportion is required, as the
letters have to balance each other so that each appears to be
in the *visual* centre between its neighbours. Bad spacing is
very easy to detect, as it tends to break up words into groups
of letters, and your aim is to get them to flow evenly so that
no single letter or group stands out aggressively in any one
word.

When you come to draw the Gill Sans serif letter you will
find that these are very much better done with geometrical
drawing instruments. The subtle beauty of the Trajan letter
depends on the relation of its thicks and thins as much as on
its proportions, but the letter of even thickness all over is a
much more mechanical affair, and its curves demand compasses. The straight lines should be truly straight, the
verticals and the horizontals truly at right angles, and they
should be drawn with the set square and the tee square. Draw
them first in pencil, perfectly, with a fine line, and then ink
them in with a ruling pen and ink compass. Then you can
fill in the body of the letters with a brush. Let the edges of
these geometrically-made letters be sharp and firm, and see
that their thickness is the same everywhere.

When setting out an inscription it is a good plan to sketch
it in freely but lightly in a red or other coloured pencil
between the bounding parallels, or guide lines, then to
improve the lines of the letters with an ordinary black lead
pencil, getting gradually firmer as you settle the shapes and
positions. Round letters, such as O, Q, C, G, S, and U, and
pointed letters, such as V, N, and W, must reach slightly
above and/or below the parallel guide lines, in order to appear
of equal height with the square-shaped letters. Finally trace

the finished words on a piece of tracing paper pinned over your first sheet and you will have nothing to erase.

The preliminary sketching out is to determine the size and spacing, and at the same time you should take into account the white spaces left between the letters. These are very important in designing lettering, and help immensely to give you correct spacing.

VOCATIONS FOR THOSE ATTRACTED TO LETTERING

To the reader who finds himself attracted to beautiful lettering and would like to make use of it in some vocation, there are various branches open. Of these, the signwriters' craft is perhaps the oldest. Nowadays it includes not only work written *in situ*, but the designing of cinema signs (now made in the studio in a variety of ingenious methods and materials) and the designing and making of solid letters in wood, glass, and metal for shops, cinemas, restaurants, and other public buildings. The most up-to-date development of this old craft is the luminous Neon electric tube letter which has made great strides during the last few years. The difficulty of bending the glass here forces the designer to use only the simplest forms, with the result that many of these signs are in very good style. Inscriptions on public buildings are usually carved on the job by the stonemason, who also does the rest of the carved stone enrichments, such as column capitals and cornices. He has to be a sculptor as well as a designer of letters.

Printing, publishing, and advertising naturally offer the greatest opportunities to profit by an interest in lettering and its uses. This branch alone is so vast as to require a section to itself to explain fully, since it deals with the production of all the printed matter in use, from the daily newspaper to the expensive edition de luxe, and from the humble circular to the huge forty-eight sheet poster—the largest poster usually printed.

The large manufacturer of to-day employs an advertising agent to prepare his publicity. The agent in his turn employs the printer to produce the finished article, and in between there are a host of artists to design the illustrations and lay-out of type for the printer to follow. The lay-out man instructs the printer what types to use and how to display them. He is usually on the staff of the advertising agent, though a few big printers employ him to help their clients. He must have a good knowledge of balance and contrast in design, and should know intimately the appearance and usefulness of the various type faces in current use. Design he can learn in an Art School, but the practical knowledge of printing types can only be learned at a printer's or at a printing school.

The correct use of type plays an important part in the layout and arrangement of all printed matter. Modern publishers are constantly on the look-out for people who can display magazine articles and books in an intelligent and interesting manner. The popular magazine of to-day is a much brighter affair than its predecessors, while many novels and works of various kinds sold at surprisingly cheap prices are extremely well designed and set in types that were unobtainable a few years ago. Allowing for the conditions under which they are produced, some of these are worthy to be placed beside the best examples of the early printers we have mentioned.

A DELIGHTFUL HOBBY FOR THE AMATEUR

EVEN if the reader does not wish to make money by his interest in lettering, he will find a course in design and lettering at his local art school extraordinarily interesting and useful. It will train him to find interest in things which otherwise he would certainly fail to notice. Allied to a habit of personal research the results can be most fascinating. He will examine lettering wherever he meets with it with a new eye, judging its suitability, its age, and the influences that went to its shaping, assessing its merits in the light of his knowledge. As well as the printed works of every age, he will find inscriptions in old buildings and churches, and on tombstones of the seventeenth and eighteenth centuries, all showing good craftsmanship and interesting forms. Research in museums will bring to light old books, engraved objects, and other forms which will well repay study. Often printed specimens can be filed for reference, and a small sketch-book carried in the pocket will be found useful for taking notes when one meets interesting forms in new developments or archaic examples.

In the suggestions for further reading which follow have been included works which the present writer has found helpful in the study of this fascinating branch of the useful arts. The reader will discover for himself many other " Books of Alphabets " which have been published from time to time. A word of warning is necessary about these ; many of them are no more than collections of widely different types gathered together with no respect for beauty or usefulness. Many ugly forms are included just because they are different and not because they are good. If the reader confines his early studies to good examples of the purer forms on the lines indicated here he will soon learn to recognise the bad ones. These are always marked by freakish distortions and consequent illegibility. The best styles keep reasonably close to their root forms in the Trajan and its derivatives. The only variations permissible are slight refinements in detail due to causes mentioned earlier.

In an age which prides itself on changing the shape of most things it may seem curious that here is an art firmly wedded to the forms established two thousand years ago. Yet when one reflects on the amount of vested capital both material and intellectual involved, it is clear that there is little likelihood of any change for a long period. Possibly future ages may see a different set of symbols used for man's printed and written records, that is, if these activities continue. At the present time our letters have the incalculable value of old-established symbols and these are always difficult to change, even were a change necessary.

BOOKS ABOUT THE ART OF LETTERING

THOSE who wish to read more about lettering and typography will find a number of books available as guides to practical work, as well as some which will appeal to those interested in the history and development of these crafts. *Writing, Illuminating, and Lettering*, by Edward Johnston, is an invaluable work for the beginner, and there have been many editions to bring it up-to-date since the book was first produced in 1906. It is concise and complete, with lucid illustrations, and the alphabet is analysed in detail, so that construction is made easy. *Manuscript and Inscription Lettering*, by the same author, is a portfolio of sixteen plates, taken from the previous work but on a larger scale. It has reproductions of several inscriptions carved in stone by Eric Gill. For a comparison of many different styles of lettering the collection entitled *Lettering from A to Z*, by Cecil Wade, is worth studying. The majority of these styles are founded on good models, but include some that are " smart " without being good. These three books are published by Pitman.

A very cheap and quite reliable handbook on the use of the broad-nibbed pen is *Pen Practice*, by Walter Higgins (Batsford). Naturally it has not the scope of the more expensive works by Johnston, but is very practical within its limits. *Alphabets Old and New* and *Lettering in Ornament*, by Lewis F. Day, are two books that were published by Batsford at the beginning of this century, and reflect the liking for intricate ornament and lettering then so popular. Bearing this in mind the reader will find them of great interest in understanding the way in which lettering and design generally are influenced by current thought. Another similar and useful historical work is *Alphabets*, by E. F. Strange (Bell).

For a useful introduction to typography, printing, and publishing processes by an expert, the reader should consult *Printing for Business*, by Joseph P. Thorp (John Hogg). In this book technical information is simply presented, with many helpful illustrations. Three books on design and lay-out that are recommended are: *Advertising Design and Lay-out*, by Charles C. Knights (Crosbie Lockwood); *Printing Design and Lay-out*, by Vincent Steer (Virtue); and *One Hundred and One Lay-outs*, by H. G. Russell (Reynolds).

THE SHAPES OF MUSIC

by HERBERT MURRILL, M.A., B.Mus.(Oxon), A.R.A.M.,
Professor of Composition at the Royal Academy of Music.

WHEN a man wants to do some constructive piece of work—to build a house, for example—two things are necessary: the materials for the work and the man's own idea of how he is going to use them. And although his idea may be different from that of most other builders, although he may be a revolutionary in his style of building, he will yet have to obey certain fundamental laws of balance and construction. If he disobeys these laws his house will look ridiculous, or be totally unsafe or it may even quite simply collapse.

A composer is a man who does a constructive piece of work with musical materials, that is, with various sorts of sound. Not every sort of sound is available for musical building, although many sorts are freely used to-day which earlier ages would have considered unusable. Thus our musical resources are widened, and there is room within modern music for all sorts of different styles and methods of construction.

Sound in itself is not music, just as bricks in themselves are not houses. A single sound is not musically significant, for music is an art *in time* : that is to say, a musical work cannot be presented to us all at once. It has to pass through our mind as a more or less orderly procession of sounds, and significance and thought can only be conveyed by this succession and forward movement. But *any* succession of sounds will not make music. Certain fundamental laws of balance and design must be followed in musical composition as well as in house-building, or our work will be ridiculous, illogical, and meaningless. In this section we shall discuss these fundamental laws as we find them obeyed in works which have stood the test of time, which have given pleasure and æsthetic satisfaction to countless critical and uncritical listeners.

We have at last arrived at what we may consider to be a neat and workable definition of music. We have called it "a succession of ordered sounds." There are many other definitions, but ours would seem to cover the essentials in the most workmanlike way. For the composition of music is a strictly workmanlike business. The romantic picture of long-haired genius lashing the piano in a fine creative frenzy is sadly misconceived. Music-making is a slow and laborious business, calling for patience, cool and clear thinking, and hard work.

Our composer has to choose the materials from which his work will be made, then set to work to weld these materials into a logical, coherent, and satisfying piece of music. If he is the best sort of composer he does not bother his head very much about trying to be original or startling or expressing his own personality. He knows that his music is bound to express his own personality, and that his originality—if he has any—is bound to be felt in his work. To bother about such things as he writes would make him awkward and self-conscious : he would forever be worrying about himself rather than about his music, and for such luxuries he has (or should have) no time.

THE MATERIALS WITH WHICH THE COMPOSER BUILDS

Now what are the materials a composer has at his disposal for the construction of his work ? In the first place he has melody or tune, that is, a succession of single notes such as you or I might sing or play upon some such instrument as the flute, clarinet, or trumpet. Secondly, he has harmony, which consists of several notes sounded at once. A single group of such notes is called a chord, and the instruments best suited to music in the harmonic or chordal manner are the organ, the piano, and the harp. Thirdly, there is the element of rhythm, by far the most difficult of the four elements to define. We must make an attempt to do so in some detail later. Lastly, there is the element of tone-colour or tone-quality, which is sometimes called by the French word *timbre*. It is the quality or colour of a certain tone which enables us to tell whether the tone is being produced by trombone, violin, oboe, or other instrument.

The composer is able to mix these tone-qualities very much as a painter mixes his primary colours to obtain more subtle shades. Thus he may write a work for two violins, a viola and a violoncello—a combination that has become extremely popular. We call it a string quartet. He may choose to write for a quintet of wind instruments, consisting, perhaps, of flute, oboe, clarinet, horn, and bassoon. In the orchestra, which is a collection of instruments with widely differing tone-qualities, he has a magnificent opportunity of combining them in a never-ending variety of ways.

Let us think of the elements of melody and rhythm, and first let us find out what rhythm really is. Music, as we have said, is an art *in time* : in fact, it has been well said that its time is its life, and that for every problem of musical thought the question of *when* is inextricably bound up with the question of *how*. It follows then, that we must have a way of measuring time, and this can be done only by dividing it into equal parts, that is, into a series of regular pulses. This is the basis of music's rhythm. Sometimes these pulses are slow, sometimes they are quick. Sometimes they are separated into regular groups of two, three, four, or even five. Sometimes a series of quick pulses will be introduced into a composition the pulses of which have up till then been slow. More often they are fairly regular in the course of any one piece of music, and their speed is known as the *tempo* of the piece.

If the pulses are regularly grouped, the grouping is called the *time* of the composition. Groups of two give us what is known as duple time ; groups of three give us triple time ; of four, quadruple time; of five, quintuple time, and so on. The first of each group is normally stressed, so that with a little practice it is easy to recognise the time of any particular composition. But the notes of our melody and the chords of our harmony need not fall regularly upon the pulses that have been established.

In certain simple forms (or shapes) of composition—in the hymn tune, for example—the melody, harmony, and pulse will coincide in this way. But in more complex forms the melody may run along more quickly than the pulses, say at double the speed, or the harmony may change only every two or three pulses. Furthermore, the melody notes and the changes of harmony need not be regular like the pulses. In a tune like *God Save the King* the notes of the melody generally do coincide with the pulses : in a tune like *Rule, Britannia*, on the other hand, they do not. In modern dance music the pulses will be shown clearly, generally by the drums and piano of the dance band, but the notes of the melody are often artfully designed so as to fall *between* the pulses, and thus give the effect known as syncopation.

RHYTHM : THE PATTERN OF THE TUNE

RHYTHM, then, is the pattern of the tune in relationship to
the underlying regular pulse beat. It is possible to tap
out a rhythm which would not fit into a regular pulse beat,
and it is possible to sing a melody in this rhythm. There is
an enormous range of possibility between such a melody and
such a rhythmically staid composition as a hymn tune. The
tendency of composers up to the seventeenth century was to
avoid a regular rhythm, and a renewal of such a tendency is
apparent in much present-day music. The tendency of the
eighteenth and nineteenth centuries was to submit to a regular
rhythm, and a good deal of the music written in these centuries
seems over-staid and dull to us to-day.

A melody so rhythmically subtle that it cannot be fitted to
the regular pulse beat would be of little use in civilised
musical composition. Occasionally for a short time such a
melody may be used, but in general the sort of melody that
is usable can be fitted into regular or only slightly irregular
bars : that is, into pulse-groups of more or less constant size
in any one composition. To make quite clear the whole
question of pulse and rhythm, one only has to think of music's
sister art, poetry. An excellent example is given by R. O.
Morris in his book on *Contrapuntal Technique*. He takes
the opening lines of Milton's *Paradise Lost :*

> Of Man's first disobedience, and the fruit
> Of that forbidden tree, whose mortal taste
> Brought death into the world, and all our woe,
> Sing, Heavenly Muse . . .

" There is no doubt," he says " as to the metre of this ; it
is the common five-foot iambic metre which is scanned thus :

$$\cup - | \cup - | \cup - | \cup - | \cup -$$

but only a very ignorant person would accentuate the lines in
this manner when reading them :

> Of·Man's | first dis | obe | dience and | the fruit
> Of that | forbid | den tree | whose mor | tal taste,

and so on. That would be the merest sing-song, in which
the metrical accents are falsely emphasised at the expense of
the natural rhythm and stress of the words." This example
serves equally well to illustrate our musical point. Substitute

pulse-groups (bars) for iambic feet and melody for words, and the whole difference between metre and rhythm will become clear.

We have dwelt at some length upon this point, because it is necessary in the first place accurately to define our terms, and also because many otherwise intelligent musicians are hopelessly vague about it. But the above example also serves to illustrate our next point, which is, that the bars or pulse-groups themselves fall into groups in exactly the same way that the metrical feet in poetry fall into groups. In poetry these groups of feet form the lines of the verse, in music they form the musical phrase or sentence. We shall return to this point later, when we are considering the building of a complete melody.

THE BUILDING OF MELODY

MUSICAL historians have often quarrelled as to which came first, melody or rhythm. Our blood flows to a regular pulse ; we tend to walk or to run with regular steps ; our emotions tend to become rhythmic ; we cannot even listen to the tick of a clock without mentally dividing the pulses into groups—*one* two, *one* two, or *one* two three, *one* two three. Is rhythm, then, the most elemental part of music ? Or do the natural inflections of our voices in speech—the falling at the end of a sentence, the rising in a moment of passion—constitute a primitive form of melody ? The point is not, perhaps, of very much importance to us to-day, but it seems clear that melody and rhythm are together the most elemental qualities in music, and that harmony is a later development. Authorities upon the musical development of primitive peoples divide this development into three stages, the Rhythm (or " Drum ") stage, the Melody (or " Pipe ") stage, and the Harmony (or " Lyre ") stage.

Although we have to consider these musical elements separately, they are, of course, so closely related and inter-woven in any one musical composition that they cannot really be studied apart. It is impossible to imagine a rhythmless melody, although the rhythm of any given melody may be extremely free and complex. In the same way, one might form a melody by composing it of the very notes that are already being sounded in an accompanying harmony. We have already defined melody as an ordered succession of single notes. What is the simplest melody that can be imagined ? What, in a word, is the unit of melody ?

KEY-NOTES : THE MELODY REACHES HOME

IF we sing a series of notes forming a simple melody, we find that we tend to linger and to end on one or two special notes rather than on the others. If we play our melody on the piano, using only the white keys, we shall probably find a tendency to end either on C or on A. These notes are " home " : our melody sounds complete and satisfactory when we end on one of them, unfinished and unsatisfactory when we do not. We call this sense of home-coming a key-sense or tonality-sense, and C or A will become the key-note or tonic of our melody. Sometimes, to give a special sense of vagueness or incompleteness, a composer will deliberately write a melody which avoids key-notes and a definite tonality. The word " atonal " (that is, without definite tonality) is sometimes used to describe this sort of music, and there are some composers living to-day who deliberately make it a part of their musical style to avoid definite tonalities in their works.

But by far the greater number of compositions, even of the twentieth century, still cling to some fixed tonality, although they may wander considerably further away from it than earlier ages would have tolerated. Our simplest melody, then, must establish its key, or it will sound vague and incomplete. And the simplest fragment of melody that will do this is the tonic rising to the note above and then falling again to establish the tonality. This little phrase of three notes may be regarded, then, as our unit of melody.

Now this, our first essay in melody-making, raises one or two further points. In the first place, why do we rise instead of fall to our second note ? This is really a question of design, and it may seem rather hair-splitting to raise it in connection with so elementary a melody. But even the simplest tune should have a definite shape, a shape dictated by rules of musical design, and I think it may safely be said that our melody rises in order to achieve, in its small way, a climax. What then is a climax ? It is a point of maximum excitement, or tension or emotional stress. Often it is the highest note in a melody, although sometimes it may be the lowest, notably in the great theme of the last movement of Beethoven's Ninth Symphony.

Our composition as a whole should lead up to and away from its climax, however long and intricate the path to and from this climax may be. As a supreme example, think of Bach's *St. Matthew Passion*—a work of tremendous length—of which the climax is the single overpowering shout of "Barabbas!" Each section or movement of our work should similarly have its climax, and so should each musical sentence, each melody. And why? Simply because our climax, and the working up to and away from it, provides the whole reason and point of our melody, movement, or complete composition.

We want to get somewhere; otherwise, why do we travel? And this "somewhere" in music will be our point of greatest emotional stress. It may be the loudest, the softest, the highest or the lowest part of the work; it may be the most exciting or the least exciting, the quickest or the slowest part. But, as in a good picture, the lines and masses will lead our eye to the one essential that the artist wished to portray, so in music our melodic lines and harmonic masses will lead us to the great moment in our work, the great reason for it all, the climax. And in a tune as simple as the one we have thought of, this climax could only have been suggested by an *upward* movement of the melody.

Mark that word "movement." Once again, music is an art in time, and significance can only be conveyed by forward movement. We must therefore slightly modify our conception of melody as a succession of single notes. It is the *succession* that is the important part of the definition : the sense of direction of movement *between* the notes, the relationships of the notes one to the other, that really give us the shape of our melody. To take a concrete example, let us sing or play a certain note and then a note some way above this. The melodic value of this fragment lies not in the two notes themselves, but in the *sense of rising* from the first to the second.

A parallel case may serve to make this point quite clear. Think of those electric sky-signs in which the words of the advertisement are spelled out by numbers of single lights. In any one letter the various points of light have to be co-ordinated, related to one another in our mind, before we can read the letter. If they were placed so far apart that our mind could not bridge the gaps, we should be unable to say for certain which letter was represented. Similarly, when some modern composers place the notes of their melodies at great distances apart, or in very unexpected places, our mind refuses to bridge the gaps, and we fail to comprehend these notes as melodies.

To return to our original melody. Why do we rise one step above our key-note, and not four or five steps, or more? Simply because such a leap would give us an intensity of climax out of all proportion to the length and importance of our melody. Over-emphasis of any sort will lead to anti-climax and bathos. On the other hand, under-emphasis will lead to dullness and monotony. A rise of one step in our particular melody is enough to give the effect of climax, avoiding equally over-emphasis and dullness.

THE GOOD ARTIST PRACTISES ECONOMY

HERE, then, we have an instance of the great principle of economy which all good artists, whatever their medium, have to respect. To go back for a moment to our very first comparison : in building a house, one would not make it larger than necessary, or higher than is safe, or more orna-mental than is tasteful. In music these words " necessary," " safe " and " tasteful " will apply to the design of our com-position. It will not be longer than is necessary for the proper development of our musical material. It will not be softer, louder, or more strenuous than is necessary for the effect we are trying to give. A perfect composition will not contain a single extraneous or misplaced note.

Finally, in our simple melody, have we established the tonality ? Well, we have begun with our key-note, we have risen to our climax, and we have returned to our key-note. With the limited means at our command it is difficult to see how we could have established our tonality more definitely.

Now, early tunes, although rather longer and more developed than ours, were exactly of the same type. Here, for instance, is part of a tune popular in the Middle Ages. It occurs in a book called *Bassarus, fabula fesivissima*, dated 1553, and Grove's Dictionary tells us that it was very often quoted in books of a similar period, so it is probably of very much earlier date.

Notice the careful way in which the tune clings around its key-note (in this case, D), and also its lack of climax. For, of course, the persistent rising of the tune to E makes this note far too common to give us any particular thrill. An earlier melody, not later than the twelfth century, shows a better sense of climax. It is the Easter hymn *O filii et filiæ*, and it is still sung in most churches to the words " O sons and daughters, let us sing." See the graceful and beautiful curve of the melody from the tonic to the climax and down again to the tonic. Here also is a delightful little tune from Adam de la Hale's pastoral play, *Robin and Marion*, which was first performed in Naples at the court of Charles of Anjou in 1285. But as the author took a number of already well-known tunes for his play, this melody is probably very old indeed. Notice the adventurous little leaps up to the climax note, and the way in which the tune lingers around this note for a moment before descending gracefully down to the tonic again.

O filii et filiae.

Adam de la Hale.

Ro - bins   m ' aime,   Ro - bins   m'a,

Ro-bins   m'a   de - man - dé - e   si m'a - ra.

Our last example is the famous hymn to St. John the Baptist, written about the year 770 by Paulus Diaconus. This is a truly amazing production for the eighth century. The melody (which is quoted in full) rises easily and naturally to its climax on the words " *Famuli tuorum*," remains there for

a while, and slips down again to the tonic in the last line.
Each line of the verse begins upon a note higher by one step
than the first note of the previous line, and so achieves a
wonderful effect of purposeful progression to the climax. It
should be remembered, in reading this example, that music
of this date was not rhythmic in the sense that we have
thought of that word here. The rhythm of the melody is the
rhythm of the words, purely and absolutely. We must not
attempt to cram this free-rhythm melody into a regular
pulse beat. It was composed three hundred years before such
a thing was thought of in music.

Ut   queant   lax - is   Re - son - ar - e   fi - bris

Mi - ra ges - tor - um   Fa - mu - li   tu - orum

Sol - ve   pollu - ti   La - bi - i   re - a - tum

Sanc - te   Io - an - nes.

CONSTRUCTING A MORE COMPLEX MELODY

WE have shown that our original three-note tune satisfies
the principles of climax, economy, and establishment of
tonality. It is a good melody so far as it goes, but obviously
it does not go very far. To be sure, large works have sometimes been based upon melodies nearly as simple as ours.
Think of the first idea of the first movement of Beethoven's
Fifth Symphony. Let us, however, apply our principles to
the construction of a somewhat more substantial melody.
How shall we begin, with the whole range of possible notes
at our command?

It is not so very difficult. Leaving out of the question the experiments of one or two very advanced composers, melody partakes of the nature of song. If a series of notes is easy or is good to sing, then it will probably be a good melodic phrase. George Dyson, in his excellent book *The New Music*, writes as follows : " The more difficult it is to sing a phrase, either actually or imaginatively, the less it partakes of the essential nature of melody, or as some would say, of music. Our ears and our æsthetic reactions are in this matter not instrumentally but vocally attuned . . . We are all singers, whether we know it or not."

So our melody will probably not skip about to notes placed excessively widely apart or in awkward places, for the voice does not tackle such problems very successfully. Melodies proceeding upwards or downwards step by step, melodies containing small leaps, easy to judge, melodies lying within the ordinary compass of a human voice—all these are good to sing and easy to listen to, for they do not demand pro-digious feats of co-ordination from our brain.

Until very recently, in fact, there have been only three particular melodic shapes, although, of course, all three might easily be used in the construction of a single melody. In the first place there is the simple progression upwards or down-wards (or both in turn) by step. The first two lines of the tune usually sung to the hymn *Christians, awake, salute the happy morn*, will provide perhaps the most familiar instance of this sort of melody, and the familiar tune to *Sun of my Soul* is based largely on simple step-wise progressions.

Other examples spring to mind : the beautiful old English melody, *Flowers in the valley*, the first line of the sea-shanty, *Let the Bullgine run*, and the main tune of the last movement of Beethoven's piano Sonata in C, Op. 2, No. 3. Beethoven was, in fact, particularly fond of melodies moving simply by step, and his most famous melody of all, the main tune of the last movement of the *Ninth Symphony*, moves almost entirely by step except for a large downward leap at the climax.

But obviously we must have some leaps in most melodies, for the sake of variety and for the sake of climax. And so we come to our second sort of melody making, which consists in basing the melody on a harmony already sounding. If, for instance, we are sounding the chord G–major, which consists of the notes G, B, and D, our melody may leap easily from one to another of these notes, as they are already firmly fixed in our mind.

Examples of this sort of melody are very numerous. The tune to *We plough the fields and scatter* begins by leaping over the notes of the tonic chord. *Darwall's 148th*, generally sung to *Ye holy Angels bright*, combines both our methods in the first line. It leaps up to its climax over the notes of the tonic chord, then falls step by step to the first note of the second line. William Boyce's fine tune to *Heart of Oak* and the American marching song, *John Brown's Body*, are precisely similar instances. Among the great composers, Brahms best loved this sort of melody making, and he has left us notable examples in the main tunes of both the first and second movements of his Violin Concerto. Other examples may be seen in the tunes of Weber's Sonata in A-flat; Beethoven's Sonatas in F-minor, Op. 2, No. 1 and in C-minor, Op. 10, No. 1; and especially the great *Appassionata*, Op. 57. Two lovely examples by Mozart occur in his Sonatas No. 14 (in C-minor) and No. 17 (in B-flat).

The third sort of melody-making is really an extension of the second method. Our melody becomes more subtle by leaping, not actually to the note we wish to reach, but one degree too far, and then returning to the note we actually wish for. Here, for instance, is a tune as Wagner *might* have written it:

It consists of two downward leaps over the notes of the F-major chord (F, A, and C), followed by a strong leap to the climax and a step-by-step descent. Here is the tune as Wagner actually *did* write it, with the ornamental notes marked thus, * :

Notice the added grace and subtlety of this second version, and the much more modern air given to a somewhat naïve tune by these very simple means. Examples of this sort of melody making could be multiplied almost infinitely from the works of Wagner, Elgar, Strauss, and others. It remains the most modern development in the construction of melodies, if we except the experiments of some very advanced twentieth-century composers.

There remain only two further points to notice. Firstly, that our melody may choose to stand still altogether, that is, it may repeat one note several times before proceeding to the next. Think of Sullivan's tune to *Onward, Christian soldiers*, or the folk-song, *Blow away the morning dew*, or the second half of *God Save the King*. Secondly, although we remain upon one note, we may choose to ornament that note with a little arabesque of added notes, as Weber has done in this well-known tune from *Der Freischütz* :

in which the little shapes marked with an asterisk are embellishments of the notes B and E.

DESIGNS THE ARTIST IN MUSIC MAY CHOOSE

WE have now studied very fully the construction of melodies. But one swallow does not make a summer, and one melody does not suffice for the creation of a musical work. How are we to proceed ? Well, here we begin to feel the necessity for some rules of design or form. " The mere ' thing '—for instance, in music, a theme or a rhythm—is in itself not the sort of material that would satisfy an artist for the creation of a work," says Igor Stravinsky, the distinguished modern composer. " It is obvious that the constituents of such material must come into a reciprocal relation, which, in music, as in all art, is called form."

The rules of design in music are similar in all respects to the rules of design in any other art, and they rest upon four main principles—the principles of repetition, alternation, contrast and balance. These rules apply as strictly to the construction of a complete melody as they do to the construction of a whole movement. They must be followed and obeyed as carefully in the composition of the longest symphony as in that of the shortest hymn-tune. Let us examine them a little more closely.

THE ENDLESS POSSIBILITIES OF VARIATION

SUPPOSING we have written our first melody, and we wish to extend it to form a short piece of music. We can do several things. We can repeat our melody, or part of it. This will make it longer, but rarely, alas, more interesting. In fact, any argument which justifies the good sense of exactly repeating a melody twice will justify the better sense of exactly repeating it two hundred times, in which case our composition will not become a well-designed, well-developed work of art, but merely a sort of aural wall-paper. This is not to say that repetition is never used. On the contrary, indeed, it is one of the major principles of design. But the repetition will rarely be exact. We may use the same notes with a different rhythm, or the same rhythm with different notes. We may begin with the same few notes, then gradually lead our melody into a different shape.

The possibilities are almost endless. Often we can construct a melody by writing responsive phrases, that is, phrases that balance our original tune without actually repeating it. By means of responsive phrases, little repetitions, new phrases in old rhythms, and so on, we can lengthen our original melody very considerably. But a pure and absolute repetition is not often used : indeed, the only composition the writer can remember which consistently makes use of this device throughout is the enormously popular *Bolero* of Maurice Ravel. And in this case the tune is so very long and so very well constructed, that each repetition comes almost with the force of a new melody, especially as the same tone-colour is never used for more than one presentation of the melody.

MAKING THE PATTERN BY ALTERNATION

INSTEAD of repetition, let us try alternation. Here at once is a more immediately fruitful method of development. We write a new melody, and then return to our first idea. We have employed simultaneously three of our principles of design. We have alternation (for we might continue in the same way to proceed to a third and a fourth new melody, so that our complete composition would be in the following form : A (first melody), B (second melody), A, C, A, D . . . etc.) ; we have contrast (for B will be unlike A in style, and C, D, and the rest will contrast with A and B and with each other) ; and we have balance (for we would not alternate say, a melody of four notes with a melody of twenty-four lines).

It is at once obvious that these principles are not applied singly, but work together in the development of our composition. We cannot write even a simple hymn-tune without a knowledge and a conscious application of all four of them. This conscious application in time becomes unconscious or subconscious, and in the case of a born genius like Mozart, it may even be intuitive. But Mozarts are not born every day, and much of our best music has been written by composers who had to learn these principles and how to apply them consciously and sometimes laboriously.

Occasionally we find a piece of music in which the composer's first tune has been extended by devices of repetition, alternation and contrast into a complete movement. Two obvious examples are Wagner's pianoforte piece called *Albumleaf* and Bach's first Prelude from the *48 Preludes and Fugues*. There are no points of rest in these movements. They flow on in one unbroken sweep from beginning to end. The ugly name of *Unary Form* has sometimes been given to such a musical shape, but examples of it are necessarily rare, since it is obviously not a form that would satisfy a composer in the composition of a lengthy work. Even in short works the form must be handled with consummate skill, or the interest of the work will sag owing to the strain imposed upon the listener's mind.

Far more common is two-part form, or *Binary Form*. In this case, Binary is the better word to use, as " two-part " in music generally refers to music written for two voices or two instruments, or for a keyboard instrument imitating two voices or instruments. In Binary form we have first a melody, which may be extended in the manner already described to form a whole section, which generally modulates. That is to say, it leads us gradually away from our tonic (or home) and comes to a halt at a new tonic. This is our point of rest, and the second section of the piece will gradually lead us back to our original tonic, perhaps making use of some of our original melodic material on the return journey.

The tune of the National Anthem is a simple example of Binary form, although it does not modulate : the same tonic is used throughout. Other examples are the seventeenth-century melody, *Barbara Allen*, many of the Bach two-part and three-part Inventions, and the Scarlatti Sonatas. In all these works we have two long sweeps of melody, with a point of rest (called a *cadence*) in between. The first section generally modulates to a new tonic, and the second brings us home again to our first key-note. And there we have the essentials of Binary form.

THE COMPOSER'S "CIRCULAR TOUR"

WE may liken Unary form to a Sunday afternoon stroll. We set out from home and we take our stroll, not with the idea of getting anywhere, but for the pleasure of strolling. We walk on and on, taking a route that will presently bring us home again another way. We have made, as it were, a small circular tour. In the same way, Binary form may be represented by a journey which we make for a particular purpose. We want to get somewhere, and when we have been there, we return by approximately the same road. This "somewhere" is our new tonic, where we rest for a moment before returning home to our first tonic.

There is, however, a third sort of journey, in which we set out for some definite destination, where we make a stay, sight-seeing or transacting business or visiting friends. The purpose of our visit over, we repeat our journey, which this time leads us home. In music this is called Ternary form, and as a particularly happy example of it, let me quote the following lovely little piece by Mozart, written when he was six years of age :

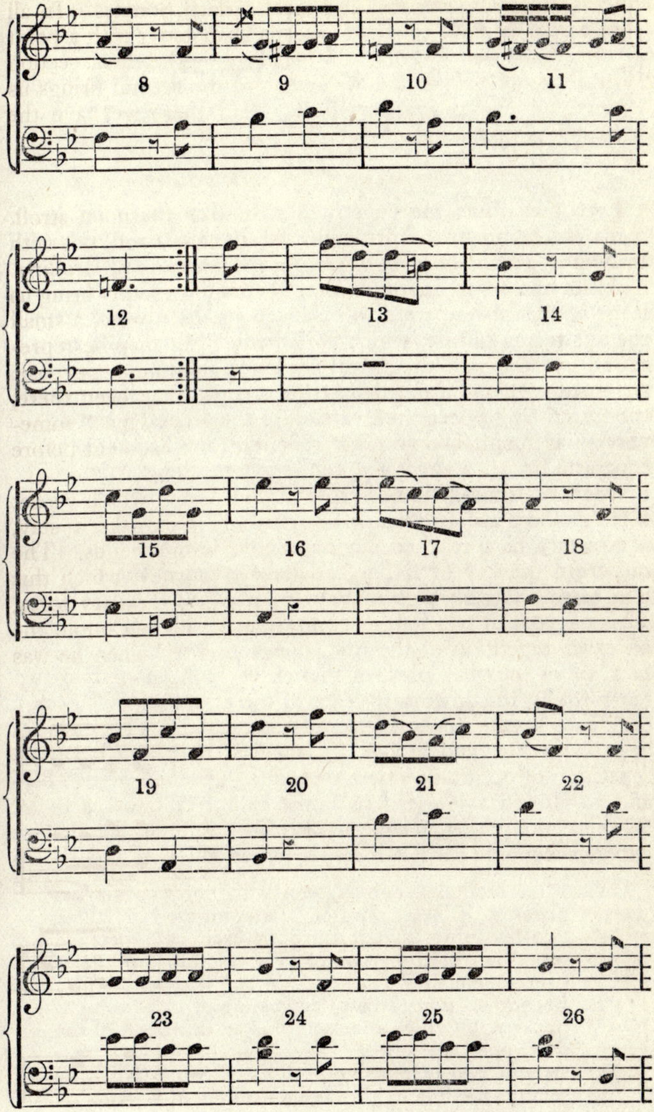
8
9
10
11
12
13
14
15
16
17
18
19
20
21
22
23
24
25
26

Let us examine the construction of this charming movement according to the principles we have already discussed. It begins with a little two-bar phrase, based largely on the notes of the tonic chord, B–flat, D and F. The downward leaps of this phrase are now balanced by the upward steps of the answering phrase, which is immediately repeated so as to round off the whole musical sentence. Now this musical sentence itself is balanced by three two-bar musical phrases, the third being a decorated version of the second. Notice this very subtle contrast : an *exact* repetition in the first sentence contrasted with a *decorated* repetition in the second. This first section is marked to be repeated, but this will not alter the form of the piece as a whole.

Now we have reached our new tonic : we have journeyed out from the key of B–flat and have reached the key of F. The second section, eight bars in length, follows immediately. This consists of two four-bar phrases, of which the second is an exact repetition of the first, one note lower. Notice also how these four-bar phrases themselves consist of two two-bar phrases, the downward leaps of the first being balanced in each case by the upward leaps of the second. This ends our second section, and at bar 20 (the last note) we begin the repetition of our first section, this time shortened by two bars, and so altered as to lead us home to our real tonic, B–flat. Were we attempting an analysis of this work for an examination paper, we should set it out somewhat as follows :

A. First section (12 bars) consisting of two six-bar phrases. These phrases are composed of three two-bar phrases, the third in each case being a repetition of the second. The section modulates from B–flat to F.

B. Second section (8 bars) consisting of two four-bar phrases, of which the second is an imitation of the first, one note lower. Each four-bar phrase consists of two responsive phrases of two bars. The section modulates through C–minor to B–flat.

A. First section repeated, with the omission of the seventh and eighth bars. The last two phrases adapted so as to end in B–flat.

For an even simpler example of Ternary form I have only to quote the traditional Welsh melody, *Ar hyd y nos* (in English, *All through the night*), in which the first section is repeated, as in the example above, and the eighteenth-century English tune, *Drink to me only with thine eyes*, built on an exactly similar plan.

Ternary form may be regarded as the basis of nearly all musical form, and indeed, the principle of saying something, saying something else, and then returning to our first statement, is one that runs through all art. We unconsciously apply it when we place the clock in the middle of the mantelpiece with a pair of vases, one on each side. Many hundreds of musical works—Nocturnes, Romances, Barcarolles, and so on—have been cast in this form, and even to-day composers use it tremendously. It is not possible here to explain the types of musical composition to which these various names apply. A list of them will be found in any text-book on musical form. But although their *character* varies very widely, their form will, as often as not, be found to be that of simple Binary or simple Ternary, and with this brief word we must leave them.

Sometimes, in long works in these forms, the *sections* themselves may be found to be in Binary or Ternary form. To such a development we apply the term compound, and say that the work is in Compound Binary or Compound Ternary form. Now the obvious development from Ternary form, in the direction of lengthening our composition, is to add one more contrasting section, returning as before to our original theme to round off the work. We may represent this form diagrammatically as A–B–A–C–A, and its two most obvious examples are *The Wedding March* and the *War March of the Priests*, both by Mendelssohn. There is nothing else new to notice in the form of these works, except that the Wedding March begins with a few bars of introduction, serving to get us into the mood of the piece, and at the end there is a short final section (called a Coda) which rounds off the whole piece in a satisfying and convincing way.

A Rondo is a very similar sort of composition, except that it is generally gay and lighthearted in style, and the sections are easily remembered, being for the most part quite short. The sections will be contrasted in key and in style, and sometimes more sections than we have considered are added, or our three sections mixed up a little further—like this, for example : A–B–A–C–A–B–A or A–B–C–B–A. A piece in this form is not always called a Rondo, however, and the following are various examples in different styles : Beethoven's *Sonate Pathétique* (Second Movement), Mozart's *Turkish March*, Grieg's *Norwegian Bridal Procession*, Martini's Gavotte called *Les Moutons*.

THE SONATA : A LONGER, DRAMATIC STORY

ALL these forms will do very well for music of a more or less lighthearted character. But for a more extended and dramatic style a rather more complex form is better. We find the very thing in Sonata form, which is really a sort of complex Ternary form, only having two main themes instead of one. A complete Sonata generally contains three or more movements, and the construction of the first of them, generally on the following plan, is the real Sonata form, as the others may be in almost any form. Here is the usual plan, then, of the first movement :—

1. *Introduction*, to get us into the mood of the piece.

2. *First main tune*, perhaps divided up into several sections.

3. *A Bridge Passage.* This is a little piece of music, generally not very important in itself, to modulate to a new key.

4. *Second main tune*, different in style from the first, and often longer. And in a different key.

5. *A Coda* to round off this section of the piece.

6. *The Development*, a section in which our themes are balanced, contrasted, played together, ornamented, and generally well-worked. Perhaps another Bridge passage, to lead us back to

7. *The first tune again*, followed by the Bridge passage, altered this time to lead us to our second tune in the same key as the first.

8. *A Coda*, sometimes recalling the Coda we had after the first section.

You will see how dramatic this form can be. If we regard our two main tunes as hero and heroine, or hero and villain of the piece, the Development will suggest all sorts of possibilities as the two are united, separated, torn to pieces, introduced unexpectedly, and so on. A first movement can be quite surprisingly exciting.

HOW THE SONATA REACHES CRISIS AND CLIMAX

THE second movement is generally slow, and may be in
Binary or Ternary form, or in Sonata form with the
Development left out. The third is often a Minuet and Trio,
that is, a stately dance with a contrasting second section and
a return to the first Minuet, this, of course, in simple or
compound Ternary form. The last movement is nearly always
quick, and may be in Sonata form or Rondo form. For
examples, look at almost any of the Sonatas of the classical
composers, but remember that before Haydn's time the form
had not been systematised, so that early Sonatas by Scarlatti,
Arne, and others are not in the form we have just discussed.

Sometimes a Theme and Variations will be used as one of
the movements of a Sonata: indeed, both Mozart and Beethoven have used this form instead of the more usual Sonata
form in their *first* movements. But such instances are rare.
In the Theme and Variations form we are given first the main
tune, which may be in Binary or Ternary form. Or it may
consist of one melodic shape only, and sometimes only of a
very few notes. This tune is then presented to us in every
conceivable sort of way, and with every conceivable sort of
decoration.

In the works of older masters such as Handel or Couperin,
the Variations were mostly decorated and super-decorated
forms of the tune. Handel's *Harmonious Blacksmith* is an
example of this sort of variation-building. But the later
masters, especially Beethoven and Brahms, treated their
themes with far greater subtlety. Let us examine some of the
ways in which a theme can be varied. It may be played in
another key. It may be played twice as fast (that is, in notes
of half the length) or twice as slow (in notes of double the
length). It may be turned upside-down, in which case all the
runs and leaps of the original tune are retained, but are taken
in the opposite direction. Here is an example of a tune turned
upside down, or inverted :

Inversion.

The tune may be played by the left hand, with a new tune above, or in the right hand with a new tune below. The tune may be left out altogether, and only the *harmony* of it used. Or we may add different harmony to the same tune. Finally, two parts may have the same tune with one of them starting a note or two after the other (as we have in a Round such as *Three Blind Mice*). Not every tune, of course, can be played against itself in this way.

Some sets of Variations are so long and important as works of art that they are not made into just one movement of a Sonata : they stand on their own feet. Beethoven wrote many sets of Variations—some upon such tunes as *God Save the King* and *Rule, Britannia*, others upon his own tunes or those of earlier composers. Brahms and Elgar have written splendid sets for orchestra, and the Russian composer, Prokofieff has a fine Theme and Variations for piano and orchestra as the second movement of his Third Piano Concerto.

We have talked of the ways of treating a tune in connection with Theme and Variations form, because in that form such devices assume very great prominence. But many examples of such treatment could be found in the development section of Sonatas, where the alterations in the tunes will assume a more dramatic aspect, for the Sonata is, as we have said, an eminently dramatic form.

Sonatas are not always piano works. There are many excellent examples for violin and piano, violoncello and piano, and so on. A Sonata for three instruments is called a Trio : one for four instruments is called a Quartet, and there are even Quintets, Sextets, Septets, Octets, and Nonets, generally in Sonata form. A Symphony is a Sonata on the grand scale for full orchestra, and a Concerto is a Sonata for one solo instrument with full orchestra. In the latter case, the first section is generally given twice, the first time by the orchestra, then by the soloist alone. A Sonatina is a sort of smaller brother to the Sonata, and is shorter and more light-hearted. Many works not actually called Sonatas are in Sonata form nevertheless.

THE MANY FORMS AN OVERTURE MAY TAKE

AMONG the orchestral forms we must notice the Overture, which appears in a variety of forms. It may be in Sonata form, or it may be a sort of medley of tunes from an opera or an oratorio. It may be a whole string of shorter pieces, loosely strung together, as is the case with Rossini's *William Tell* Overture. The Symphonic Poem is a musically descriptive piece of work, and its form is dictated by whatever story the composer is seeking to describe. Thus in the *Don Quixote* of Strauss (the great master of the Symphonic Poem) we have, musically represented, the knight's attack on the windmills, the adventure with the sheep, the flight through the air, and many other incidents of Quixote's career. But Strauss generally manages to conform *somehow* to a musical pattern : *Don Quixote* is a set of Variations ; *Till Eulenspiegel* is a Rondo. The Swiss composer Honegger has written *Pacific* 231, a musical picture of an express train, and *Rugby*, a sort of musical scrum !

Choral works, in the same way, generally mould their forms to the literary requirements of the text, and Oratorio, Opera, and the Mass may generally be regarded as a series of pieces rather than one complete piece, as may also the Suite for orchestra or solo instruments.

The Fugue, which may be for orchestra, choir, or keyboard instrument, is a sort of very extended Round. The voices or instruments enter one by one or group by group, and all work at the same melody. If the fugue is for a keyboard instrument, the hands have to employ themselves in playing three, four, or even more separate melodies, and keeping them distinct— often an extremely difficult business. The whole work is based upon its one melody, which appears in all sorts of altered forms—in inversion, in notes of double or of half length, sometimes even played backwards ! A wit once described the Fugue as a composition in which " the voices one by one come in, and the people one by one go out " ! But not all fugues are dull by any means.

Little has been said about harmony or about tone-colour, because shape in music is primarily a melodic and a rhythmic business. An appreciation of form means, in the first place, an ability to " follow the tune," and most people's objection to modern music rests upon the fact that they are unable to follow the tune, or often, indeed, to hear any tune at all ! But, of course, the tune is there all the time, and an attempt to follow it not only means that we are learning to listen intellectually instead of just wallowing in what we like, as though music were a sort of aural hot bath, but also adds tremendously to our enjoyment of the pieces we know, and

II

leads us to discover unsuspected beauty in things which previously we thought were dull, abstruse, or " beyond us."

Composers sometimes break the rules, and blur the edges of their musical shapes, so that it is really difficult to tell what form their work is in. In the same way, a poet or an author will cheerfully break grammatical rules if by doing so he can express what he wants to express with more force and with greater point. You really cannot expect a composer of creative genius to keep rigidly to any particular set of rules, for these rules are meant to help, not to hinder, his musical structure.

He may, for instance, join up all the movements of a Sonata or Symphony so as to form one long, complete, unbroken work. It makes the listener's job harder, but he has his reward. The great library of musical masterpieces awaits him, and it only requires an effort of appreciation, an intellectual approach, intelligent listening instead of careless hearing, for these masterpieces to become in a very intimate way *part of himself*. The whole realm of art is our heritage, and it invites us to accept it for ourselves. But we ourselves must take the first step.

A GUIDE TO THE STUDY OF MUSIC BY BOOKS

From a general standpoint the *Listener's Guide to Music*, by Percy Scholes (Oxford University Press), and *Music and its Appreciation*, by Stewart Macpherson (Joseph Williams), are both excellent. In a rather more technical style, *The Structure of Music*, by R. O. Morris (Oxford University Press), is excellent, and Stewart Macpherson's *Form in Music* (Joseph Williams) has deservedly become a standard work. Of the many other books on Musical Form one must mention H. A. Harding's *Analysis of Form* (Novello) and C. Egerton Lowe's *Form in Pianoforte Music* (Hammond). The construction of the Sonata is especially dealt with in W. H. Hadow's *Sonata Form* (Novello).

THE STORY OF MUSIC

by HERBERT MURRILL, M.A., B.Mus. (Oxon), A.R.A.M.,
Professor of Composition at the Royal Academy of Music.

THE story of music is as long as the story of man himself, but it is no longer. There may have been a time when the earth was silent ; when there was no air to transmit the vibrations which we call sound ; when there was no living creature to make such vibrations and no aural apparatus to receive them. The story of music is not, however, the story of sounds, but—as Dr. P. C. Buck well says—" the story of the conscious effort of man to manipulate them." And so our art begins with the first men who sang a rough sort of shanty to keep them together in some piece of work, or with the first woman to croon her child to sleep.

It is not our purpose here to attempt a complete account of the rise of music from these humble beginnings to its amazing variety of manifestations to-day. The development of Eastern music, so tremendously different from ours ; the slow piecing together of small scraps of evidence to form some coherent account of Greek and Roman music ; the whole fascinating subject of primitive and savage music; all these would require a very much larger book than this for adequate treatment. We must confine ourselves to an account of music in Europe, starting at about the time when it began to take a form in which it would be intelligible to modern ears.

Early music centred, as did every form of art, around the Church. It was melodic, and very free as to rhythm. There were no generally recognised ways of writing it down, and there were—in the modern sense—no composers. By the fourth century there were a number of traditional melodic shapes, and these were handed down orally from generation to generation of singers. Ambrose of Milan in the fourth century, and Gregory the Great in the sixth, did something to systematise these melodic shapes, which became known as Plainsong. Some of Gregory's shapes are still used, and his name survives in the Gregorian chant of the modern Church.

In the tenth century the problem of how to write down the plainsong of the Church was seriously tackled. As an aid to memory, little marks—curiously like shorthand symbols—

had sometimes been made above the words to be sung. These showed whether the melody was to rise or fall, but could not indicate how far up or down it was to go. By ruling a straight line through the marks, three notes were fixed with absolute certainty—the note on the line, and the notes immediately above and immediately below it. Of course, this excellent idea was pushed to extremes. More and more lines were added, until at last as many as ten or eleven were used ! It was extremely difficult to read accurately with such a cumbersome apparatus, and a set of four, five or six lines was generally adopted. But the eleven-line stave still remains, be it noticed, in our pianoforte music, although the middle line (for middle C) is only written when necessary.

Even with this step forward, however, progress was slow and we find ourselves in the twelfth century before any workable method of measuring the *length* of notes is suggested. The very complex system of mensuration which was devised gradually simplified itself, but even so, bar-lines were not introduced until the beginning of the seventeenth century, and our method of grouping notes was adopted only just before the eighteenth. It is difficult for us to realise the amount of careful and patient research which accompanied every step forward in the development of the factors we take for granted to-day.

Now, as to the music itself. Until the eleventh century the basis of all music was, as we have said, the plainsong of the Church. Imagine, then, a crowd of men with mixed voices—some high (tenors) and some low (basses)—singing together. If the plainsong fits the voices of the basses, it will be too low for the tenors. If the tenors can sing it comfortably, it will be too high for the basses. As a compromise, both sang it together at the pitch best suited to their voices. This system of parallel doubling of plainsong is called Organum, and it remained for centuries the only sort of harmonic music generally practised.

In the eleventh century some advance was made by permitting, under certain conditions, one voice part to remain stationary whilst the other moved about more or less freely. The idea that the two parts might be made quite independent as melodies slowly began to take root, and by the end of the century another sort of part-singing had begun to be practised. This consisted simply of the simultaneous singing of several of the Church plainsongs. The effect may be imagined better than described! The examples that have come down to us sound merely ludicrous, but the idea of independence of parts which lay behind the composition of these Motets (as they were called) was a sound and, ultimately, a fruitful one.

Meanwhile, a school of secular music had sprung up in the Troubadours, the Trouvères, the wandering minstrels, and later the Minnesingers and the Mastersingers. These poet-musicians carried the story of music into more gay and adventurous paths than it would have reached in the hands of the Church musicians. The Troubadours (one of whom was our own king, Richard Cœur de Lion) and the Trouvères (the best-known of whom was Adam de la Hale) in France, the Minnesingers and Mastersingers in Germany, carried their music to the courts of the princes. The humbler minstrels sang their songs in the market-places and fairs of the common people.

Not only was their music more gay and acceptable than the grim organum of the Church (and much of it can still be enjoyed to-day, whereas the Church music of the time is unbearable), but also they began to use instruments such as the lute, violin, and pipe to accompany these songs, and their combined influence lasted for hundreds of years. Thus, the Troubadours and Trouvères flourished from about 1087 until the late thirteenth century, the Minnesingers from the twelfth until the thirteenth century, and the Mastersingers from about 1300 until comparatively recent times. Their influence was negligible after 1600 or so, but the last Mastersinger society was not disbanded until 1839 and its last member died in 1876.

THE GRACEFUL WORK OF AN UNKNOWN GENIUS

OF musical progress in England during the twelfth and thirteenth centuries little is known. The wonderful six-part Round, *Sumer is i-cumen in* probably dates from 1240, and it is one of the very earliest works which can still be heard with pleasure to-day. Few works of the next two centuries can rival its grace and formal perfection, and we are forced to the conclusion that it is the composition of an unknown genius, born a century or two before his time. On the Continent, Guillaume de Marchault is the only composer of note, for he produced, in addition to the light-hearted chansons and ballades made popular by the Troubadours, a number of motets and a Mass for the Church.

The only name worthy of mention in the fourteenth century is that of an Englishman, John Dunstable, who directly influenced the first great composer of what is called the Netherlands period—William Dufay. France and England were at this time so busied with every sort of internal strife that the Netherland school of composers took the lead, and might have become much more important than they actually did. But in their hands music became a sort of puzzle, unintelligible to any but professional musicians.

Their energies were directed into every sort of channel but that of pure music : thus it would be their delight to write a composition in which one voice sang a tune, another sang the same tune backwards and a third began in the middle. Sometimes only the one tune was written out, and a riddle was written above, the solution of which told the performers how to construct the composition from this one tune. In a maze of such tricks music lost its way, and it remained for Josquin des Prés to set it once again upon the right road. The excellent work of Josquin and his pupils prepared the way for the greatest period of vocal music—the sixteenth century— and for its greatest master, Palestrina.

Great men generally come at the end of a period, and they sum up in their work all that has been attempted by lesser men preceding them. Thus Palestrina comes at the summit of the vocal period in music, and he sums up in his work the aims of all these earlier composers. His work is contrapuntal, or polyphonic : that is, it is written for a definite number of voices, all of whom have independent and interesting tunes to sing. The harmony resulting from the combination of these tunes is generally very simple, but it is, of course, completely satisfying. The harmonic aspect of Palestrina's work is, however, not the most important part of it. If we listen to a hymn tune, the highest voice will give us the tune itself. The other voices add notes which, of course, fit the tune and provide the harmony for it. But their tunes may not be half as interesting as the main tune, and in many hymn tunes the accompanying parts are very dull indeed.

In Palestrina's music, however, all the parts are interesting; and, what is more, they are rhythmically independent. The great glory of the contrapuntal style is not so much that it combines tunes, but that it combines rhythms. This interplay of contrasted rhythms gives the works of Palestrina and other contrapuntalists a peculiar charm and vitality, and this, combined with a simple harmonic scheme, imbues their work with the serene dignity that is the glory of sixteenth-century music.

The whole of Palestrina's very large output consists of vocal music, and he definitely established Italy in the place of the Netherlands as the musical centre of the world. The Netherlands did, however, produce one master of comparable stature in Orlando di Lasso, who was born in 1520, eight years before Palestrina. Spain gave us Morales and Vittoria, both great masters of the contrapuntal style, and the Dutchman, Sweelinck, born forty years after Palestrina, merits greater recognition than he has so far received for his magnificent choral works and for his organ pieces.

In England there was much musical activity, and Henry VIII himself was an excellent musician. The composers of this time produced works which were scarcely inferior to those of Palestrina himself, although often they were considerably more daring and experimental in their harmony. John Taverner and Christopher Tye were, perhaps, the fathers of the group, and John Merbecke wrote a musical setting of the English service for the new *Booke of Common Praier*. This setting is still sung, as is sometimes the Mass of Tye, based on a tune called *Westron Winde*. But the really great names of the century are those of Byrd and Tallis, the bulk of whose music—especially the versicles and responses of Tallis—is still in constant use. Byrd also produced some of our earliest keyboard music, and both he and Tallis wrote anthems and services for the Catholic and Protestant service alike.

WHEN ENGLAND LED THE WORLD OF MUSIC

IN Elizabeth's reign we come to what has been called the Golden Age of English Music. Never has this country produced in one period so many composers of such brilliance, and there can be no doubt that at this time English music was the finest in the world. Morley wrote music in all the known forms, and also published his famous *Plaine and Easie Introduction to Practicall Musicke* in 1597 ; Weelkes and Wilbye wrote unsurpassed madrigals ; Dowland produced vocal music and delightful pieces for the lute ; the church music of Orlando Gibbons is one of the chief glories of the period, and he also wrote keyboard works in company with John Bull, who, with Peter Phillips, produced some of our earliest organ music. The list might be greatly prolonged, for there are many other names worthy of mention.

There seems to have been a fashion at this time for collections of representative works. In 1601 appeared a magnificent collection of twenty-five madrigals made by the best composers of the day in honour of the Queen, and called *The Triumphes of Oriana*. The idea came from a similar set published some ten years earlier in Venice, and each madrigal ends with the refrain, " Long live fair Oriana." The famous *Fitzwilliam Virginal Book* contains over two hundred and ninety keyboard pieces, mostly by English composers, and is written out by hand : *My Ladye-Nevells Booke* is a collection of forty-two keyboard pieces by Byrd ; *Will Forster's Virginal Book* (1624) has seventy-eight pieces, and *Benjamin Cosyn's Virginal Book* has ninety-eight. The first printed volume of keyboard music was called *Parthenia, or The Maydenhead of the first musicke that euer was printed for the Virginalls, Composed By three famous Masters William Byrd, Dr. John Bull and Orlando Gibbons Gentilmen of his Maties most Illustrious Chappell*, and it appeared in 1611.

Besides keyboard music, composers began to turn their attention to music for the viols, and many sets of madrigals are described upon the title-page as being " apt for voices or viols," which shows that music for these instruments was conceived in exactly the same style as the vocal music of the day. Keyboard music had to be somewhat different, because the instruments of that time had no power of sustaining the notes, which died away as soon as they were played. And so keyboard music, whilst based on the vocal style, and often founded upon a well-known tune, yet came to have a peculiar style of its own—a style which made great use of rapid runs, trills, and grace-notes. Organ music—since the organ can sustain notes indefinitely—was much nearer to vocal music in style.

MUSICIANS TURN FROM SONG TO INSTRUMENTS

THE turn of the century brought a change both in musical style and also in the preferences of its composers. The great age of choral music passed with the sixteenth century, and with the beginning of the seventeenth, composers turned their attention more towards instrumental music, which soon began to show a distinctive style of its own. England still led the world, as she did until the advent of Handel, and produced outstanding masters of the new music as she had done of the old.

Music for lute and for viols came to be much in demand, for the sixteenth and seventeenth centuries had a performer-ideal and not, as we have, a listener-ideal. People preferred to make music for themselves, and the professional performer was almost unknown. What we should call instruction books or tutors were published, the most famous of which were *Musick's Monument* for the lute, and *The Division Violist* for the viols, and composers worked brilliantly to satisfy the demand for instrumental music. John Jenkins, Thomas Tomkins, William Lawes, and Matthew Locke were among the best of these composers, and Locke, together with Henry Lawes and Simon Ives, produced incidental music to pastoral plays and masques. The seventeenth century ended in England with a blaze of fine instrumental composition, but meanwhile another sort of music had begun to be practised in Italy.

This " New Music," as it was called, was nothing less than the beginning of what we now call Opera and Oratorio. The guiding spirits in the movement were Peri, Caccini and Cavaliere, who, with the poet Rinuccini, used to meet at the house of Count Bardi in Florence. It was their aim to re-create in their own style the Greek dramas, which they believed had not been declaimed, but sung to a musical chant. No examples of the Greek chant—if it existed—had survived, and these men resolved to invent the nearest thing to it they could. They called the result *musica parlante*, and its modern counterpart is what is known as recitative. Good recitative preserves the natural rhythm and stress of the words, is scarcely more elaborate than the ordinary inflection of the speaking voice, and is accompanied by simple harmonies.

Early examples of the works of this little band are lost, but Peri's *Euridice*, which was first performed in 1600 as part of the wedding festivities of Henry the Fourth of France and Maria de Medici, has survived, and may thus be taken as the earliest opera. It consisted of much *musica parlante*, a few choruses, and some short passages of instrumental music. The accompaniments were played upon an orchestra of viols, lutes, guitars, and a keyboard instrument called a cembalo. In the same year Cavaliere produced *La Rappresentazione dell, Anima e del Corpo* in the Oratory of Santa Maria in Vallicella at Rome. Except for its sacred character, it was a very similar sort of work to *Euridice* in style, and was accompanied by an orchestra of similar instruments. It is tempting to think that the name Oratorio was given to works of this kind because of the performance of Cavaliere's work in the Oratory of Santa Maria, but actually the name was not applied until some time later.

These early pioneers in the operatic field prepared the way for Claudio Monteverdi, who stands head and shoulders above them as a composer. His opera *Orfeo*, produced only seven years after Peri's *Euridice*, shows a tremendous advance in musical and dramatic feeling. Monteverdi used a much fuller orchestra, which included cornets, trumpets, and trombones, and even small organs, and his effects were much bolder than anything that had yet been attempted.

THE GROWTH OF OPERA IN ITALY

OPERA now became extremely popular in Italy, and it is said that Venice had no fewer than eleven opera houses. The genius of Monteverdi overshadowed the composers who followed, as well as those who preceded him ; but Cavalli, his pupil, and Antonio Cesti carried on the tradition, and twenty-six of Cavalli's operas are still preserved in the library of St. Mark at Venice. Cesti's master, Carissimi, and Carissimi's pupil, Stradella, wrote mainly church music, and both produced magnificent oratorios. In Germany, Heinrich Schütz, who had studied the new music in Venice, introduced opera in his setting of *Dafne*, a German translation of Rinuccini's libretto previously used by Peri.

It was not until 1647 that opera was introduced into France with the production of Peri's *Euridice*, and it found little favour with the French audiences, who preferred more lively works containing a good deal of dancing. Now there was at the court of Louis XIV a young man named Lulli, who had gained great favour by his ability to write the sort of dances the King liked. Louis therefore gave him the sole right to produce opera in France, which he proceeded to do in the most spectacular way. He interspersed the choruses and recitatives with dances, very much to the French taste, and he gave to the music of that country a character and style which are still apparent in the works of its composers.

In England little was known of the new music, and the only sort of dramatic music was that used in the pastoral plays and masques. With the recall of Charles II to this country, however, the influence of the French style came to be felt, for the King had no taste for the austere contrapuntal style, and even introduced viols and a much more lively style of music into the Chapels Royal—to the great scandal of many devout die-hards. Evelyn wrote in his diary for December 1662 :

> " One of his Majesty's chaplains preached, after which, instead of the ancient, grave, and solemn wind musique accompanying the organ, was introduced a concert of twenty-four violins between every pause, after the French fantastical light way, better suiting a tavern or playhouse than a church."

Of course, the composers and organists of the day were unable to produce this new sort of music at the mere order of the King, and he sent a very talented chorister, Pelham Humphrey, to France in order to study the French style. Upon Humphrey's return he became the leader of the new school of composers, although he himself only lived to the age of twenty-seven. John Blow (twice organist of Westminster Abbey) and Michael Wise produced some very fine work in the new manner, but their fame is overshadowed by that of Henry Purcell, whom some regard as England's greatest composer.

THE YOUTHFUL WRITER OF "THE PERFECT ENGLISH OPERA "

PURCELL'S life was a short one—he lived only thirty-seven years—but he managed to produce an amazing amount of music in that time, in every sort of form then known. John Blow thought so highly of his pupil that he resigned the organistship of the Abbey in Purcell's favour, taking it again after Purcell's death in 1695. As Organist of the Chapel Royal and Composer to the King, Purcell had to write Coronation Odes, Birthday Odes, and music of a like character. Apart from these works he produced a great deal of church music, as well as songs, sonatas for strings, keyboard works, and cantatas. He is at his greatest, however, in his stage works. Although he only wrote one opera—the exquisite *Dido and Æneas*, which has been called " the perfect English opera "—he produced incidental music for over forty plays, most of which is of the very highest order. His orchestra consisted of strings, with the occasional addition of oboes, cornets, trumpets, and drums.

Although Purcell's style is eminently English, he studied

and assimilated the current French and Italian idioms. Thus
he writes in his preface to *Dioclesian* (1691) :—

> " Whereas Painting and Poetry have arriv'd to
> their perfection in our own Country, Musick is yet
> but in its Nonage, a Forward Child which gives hopes
> of what it may be hereafter in ENGLAND, when the
> Masters of it shall find more encouragement. 'Tis
> now learning ITALIAN, which is its best Master, and
> studying a little of the French air, in order to give it
> somewhat more of Gaiety and Fashion."

Since Purcell, England has had no native composer of the
first rank until comparatively modern times. It is generally
said that the advent of Handel, fifteen years after Purcell's
death, effectively strangled our own composers' utterances ;
but it must be remembered that the story of English music
up to Purcell is an especially glorious one. For the four centuries after the year 1000 we had led the musical world, and from
1400 to about 1700 we have a splendid record of contrapuntal
and early instrumental music. The Netherlanders were
supreme for only two centuries, and Italy for a shorter period.
Germany's mastery lasted similarly for two centuries only,
although we are apt to exaggerate the importance of this period,
since all the works we are accustomed to call " classics " were
written in the eighteenth or nineteenth centuries. It was surely
time, at the beginning of the eighteenth century, for English
music to take a rest. The pity is that it rested so long !

THE SCHOOL THAT WAS FOUNDED BY SCARLATTI

To return to Italy. In the latter half of the seventeenth
century the great Neapolitan school of composers arose,
headed by Alessandro Scarlatti. As a school it is famous for
its developments in the field of vocal music, and Scarlatti—
although he wrote a good deal of church music—is remembered
chiefly for his operas. Of these he wrote over one hundred,
carrying the earlier operatic tradition to a higher standard of
technical brilliance. They were generally preceded by an
instrumental overture in three or four movements, and this
ultimately developed into the modern Symphony.

In the field of instrumental music Italy produced Domenico
Scarlatti, son of Alessandro. Like his father, he wrote
operas, but he is remembered to-day for his harpsichord
music. Corelli was the first composer to write for the new

type of violin which at the time was beginning to be made in the workshops of Amati and Stradivarius. The greater brilliance of tone and the technical advantages of the new instrument as compared with the old viols soon began to capture the imagination of composers and performers alike, and Vivaldi, Locatelli, Tartini, and others followed Corelli in the formation of the great school of Italian violin masters. In the field of organ music the names of Buxtehude, Fresco-baldi, Froberger, and Sweelinck are still remembered, and in France the harpsichord music of Couperin and Rameau—the first great French master—remains as the great contri-bution of that country to the music of the early eighteenth century.

THE RELATIVE CLAIMS OF HANDEL AND BACH

IT has become the custom to think and to speak of Bach and Handel in the same breath, but, as a matter of fact they have very little in common save the date of their birth—1685. In the story of music, Bach's name stands very high, but Handel must be content with a lower place. For Handel remains in and of the eighteenth century, summing up the latest developments in opera, oratorio, and instrumental music. But Bach looks forward to the present day, and his influence on modern composers has been incalculable. In his splendid little book on musical history Dr. P. C. Buck says of Handel :—

> " That he was a Colossus will be denied by no one who has ears to hear, though for 150 years he strangled English music. But no denial of his claims to great-ness is involved in expressing a doubt as to his im-portance in the evolution of any branch of music save oratorio."

In his operas Handel followed the Italian style, but added a breadth and a geniality all his own. They were immensely popular in their day, and many arias taken from them are still sung. His church music is splendid in a very massive, solid way, and his instrumental works—based again upon the Italian model of Corelli—are replete with full-blooded vigour. But his oratorios stand entirely in a class of their own. His treatment of voices and instruments in the mass is superb, and the success of the *Messiah* in 1742 has been continued until this very day. Its element of religious heartiness has been sought in every subsequent oratorio, and critics and public alike have frowned upon any composer who has dared to produce a work in a more penitential or humble style. The frigid reception given, for example, to Stravinsky's Psalm-Symphony (1931) in this country is partly due to the ideal of the *Messiah* which most of us still carry in the back of our minds.

But a knowledge of the music of Bach adds to our appreciation of the moderns, for in many ways he foreshadowed them. He is generally regarded as the greatest of the contrapuntalists, but his true place is midway between them and the harmonic composers. He is not a true contrapuntalist, because in his works the harmony is the important feature, which was never the case with the earlier writers. His work *is* contrapuntal because he had a marvellous gift for writing interesting and often intricate melodies in all his voices. But these melodies are not rhythmically free in the manner of the true contrapuntalists, and when—as sometimes happens— Bach has to choose between writing a good melody in one voice which leaves the harmony bare and uninteresting, or writing a full and interesting harmony which makes the vocal melody awkward and distorted, he always decides in favour of the full harmony and leaves the melody to look after itself. And often he writes a piece—such as the first Prelude of the *Forty-eight Preludes and Fugues*—which is purely harmonic throughout.

In his three great appointments—as musician to the Duke of Weimar, chapel-master to Prince Leopold of Anhalt-Cöthen, and cantor of St. Thomas's School, Leipzig (where he had to arrange the music of the churches of St. Thomas and St. Nicholas)—Bach explored every single musical field with the single exception of opera. At Weimar he produced incomparable organ works, at Cöthen he wrote mainly orchestral and chamber music, and at Leipzig he devoted himself largely to the composition of church music. He produced no fewer than two hundred and ninety-five cantatas, the great Mass in B–minor, and four settings of the story of the Passion, of which two have remained. The *St. Matthew Passion*, a tremendous work, is regarded by many as music's greatest masterpiece.

A CHILD OF BACH WHO FRAMED THE SONATA

OF Bach's many children perhaps Carl Philipp Emanuel is the most important in music's story, for in his concertos, symphonies, and sonatas he laid the foundation of Sonata Form upon which Haydn, Mozart, and Beethoven were to build. In style his music sometimes resembles that of Beethoven to a surprising degree, but his fame as a composer is overshadowed by that of his great father and of the three musical giants who were so soon to follow him.

Haydn, Mozart, Beethoven, and Schubert form what is known as the Viennese School. In the hands of Haydn, the Sonata began to take the shape which now we associate with that form, and in his hundred and fifty symphonies, seventy-seven string quartets, thirty-one concertos, and thirty-five sonatas he combined a delicacy, a grace, and a genial sense of humour that won for him the affectionate nickname of " Papa Haydn."

Mozart, born twenty-four years later (in 1756) based his musical style upon a study of C. P. E. Bach and Haydn. He was a born composer, producing perfect little works at the age of six, and a complete opera at the age of twelve. He and Haydn worked together in the development of Sonata Form, although Mozart added his own especial gift for graceful melody, and also enlarged the size of his orchestra. His immense output was conceived very largely in Sonata Form, and he brought particular glory to the Concerto, and especially to the piano Concerto. Both he and Haydn wrote church music and operas, but whereas we remember the church music of Haydn (particularly *The Creation* and *The Seasons*), that of Mozart is nearly all forgotten, and we enjoy instead *Figaro, Don Giovanni, Cosi fan tutte,* and the *Magic Flute.*

BEETHOVEN INTRODUCES THE DRAMATIC ELEMENT

WE have now travelled far from the true contrapuntal style of Palestrina and the harmonic-contrapuntal style of Bach. We might sum things up by saying that now we have Melody instead of melodies. The harmony is added as an accompaniment to the principal melody, and does not result from the individual movement of various under-melodies. In a composition for voices, the underneath parts are definitely less interesting than the main tune on top, or—if the main tune happens to be at the bottom or in the middle—the top parts will be less arresting than the one part the composer wishes to emphasise. From the eighteenth century to the beginning of the twentieth the important element in music was that of harmony.

But with Beethoven, a new element is introduced—a *dramatic* element. Music is dictated, not by the formal development of the material only, but by the illustrating of some external idea, some state of mind, some definite event. Of the first class we have examples in Beethoven's *Pastoral Symphony*, where movements are headed *By the Brook*, *The Storm*, *Peasants' Merry-making* : of the second class the *Pathetic* and the *Appassionata* Sonatas are instances : the third class might be illustrated by the *Battle of Vittoria*.

Now the Sonata provides an admirable form for such dramatic conceptions. Its two subjects form an example of contrast that, exaggerated, might easily portray strife or emotional conflict. Beethoven found in the sonata exactly the form best suited to his dramatic conceptions, and by far the greater number of his works are in this form—sometimes used upon a gigantic scale, as in the Ninth Symphony.

"CLASSICAL" AND "ROMANTIC" IN MUSIC

BEETHOVEN died in 1827, shaking his fists in fury at a violent thunderstorm — a fitting end for a dramatic musician. With him began what is called the Romantic period in music, which lasted until immediately before the World War. Many definitions of the words " Romantic " and " Classical " have been given, but I think it safe to say that a work in which the development follows as a natural result of the extension of the musical ideas it contains could be called a Classical work. A work, on the other hand, in which the development is suggested by any non-musical, literary, or dramatic argument is a Romantic work.

It is strange to relate that Beethoven produced only one opera,[1] although it is safe to assume that he would have written others had he been able to find a story which pleased him. His especial contributions to our story are, then : the extension of Sonata form into a dramatic means of expression (which meant, of course, the blurring of the clear edges of the form, since the development of any one work was dictated by non-musical reasons, which might or might not be satisfied by a rigid adherence to the set form) ; an enlargement of the orchestra to something like its present size, and the intro-

[1] *Fidelio.*

duction into it of new instruments such as trombones[1]; the addition of a new element into music, best described as a *dramatic* element.

GLUCK COMES TO THE RESCUE OF OPERA

IT was Gluck who, in the latter half of the eighteenth century, rescued opera from the dreadful state in which he found it. In France and Italy it had degenerated into a mere means of showing off the voices of the great singers of the time, and musically it was of little account. The production of *Orfeo* in 1762, in the composer's forty-second year, and *Alceste* five years later showed that Gluck had a higher conception of the composer's function in opera, for he wrote the sort of music he imagined would best suit the story, without caring very much whether it showed off the singers' voices or not. He aroused, of course, a good deal of opposition, which came to a head in Paris in 1779. To settle the question once and for all, Gluck and Piccini—a representative composer of the more popular school—set the same opera, *Iphigénie en Tauride*. Gluck's setting was acknowledged to be infinitely the finer, and so the battle was won.

The composers who followed Gluck's lead are not in themselves of great importance in the story of music, but the principle for which he fought is supremely important, as—for one thing—it greatly influenced Mozart, who visited Paris at the height of the battle.

The operas of Schubert, the second of our great Romantics, are now forgotten, and formally he accepted the Sonata as Haydn and Mozart left it. The *Unfinished Symphony* and the tremendous C–major Symphony do not develop the form to any extent. We remember him for his songs, of which he has left over six hundred. He developed the song form into a marvellously expressive and often dramatic commentary upon the poem set, using his great harmonic sense to bring out every shade of meaning in it. Schubert's Church music is not often performed now, and indeed, the Church music of this period is rarely of the first order. Cherubini carried on the contrapuntal tradition of the sixteenth century, and he is important for his Church music, his operas, and his string quartets.

---

[1] The trombone had, of course, been known and used for very many years, but was not introduced into the Symphony Orchestra until Beethoven used it in the finale of his C–minor Symphony.

MENDELSSOHN : A MASTER WHOSE VIRTUE WAS ELEGANCE

AND so we come to the nineteenth century, and our first important name is that of Mendelssohn. As a penalty for unprecedented success during his life, he has had to suffer contumely and neglect in recent years. The chief quality of his work is elegance, and elegance is a quality not very highly prized to-day. To music he gave a delicacy and poetic feeling which we ought to value more highly than some of the very oppressive greatness of the accepted masters. The " grand manner " in any art can verge dangerously on pomposity, and Mendelssohn reminds us that a water-colour can be as perfect and finished a work of art as a six-foot oil painting.

Weber in his orchestral works and Schumann in his pianoforte compositions and songs carry on the Romantic tradition. " There never was a composer who in his music was influenced by literature, and by ideas derived from literature, to a greater extent than was Schumann," says Herbert Bedford in his book upon the composer. On the other hand, Chopin—the most Romantic of the Romantics—did not attempt definite illustration or description in his music. His pianoforte compositions—and he wrote almost entirely for the piano— are mood-pictures, musical states of mind. In this sense, and in his use of harmony and his style of writing for the piano, he is the musical father of the twentieth-century keyboard masters, notably Debussy and Ravel.

THE ARRIVAL OF "STORY-TELLING" MUSIC

WITH Liszt and Berlioz we enter the period of programme-music, that is, of music which definitely *does* set out to tell a story or to illustrate a situation. They did not invent the idea : descriptive music dates at least from the sixteenth century, when an old composer named Jannequin wrote *Le Chant des oiseaux* imitating the songs of various birds, *La Guerre*, the first of the " battle-pieces," and *La Chasse*, a musical hunting-print. From Jannequin and Byrd to Strauss and Honegger, composers have flirted to a more or a less serious degree with purely descriptive music, and the test of such music is—does it satisfy us as music without a knowledge of the story behind it ? Sometimes it does, and is therefore good music ; often it does not, and then—however well-written or clever it may be—it remains a trick, an illusion, a pun : anything but music.

Berlioz in his *King Lear*, *Romeo and Juliet*, and *Harold in Italy*, Liszt in his *Faust Symphony*, *Dante Symphony*, and *Hamlet*, have written fine music, generally unsatisfying formally because of its literary rather than its musical impulse. Both, however, in their use of the orchestra, and Liszt in his use of the piano, have left models which have had the greatest possible influence on later composers. Their Symphonic Poems (the very apt title invented by Liszt himself) lead directly on to those of Richard Strauss, whom we shall discuss later.

WEBER : GERMANY'S FIRST GREAT WRITER OF OPERA

WE have referred to Weber's orchestral works, but his great position in our story is that of Germany's first great opera composer. In *Der Freischütz* and *Euryanthe* he tries to portray in his music whatever character happens to be singing at the time. In this, and in the use of various combinations of instruments to suggest various moods or situations, he directly influenced Wagner, the greatest of the German operatic writers and an acknowledged musical father of many modern composers. The influence of Weber and of Beethoven, for whom he had an intense admiration, may easily be traced in much of Wagner's work, and in his early operas there are some traces of the Italian style.

But as he grows older, Wagner gradually throws off the old operatic conventions, and forges for himself an operatic style upon which the greater number of modern operas have been based. He strove above all for unity in the various arts which go to make up opera, and himself wrote the poems for his works. He abolished the division of the acts into set solos, duets and choruses, and by writing sets of themes for the characters, situations and even the material objects of his story (such as the sword and the anvil in *The Ring*), he manages to weave a gigantic, continuous web of melodies, lasting unbroken for a complete scene or act.

This new sort of theme-development, his extraordinary richness of harmony, his skilful use of a very large orchestra : these, together with his new conception of opera as *music-drama*, form the reasons for his important position in the story of music. His own music is very great in its own way, but in its effect upon succeeding composers it becomes most vitally important. Neither the man nor his music can ever

be ignored, for with him the whole period of modern music
may be said to begin.

THE WIT AND LIGHT-HEARTEDNESS OF ROSSINI

MEANWHILE in Italy, the operatic school had produced two
composers of note, Rossini and Verdi. Rossini's career
was a series of triumphs—musically and financially—so that
this fat, lazy, incredibly facile composer was able to live the
last thirty years of his life in retirement. His fifty operas are
the antithesis of Wagner's in style, for instead of the " grand
manner " he brought wit and a sort of cheeky light-heartedness
into music. He had an amazing gift for vocal melody, as
had also his immediate successors, Donizetti and Bellini.
William Tell and the *Barber of Seville* of Rossini, the *Daughter
of the Regiment* of Donizetti and *La Sonnambula* of Bellini
are full of the jolly, artless tunes that form the chief contribution of this group to the story of music.

Verdi as a composer stands head and shoulders above any
Italian musician of the day. In his management of every
operatic problem he shows consummate mastery, but formally
he follows the general Italian model in his early operas
(including *Il Trovatore*, *La Traviata*, and *Aida*). *Otello* and
Falstaff, produced in the composer's seventy-fourth and
eightieth years, have been called " masterpieces of expressive
force and technical skill," and reveal an amazing melodic
sense and a great orchestral mastery. They also show some
Wagnerian influence.

The French opera composers are less important, although
no less a person than Wagner praised the work of Auber.
Gounod is remembered chiefly by *Faust,* and Bizet by *Carmen.*
Saint-Saëns brought a gift for exquisite workmanship into his
music, and his *Samson and Delilah* and the five piano concertos
are perfect works in a somewhat facile manner. In England,
Sullivan (in brilliant collaboration with W. S. Gilbert)
perfected his own sort of opera, and his music still enjoys a
well-deserved popularity.

Brahms, like Handel, is a composer who sums up what has
gone before. We feel that, whereas some masters founded a
particular school of composers, others appear as the final,
comprehensive product of a particular period. Thus Brahms
is said to sum up Bach in his counterpoint, Beethoven in his
construction, and Schumann in his romantic feeling. Broadly
speaking, this is true enough. But he has never been sufficiently

praised for his truly wonderful subtlety of rhythm, which in its freedom recalls the great age of contrapuntal music and also looks forward to the rhythmic experimenters of the twentieth century. He freed German music from a certain " four-square " feeling which it had often showed, and herein lies his greatest contribution to our story.

Richard Strauss, the master of the Symphonic Poem, is important as a technical rather than a musical innovator. His musical resources are the logical outcome of the nineteenth century, but in his degree of realism (that is, actual *imitation* of natural sounds), in his power of development, and most of all in his simply amazing orchestral mastery, he is quite unsurpassed. Since Strauss, no composer has dared to orchestrate badly.

THE BRITISH COMPOSER WINS A PLACE

IN the last few years of the nineteenth century England began to shake off the influence of Handel and Mendels-sohn, and, under the guidance of such men as Stanford and Parry, produced—somewhat shakily at first—music which owed nothing to German influence. Elgar is the great representative of this phase of English music, and Delius is responsible for the development of a certain sort of highly-developed harmony and a very personal method of orches-tration. Elgar, in his orchestral technique, is a worthy rival to Strauss, and he has been called " the most *English* composer who ever lived."

Now Elgar never uses folk-tunes, or imitation folk-tunes in his work. Its own special style is so different from that of any foreign composer's music that we have to call it " English " for lack of a better word. But there are composers who do achieve a nationalist feeling in their music by deliberately borrowing or imitating the folk-music of their own country. The movement began with Glinka, then The Five (Balakirev, Cui, Borodin, Rimsky-Korsakov and Moussorgsky) in Russia, Grieg in Norway, Smetana in Bohemia, Dvořák in Bohemia and in America ; and it dates from the second half of the nineteenth century.

In the twentieth century the movement continues, and has included many of the chief figures in contemporary music. The movement has now practically died out—for two reasons : in the first place the folk-song tendency became mannered and " arty " and incapable of further development, and in the second place most of the composers who used folk-song soon found their own style (which sometimes owed a great deal to the folk-music they had studied, sometimes was completely different in manner), and so they proceeded to write in a personal instead of in a national style. Thus, Béla Bartók in Hungary, Hans Pfitzner in Germany, Manuel de Falla in Spain, Pizzetti and Malipiero in Italy, Gustav Holst and Vaughan Williams in England all found their own personal language in music through the folk-song of their own country.

THE VIOLENCE AND COMPLEXITY OF STRAVINSKY'S MUSIC

STRAVINSKY, the most important figure in the music of this century, started as a Romantic nationalist composer, in the direct line of The Five, but in a rather móre primitive and barbaric manner. His unbelievable orchestral powers, his increasing complexity of harmony, and his violent and irregular rhythms led him, in 1913, to the composition of *Le Sacre du Printemps*, which may be regarded as illustrating the limit of complexity possible with music' built upon a traditional basis. The element of rhythm is the most important element in this and in all Stravinsky's early works. The simple melodies (often mere patterns of four or five notes), the blocks of harmony, the sharply-contrasted orchestral colours, all serve to add force and point to the interplay of rhythm which is the ultimate basis of the work.

The development of rhythm to its highest possible point of complexity in the early works of Stravinsky is balanced by similar developments in counterpoint and in harmony mainly due to the work of Schönberg and Debussy. Schönberg begins with a Wagnerian harmonic vocabulary, which he extends to include almost any combination of notes. Debussy does not innovate in the harmonic field, but uses the harmony of his predecessors in an entirely novel and personal manner.

He has been called an Impressionist composer, and this label fits him well enough if we remember Pater's definition of Impressionism as " a vivid personal impression of a fugitive effect." His musical vocabulary consisted of that of his predecessors, enlarged by a study of Wagner and of The Five, influenced by the pianoforte style of Chopin, enlarged by a knowledge of Javanese and Chinese music and the old Gregorian music of the Church. This bewildering mass of influences he moulded into a personal style by his impeccable taste, a very sensitive ear, and a mastery of instrumental technique.

His use of music to suggest " abstract mental images induced by a thought, an emotion, a perfume, a colour, a poem, a scene, any definite object, suppressing unnecessary detail, and reproducing not the reality but the *emotion* evoked by the reality " led to an entirely new use of harmony. Thus Debussy uses chords for their own sake, and not merely as units in a harmonic scheme. His harmony remains, of course, a succession of chords, but now it is not the *succession* that is the important part of the business, but each separate chord in itself.

TWO PATHS FOR THE FUTURE

BY 1913, then, music had reached the limit of harmonic, rhythmic, and contrapuntal complexity possible under the present system. There were only two possible paths for the future. Either a new system must be found, or else the older systems must be used in a new way. In spite of the experiments of composers along both these paths, the problem remains to-day, and future generations of composers must either invent new systems or view the old from a different standpoint.

Schönberg and his followers—among whom we must mention Alban Berg and Anton von Webern—have actually invented a new system, which has to be understood before we can listen to their music with any sort of critical appreciation. Most of us have neither the time nor the inclination for such a task, and it is a moot point whether future generations of listeners will care to master music made in two (or even more) different systems. Other composers extend the old systems by the use of quarter-tones, the simultaneous use of two or more key-centres, or the complete abolition of tonality. With them we have more sympathy, for it is easier for us to follow music which keeps one foot, at least, upon a traditional basis.

But by far the greater number of post-war composers model their music upon the music of the past, contrasting and mixing their styles as a painter contrasts and mixes his colours. Thus Poulenc in France may use, in one movement of a work, the eighteenth-century style, tunes reminiscent of Mozart, a touch of Victorian sentimentality, and a modern harmonic vocabulary. Superficial critics call this the " scrapbook " method of composition, but music must be judged by its sound, and if such a work sounds coherent and aesthetically satisfying, who will condemn it ?

We have thus reached a classical (or, as some say, a neo-classical) period in music. The constructive side of our work is the more important side : we do not say now, " What has he done ? " but " How has he done it ? " and if he has done it well, we do not grumble when we recognise here a touch of Mozart, there a hint of Scarlatti, somewhere else a flavour of Mendelssohn. Thus Stravinsky in his later works recalls sometimes Bach and Handel, sometimes Glinka and Tchaikovsky, sometimes even Liszt and Chopin. In these days a composer trusts to the strength of his own individuality, which should make his works—whatever their style—personal to himself, and to himself alone.

Stravinsky may be said to head the modern classical school, and most modern composers, in their post-war productions, can be said to belong to this school. Bartók, Ravel, Casella, Falla, Hindemith, Prokofieff, Vaughan Williams, and even Sibelius are more classical than romantic in their latest works, although the Romantic tradition still persists in such composers as Delius, Bax, and even in Schönberg.

MUSIC FOR SOME AND MUSIC FOR ALL

THE intense complication of much modern music—particularly that of the first fifteen years of this century—made it quite impossible for any but a very highly-trained musician to appreciate. The Schönberg school in Germany was so far removed in style from any music that the ordinary listener was acquainted with, that a new school of composers arose, whose object was to write music that the ordinary listener could appreciate. They called this new music *Gebrauchs-musik*, or music for everybody, to distinguish it from the *Luxusmusik*, or music for the highly-trained few. It was not an attempt to " write down " to the public, but an attempt to use all the devices and the freedom of modern musical style in the creation of an art that should appeal to the listener with little or no technical knowledge.

The problem was most acute in Germany, and so the names of the composers of Gebrauchsmusik will mostly be German names. Hans Eisler writes music for workmen's choirs, Kurt Weill produced the *Lindberghflug*, a sort of oratorio based upon Lindbergh's flight across the Atlantic ; Ernst

THE BRITISH COMPOSER WINS A PLACE 345

Krenek wrote the jazz opera, *Jonny spielt auf*, and Hindemith
has composed instrumental and keyboard works so simple
that amateurs can play them, music for films, and even
waltzes for the mechanical piano.

The use of jazz is not confined to the creation of a popular
style of music. Most composers have flirted with the dance
music of their time, from the seventeenth century onwards,
and modern composers have been attracted in turn by nineteenth-century dance music, ragtime, and jazz. William
Walton, the most promising of the English composers, has
delicately burlesqued the Victorian waltz and polka in *Façade*;
Constant Lambert has used jazz rhythms in his *Rio Grande* and
in his Sonata and Concerto for piano; Stravinsky produced a
Ragtime and *Piano-Rag-music*, and has used jazz rhythms in
many of his works; Milhaud used a sort of mixture of Bach
and jazz in his ballet *Le Création du Monde* ; Ravel wrote a
foxtrot called *Five o'clock* ; and even Debussy produced a
Golliwog's Cakewalk. Schulhoff and Wiener write jazz pieces
also, and Tansman has produced a complete jazz sonata, called
Sonatine Transatlantique.

In my own jazz opera, *Man in Cage*, produced in London
in 1930, I found that it is almost impossible to work in
large movements in the jazz style. Its melodies are short-
winded, its very restricted rhythmic conventions are apt to
grow wearisome, and its characteristic harmony tends to pall.
Long works in jazz idiom almost always tend to fall into
separate movements, as a rhythm based on the blues, foxtrot,
or charleston can be endured only for about the length of a
ten-inch record. After that, one can only make an abrupt
change to a new rhythm, which in turn becomes tiring in a
few minutes.

JAZZ AN INGREDIENT BUT NOT A STYLE

THUS the long works written in jazz style tend to be scrappy
and unsatisfactory from a formal point of view. Gershwin,
who has written some fine music in his *Rhapsody in Blue*, in
the *American in Paris*, and in his piano Concerto, fails to
combine his ideas into one convincing whole, and never
quite knows when to stop. The same defect is found in
Lambert's *Rio Grande* and in the works of Louis Gruenberg,
the American. It seems clear that jazz is useful as an in-
gredient but not as a style in itself. Its contribution to
" serious " music will probably be in the first place an added

346 THE STORY OF MUSIC

vitality of rhythm, and in the second an improved standard of instrumental technique. The standard of trumpet and clarinet-playing, for example, in the best jazz bands is far higher than that in most symphony orchestras, and in the future the members of symphony orchestras will have to raise their standards of performance, and also learn the new technique of playing that the performance of works in the jazz style will demand.

We have stated the problem that awaits the composers of the future. Since no further advance in violence of rhythm, discordance of sonority, or angularity of melodic line can now be made, the music of the future will probably consist of a new working-out of traditional material. It seems likely that, as life itself becomes faster and more complex, music will become clearer and more simple. And few of us, we imagine, would have it otherwise.

BOOKS WHICH TELL THE HISTORY OF MUSIC

PRIDE of place must be given to Dr. Percy Buck's wonderful little book, *A History of Music*, which, in less than eighty small pages, gives a complete bird's-eye view of music, working back from to-day to the infancy of music, and avoiding as far as possible a mass of biographical details and names. Music in this country is fully dealt with in *English Music*, by W. H. Hadow (Longmans) and *A History of Music in England*, by Ernest Walker (Oxford University Press). Parry's *Summary of Musical History* (Novello) and *An Outline of Musical History*, by T. J. Hewitt and Ralph Hill (Hogarth Press, 2 volumes), are comprehensive and complete, but do not deal with modern music. W. H. Hadow's *Music: Earlier Times—1925* (Home University Library, Thornton Butterworth Limited), deals fully with the great musical classics and carries the survey almost to the threshold of the modern period.

For an introduction to modern music, read *This Modern Stuff* (Denis Archer), a racy and amusing little volume by Gerald Abraham, and continue with George Dyson's *The New Music* (Oxford University Press). The same author's *Progress of Music* (Oxford University Press) and Percy Buck's *The Scope of Music* (Oxford University Press) are valuable and informative, and Marion Bauer, in her *Twentieth Century Music* (Putnam), prefaces the modern part of her book with a review of the development of music from the ninth century. *How Music Grew* and *Music Through the Ages* (both by Marion Bauer and Ethel Peyser, published by Putnam) are excellent histories, as is also *The Growth of Music* (Oxford University Press, 3 volumes), by H. C. Colles.

For those with longer pockets, the *Columbia History of Music, Through Eye and Ear* may be recommended. So far, four volumes have been published, bringing the story up to the time of Balakirev. Each volume consists of eight records and a text-book, or the text-book may be purchased separately. (Columbia Graphophone Company and the Oxford University Press). The Parlophone Company publishes a set of twelve records called *Two Thousand Years of Music*.

THE MEANS BY WHICH MUSIC IS MADE

by J. A. WESTRUP, M.A., B.Mus.(Oxon)

As painting and sculpture appeal to the eye, so music appeals to the ear. Its medium is sound. Sound is the name which we give to the effect produced on the human ear by vibrations. In music these vibrations are specially controlled so as to give out notes of definite pitch (except in the case of one or two rudimentary instruments, such as the side-drum or tambourine). The vibrations may be produced, or, in other words, the notes may be sounded, by the human voice or by instruments specially constructed.

Though the fundamental principle of the production of sound by vibrations is common to all instruments and to the human voice, both the exact method of production and the quality of the sound produced vary according to the instrument employed. In the case of wind instruments the sound is produced by the vibrations of a column of air ; in other instruments the vibrations are set up by material of some kind— gut, wire, skin, metal, or wood. In all instruments the height or depth of the notes, to use the common designation, is determined by the length (and in the case of elastic materials, the tension) of the vibrating substance. Thus a long air column will produce a deeper note than a short column, if both are set vibrating in the same way. A long string will give a deeper note than a short string, as anyone can see by examining an ordinary piano. Further, if the string is stretched tighter it will produce a higher note. If it is slackened the note will be lower. The density of a string also affects the pitch. A thicker or heavier string vibrates more slowly and so gives a lower note.

EFFECTS WHICH CALL FOR COMBINED INSTRUMENTS

Musical instruments and voices may obviously be used either by themselves or in combination. Most instruments (and, of course, voices) are incapable of sounding more than one musical note at a time and so cannot do more than play a melody without accompaniment if left to themselves. But music is something more than melody. From the Middle

Ages to the present day it has tried to solve successfully the problem of combining sounds. The success of that experiment may be judged by the ease with which we listen to and assimilate combinations of sounds which at one time seemed new and strange. The combination of sounds involves the combination of instruments, unless one is content to rely solely on the few instruments which are able to sound several notes at the same time.

When a large number of instruments is assembled in accordance with a certain definite plan for the purpose of producing a combination of sounds, the whole, of which they are the parts, is called an orchestra. The word is Greek and meant originally a " dancing place," since in the Greek theatre a large space in front of the stage was reserved for the chorus, whose dancing and singing was an important part of a dramatic performance. Modern European languages applied the word to that part of the theatre where the musicians sit. By a natural transference it came to be used also of the actual body of instrumentalists. The composition of orchestras, the ways in which instruments have been combined, as well as the actual mechanism of the instruments themselves— all these have developed and changed in the course of time. Instruments were at first cumbrous in manufacture and were often combined in a haphazard way, dictated by convenience rather than by principle.

It was not till the eighteenth century that anything like a standardised combination of instruments existed. Since that date the tendency has been, while maintaining on the whole the basic structure of the orchestra, to extend its possibilities by increasing the number of instruments or by adding new ones. Since the modern full orchestra contains nearly every musical instrument in common use to-day, it will be convenient to begin by examining this vast combination and its component parts and then to pass on to a discussion of smaller combinations and the single use of individual instruments.

An orchestra is described as " full " if it is composed of the full complement of instruments prescribed by contemporary practice. What constitutes a full orchestra has naturally varied in the course of time, as we shall see later on. A small orchestra is one in which the same principles of relationship between the component parts are observed but the actual number of instruments is considerably smaller.

STRING INSTRUMENTS : THE BODY OF THE ORCHESTRA

THE most important section of the orchestra is the body of
string instruments. It is true that there are composers
to-day who resent this supremacy and write works in which
the strings are reduced to the minimum or eliminated altogether ; but our generalisation is true of most works which
have been written for the orchestra. The string instruments
which form this body are the violin, the viola, the violoncello
(or cello, to use the abbreviated form common in this country),
and the double-bass. (The harp is a string instrument, but
the method of producing sound is different, as well as the
whole structure of the instrument; it is always treated as an
independent instrument and will be dealt with later on.)

The principle of these four instruments is the same. Over
a hollow wooden body, which acts as a resonator or sound-
board, are stretched four [1] strings of gut, the thicker strings
being covered with wire. The strings are attached to pegs at
the upper end, or neck, of the instrument and can thus be
tightened or relaxed at will. A wooden " bridge " towards
the lower end of the instrument holds the strings in place and
enables a satisfactory tension to be secured. Only that part
of the string which lies between the bridge and the upper end
of the " finger-board " (just below the pegs) is actually called
upon to vibrate. The four strings are tuned to definite notes ;
the thicker strings, giving the lower notes, are on the left of
the instrument as one faces it, the thinner strings on the right.

Vibration of the strings is produced in two ways : by
drawing across them a bow consisting of horsehair stretched
to the requisite tautness on pliable wood, and by plucking
them with the finger. The latter method is known in Italian,
and in most other languages, as " pizzicato." In order to
play notes other than those which the four strings naturally
sound it is necessary to shorten the length which vibrates by
pressing the fingers firmly on the finger-board, i.e. at the upper
end of the string. Since the vibrating length of the string
is thus shortened it naturally gives a higher note. A player
therefore who wishes to play a scale will begin by pressing
down his fingers on a particular string until he has reached the
point where he can change over to the next string, unless for
particular reasons he wishes to stay on the original string.
To take a simple example, if a cello player wishes to play

[1] The double-bass sometimes has five.

a scale of C major, beginning with his lowest note, the first note, C, will be played on the open string ; the next note, D, will be played by pressing the first finger of the left hand on the C string at the correct point, thus shortening the vibrating length ; the next note, E, will be played by pressing the third

Tuning of String Instruments

Violin.

Viola.

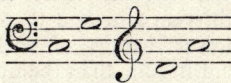

Cello.

¹ Double-bass.

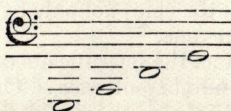

¹ These are the actual notes sounded by the strings. For convenience in writing and reading, however, music for the double-bass is always written an octave higher than it sounds, so that the notes of the four open strings would be written

thus : [musical notation] . Some players use different

tunings, *e.g.* [musical notation] or [musical notation]

as composers often write the lower notes. The difficulty is also solved by using a double-bass with five strings, tuned thus :

[musical notation] or even [musical notation]

finger on the string, and the fourth note, F, by pressing down the fourth finger. He can then either change on to the next string, which will sound G without any stopping, or move his hand up to a new position on the C string and begin again with the first finger. It is possible to play on two strings simultaneously, and chords can be played across three or even four strings by a vigorous movement of the bow. By touching the strings (without pressure) in certain places notes of a clear, bell-like quality (called "harmonics") are produced.

As the four instruments vary considerably in size, the violin being the smallest and the double-bass the largest, it is obvious that the distance between one note and the next on a string varies according to the instrument. On the violin the semitones are very close together, whereas on the double-bass there is quite an appreciable distance between them. Hence the fingering differs on the different instruments. Besides the difference in size there is also a difference in tone. As the lower strings of each individual instrument are less brilliant in tone than the upper ones, so the larger instruments are less brilliant than the smaller. Thus it is possible to distinguish the viola from the violin (both of which are held under the chin) not only by its larger size but also by its richer, darker tone.

On all the instruments of this family the tone can be varied in a number of ways. On the violin, viola, and cello (less commonly on the double-bass) it is usual to oscillate the left hand while any particular finger is pressed on a string, except in rapid passages or where the effect is not desirable. The oscillation affects the finger which is pressed on the string, so that the vibrating length of the string is alternately increased and diminished by a minute fraction. The rate at which this happens depends on the player. The listener hears the effect, not as a subtle variation of pitch, but as a throbbing which adds expression and poignancy to what is being played. The tone is also affected by the distance of the bow from the bridge.

It is even possible to hit the strings with the wooden part of the bow. The effect is not very pleasing but has been used by composers occasionally for special reasons. The dry, brittle sound which is produced in this way is particularly effective, for instance, in the first number, *Mars*, of Gustav Holst's suite *The Planets*. Lastly, by fitting to the bridge a special attachment known as a mute (in Italian, *sordino*) the vibration of the strings is hampered and the tone is consequently veiled and mysterious.

HOW THE STRINGS ARE COMBINED

THE string section of the orchestra consists of a number of instruments of each kind. The numbers naturally vary according to the size of the orchestra, but they are governed by a fairly well-established proportion. A normal number of strings in an ordinary full orchestra would be : 16 first violins, 16 second violins, 12 violas, 10 cellos, 8 double-basses. These numbers will be modified to suit individual requirements or preferences. Some conductors like to have slightly more first violins than second, or prefer to have twelve cellos and ten double-basses. The second violins differ from the first only in the music which they have to play. There is no difference in the instruments used, and the players are supposed to be just as competent as the first violinists. The various parts of a piece of music may be divided between these groups of instruments in a large variety of ways. The compass of the instruments is naturally a limiting factor ; apart from this, the distribution of parts is determined by the particular quality of tone which the composer wishes to pre-dominate.

We may take a simple example of this branch of instrument-ation by seeing how the first line of *God Save the King* might be arranged. This would ordinarily be in four-part harmony :

If no special effect is desired, the first violins will play the melody, the second violins will play the second or alto part, the violas will play the third or tenor part, and the cellos will play the bass. The double-basses will reinforce the bass by playing it an octave below the cello, the effect being something like the use of the pedal notes on the organ.

This arrangement of parts is that normally used in the orchestra for all string music in which no special effect is desired. The double-bass could, of course, be omitted ; the effect of the whole would then be lighter. But it would be unsatisfactory to omit the cello, as the deep notes of the double-bass would by themselves hardly supply the firm foundation of tone which is wanted here. Alternative arrange-ments of the string body and possible sub-divisions of the individual sections are numerous.

12

HOW THE REST OF THE ORCHESTRA IS MADE UP

THE strings, then, are the foundation of the orchestra. Indeed they may be said to constitute a limited orchestra in themselves and a very large number of works have been composed for this combination alone. But the full orchestra contains several other departments. In addition to the strings there are wind instruments and percussion instruments— made to sound by being struck or beaten. The principal difference between all these instruments and the strings is that, while the strings, as we have seen, have several players to each part in the ordinary way, in the wind and percussion departments it is usual to have only one player to each part. This means that if a work contains parts for four horns, each horn will have its own independent part. They may for the sake of emphasis be called upon all to play the same passage in unison, but this does not alter the fact that the four players are essentially soloists. The same is true of the other wind instruments and of the percussion instruments.

The wind instruments may be classified in various ways, but the simplest and most common division is into two main groups—wood-wind and brass. The names of the groups must not be interpreted too literally. A flute belongs to the wood-wind group even though it is made of silver, and so do the saxophones, which are regularly of metal. The difference is more in methods of construction and tone production than in the material employed.

THE WOOD-WIND FAMILY

THE basic principle of all wood-wind instruments is the same. A column of air is set in vibration and is then shortened by uncovering in succession holes in the side of the instrument, starting from the end nearest the opening where the sound emerges. An ascending scale can thus be played, until all the holes are uncovered. The fingers are then placed on the holes once more and by increased wind pressure (supplemented in many cases by a mechanical device) a higher note than that originally played can be produced ; from this point a new ascending scale is played by uncovering the holes as before. The distance between this higher note and that originally played is not the same in all the instruments of the family, and the method by which the highest notes of all, above the second series, are obtained varies also and is too complicated to be described here.

Intermediate notes and semitones not in the original scale of the instrument are obtained by a further series of keys and holes. Each instrument is built in a particular key, *i.e.* in the simplest type of instrument, if the six principal holes are uncovered in succession as described above it will play the first seven notes of a scale. The principle is thus similar to that of the string instruments. There the string was shortened by pressing the fingers on it ; here the air column is shortened by uncovering holes.

The wood-wind instruments normally used in the orchestra are of three main types : those in which the column of air is set vibrating by the lips alone, those which employ a single reed set in vibration by the lips, and those which employ a double reed. To the first class belong the flute, bass flute, and piccolo ; to the second, the clarinet and bass clarinet ; to the third, the oboe, cor anglais, bass oboe, bassoon, and double bassoon. In the flute and piccolo (or small flute), whose appearance is too familiar to need description, the player blows across a hole cut in the side of the tube at one end. The natural scale of the flute (in the sense mentioned above) is D major. That is to say, by covering the six principal

holes with the fingers the note is sounded. By

uncovering the first hole from the right the next note, E, is produced. By further uncovering the second hole, F♯ is obtained, and so on. In the modern orchestral flute this system has been modified, but the principle remains the same.

For practical purposes the compass of the flute is

8ve higher.

from to . The tone in the middle

part of its compass is mellow and expressive, and in the upper register has a crystal clearness which is quite un-mistakable in the orchestra. The lower notes have a character of their own, but often tend to sound flat, not so much in pitch as in tone. The tone of the instrument still further varies according to the material used and the ability of the player. The flute can be used for all kinds of solos, whether sustained or rapid. An example of the former will be found in one of the entra'ctes in Bizet's *Carmen*, of the latter in Beethoven's *Leonora* Overture No. 3.

The piccolo, particularly in the upper part of its compass, has a shrill and piercing quality which makes it easily audible over the full orchestra.   Its compass is

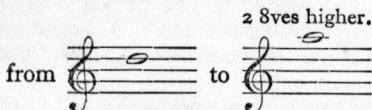

(or even higher), and its music is written an octave lower than it sounds. The bass (or alto) flute is slightly larger than the ordinary flute.   It is rarely used in the orchestra.

THE OBOE AND ITS RELATIVES

THE members of the oboe family all have a double reed, *i.e.* two thin pieces of cane through which the air is forced. The resultant tone has a curious nasal quality which is more pronounced in the upper instruments. The natural scale of the oboe, like that of the flute, is D major, but the compass is generally carried down by extra keys so that it is actually

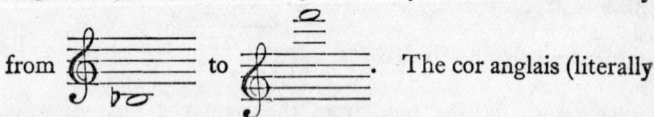

" English horn ") is not very well named, since it is neither a horn (in the ordinary sense of the word) nor particularly English. Its relation to the oboe is similar to that of the viola to the violin. It is larger than the oboe, and its bell is of a different shape. Its tone is richer than the oboe's, and is very suitable for pastoral or plaintive melodies. The famous solo in Rossini's *William Tell* overture is played on this instrument. Another excellent example is in the beginning of the third act of Wagner's *Tristan*, where it represents the shepherd's pipe.

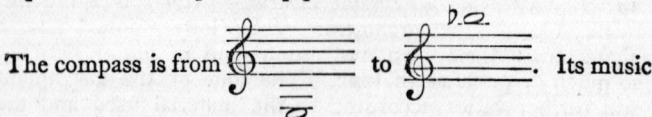

is written a fifth higher than the actual sounds, so that the fingering is the same as that of the oboe.

The bass oboe is also known as the heckelphone, after its inventor Heckel. It has a compass an octave below that of the oboe. It is rarely used. The natural bass of the family is the bassoon, called by the Italians from its odd appearance *fagotto*. Its natural scale is G, but extra keys extend the

compass, which is actually from ▦ to ▦

though the high notes are pinched and unsatisfactory. The tone is well adapted either for pathos or for merriment, and it is a most useful instrument for filling in harmony unobtrusively. The double-bassoon (or *contrafagotto*) has a

compass from ▦ to ▦. As in the case

8ve lower.

of the double-bass the music is written an octave higher than it actually sounds. The rich reedy tone of the lower notes of this instrument is quite unlike anything else in the orchestra. It is an invaluable supplement to the double-basses, and provides a firm foundation for the whole body of wood-wind.

HOW THE CLARINET NOTES ARE PRODUCED

THE clarinet, unlike the oboe and the bassoon, is played by means of a single reed, *i.e.* a single piece of cane laid against the wood of which the mouthpiece is composed. The air is then forced between the reed and the wood. It differs also from the oboe and the bassoon in having a cylindrical tube, whereas they are conical, *i.e.* the diameter of their tubes decreases from the bell to the mouthpiece. This difference is responsible for a difference in the notes produced by increasing the wind pressure, or as it is technically called, " over-blowing." The conical tube of the oboe and bassoon enables the player to get a note an octave higher by overblowing. But the cylindrical tube of the clarinet, aided by a special key operated by the thumb, sounds a note a twelfth higher when overblown.

By starting with all the six principal holes covered, and uncovering them in succession without using the special key (though with the additional use of a key for the last note) one can play on the simplest form of B♭ clarinet [1]:

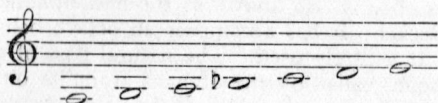

With the aid of the special key and the same fingering one produces the notes :

exactly a twelfth higher throughout than the original series.

Extra keys enable one to play :   without

using the special key, and with the special key :

. The notes in between   and

are produced by uncovering a thumb-hole and

using keys.

The peculiar system on which the clarinet works has been described in some detail, as it is important to understand the difficulties with which the player has to contend, though those difficulties are considerably lessened by the modern system of fingering and keys which is generally used. The tone of the clarinet can be made to vary considerably ; it can sound at will rich and mellow or hard and biting. The low notes in particular, when played softly, have a velvety quality which

[1] The term " B♭ clarinet " means that when the note C is written the instrument sounds B♭. This may seem curious, but the practice dates from a time when instruments were imperfect, and it was convenient, for ease of execution and accuracy of intonation, to have instruments in several keys on which the fingering would correspond to the written notes, while the sounded notes differed according to the instrument used. The A clarinet, which is still used, is built a semitone lower than the B♭.

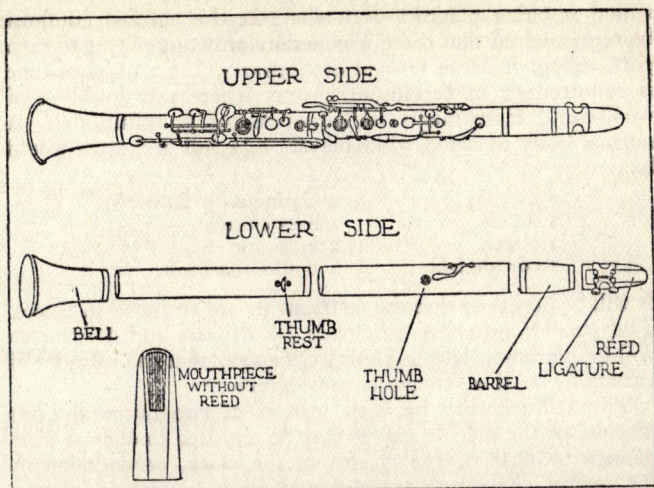

UPPER SIDE

LOWER SIDE

BELL
THUMB REST
MOUTHPIECE WITHOUT REED
THUMB HOLE
BARREL
LIGATURE
REED

30. HOW THE CLARINET IS BUILT

The Clarinet, a wood-wind instrument, is played by means of a single reed laid across the wood of the mouthpiece. Its natural scale has been extended by means of special keys which enable it to play the intermediate semitones.

is often used to advantage by composers. The notes in

between [musical notation] and [musical notation] *i.e.* in between the two

main series which I have described, are comparatively weak and less attractive. The compass of the B♭ clarinet

is from [musical notation] to [musical notation]

The compass of the bass clarinet, which has a turned-up bell rather like those of the larger saxophones, is an octave lower.

THE WOOD-WIND ENSEMBLE

THE number of wood-wind instruments employed in a full orchestra varies according to the particular composition which is being played. But whatever the number, it must be remembered that there is generally only one player to each part, except in large festival orchestras where a mass of tone is required or in certain orchestras where the doubling of wood-wind instruments in loud passages is traditional. A normal body of wood-wind players in a full orchestra would be :

1 piccolo	2 clarinets (in B♭ or A)
2 flutes	1 bass clarinet
2 oboes	2 bassoons
1 cor anglais	1 double-bassoon.

It will be observed that the instruments are arranged in threes. The smaller numbers employed by Mozart and Beethoven will be discussed later. Here we may say that the number of variations on this scheme is considerable.

Three flutes may be used instead of two flutes and one piccolo, or the piccolo player may be required to change from piccolo to flute in the course of the work, or occasionally for special effect two piccolos may be used instead of one. Similar modifications and additions are possible in the other groups. A small clarinet in E♭ may be added to the others. Three oboes may be used instead of two. The number of bassoons, in particular, varies. Some composers write for three, while French composers sometimes require four. Here as elsewhere in the orchestra the tendency has been not only to improve the mechanism of the instruments, but to increase the number used in the orchestra.

While each of the instruments in this group can be used for solos (even the piccolo and the double-bassoon), they can also be combined in an innumerable variety of ways, either with each other or with the strings. The art of orchestration consists in skilfully blending the many tonalities which the orchestra offers, much as painting calls for a skilful blending of the colours on the palette.

THE SAXOPHONE : A HYBRID INSTRUMENT

THE saxophone, though familiar enough in jazz bands, is still not very often seen in the orchestra. It is in a sense a hybrid instrument. It is named after its inventor, Adolphe Sax, and dates from about the middle of the last century. Though a member of the wood-wind family, it is made of metal. The mouthpiece and reed are similar to those used for the clarinet but the tube, instead of being cylindrical like that of the clarinet is conical or tapering like that of the oboe, and so " overblows " at the octave. It is therefore free from the special difficulties of the clarinet.

There is a whole family of saxophones, from soprano to double-bass. The tone is peculiar, having a certain affinity with that of the human voice and of the string instruments. It is often abused in jazz bands ; the excessive " vibrato " which some players affect is no more representative of the true saxophone tone than " crooning " is representative of the human voice.

THE BRASS INSTRUMENTS : PRODUCERS OF THE " HARMONIC SERIES "

THE chief characteristic of all the brass instruments is that a whole series of notes can be obtained by gradually increasing the tension of the lips. We have seen already how notes an octave higher are produced, for instance, on the oboe by this method. But in the case of the brass instruments the application of the principle is far more extensive. If one were to take a brass instrument on which with a very loose lip the

note could be produced, then by gradually

tightening the lips the following series of notes could also be obtained :

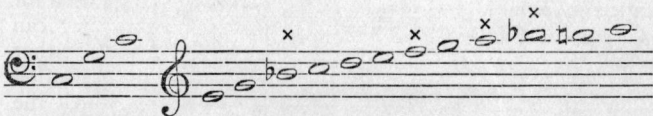

Of these notes those marked with a cross are not in tune with our ordinary scales, and the possibility of playing the extreme high notes depends on the particular instrument and skill of the player.

This series of notes is called the " harmonic series." That its existence (which is one of the fundamental laws of acoustics, or the science of sound) is not confined merely to brass instruments can be seen by any one who cares to make a simple experiment with the piano. Press down the right-hand or sustaining pedal (often erroneously called the " loud "

pedal) and play quite loudly and firmly 𝄢———. If you
listen carefully you will hear some at least of the notes
given above, sounding with a clear bell-like tone which is
quite different from the sound produced if the notes are
played in the ordinary way. The note 𝄞———— will
probably sound with particular clearness. (The notes can be
heard more easily if the front of the piano is removed.) It
is the same principle that enables the player to produce on
a string instrument those special notes called " harmonics "
which are obtained by touching the string in certain places.

HOW THE BUGLE WORKS

THE most familiar example of the practical application
of this principle in a brass instrument may be seen in
the bugle. The notes ordinarily employed on a bugle
are : 𝄞————————. The actual sound is :

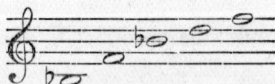

Here we have only some of the notes of the harmonic
series. Neither the lowest note (or " fundamental," as it is
called) nor the higher notes are practicable on this instrument
on account of its size.[1] The longer the tube of a brass instrument, the greater the number of notes which can be produced
by increased tension of the lips. If all brass instruments
were constructed like the bugle, it would be impossible for
them to do anything more than play the notes of the harmonic
series, which would obviously restrict their activities considerably.[2]

[1] Two notes higher than those given are practicable, but they are
not used.

[2] As a matter of fact, the trumpets and horns for which the classical
composers wrote were so restricted. They could only play the notes
of the harmonic series. Hence in order to make it possible for them
to play in any particular piece it was necessary to use pieces of tubing
of varying lengths (called " crooks ") to obtain harmonic series which
would fit in with the key of the piece. The problem was similar to
that of the clarinet, but much more complicated.

COR ANGLAIS
SAXOPHONE
TUBA
TROMBONE
BASSOON

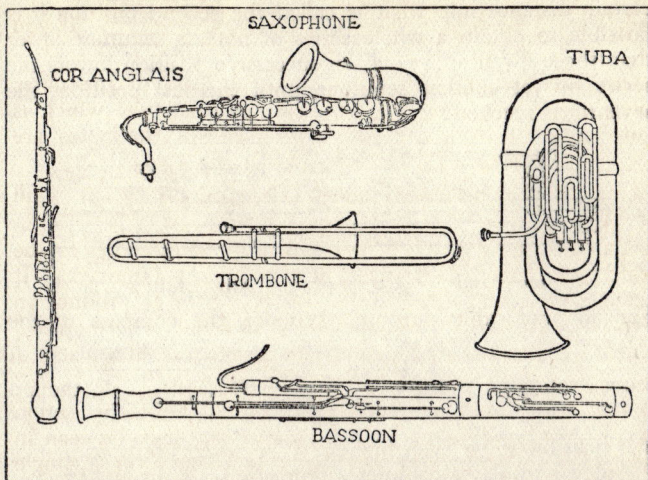

31. RICH-VOICED INSTRUMENTS OF WOOD AND BRASS

The Cor Anglais, Bassoon, and Saxophone belong to the wood-wind group, and the Trombone and Tuba to the brass. Note that the instruments are not drawn to scale.

Hence it is necessary to have some system by which the player can instantaneously lengthen his tube and thus obtain extra sets of harmonic series, until he has enough to build up a complete scale. The simplest system is that used for the trombone, where the player pushes out a movable slide in order to lengthen his tube. The way in which this enables him to play a complete chromatic scale (*i.e.* with all the semitones) may be briefly explained.

THE TROMBONE AND ITS SLIDE

IF the slide of the tenor trombone is kept closed (or brought home by gently pressing the slide towards the lips), the player can produce the following series (omitting the lowest or fundamental note, which is quite playable but not very often

used) : This

is called the first position. By extending the slide a

certain distance into what is called the second position it is possible to obtain a whole series of notes a semitone lower than those given above. Each successive position lowers the series by yet another semitone until the last position, the seventh, is reached:

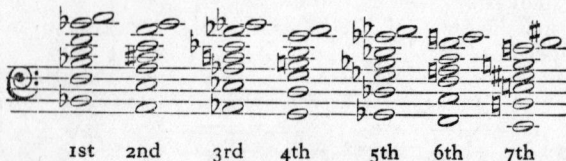

1st   2nd   3rd   4th   5th   6th   7th

For all practicable purpose, therefore, the compass of the

tenor trombone is from to , though

it is possible to go even higher. The seven positions enable the player to play a complete chromatic scale throughout this compass. In order to play any note two things are necessary: the correct tension of the lips and the correct position of the slide. The positions necessary for playing the first line of *God Save the King* (an octave lower than in the example) would be:

The other way of providing a complete chromatic compass is by *the use of valves*. Three pieces of extra tubing (or in some cases four) are attached to the main tube as by-passes. They are controlled by pistons. If a piston is pushed down the air is diverted through the extra piece of tubing, from which it passes once more into the main tube ; the air column is thus lengthened. The three pieces of extra tubing, which are of different lengths, used individually or in combination enable the player to fill up the gaps between the notes of the harmonic series. The first piston lowers the pitch a whole tone, the second a semitone, and the third (or first and second together) a whole tone and a semitone (a minor third). By combining the pistons still further, it is possible to play the same number of semitones below the original (or " open ") note as the trombone player gets by extending his slide.

The valve or piston system is used on the trumpet, the cornet, the horn, and all members of the saxhorn family, including the euphonium (which has a fourth piston lowering the pitch a whole fourth) and the tuba (which also very often has a fourth piston). Trombones are also made with pistons instead of slides, but they are not often used in this country. The first line of *God Save the King* would be played on the trumpet in C as follows (the figures refer to the pistons ; the figure o means that no pistons are used) :

BRASSES THAT ARE USED IN AN ORCHESTRA

THE brass instruments generally used in the orchestra are the trumpet, the horn (often called the French horn), the trombone, and the bass tuba. Other instruments are used occasionally or in military bands. The clear, bright tone of the trumpet—it sometimes breaks through the orchestra like a sudden blaze of light—is well known. The pistons enable it to play rapid music with comparative ease. Its compass

(if in C) is from to .

The number of trumpets in a full orchestra is generally three at the present day, though some composers require more. Some French composers have written for two trumpets and two cornets. The latter instrument, which differs from the trumpet in one or two respects, is discussed later on.

THE HORN'S SPECIAL CHARACTERISTICS

TWO things strike one at once about the horn. One is the bell, which opens to an unusual extent, the other is the mouthpiece. The other brass instruments generally use cup-shaped mouthpieces, whereas the horn mouthpiece is funnel-shaped. This difference has an effect upon the tone, which is much smoother than that of the other brass instruments (at any rate as made in this country) and makes it an ideal instrument for solos. The solo in the Nocturne of Mendelssohn's music to *A Midsummer-Night's Dream* is a well-known and typical example.

Another reason for its individual tone is the method of holding the instrument. The player generally holds it with his left hand and inserts his right hand into the bell, without, however, in any way blocking the passage of air. The correct placing of the hand is of some importance in securing a good tone. The instrument is, of course, a highly developed form of the old hunting horn. For many years after it was introduced into the orchestra it remained a " natural "[1] instrument, until the invention of pistons extended its scope. As a " natural " instrument, *i.e.* before the invention of pistons, it had the same disabilities as the " natural " trumpet, and it was necessary to write for horns in D, E♭, G and so on. It was possible, however, to play notes other than those of the harmonic series by partially closing the bell with the right hand. The effect was not pleasing. The tone was always dull, and sounded stopped or muted; but it was the best that could be done in those days. Even with the coming of pistons it was still customary to write for horns in various keys, partly because the tone differs according to the crooks used. The tone is richer if the larger crooks (*e.g.* the E♭, D and C) are used, less satisfying if the smaller crooks are used.

Gradually as time went on the horn in F was found to be the most convenient as occupying an intermediate position. Nowadays most players confine themselves to this horn, which is also made abroad with a special attachment for pitching it a fourth higher in B♭. Music for the horn in F is naturally written a fifth higher than it actually sounds. The first line of *God Save the King* (in the key of G as before) would be written thus (the figures indicate the pistons used) :[2]

As so many of the older composers (and all who wrote before the introduction of pistons) wrote for horns in various keys, the player spends a good deal of his time transposing the part which is in front of him. (Trumpet players have to do the same thing for a similar reason.) The only alternative would

[1] By a " natural instrument " is meant one without any mechanical device to fill up the gaps in the harmonic series.

[2] Alternatives are possible.

be to use a different crook each time, but that is upsetting, and means also that the valve tubings would have to be specially tuned each time a new crook was used.

The horn player has to face one particular difficulty which makes this instrument one of the most awkward to play properly. The construction of the instrument makes it possible to use a far wider range of harmonics than are available on the other instruments. The horn in F can produce the following notes without *the aid of pistons* :

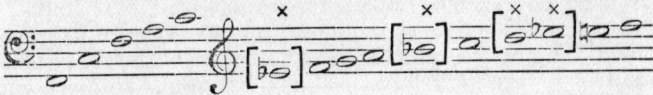

(The notes marked with a cross are those which are not in tune with our ordinary scales.) It will be noticed at once that the higher notes are very close together, so that it obviously requires great care and long practice in accurately adjusting the tension of the lips before it is possible to play correctly, especially as the notes which are not in tune must be avoided. Everyone has probably at some time or another heard horn-players " bubble " ; this means that instead of hitting a particular note cleanly, owing to tiredness or carelessness, they have not quite accurately adjusted their lips and their breath pressure, and so have fallen, as it were, between two stools. Difficulties of this kind naturally exist on all brass instruments (high notes, especially if they are to be played softly, are never easy) but they are accentuated on the horn.

The customary number of horns in the orchestra is four, but some modern composers write for six or even eight. Little is gained except volume of tone by using more than four. The instruments blend well together and are admirable for sustaining harmony either softly or loudly. It is common in modern instrumentation to use all four in unison to reinforce a melody played by cellos or violas. Rapid passages, though quite possible with the pistons, are neither particularly easy nor particularly effective. The chief virtue of the instrument is its tone, warm and restful in soft passages, hard and brassy in loud passages, and this is best exploited by music that moves at a reasonable pace.

HOW THE TROMBONES ARE EMPLOYED

THE trombone has already been described. The tone is brilliant, and if the instrument is played loudly it can easily dominate the whole orchestra. It is usual to employ three trombones—two tenors and one bass. The tenor trombone, as we have seen, sounds the harmonic series starting from B♭ if the slide is closed. The bass trombone sounds a similar series starting from G. The instruments have the following compass :

Tenor trombone :   to

Bass trombone :   to

In addition, it will be remembered that some extremely low notes outside this compass are possible with a very slack lip,

starting (on the tenor trombone) from   downwards.

These notes are often called " pedal notes." The power of the trombone makes it useful for bringing to the fore some broad and dignified melody to the accompaniment of the full orchestra. A good example of this is Wagner's over-ture to *Tannhäuser*, where all three trombones play the Pilgrims' melody. In spite of certain disadvantages imposed by the slide, it is also possible to play quite rapid passages. An example of a quick melody played by trombones is the in-troduction to the third act of Wagner's *Lohengrin*. But more valuable than their use as melodic instruments is the oppor-tunity of using them to fill up the harmony, whether in soft or loud passages. For all its power the trombone can be played extremely softly ; quiet chords on the three trombones are often used by composers with great effect. Wagner extended the possible compass of the trombones by writing for a contra-bass trombone with a compass an octave lower than that of the tenor trombone. The instrument is tiring to play, but extremely effective in its place. It has not been much used by other composers.

THE SAXHORNS : LATEST MEMBERS OF THE BRASS FAMILY

THE last member of the brass family in the orchestra is the bass tuba. This instrument, which is made in various keys, is the largest member of a particular group known as saxhorns, after Adolphe Sax, who was also the inventor of the saxophone. The principal characteristic of the saxhorn is the shape of its tube. The tube of the trumpet and of the trombone is cylindrical (in other words, the diameter remains the same) until the bell is reached. In the saxhorn, as in the bugle, the diameter of the tube increases throughout its length. The practical effect of this is to give a broader, rounder tone, which is particularly valuable for playing low notes. At the same time, the tone lacks the purity of the trumpet and trombone and in some members of the family may easily become coarse if not carefully controlled by the player.

PERCUSSION : THE SOUNDS PRODUCED BY STRIKING

PERCUSSION instruments may be divided into two main classes—those which produce musical notes of definite pitch and those which produce indeterminate sounds. To the first class belong the timpani (or kettle-drums), tubular bells, the glockenspiel and the xylophone ; to the second, the bass drum, the side drum, the tambourine, the triangle, the gong, the cymbals, the castanets, and other instruments of the same kind. At least three timpani are used in the modern orchestra. Each drum consists of a skin stretched over a large metal bowl. The tension of the skin is controlled by screws acting on an iron ring. By tightening or relaxing the tension it is possible to raise or lower the pitch. The three drums are normally tuned to notes which are most likely to be useful in the course of a piece; the composer writes at the beginning the tuning he wants : *e.g.* timpani in D, C, and G, often

marking the actual notes, thus : . If necessary, the tuning of any or all of the drums may be altered in the course of the piece.

The compass of the three drums is roughly, beginning with the smallest :

There is a mechanism used on some drums which enables the

player to control the pitch by means of a pedal, without having to turn separately all the screws. For this reason some composers write whatever notes they want for the timpani, and leave the player to make the necessary adjustments with the pedal as he goes along. The three timpani are usually all played by one performer. If there are more than three it may be necessary to have a second player. One of the most familiar effects obtainable on the timpani is the roll. The player rapidly alternates the two sticks (made of cane with felt heads) on the skin, thus producing a curious rumbling sound, which can be mysterious when soft and overpowering when loud.

BELLS, DRUMS, AND CYMBALS

THE other percussion instruments need not detain us long. The tubular bells explain themselves. They are long tubes of metal open at the ends, of different lengths, tuned to definite notes and hit with hammers. The glockenspiel (German for a " play of bells ") consists of a number of short metal bars of different lengths arranged like the keys of a piano. The bars are struck with small hammers and give forth a clear bright sound which can be heard quite distinctly, even when the rest of the orchestra is playing loudly. The xylophone (derived from the Greek *xylon*, " wood," and *phōne*, " sound ") is similar to the glockenspiel, but the bars are made of resonant wood instead of metal. The dry, brittle sound produced when the bars are struck is highly effective. Other instruments, originally of native manufacture and similar to the glockenspiel and xylophone, exist but they are not often used in the orchestra.

The percussion instruments with no definite pitch are mostly familiar to everyone. The bass drum gives a low dull sound which can be very useful in emphasising a heavy rhythm. The tone of the side-drum, on the other hand, has a dry, hard rattle, which is more effective for accentuating a brisk rhythm. The function of all these instruments, since they cannot produce musical notes of definite pitch, is to underline the rhythm or mark a climax. For marking a climax the cymbals (plates of metal clashed together) are particularly useful. Their entry at the end of Wagner's overture to *The Mastersingers* is unforgettable. The clicking of the castanets, the metallic rustle of the tambourine, the " ping " of the triangle and the hollow boom of the gong perform a similar function. They are all instruments which are very effective in their place but can easily be abused and degenerate into mere noise-makers.

FOUR INSTRUMENTS WITH INDIVIDUAL TRAITS

IN addition to the instruments mentioned above, there are four special instruments which are also used in the orchestra —the harp, the celesta, the piano and the organ. All these instruments are capable of playing several notes at the same time and so differ in a very important point from the other instruments of the orchestra.[1] The harp has a series of strings of varying length, which are plucked by the fingers and (in the instrument most frequently used) controlled by pedals which alter the pitch, so that it is possible to play in any key. Each pedal controls all the notes of the same name. Thus by pressing down one of the pedals one raises the pitch of all the C♭ strings (in whatever octave) to C♮. In this position the pedal can be fixed ; by pressing it down still further, however, the pitch of all the strings affected can be raised another semitone, so that all the C♭ strings (which were first raised to C♮) are now raised to C♯. There are in all seven pedals,

and the compass is from   to

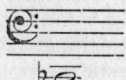

The number of harps in the ordinary orchestra is one or two ; Wagner actually wrote for six, but the increase in numbers is hardly answered by a corresponding increase in effect.

The celesta, invented in 1886 by Auguste Mustel of Paris, is constructed of metal plates of varying lengths suspended over wooden resonators and struck by hammers, which are controlled by keys like those of the piano. The principle is similar to that of the glockenspiel, but the keyboard enables chords to be played. The ethereal, silvery tone of this instrument has appealed to modern composers, who

[1] It is true that string instruments can play more than one note at a time, but their ability to do this is very limited in comparison with the harp or piano.

use it frequently.   It has also found its way into jazz

2 8ves higher.

bands.   The compass is from 🎼 to 🎼.

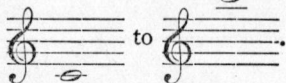

HOW THE PIANO AND ORGAN ARE USED

NEITHER the piano nor the organ can be considered normal members of the orchestra. They are both primarily solo instruments. If they are used in combination, the piano is most effectively joined with only a few instruments, while the organ blends best with voices. However, they both make their appearance occasionally in the orchestra, the organ in particular being often used in large works for choir and orchestra, where it helps to support the chorus.

The piano, like the celesta, is really a percussion instrument. Strings of varying lengths stretched on a frame, with an unfilled space behind or underneath to act as resonator, are struck by wooden hammers (with felt heads) controlled by keys. So long as a key is depressed the string or strings (all except the lowest notes have two or three strings each) will continue to vibrate, and on a good piano the note will continue sounding for some time ; as soon as the finger is lifted off the key, a felt damper falls on to the strings and stops the sound. By means of the right-hand or sustaining pedal (often popularly known as the " loud " pedal) the player can lift all the dampers from the strings so that any note or notes which he plays will continue sounding, while other strings will also vibrate " in sympathy." The correct use of this pedal is of great importance in piano playing. It is sometimes called the " soul " of the piano. If properly employed it lessens to some extent the undoubted weakness of the piano, namely, its inability to sustain notes with a constant amount of tone.

The second pedal at the disposal of the player reduces the tone either by bringing the hammers nearer the strings so that the impact is less sharp, or by shifting the keys slightly to one side so that not all the three strings of each note are struck by the hammer. Some pianos have also a third pedal, placed between the other two. The function of this is to sustain only those notes which are pressed down at the moment that the pedal is used. The compass of the piano is from

2 8ves higher.

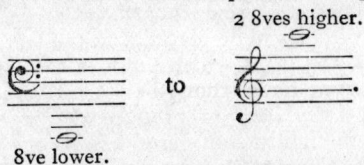

8ve lower.

Further experiments in manufacture in recent years have included the Moór Duplex piano, which has two keyboards, one an octave higher than the other, and the Neo-Bechstein, in which the fundamental weakness of the piano is obviated by means of amplifiers which enable the tone to be sustained.

In the orchestra the piano (when not used as a solo instrument, *i.e.* in piano concertos) is employed either as a substitute for the harp or to reinforce the higher notes with its clear, percussive tone. In the latter capacity, as a percussion instrument, it is quite useful. Many of Percy Grainger's compositions contain effective examples of the particular contribution which the piano can make to the sum total of sound in the orchestra.

"THE KING OF INSTRUMENTS"

THE organ is not only one of the most complicated of all instruments in its construction but also one of the most difficult to play. It is in essence a mechanical wind instrument. In the ordinary wind instrument the player supplies the wind, and by making modifications in the tube itself and in the pressure of his lips succeeds in playing a number of different notes. In the organ the wind is supplied from bellows worked either by an assistant or by a motor of some kind, while, instead of modifying a single tube, it is necessary to have a whole series of tubes or pipes, one for each note, the air being released when the key is depressed.

But the organ is not content with one series of pipes giving only one sort of tone. It has a large number of such series, each with a different tone quality or power and many of them sounding notes an octave or two octaves higher or lower than those normally produced by the keyboard of the piano. Each series is controlled by a stop within reach of the player. By drawing any stop (which will be labelled for his convenience), he brings into action a particular series of pipes. He has then only to press down the keys and the corresponding pipes in that series will sound. To make it easier to contrast two or more stops of different character, or whole batches of stops of different character, several keyboards are employed, as well as a row of notes to be played with the feet, called pedals. It is here that the stops which produce sounds an octave or even two octaves lower than the normal are of particular importance. They help to produce that deep, impressive sound which is rightly considered one of the characteristics of the organ. The actual compass of the organ keyboard is

normally from to but its sounding

compass is greatly extended by the stops.

INSTRUMENTS USED IN A MODERN ORCHESTRA

IT may be useful to run through once more the instruments ordinarily employed in the modern orchestra. They are :

Wood-wind
- 1 piccolo
- 2 flutes
- 2 oboes
- 1 cor anglais
- 2 clarinets
- 1 bass clarinet
- 2 bassoons
- 1 double bassoon

Brass
- 4 horns
- 3 trumpets
- 3 trombones
- 1 bass tuba
- 3 timpani
- 2 harps

Strings
- 16 first violins
- 16 second violins
- 12 violas
- 10 cellos
- 8 double-basses

In addition to these there may be extra instruments in any one department, e.g. 3 flutes instead of 2, a tenor tuba as well as a bass tuba, various percussion instruments, and celesta, piano or organ. The orchestra has grown to its present size gradually. By the time it became more or less standardised in the eighteenth century it had not reached anything like its present proportions.

What we may call the " classical " orchestra consisted of a smaller body :

- 2 flutes
- 2 oboes
- 2 clarinets
- 2 bassoons

- 2 horns
- 2 trumpets
- 2 timpani

and strings in smaller numbers than those employed to-day. Even the clarinets were comparative late-comers. Some of Mozart's symphonies have no parts for them. Trombones had long been used in sacred music to accompany the singers, but it was some time before they were introduced into symphonies. Mozart used them in his operas only for effects of special solemnity. There are no trombones in six out of Beethoven's nine symphonies. It was Wagner particularly who increased the number of wind instruments, as well as calling for larger numbers of string players.

What the future development of the orchestra will be it is impossible to say. Experiments have been made by leaving out part of the normal orchestra but they have not been very successful. The orchestra is a combination which has proved its value and possibilities by many years of development and progress. Any further developments are more likely to be on similar lines to those in the past than in the form of radical changes.

HOW THE MUSIC IS ARRANGED

MUSIC for the orchestra has to be in two forms—the score and the parts. The score, which is used by the conductor, contains the parts for every instrument, written one above the other in the order in which the instruments have just been mentioned, that is to say, the piccolo line is at the top of the page and the double-bass line at the bottom. If the work is for voices and orchestra, the voice parts will probably be written just above the string parts. Thus the conductor has in front of him everything that is to be played, complete with marks of time and expression. It is his duty to see that the composer's intentions are duly carried out, to make certain that instruments come in at the right time, and generally to weld all the parts into a consistent whole.

The parts for the individual players are copied from the score (generally by some one other than the composer, who has had quite enough of writing by the time he has finished the score); they contain all the same marks of time and expression as are in the score. When an instrument has nothing to play, the number of bars during which the player is to be silent is marked in his part, and it is his duty to count them. If the period of silence is fairly long, the copyist will write in at the end of it a " cue," *i.e.* a bar or two in which the music played by some prominent instrument is quoted so that the player can recognise it and check his counting. The provision of cues is much more common at the present day than it used to be. It is almost essential if a work is to be performed with little or no rehearsal.

The way in which the instruments of an orchestra are placed varies ; a common arrangement is shown in Fig. 32. The important thing in any arrangement is that the members of each family should be together as far as possible. Some conductors prefer to put the second violins where the cellos are in the plan, and vice versa. The reason for this is that if the second violins are on the conductor's right their instruments are turned away from the audience and there is a loss of tone. In the opera house the arrangement varies according to the size of the orchestra pit, which may be very cramped.

THE DIFFICULTIES OF THE MINIATURE ORCHESTRA

THE full orchestra is not the only possible combination of a number of instruments. Smaller groups are possible, as we have seen, in which the proportions between the various sections are roughly maintained. It is also possible to have an orchestra composed of strings only. When the numbers sink below a certain level and it is found that there are not sufficient instruments for adequate performance, a piano and often a harmonium [1] as well are used to fill up the harmony. This is often the case in restaurant orchestras, but the method cannot be regarded as anything but an inadequate substitute for the real thing. It is unusual for music to be written specially for such a combination. Restaurant orchestras are mostly condemned to play arrangements.

HOW A MILITARY BAND IS FORMED

AN entirely different type of organisation is the military band, in which only wind instruments are used.[2] Here the clarinets, of which a large number are used, represent the higher string instruments of the orchestra, while the euphonium and tubas, reinforced by several saxophones, stand for the cellos and double-basses. The flutes, oboes, and bassoons

[1] The harmonium is a keyboard instrument in which the keys act on reeds, through which air is forced by means of bellows worked by the feet of the player. The tone, like that of the single-reed instruments in the orchestra, tends to be rather nasal.

[2] String double-basses are often used as well for concert performances.

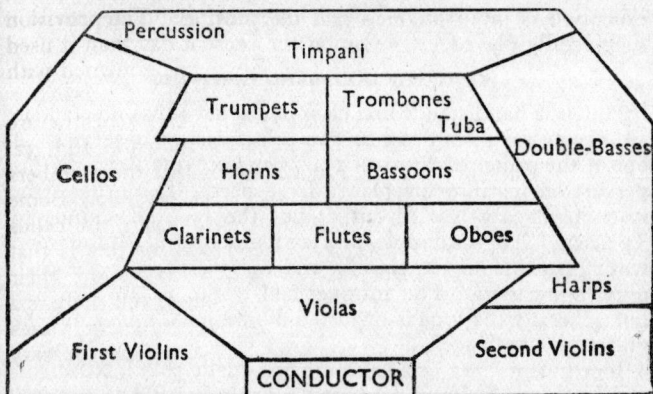

32. GROUPING THE PLAYERS TO FORM AN ORCHESTRA

The detailed arrangement of the orchestra depends on the conductor, but he will be certain to group the instruments according to their families. The violins, for instance, will never be placed among the brass—trumpets, trombones, etc. The grouping shown here is a usual one.

play much the same part as in the orchestra. Cornets[1] are generally used instead of trumpets; the rest of the brass instruments are the same—two or four horns, and three trombones. Many orchestral works have been arranged for military bands; a good band can perform the most elaborate music.

One of the most important instruments in the military band is the euphonium, a member of the saxhorn family. Not only is it a valuable bass instrument, but its rich and mellow tone makes it very useful for solos. In operatic selections arranged for military band, bass or tenor solos are commonly assigned to the euphonium. The brass band is a different combination still. As its name implies, it is composed exclusively of brass instruments. Here some members of the saxhorn family not used elsewhere make their appearance. Other unusual instruments, such as soprano cornets in E♭, are also found. As in military bands, a high standard of

[1] The cornet (generally in B♭) is a sort of hybrid instrument, midway between the trumpet and the bugle in shape. It has three pistons and is very suitable for light and rapid passages as well as for sustained solos.

execution is often attained and the most elaborate music is successfully played.

THE jazz band stands in a class by itself. It has no standard organisation, but one or two principles are observed. As one of the principal duties of a jazz band is to mark the rhythm, percussion instruments play a large part. The usual string instruments are less favoured, but the plucked sounds (or "pizzicato") of the double-bass are found useful. Of the wood-wind instruments the clarinet and more especially the saxophones are used. The trumpet and trombone are also used but generally the tone is distorted by means of mutes or other grotesque appliances.

Instruments in a jazz band are essentially solo instruments, and instrumentation for a jazz band consists not so much in fusing different kinds of tone into a whole as in bringing to the fore in turn strongly contrasted tones. The piano plays an important part in filling up the harmony and maintaining the rhythmic background, which is also supported by banjos, guitars and other plucked instruments.

THE DIFFERENCE BETWEEN CHAMBER AND ORCHESTRAL MUSIC

INSTRUMENTS are not only combined together in large numbers to form an orchestra. A good deal of music exists for much smaller combinations, composed of only a few instruments, each one of which plays the part of a soloist. The name given to music of this kind is "chamber music," since the few players necessary to perform it can easily meet in an ordinary room, whereas the orchestra needs a large hall. There is a further distinction between chamber music and orchestral music. Orchestral music is practically always played before an audience, whereas one of the beauties of chamber music is that it can be played in private simply for the delight of the players in their task. It is, of course, also performed in public, but there is a quality of intimacy about it which makes a purely private performance, with (perhaps) one or two friends listening, particularly appropriate and satisfying. Taking part in chamber music is one of the most enjoyable experiences anyone can have.

The commonest of these small, intimate combinations is the string quartet, which consists of four instruments only—two violins (first and second, playing different parts as in the orchestra), viola and cello. To these four instruments it is possible to add other string instruments or wind instruments or the piano. Thus the addition of another viola or another cello makes the string quartet into a string quintet. The addition of a clarinet or oboe will make a clarinet or oboe quintet. The addition of the piano will make a piano quintet. In each case it is assumed that the string quartet is the foundation, and the distinctive name of the combination is taken from the particular instrument which is added, when that instrument is not itself a string instrument.

Larger combinations are also possible. Beethoven wrote a septet for clarinet, bassoon, horn, violin, viola, cello, and double-bass, and Schubert an octet for the same instruments with the addition of a second violin. The number and variety of possible combinations is practically unlimited. There is always, however, a danger that too many instruments will tend to do away with the essential intimacy of chamber music and make the combination a small orchestra. Hence chamber music combinations are as a rule restricted to comparatively few players. Combinations for wind instruments alone or with piano are also found.

Smaller combinations than those already mentioned are frequent. Three string instruments by themselves are a string trio ; with piano, a piano quartet. A piano trio consist of violin, cello and piano. If some other instrument is used it will probably give its name to the combination. Brahms's trio for violin, horn, and piano is generally called a horn trio. The combination of two instruments has not as a rule any distinctive name, though the term " duo " is sometimes used. The commonest combination of two instruments is the piano with violin, viola, cello, or one of the wind instruments. Works for two string instruments or two wind instruments are not often satisfactory ; they tend to sound empty. Two pianos are often played together, but the effect is not wholly satisfying, largely because of the difficulty of distinguishing between the tone of two similar instruments.

INSTRUMENTS THAT CAN STAND ALONE

FINALLY we come to instruments by themselves. As was said earlier in this section, solos for string or wind instruments without accompaniment are a little unsatisfactory. Wind instruments cannot play more than one note at a time,[1]

[1] A freak effect of chords can be produced on the horn, but they are very difficult and practically never used.

and though string instruments can do so, their natural limitations soon become apparent in the course of a performance and one feels a sense of strain and deliberate conquest of difficulties which interferes with one's enjoyment. Apart from the harp, whose possibilities as a solo instrument are also limited, the only instruments which can comfortably stand on their own feet are the two keyboard instruments—the piano and the organ. Both these instruments have their weaknesses, even at the present day, but composers have done so much to take advantage of their special capabilities that a vast amount of music written for them can be played and listened to without any feeling of incongruity. At the same time, these instruments must not be considered to be the most important because they stand by themselves.

Ability to play the piano is not essential to a knowledge of music, though it is a great assistance. There have been composers who have either played the piano badly or been unable to play it at all. Indeed, from the point of view of a composer for the orchestra or string quartet, it may even be a handicap to be too much tied to the piano. It is necessary to think in the medium for which one is writing ; to compose a work at the piano may be a very dangerous way of writing music, unless one is gifted at the same time with a very lively imagination and a fair amount of self-discipline.

INSTRUMENTS OF THE PAST AND FUTURE

IT has been impossible to mention in this section every musical instrument. The reader will very probably come across others which are not in regular use at the present day except in performances of old music for which they are required. Such are, for instance, the harpsichord (a keyboard instrument, in which the strings are plucked by pointed quills), the viols (string instruments in regular use in the sixteenth and seventeenth centuries) and the recorders (flutes played from the end in much the same way as the penny whistle). These and many other instruments too numerous to mention here have been revived for the performance of old music in modern times, largely through the energies of Arnold Dolmetsch, who has devoted a large part of his life to the study and manufacture of these instruments and to the literature of the subject. They often sound odd to those who are quite unfamiliar with them, but a second hearing and increased acquaintance soon remove the feeling of strangeness. There is a good deal to be said for using the proper instruments to play old music, even though the ideal is impracticable for many people.

These are instruments of the past. But we also live in an age of experiments which look forward to the future. Scientists have occupied themselves in recent years with constructing electrical instruments of various kinds which will enable the tone of several instruments to be imitated by one machine. The experiments have not been wholly successful from the musical point of view, though some of the instruments of this kind have actually been used in modern compositions. A more daring experiment, the developments of which will be watched with interest, is the use of apparatus similar to that employed in making talking-films, for constructing straight away, without reproduction from actual instruments, the sounds of a whole orchestra.

MORE BOOKS ABOUT ORCHESTRAL INSTRUMENTS

BOOKS on the orchestra are mainly of two kinds : those which simply describe the instruments, and those which in addition give instruction in writing for the orchestra. Knowledge of the technique of instruments is obviously essential for a composer who wishes to write for them effectively. A great many popular books on the constitution of the orchestra have been published. Most of them cover much the same ground as this section. Adam Carse's *Orchestral Conducting* (Augener) may be recommended to anyone who wants more detailed information about the instruments than can be given here. There are some excellent diagrams. The same author has written a *History of Orchestration* (Kegan Paul), which should be useful for those who are anxious to pursue this part of the subject.

A brief but practical treatise on the art of writing for the orchestra is Gordon Jacob's *Orchestral Technique* (Oxford University Press). More elaborate and generally the most comprehensive book on the subject in English is Cecil Forsyth's *Orchestration* (Macmillan). There are a number of excellent illustrations. Interesting from the historical point of view is Berlioz's *Traité de l'Instrumentation* (English trans., Novello), which was in its day an epoch-making work and is still worth reading. A German edition, revised by Richard

Strauss, is published by Peters. Another celebrated composer who wrote about the orchestra is Rimsky-Korsakov. The greater part of his *Foundations of Instrumentation* consists of examples drawn from his own works. For information about particular instruments see also the separate articles in Grove's *Dictionary of Music and Musicians* (3rd edition, Macmillan), which contains a number of plates.

Practical study of orchestral instruments can, of course, only be made under a competent teacher. Anyone who can read music should try following orchestral works with miniature full scores. All the standard works can be obtained in this form at a fairly moderate price. Catalogues of the " Philharmonia " series can be obtained from Boosey and Hawkes, and of the Eulenburg series from Goodwin and Tabb.

MAKING MUSIC WITH THE VOICE

by EDMUND RUBBRA

THE first music was sung music. The first instrument was
the human voice. From the " seed " of the voice all the
varied orchestral instruments of our day, except those
of a purely percussive nature, such as drums and cymbals,
have sprung. If modern composers have found other, percussive, uses for these orchestral instruments, their nature
nevertheless remains fundamentally a vocal one, evolved by
the desire of man to extend the limited range and power of
the human voice. The white light of the voice is split up into
the primary colours by the orchestral prism of wood-wind,
brass, and strings, and out of this new palette the great composers have been able to portray increasingly deeper visions.
Even that beautiful hybrid the piano, which can only produce
sounds by means of the percussive blows of felted hammers
on strings, needs but a sympathetic approach to legitimatise
its kinship with the voice.

Many are the forms that have evolved in Western European
music, but all the music that lives has its roots in melodic
inspiration. The voice remains the means, par excellence,
for expressing the intimate experiences of human life, either
of deep joy or of deep agony, disillusionment or hope. The
wealth of folk-song that has been discovered shows what a
single unaccompanied voice part can achieve in expressiveness.
Harmony is a comparatively recent growth in the history of
music, but even this element evolved from the fusion at any
one point of many separate and independent vocal lines. If
composers have now severed the cord linking harmony with
its parent melody, yet still its main use is to intensify the
melodic emotion.

We have seen then that the vocal element in music turns up
in most unexpected places : that the purpose of the high flute
and deep bassoon of the orchestra is but to add extensively
to the normal one-and-a-half to two-octave range of the
human voice, in the same way that the piano key adds to the
natural extension of the pianist's finger ; and that what we
call harmony originated in viewing music vertically instead of
horizontally.

THE IMPORTANCE OF BREATH-CONTROL

To sing is to put ourselves in touch with the very heart of the musical universe. Out of this centre spring the symphony, the opera, the string quartet, as well as the smaller form of the song. The smallness of the form of the latter is, however, not a proof of its comparative insignificance. As the length of a violin is conditioned by the length of the normal arm, so is the song-form conditioned, first, by the physical capacities of the singer, namely, the amount of breath that can be inhaled and the strength of the vocal cords ; and secondly, by the length and emotional scope of the poem. If, however, the song-form is strictly limited to the physical capacities of the normal adult human being, how is it that a large percentage of songs are physically inaccessible to the ordinary person ? Does it not seem that Handel, for instance, wrote some of his arias, with their long and uninterrupted cascades of notes, for singers with super-lungs ? And yet it is doubtful if even the famous Farinelli, Handel's contemporary, had lungs of exceptional size.

The secret, of course, lies in the expenditure of the breath once it is inhaled. Breath-control is the first step leading to Farinelli's famous feat of virtuosity, commencing a note with the utmost softness, increasing it very gradually to an enormous volume and dying away again equally slowly. Such virtuosity is, of course, meaningless by itself : only when it is applied to a musical phrase can it have any emotional meaning. Giotto's perfect circle only acquired significance in the marvellous emotional curves of his kneeling figures.

VOICE A UNIVERSAL GIFT

In so far as we all possess both lungs and vocal cords so are we all potential singers. Indeed from childhood up the most common form of emotional expression is through the voice : the baby's croon of contentment or cry of hunger, or a boy's shout in a game are definitely vocal expressions of emotion, primitive perhaps, but nevertheless real. When these early emotions are, by life-experiences, lifted on to a higher plane and at the same time are intense enough, then comes the desire of the artist to give these experiences a permanent form.

In music, an emotion frequently pours itself into the mould of a song because of the presence of a poem which responds to and clarifies the composer's own experiences. The more

subtle the emotional core of a song, the more subtle must be
the interpreter's technique of expression. Singing is a natural
accomplishment only if the emotional and technical demands
of a song are of a simple order, such as those found in most
folk-songs. Folk-songs are not spoilt by being sung by an
untrained voice : indeed an added freshness is often imparted.
This is because a folk-song is instinctive and " unmental,"
and an untrained voice is able to meet it on its own ground.

THE BREACH BETWEEN ART-SONG AND FOLK-SONG

MANY excellent singers of folk-songs are entirely at a loss
when confronted with what are called " art-songs." In the
latter the instinct is directed by a conscious intelligence and
guided into moulds formed by many influences, chief among
which is the particular art-form uppermost when the song is
composed. Songs composed, for instance, under the influence
of Italian operatic singing are ornate and " showy " with the
accompanimental background reduced to a minimum (Mozart
reached the highest point in this style), while those songs
influenced by the deeper and more philosophical seriousness
of the German symphony have a thicker, more important
texture, in the accompaniment, and a vocal line relieved of all
unnecessary " roulades " and ornamentations (Hugo Wolf is
the finest composer of this type of song).

The question then of the value of a trained or untrained
" natural " voice entirely devolves upon the type of song one
intends to sing. The best art-song—a bad word, but no
other is available—demands for its adequate performance a
cultural background, mental, emotional and instinctive, as
complete as that of the composer, whereas a folk-song only
demands an every-day social background for its immediate
appreciation. The breach between the two forms is often
further widened by the words used. The words of a folk-
song are mostly either straightforward accounts of love in
happy or unhappy circumstances, or are fantastic and often
meaningless, such as :

> This old man, he played one,
> He played nick-nack on my drum ;
> Nick-nack paddy-whack, give a dog a bone,
> This old man came rolling home.

The words of art-songs are, on the contrary, usually the work
of poets concerned with deeper and more subtle experiences

13

than surface ones. The cultural background of the poem must therefore be shared by the singer.

WHAT THE DRAWING-ROOM BALLAD DEMANDS OF THE SINGER

So far we have discussed two extremely differentiated types of song, the folk-song and the art-song. There is, however, another class of song, the drawing-room ballad, which may be said to lie in the neutral area between these two extremes. But it is a mistake to suppose that the technical equipment necessary for the singing of a drawing-room ballad need be in but a half-evolved condition, lying somewhere between the untrained "natural" voice of a folk-song singer and the highly-trained voice of the Lieder singer. The two extremes of the folk-song and the art-song touch in one particular : they are both the result of an emotional drive, an urge for expression within the composer.

The popular ballad, however, cannot be said to have its origin in a divine urge ; most often its genesis is an opposite urge from within the pocket. This fact, far from simplifying the matter for the singer, makes it doubly difficult, for the whole life of the song depends upon the capacity of the singer to emphasise all the sentimental high lights intended by the composer to " bring the house down." That last long-held top note, for example ; does it not demand for its true effect a highly-cultivated beauty of tone and a controlled exhalation ? A wobble or a crack would make the whole song ludicrous. Singing teachers are constantly being blamed by high-minded musicians for giving " ballads " to pupils, but the teachers are wiser than appears on the surface. They know that the ballad offers excellent material for pure tone-production with few or no distractions of interpretation.

THE FOLK-SONG NEEDS ACTION

THE folk-song does not necessarily demand either a trained voice or a highly evolved cultural-musical background. The singer, however, must have a natural histrionic or acting sense, for to sing a folk-sing " straight," with immovable limbs and a smile that is more the result of a mental command of the facial muscles than of an inner feeling, is simply to misunderstand the whole meaning of folk-art. Folk-art is near to the earth and summarises in a permanent form the freely-moving gestures and emotions of everyday life. It is to be noted that the musical value of the singing, as such, does not in the least matter. A highly-trained singer is usually so concerned with producing a beautiful tone that any accompanying stage-action is liable to be of a very primitive and stylised kind. (See any opera for a proof of this.)

It is well for the beginner to start with the numerous English Folk-songs, excellently arranged by Cecil Sharp and Vaughan Williams. Afterwards the fascinating folk-music of other nations can be explored, notably the Red Indian Folk-songs arranged by Dr. MacMillan of Toronto University, the Spanish Folk-songs of Manual de Falla, the Hebridean Folk-songs of Mrs Kennedy Fraser, the Manx Folk-songs of Arnold Foster, and the French chansons.

THE BALLAD DEMANDS THE TRAINED VOICE

ONE cannot place the drawing-room ballad among serious art because its ultimate aim is an objective effect rather than the transmission of a deeply-felt inner emotion. Yet for this very reason it demands a cultivated voice, without, however, owing to the nature of the words and the musical idiom usually employed, a correspondingly cultivated musical taste. The ballad has distinct advantages as a practising-ground for tone and word production. Once beauty of tone and breath-control becomes a natural thing the wise teacher will see that the pupil is given music upon which to test his or her powers of interpretation.

Ballads are of course widely differentiated in musical value. Some songs, such as those of Roger Quilter, Cyril Scott and Reynaldo Hahn lift the ballad form on to a higher plane, and are useful as stepping-stones to the German Lieder. Below is a list of songs useful for various purposes :

SUSTAINED ENGLISH SONGS (BALLAD TYPE)

For deep voice or mezzo-soprano.

Lie there, my lute.	*Hamish MacCunn.*
Break, break.	*Walthew.*
Songs of Sorrow.	*Roger Quilter.*
The Silver Swan.	*Thiman.*
Brittany.	*E. Farrar.*
Life and Death.	*Coleridge Taylor.*
Peace.	*Eric Fogg.*
Twilight.	*Walter Rummel.*
Dreary Steppe.	*Gretchaninoff.*

Sea Pictures.	Elgar.
O that it were so.	Frank Bridge.
Lament of Isis.	Granville Bantock.
Slow horses, slow.	Mallinson.
England.	Edward German.
Little silver ring.	Chaminade.
Starry Woods.	Montague Phillips.
So we'll go no more a-roving.	M. V. White.
She is far from the land.	Walford Davies.
Hame.	"

For soprano.

Magdalen at Michael's Gate.	Lehmann.
Solvieg's Song.	Grieg.
Blackbird's Song.	Cyril Scott.
Do not go, my Love.	Hageman.
Blackbird's song.	Martin Shaw.
The Song of the Palanquin-Bearer	"
I know a Bank.	"
Sylvan.	Landon Ronald.
A Memory.	Goring Thomas.
A Summer Night.	"
Waters of Minnetonka.	C. W. Cadman.
Hey Derry.	Edward German.
The Fields are full.	Armstrong Gibbs.
The Songs of Michael Head and Roger Quilter.	

LIGHTER ENGLISH SONGS (BALLAD TYPE)

For deep or mezzo-soprano voice.

The Jocund Dance.	Walford Davies.
When Childer plays.	"
A Birthday.	Cowen.
Song of the Open.	de la Forge.
Five Eyes.	Armstrong Gibbs.
The Flower Song from " Faust."	Gounod.
Invitation to arise.	Graham Peel.
Sing, joyous Bird.	Montague Phillips.
Wake up.	"

For soprano.

Waltz Song from " Tom Jones "	Edward German.
Good morning, Brother Sunshine	Liza Lehmann.
Cherry Ripe, arranged by.	"
Songs my Mother taught me.	Dvorak.
St. Nicholas Day.	Easthope Martin.
Cuckoo Song.	Martin Shaw.

Go not, happy Day.	*Mallinson.*
Ecstasy.	*Walter Rummel.*
Ferry Ahoy !	*Herbert Brewer.*
Fairy's Lullaby.	"
Fairy went a-marketing.	"
Morning.	*Henschel.*

SUSTAINED ITALIAN AND FRENCH SONGS

Ombra mai fu.	*Händel.*
Lascia ch'io pianga.	"
Che faró senza Euridice.	*Glück.*
O don fatale.	*Verdi.*
O mio Fernando.	*Donizetti.*
Connais-tu les pays.	*Thomas.*
Le Miroir.	*Ferrari.*
Il est beau.	"
Crépuscule.	*Massenet.*
Le Lilas.	*Rachmaninoff.*
Le temps des Lilas.	*Chausson.*
Aria de Jeanne d'Arc.	*Tschaikovsky.*
Album of Songs.	*Narini.*

LIVELY ITALIAN AND FRENCH SONGS

Il segreto per esser felici.	*Donizetti.*
Stride la vampa.	*Verdi.*
Ouvre tes yeux bleus.	*Massenet.*
A des oiseaux.	*Hüe.*
Papillon.	"
Habanera.	*Bizet.*
Pastorelle.	"
Chanson en route.	*Chausson.*

THE SIREN CALL OF SONG

WHAT we have called the art-song includes all the German Lieder (Schubert, Schumann, Brahms, Mahler, Wolf, and Strauss), the songs of Debussy, Ravel, Fauré, Delius, Sibelius, the lute-songs of Dowland (1562–1628), the songs of Purcell, the oratorio arias of Bach, Handel, and Haydn, the opera arias of Monteverdi, Mozart, Verdi, Wagner and Puccini. The singer wishing to go beyond the confined area of folk-songs and drawing-room ballads has, therefore, an abundance of material of every mood and variety of style to draw upon.

The voice has saturated Western music for at least a thousand years. Only one composer, Scriabin (1872–1915), has failed to succumb to its siren-call (unless we include the choral part in the orchestral tone-poem *Prometheus*), for even Chopin, usually so deaf to the claims of the voice, published as his Opus 74 seventeen fine Polish Airs arranged for voice and piano. Whether these were done for his own satisfaction is a moot point.

Some composers are, of course, primarily song composers : such as Schubert [1] (1797–1828), Hugo Wolf (1860–1903), and it is among the works of these composers that we should naturally find the finest examples. Other composers, such as Schumann, Beethoven, Brahms, Liszt, Mahler, and Strauss only spasmodically resorted to song writing, perhaps in accordance with the old adage " a change of work is as good as a rest." In the case of Brahms in particular this change of work resulted in some remarkable songs, full of warm-hearted and rich romanticism.

Beginners can attempt the simpler Lieder such as *Lullaby* (*Wiegenlied*), by Brahms ; *An die Musik* or *The Nun* (*Die Noune*), by Schubert; *Lotus Flower* (*Die Lotosblume*), by Schumann; and *Still wie die Nacht*, by Bohm.

FINGERPRINTS IN SONG

THE viewpoint of all of the songs of the above-mentioned composers is intensely personal. Any singer approaching them should not only have a complete command of vocal technique, but enough of a musical background to be able to objectify the particular style of the song. We have all heard singers who approach every type in exactly the same way : the same vocal trick or mannerism has to do duty for everything from a Monteverdi aria to a song by Debussy.

As Ernest Newman has persistently and rightly pointed out, every great composer unconsciously rings the changes on quite a few formulæ. It is even suggested that some composers such as Schubert always gravitate towards a certain key for similar moods. But it is only by thorough and minute examination of all the works that we can put our finger on the exact identity marks. Only the lesser composer wears his formulæ on his sleeve. It is literally true, therefore, that any simple succession of notes, such as an upwards movement from C to D, means a different thing for different composers. The slightest inflexion, the slightest weight will turn a neutral phrase into a well-defined style.

[1] One of the best studies of Schubert's songs is Richard Capell's book, *Schubert's Songs*, published by Benn.

THE VALUE OF A CRITICAL EAR

THE factor that is all-important, not only for the trained or untrained singer, but for performers on any instrument is a critical ear. Ear-training forms a part of the curriculum of every school of music, and its object is to create listeners instead of hearers. The distinction between the two is vital, for listening is hearing plus attention. (It is a misuse of a word to call all wireless enthusiasts " listeners-in " ; ninety per cent. are but " hearers-in.") In listening an act of the will is demanded, otherwise we merely revel in a bath of sound from which we emerge with our backs like that of the proverbial duck. No music will yield up its secret unless we, by an effort of attention, let each note and each phrase penetrate farther than the surface of the mind. Then, and only then, shall we be able to relate the various parts and see the structure taking shape. Memory enters largely into critical listening, for music is not seen whole as a painting but is gradually unfolded, and has only a shape by virtue of our capacity for retaining in our minds the salient ideas. These ideas then become definite personages, and the excitement of following their various adventures is one of the thrills of listening.

LISTENING TO OURSELVES

THIS type of listening, however difficult for the beginner to acquire, owing to what psychologists call our limited " span of attention," is yet easier than the second type. This is when the critical and listening faculties are turned in upon ourselves as performers. It is one thing to be a critical listener of the performance of others and quite another to critically dissect our own playing or singing. We can be hyper-critical of others : it gives us a feeling of superiority, but pride (or laziness !) prevents us from being adequately critical where our own efforts are concerned. In any real practice the pupil and teacher are rolled into one.

This faculty of self-criticism is a basic one. It is not merely a question of detecting faults of intonation, although this is very important, but of detecting wrong emphasis, unsuitable phrasing, unsteady breath-control and bad enunciation (commonly, but wrongly called " diction "). Moreover it is not an element that need only enter fairly late in the pupil's apprenticeship to the art of singing or playing, for every step of progress made is the result of a struggle between the will or desire and the natural inertia of the body. Of course, the critical faculty can only be fully effective if the pupil knows exactly what he wants, and what should be the physical sensations in tone-production. In the beginning this knowledge is hazy and almost non-existent, and it is the function of the teacher, especially in the early stages, to give a direction to the pupil, and to make clear to him what, according to the teacher's experience and the experience of many others, is the aim at any one point of his study.

The benefits resulting from such an attentive listening will manifest themselves not only in the work accomplished but in the appreciation and enjoyment of music made by others. Music which hitherto seemed to be but an agreeable or disagreeable mass of sound, a tangled skein of notes, will gradually sort itself into recognisable shapes, and we shall perceive unsuspected inner beauties. The critical ear is the X-rays of music : by it we are able to pierce through the outer skin and see the bones and skeleton, the framework of the music. Debussy (1862–1918), the greatest modern French composer, once wrote deploring the action of certain critics in dissecting music like a " watchmaker taking a watch to pieces and thus depriving it of all mystery." But this is a false analogy, because a watch is never more than a collection of separate parts fitted together for a definitely utilitarian purpose, whereas the finest music is greater than the sum of the separate parts. The escapement or the mainspring of a watch exists as a complete entity, but a phrase from a Beethoven or a Sibelius Symphony is not complete by itself : it exists only in relation to all that has led up to it and all that follows it.

The true function, then, of the critical and alert ear is to relate the parts of a piece, and to discern the various disguises that the principal characters (themes) assume in the unfolding of the drama. If this is to deprive music of its mystery, then the continuous and minute analysis for two hundred years of Bach's fugues should have resulted in an entire lack of interest in the music. But the cult of Bach shows that the poetry of his music is still appreciated.

THE CHOIR A FINE TRAINING GROUND

ONE of the best training-grounds for the student of singing, especially for the English student, is the choir. The voice expands freely in group singing because we are not conscious of listeners. We can lose ourselves in the sheer physical joy of making beautiful sounds, knowing that there are no listening ears to criticise our efforts. In later stages, of course, we can do away with the crutches that choir singing gives. In another direction however the choir gives us a singularly good practice in independence, for the fact of having to hold our own part against a number of other conflicting parts gives invaluable help in accurately pitching notes. Moreover, being communal music making, the ear is trained to relate our volume of sound to that of the others. If, then, the pupil has reached the stage when right production is a matter of habit (this is important, for it is easy to relapse into old habits if the critical ear of the teacher is absent) many joyful and profitable hours may be spent in singing with others.

Opportunities for joining choral societies in England are legion. It was mainly through the local choral society that the spark of music was kept glowing in the dark days of native musical production in Victorian England. The annual performances of Handel's *Messiah* or Mendelssohn's *Elijah* never seemed to lack enthusiasm, and if this enthusiasm was often wasted on such pieces of threadbare banality as Stainer's *Crucifixion* it did serve to keep the choral forces in training for the finer modern works beginning with Stanford's *Revenge* and Elgar's *Dream of Gerontius*. (Stainer's work was definitely a hyphen between one period of production and another. Unfortunately this hyphen bore a strange resemblance to the minus sign of algebra.)

THE ELIZABETHAN FASHION FOR DAILY PRACTICE

THIS long choral tradition probably owed its vigour to the fashion in Elizabethan times for members of a family to meet daily for the " exercise of Musicke." Indeed this was practically the only way of hearing secular music, for public concerts did not begin until the end of the seventeenth century. This daily practice was an excellent training-ground for sight-reading, and in the introductory dialogue of his *Plaine and Easie Introduction to Practicall Musicke*, Morley tells of the discomfiture of a young man when after supper :

> " the mistresse of the house presented me with a part, earnestly requesting me to sing. But when after manie excuses I protested unfainedly that I could

not : everie one began to wonder. Yea, some whisp-
ered to others, demanding how I was brought up :
so that upon shame of mine ignorance, I go nowe to
seeke out mine olde frinde, master Gnorimus, to
make my selfe his scholler."

Henry the Eighth could sing at sight, and no gentleman's
education was considered complete without a knowledge of
music, which usually meant being able to sight-read. When
public concerts, initiated by John Banister, became the vogue,
this domestic music-making was bound to widen its scope,
and, as so often happens in the history of art, a figure appeared
whose music demanded these increased forces. This figure
was Henry Purcell (1658–1695). Since Purcell's time,
especially since the first production of Handel's *Messiah* in
Dublin in 1742, the choral tradition in England has grown
steadily in strength, finally crystallising into such fine
organisations as The Philharmonic Choir, The B.B.C. Choir,
The Oriana Madrigal Choir, The Bach Choir, and The Royal
Choral Society.

CHOIRS AND RULES FOR MEMBERSHIP

ALL these choirs have their headquarters in London, but
it must not be supposed that the provinces lack equally
fine organisations. The Glasgow Orpheus Choir (conducted
by Sir Hugh Roberton) and the choirs drawn upon for the
Leeds Festival have claims to artistic recognition equal to the
more widely known London choirs. A brief account of one or
two of the most important choral organisations is here given.

A unique place is held by the Oriana Madrigal Society
" founded in 1904 for the primary purpose of extending
interest in unaccompanied English choral music of the
sixteenth and seventeenth centuries, both by performing and
republishing it." Three concerts are given yearly (usually
in December, March, and June), and although the programmes
contain a large percentage of native unaccompanied Elizabethan and Stuart music, an increasingly large place has been
given to modern British choral works. The choir consists
of about eighty voices, and sometimes the assistance of vocal
or instrumental soloists is obtained. Amateur members can
join the choir by payment of £1 11s. 6d. per annum, but
special terms can, at the discretion of the committee, be made
for professional singers. Intending members should write
to the conductor Charles Kennedy Scott, Oriana Madrigal

Society, Leighton House, Holland Park Road, Kensington, W., asking for an audition, which usually takes place on Mondays.

Other choirs under the same conductorship are The Philharmonic Choir, founded in 1919 for the performance of large-scale choral and orchestral works, both old and new : (before being admitted to the choir, intending members must pass a voice test and pay an annual subscription of one guinea); the Junior Philharmonic Choir : (this is affiliated to the Trinity College of Music, and was formed for giving a training in vocal music to the young and keen musician. For this reason no tests have to be passed. Promotions are from time to time made to the larger Philharmonic Choir. The subscription is 10s. 6d. per annum); the Bach Cantata Club, founded in 1926 by Charles Kennedy Scott, E. Stanley Roper, and Hubert Foss.

One of the oldest and biggest of the choral organisations in London is the Royal Choral Society. When the Albert Hall was opened in 1871 a choir was formed by Charles Gounod, the well-known composer of the opera *Faust*. The following year it amalgamated with Barnby's Choir and became The Royal Albert Hall Choral Society. This title was changed to the present Royal Choral Society in 1888 by command of Queen Victoria. The accoustics of the Albert Hall, while demanding a large volume of tone, negative subtlety of effect ; for this reason only works conceived on broad lines can be successfully given. Intending members should write to the Secretary, Royal Choral Society, Albert Hall, Kensington, S.W., asking for an audition. This includes sight reading as well as voice tests. There is no subscription.

THE SINGER IN TRAINING AND PRACTICE

HAVING chosen to enter the singing profession, the first and most important task is to find a suitable teacher. If the student reads the many books on singing that have been published he will most probably find himself completely confused, even on such a seemingly simple matter as breathing. But his confusion will be worse confounded when contradictions occur about the very fundamentals of the mechanical bases of singing. In reading any book on singing we should therefore be hyper-critical and question by our commonsense the many dogmas that are as unthinkingly accepted as the dogmas of science and religion. If read in this way they will be most helpful to the student, but in no case should they be accepted as bases for voice-training without the guidance of a teacher.

The choice of a teacher is an individual matter dependent on personal circumstances and taste. Recommendation is perhaps as good a guide as any.

If the desire of the student is for a more specialised form of singing such as opera, a very good training can be obtained at the New Operatic Academy. Classes in gesture, including poise, balance, graceful walking, curtseying, taking calls, etc., are given as well as in acting and mime. The more general institutions, The Guildhall School of Music, The Trinity College of Music, The Royal College of Music, and the Royal Academy of Music, also give excellent training in operatic work. An additional advantage to the student is that in these general institutions the specialised study of one branch of music carries with it the right of entry into other classes, such as Ear training.

HOW THE SINGER CAN OBTAIN AN AUDIENCE

At the moment the demand for opera singers in this country is exceedingly limited, but with the advent of television opera is a form of art which may well be prosperous in the future. Again, the " talkie " film is opening out new fields for the singer. If old forms are breaking down, new ones are certainly rising up to absorb the waiting talent.

How can one be heard ? By singing at every opportunity ! Plenty of chances for performance are given to students at all of the above-mentioned institutions. Operas and concerts are regularly given, and any talent manifesting itself will not be overlooked. It is usual for singing students on completing their training to give a public recital. This has distinct advantages as publicity, for the singer reaches a wider public not only through the audience but through the press. A recital can easily be arranged through an agent, but the young recital-giver must not expect any financial return for the expenditure of £50 or £60. It is purely a form of advertisement.

If the student cannot afford the expense of a public recital, he or she should write for an audition with the British Broadcasting Corporation, for where an audience is numbered by millions any engagement on the " wireless " can have far-reaching effects.

BEFORE the War an ideal way for the young and talented singer to get a first hearing was to obtain an engagement at one of the numerous "At Homes." This not only gave an opportunity for proving one's voice, but the intimate social atmosphere enabled one to build up a public based on personal acquaintance. Unfortunately "At Homes" are no longer so fashionable, and the young singer must rely on other modes of building up an interested public, such as teaching.

The young teacher would do well to take the recognised examinations qualifying for the Licentiateship of the Royal Academy of Music or the Associateship of the Royal College of Music. If they do not add to one's artistic stature, they have a certain public value if one is unknown. These examinations are held three times yearly, and the fee is five guineas. Syllabuses giving full particulars can be obtained from the Royal Academy of Music and the Royal College of Music. As education authorities and heads of schools, wishing to fill vacant music-teaching posts, usually apply through the recognised schools of music, the successful student at these institutions will have a good chance of finding work.

The rewards of music-making are chiefly rewards of the spirit : money rewards are, or should be, a secondary consideration. If approached in this way, the world of music will yield delights of mind and spirit unobtainable elsewhere.

> "There is not any musicke of Instruments whatsoever, comparable to that which is made of the voyces of Men." (*William Byrd*).

WHERE THE SINGER CAN READ ABOUT HIS ART

THE reader wishing to deepen his knowledge of the craft of singing will find no lack of material for study, but judicial selection is necessary if the student wishes to avoid complete confusion. An attempt is therefore made below to select from the mass of available material those books which are likely to be valuable as an introductory course of reading.

It is a regrettable fact that few books written by professional musicians on singing are based on sound physiological principles. One must therefore extend a welcome to a book, written by a medical doctor, which provides a more scientific approach. This is *The Voice*, by W. A. Aikin (Longmans, Green and Co.). While mainly an introduction to practical phonology, it contains a very thorough discussion of all the elements in singing. A valuable inclusion is the pronunciation chart.

Voice and Verse, by H. C. Colles (Oxford University Press), while not touching on technical problems in voice production, is invaluable to the student interested in the relations between words and music throughout the history of Western music. Plunket Greene's *Interpretation of Song* is a classic in its own sphere, and is the outcome of a wide experience in song interpretation. Students wishing to take up school work will find Dr. W. G. Whittaker's *Class-singing* (Oxford University Press) an admirable book. An appendix contains an exhaustive list of useful part-songs. (The old fallacy of the " registers " of the voice is given prominence, but this is a detail in an otherwise sound book.)

Four other books will be found valuable for throwing light on various aspects of singing : *The Control of the Breath*, by G. Dodds and Lickley (Oxford University Press); *The Singing of the Future*, by Ffrangçon Davies (John Lane); *The Brain and the Voice in Speech and Song*, by F. W. Mott; and *Music for the Films*, by Leonard Sabaneev. Edgar T. Evetts' book, *Vocal Disorders : Their Cause and Cure* (J. M. Dent and Sons) gives excellent breathing exercises in addition to remedies for sore throats caused by wrong singing or speaking, and special defects, such as stammering and cleft palate, are dealt with.

For modern vocal technique the reader is recommended *The Gentle Art of Singing*, by Henry J. Wood, 4 vols. (Oxford University Press).

HOW TO READ MUSIC

by H. V. JERVIS READ, F.R.A.M.

READING a piece of new music is an adventure : it may lead you to the Isles of the Blest : it may take you to a land where no water is. It is like cutting the pages of a new book. Anyone whose interest in music is not entirely superficial and ephemeral must obtain mental stimulation from its practice. Music may be read at the instrument for which it is written, or it may be read away from an instrument and read as a book is read. The second method is, probably, the harder. It requires very considerable concentration and knowledge. It requires a certain amount of natural aptitude or talent ; and it requires, certainly, musical intelligence above the average.

In spite of the difficulties the practice can be fostered and, granted a certain natural aptitude and musical intelligence, the mental study of music with the aid of the eye only, can be acquired.

Reading music away from the instrument is obviously more complicated than reading a book. Obviously, too, you have to hear the sounds in your head, without the aid of the outer, physical ear. It is often affirmed that the eye is of no importance and of no value either in the study of music, or in the understanding and assimilation of music, and cases of blind musicians are cited to support this statement. It is true that a blind musician, lacking as he does the sense of sight, develops an amazing capacity which enables him to understand and assimilate music through the aural sense alone. He will learn to play a piece of music, even a piece of complicated music, studied, not at the instrument aided by sight and so " learned by heart," but through the sensitive and sure touch of his finger tips passing along the page of signs denoting, in Braille, the notes, dots, dashes, words, and abbreviations which, taken together, form music's notation. By this means he will commit to memory even a complex piece of music.

But those who possess sight have not, as a general rule, so highly developed a memory for music which has not been heard. The eye *is* of value in the study of music, and in the understanding and assimilation of music. It is an immense aid to be able to study intelligently a piece of music through the eye, and it is not, as is sometimes alleged, the hall mark of an intellectual snob to insist on and to practise this.

READING MUSIC AWAY FROM AN INSTRUMENT

THERE are three causes which, taken together, account for the difficulties encountered in reading music away from an instrument. And these three causes prove that it is harder, certainly, to read a piece of music than to read a book. The first difficulty consists in the Notation, or the Elements, of Music, and in the Theory of Music. These are analogous respectively to the alphabet and the grammar of a language. The second difficulty arises because music is not, except in its simplest aspect, written along one horizontal line ; the third is due to the inability of most people to appreciate musical sounds apart from, and unaided by, the outer ear.

As regards the first cause : the notation and the grammar of music are as easy to learn as the alphabet and grammar of any other language. As regards the second cause : the eye can be trained to follow more than one line at one and the same time, and it is a part of a musician's equipment to be able to do this. As regards the third cause : one can learn to appreciate musical sounds, one can learn to appreciate, even, the aural effect of many sounds sounding simultaneously without the aid of the outer ear.

The first and second of the three difficulties enumerated cannot be explained or simplified until both the Elements and the Theory of Music are learned and understood. The third difficulty is rather different and may be expounded here.

The *actual pitch* of a note is of no importance in hearing and reading music without the aid of an instrument. You may call the process either hearing or reading or both, for it is clear that in this case, hearing and reading are one and the same thing ; the eye conveys the sound to the brain direct : the sound is not conveyed to the brain by means of the eyes and the fingers and the aural sense.

There are two modes of scale in general use. Whichever note you start on, the size of the step to the next note is an ordained interval. Therefore the main thing to be sure about is which note of a scale, the first or seventh or any other you are starting on.

Here is the beginning of a tune. It is a phrase, four metrical accents, and is the half of a complete musical statement :

The elements of music will teach you the meaning of the various signs employed. The theory of music will teach you that the tune starts on the third note (called the Mediant) of the scale or key of G.

Auralise (if you understand *visualising*, seeing mentally, you will understand that *auralising* means hearing mentally)—auralise a keynote, or tonic : any note that comes to you will do. Having fixed this tonic you should have no difficulty in imagining the third note of the scale. Look for the time-signature, in this case two-four, which signifies a stronger pulse followed by a weaker in each bar. The stronger pulse, or stress, in rhythmically regular tunes, is invariably the note immediately succeeding the bar-line. Now, think of this tune, auralise it, keeping time—third of the scale, fifth, tonic, and so on. When you get to the end and it feels like a comma and not like a full-stop, you will have auralised the tune correctly.

Now try to imagine a part added beneath the title tune. Remember it is only half a tune.

You will note that the lower part is quite a good tune too, that is to say, it has a certain character of its own. It is not note against note, but possesses an independent, though simple, scheme of its own. It starts on the Tonic or keynote of the scale : this helps you to feel the Mediant (third note of the scale) in the top part. The underpart ends on the Dominant, or fifth of the key : this helps enormously to give a feeling of taking a breath, a comma : there is no finality. This counter-point, which is the name given to a tune sung or played together with a set tune (called the *Cantus Firmus*) proceeds from the keynote down to the Mediant scale-wise, that is to say, conjunctly : then a fairly big jump to the tonic, and so on.

Look at it hard : try to auralise it. It is great fun.

THE ELEMENTS OF MUSIC : CLEFS AND NOTES

THE notes in music are named after the first seven letters of the alphabet. These notes are written upon five horizontal lines called the Staff. At the beginning of a line of music a clef is placed. This clef is the key which determines the names of the notes written on the Staff. It also determines their pitch.

There are two clefs in general use : the Treble or G Clef, and the Bass or F Clef.

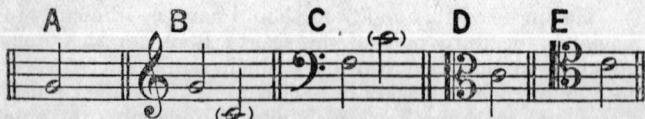

In this example, A means nothing at all. In B the Treble Clef is the *key*. The other name for Treble Clef is G Clef, meaning that the second line of the Staff is G : the G next above middle C on the piano. You can easily find middle C. It is printed alongside the G in the example (B) given above. In C the Bass, or F Clef, is the *key*. This clef makes the fourth line F : the F next below middle C on the piano. This note is printed after the F above.

There are several other clefs : most of these are obsolete, but the Alto and Tenor clefs (examples D and E) remain. Both are C clefs.

The third line in the Alto Clef is middle C on the piano, and the fourth line in the Tenor Clef is exactly the same note. The Alto Clef is used for viola music and the Tenor Clef is used both by violoncello and bassoon players, and for the higher notes of the trombone.

Understand clearly that *each note* shown in the next example is the same note, namely, middle C.

HOW MUCH EACH OF THE NOTES IS WORTH

THE notes are of varying lengths. The largest note, called a *breve*, is practically obsolete, and need not be considered. A *semibreve* equals one. This is the unit from which all divisions of notes are calculated. A *minim* equals two, a *crotchet* equals four, a *quaver* equals eight, a *semiquaver* equals sixteen, and a *demisemiquaver* equals thirty-two. There are, then, two minims in a semibreve, or four crotchets, or thirty-two demisemiquavers. There are eight semiquavers in a minim, and two crotchets in a minim. A semibreve is a note-head only, a minim consists of a note-head and a stem, a semiquaver of a note-head, a stem and two tails.

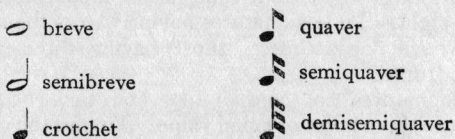

A dot placed after a note increases its length by one-half. This prolongation of a note can also be expressed by means of a tie.

In this example, A shows the minim G equalling *three* crotchets, not two crotchets. B shows the crotchet D equalling, not two quavers, but *three* quavers *and a semiquaver*, because a *second* dot is equal to half the first dot.

DETERMINING THE PULSE-RATE OF MUSIC

TIME is the procession of the beats : rhythm is the progression of the music. Perpendicular lines placed on the staff are called bar-lines, and the space between two bar-lines is a bar, or measure. Marches, Dances, and Hymn-tunes are familiar examples of music having a regular succession of beats, or pulses, in every bar. The number of pulses in each bar, and which are the stronger and which the weaker, is shown by means of time-signatures. For instance, two over four signifies two crotchets (or quarter notes) in each bar, or expressed in a different manner, one-half of a semibreve (this is always the unit) in each bar ; in addition, it signifies a down and an up beat—a

stronger and a weaker—in each bar. So the numerator of
the fraction designates the number of beats, or pulses, in a
bar, and the denominator expresses the fractional part of a
semibreve, and so shows the value of each beat.

Time is either simple or compound. The simple time-
signatures are those in which each beat can be divided into
two notes of equal value. In two-four time, for instance,
each of the crotchets can be divided into two quavers. The
simple time-signatures in common use are two-two, two-four,
three-four, three-eight, four-four (also called common time)
and four-eight. Time-signatures having two as the numerator
are known as duple times ; those having three, as triple ;
four, quadruple.

Time-signatures are compound when each beat can be
divided into three notes of equal value. To find the compound
form of a simple signature, multiply the numerator by three,
and the denominator by two. To convert compound to simple,
divide by three and two respectively. Applying this process
to the simple time two-four, six-eight results, signifying six
quavers in a bar, or two dotted crotchets, and the simple,
duple signature becomes a compound duple.

The corresponding compound forms of the simple time
signatures enumerated are then : four-six, six-eight, nine-
eight, nine-sixteen, twelve-eight, and twelve-sixteen. A
common error is a confusion of thought over six-eight. It
should be clear that six-eight signifies two dotted crotchets.
Being a compound duple time signature it does not express
three crotchets ; that would be simple triple time.

A comparison of A and B in this example will prove the relationship of two-four and six-eight. Example C has the same number of quavers in a bar as B; the metrical effect, however, is different: both simple and compound duple express a stronger pulse followed by a weaker, while simple triple is a stronger pulse followed by two weaker ones.

Three notes in the time of two is called a triplet, and two notes in the time of three, a duplet. There are other irregular divisions; quadruplet, four in the time of three; quintuplet, five in the time of four; sextolet, six in the time of four; and so forth. By means of these irregular groupings we may obtain the effect of a simple time while using a compound time-signature, and *vice versa*. But this is merely one example of the boundless rhythmical fluidity resulting from their use.

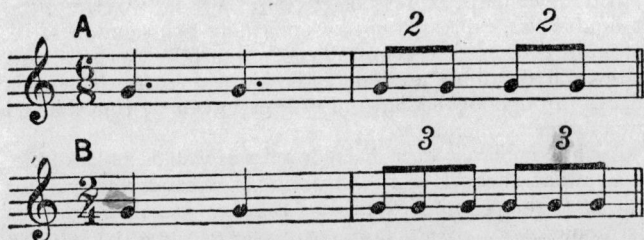

HOW THE RESTS IN MUSIC ARE USED

MOZART said that the rests were the best part of his music! There is a rest corresponding to each note.

This example shows each note together with its equivalent rest. A rest may be dotted in the same way a note is dotted: its duration is then lengthened by one-half. The following shows the use of rests in various times:

THE EFFECT OF SHARPS AND FLATS

A NOTE may be inflected by means of an accidental. A sharp raises a note by one semitone. A flat lowers a note by one semitone.

The accidental in the first bar of this example raises G one semitone to the black note next above it on the piano. The accidental in the second bar lowers G one semitone to the black note next below it on the piano.

A double sharp, expressed ××, raises a note two semitones. A double flat, expressed ♭♭, lowers a note two semitones. A natural, expressed ♮, contradicts a sharp or a flat. An accidental continues to inflect the note against which it is placed throughout the bar, unless it is previously contradicted by another accidental.

A white note may be a sharp or a flat as well as a black note. A semitone above E is E–sharp, and it is often necessary to call it E–sharp rather than F. E–sharp is called the enharmonic of F. Every note (with one exception) has three names: or finstance C–, B–sharp, and D–double–flat are each enharmonics of one another. The exception is G–sharp and A flat.

SCALES : THE CLUE TO MUSIC'S TONE

THE first degree of a scale is called the tonic, or keynote; the second, the supertonic; the third, the mediant; the fourth, the sub-dominant; the fifth, the dominant; the sixth, the sub-mediant; the seventh, the leading-note.

When notes are required outside the compass of the five lines comprising the staff, leger-lines are employed.

A scale is an alphabetical succession of notes arranged in relation to a keynote, or tonic. A semitone is the smallest interval on a keyboard instrument. A tone is two semitones. Scales are of two modes, major and minor. On whichever note a major scale begins, the arrangement of tones and semitones is similar. The same rule applies to minor scales. Let us then take C as our starting-point:

Here is an alphabetical succession of notes. C to D is a tone; if you look at the piano you will see there is another note in between (in this case a black one). D to E is a tone, E to F a semitone, and so on. There is a semitone between the seventh and eighth degrees, B and C.

Hence we find that the semitones in a major scale fall between the third and fourth and seventh and eight degrees. Wherever you start a major scale, and one may be started on any note, black or white, the semitones must fall in these two places. If you play up eight notes, starting on G, you will find it sounds different; there is no tonic. There will be the correct succession of notes and semitones as far as the seventh degree. Raise this seventh degree to the black note immediately above it, and the tonality, or key-feeling, will be satisfactory. Similarly, if you start a scale on D, including the F–sharp you used in the scale of G, you will hear the same unsatisfactory result between C and D you heard when you started on G, between F and G. Repeat the process you practised in G, sharpen the seventh note, and the effect is satisfying.

The scales using sharps for inflection arise in perfect fifths from C. Each scale represents a key.

This example represents the key-signatures of the scales employing sharps. The tonic of each scale is shown, and you will note that the tonics are successively a fifth apart. The change of pitch is a convenience merely, and avoids the use of leger lines.

Now start a scale on F, employing white notes only. A semitone will be found between the leading-note and the tonic; between the mediant and sub-dominant there is a tone. Lower the sub-dominant by one semitone to B flat and the required semitone results. Start another scale on B♭ and you will find the E has to be flattened.

The flat scales, then, arise by perfect fourths from C, and the sharp scales by perfect fifths from C. The last flat added to the key-signature is the fourth degree of the scale, while the last sharp added to a key-signature with sharps, is the seventh.

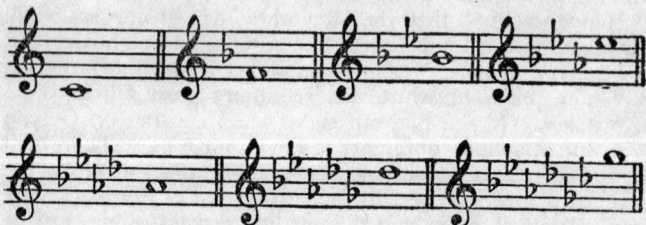

This example represents the key-signature of the scales employing flats, and the key-signature in the last bar shows that the scale of G–flat is the enharmonic of the scale of F–sharp. Theoretically, then, each scale is similar, and, theoretically, each key sounds the same. Æsthetically and practically (curious these two apparently dissimilar adverbs should be used in conjunction), the difference is as the difference between right and wrong.

HOW DIFFERENT MINOR SCALES ARE MADE

SCALES are of two modes: major and minor. The third and the sixth degrees of a major scale are major; the third and the sixth degrees of a minor scale are minor, and each contains one semitone less than the corresponding major interval. Minor scales are of two kinds: harmonic and melodic, or arbitrary.

If you start a scale on C and flatten the third and sixth degrees, the harmonic scale of C–minor is obtained. The key-signature of a minor scale is that of the major scale a minor third higher : thus, the key-signature of C–minor is that of E–flat major, and these two keys are called the relative. major and minor of one another.

The semitones in the harmonic minor scale occur between the second and third, the fifth and sixth, and the seventh and eight degrees. In order to obtain the semitone between the seventh and eight degrees, the seventh note of the scale is raised one semitone by means of an accidental. Hence in the scale of C–minor the leading-note B will always require a natural. The interval of the augmented second between the sixth and seventh degrees results. The seventh degree of a harmonic minor scale, then, is inflected one semitone up by means of an accidental.

The use of the interval of the augmented second is often undesirable. The melodic form of the minor scale eliminates this interval. It is formed by raising the sixth as well as the seventh degree a semitone *ascending* and by flattening both these degrees *descending*. Hence in an ascending melodic minor scale both the sixth and seventh degrees require accidentals.

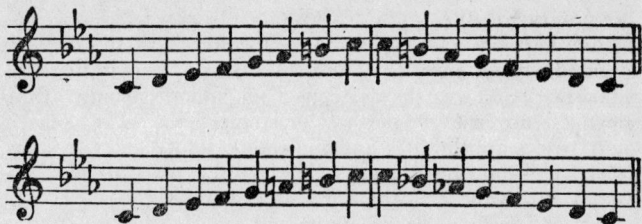

The above example shows, in the top line, the scale of C–minor, harmonic form, and in the bottom line, the melodic form. C–major and C–minor are known as the tonic major and minor of one another. C–major and A–minor are relative major and minor. C–minor and E–flat major are relative minor and major. Diatonic means according to the key-signature. Major and minor scales are diatonic. Chromatic means contrary to the key-signature. A chromatic scale may start on any note. It proceeds by semitones.

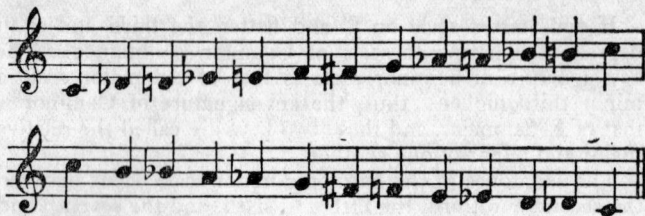

This is the chromatic scale of C. Actually in a piece of music the enharmonics of many of these notes are written. The scale given above, though, is the correct one theoretically.

A piece of music, then, is written in a certain key or scale : this key decides its tonality. This does not mean that a piece of music remains in one key ; this would be like a picture painted in one colour only : the picture would have no " colour." Few pieces of music with any pretensions to completeness remain in one key throughout ; fresh keys are employed ; new lands entered. Modulation, as change of key is called, may be effected smoothly and by almost imperceptible steps, or a new key may be jumped into like jumping a dyke.

THE INTERVAL : A BRIDGE FROM NOTE TO NOTE

AN interval is the numerical distance between one note and another : whether the notes forming the interval are sounded simultaneously or successively is immaterial. Intervals are of two kinds, consonant and dissonant. Consonances are either perfect or imperfect. The perfect consonances are the fifth and the octave, and their inversions, the fourth and the unison. These intervals are called the perfect intervals, and their use is governed by rule. The imperfect consonances are sixths and thirds.

The dissonances are seconds and sevenths, and all augmented and diminished intervals. The quantity of an interval is *the number of notes of a scale* contained within its limits. Intervals are counted inclusively, hence, C to E is a third. The quality of an interval is determined by *the number of semitones* contained within its limits. Intervals are reckoned upwards. The intervals above the tonic of the major scale are either perfect or major : thus, perfect unison (or first), major second, major third, perfect fourth, perfect fifth, major sixth, major seventh, perfect octave (or eighth). The intervals above the tonic of the minor scale in its harmonic form are perfect, major, or minor. Thus, perfect unison, major second, minor third, perfect fourth, perfect fifth, minor sixth, major seventh, perfect octave. The melodic form of the minor scale contains a major sixth ascending, and a minor seventh and minor sixth descending.

An interval is described as minor when it is one semitone less than major. An interval is augmented when it is a semitone greater than perfect or major. An interval is diminished when it is a semitone less than a perfect or a minor interval. The quantity of an interval, then, is constant : a third, for instance, remains a third, although the quality of the third may vary. Perfect intervals may be changed in quality by one semitone only. Major and minor intervals may be inflected, or changed in quality, by two semitones.

A shows a perfect fifth because both notes occur in the scale of C. B shows an augmented fifth because the interval is a semitone greater than perfect. C is a sixth in quantity : to determine its quality, consider E its tonic. C–sharp is contained within the scale of E, therefore the interval is a major sixth. In D, B–flat is the lowest note. D is then the major third. D–sharp is a semitone greater : the interval, therefore, is an augmented third.

An interval is said to be inverted when the relative position of the two notes comprising it is reversed. In quantity, therefore, it changes. The sum of an interval and its inversion equals nine.

The quality of an interval changes on inversion also. Perfect intervals remain perfect, major intervals become minor, and minor become major ; augmented intervals become diminished, and diminished, augmented.

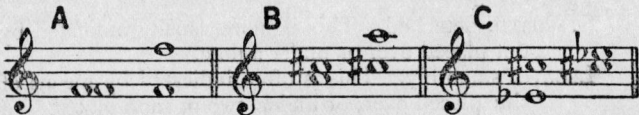

A is a perfect unison, which, inverted, becomes a perfect octave; B is a major third and, inverted, a minor sixth; C is an augmented sixth, its inversion is a diminished third. Note that if we enharmonically alter one of the notes forming an interval, the quality of the interval will remain the same, but its quantity will be different. For instance, if we take example C and name the notes E–flat and D–flat respectively, the interval will still contain ten semitones, but its quality will be a seventh.

All the intervals named have been simple intervals. Compound intervals are intervals greater than an octave. Although for convenience we speak of a tenth or of a thirteenth, the essential features of a tenth and a third, of a thirteenth and a sixth, are identical.

TERMS WHICH TELL THE MUSIC'S CHARACTER

TIME, in music, has been defined as the procession of the beats. The tempo of a piece of music is the speed at which it is played. The tempo is indicated by a direction placed at the beginning of the piece. The tempo may change once or many times during the course of the piece. The tempo indications in common use are :

PRESTO, quickly, and its superlative, PRESTISSIMO.
ALLEGRO, quickly, and its diminutive, ALLEGRETTO.
ANDANTE, moving (a little slowly), and its diminutive ANDANTINO.
LARGO, LENTO, ADAGIO, all signify slowly.

Each direction possesses a distinct *feeling* and character of its own. A piece marked *Presto* is entirely different in feeling and character from one marked *Allegro*.

Other indications are used, often in conjunction with the tempo indications, to express more clearly the mood of a piece of music. Of this nature are :

CANTABILE, singingly.   LEGGIERO, lightly.
EXPRESSIVO, expressively.   PESANTE, heavily.
MAESTOSO, majestically.   CON BRIO, brightly.
MESTO, sadly.
STACCATO, detached. This is more usually indicated by a dot placed over or under a note.
LEGATO, smoothly. This is often indicated by means of a slur placed over, or under, two or more notes.

CRESCENDO, or ◁◁, gradually getting louder.
DIMINUENDO, or ▷▷, gradually getting softer.
RALLENTANDO, gradually getting slower.
ACCELERANDO, gradually getting quicker.

Softly is indicated by *p* (*piano*), very softly by *pp* (*pianissimo*); loudly is shown by *f* (*forte*), and the superlative is *ff* (*fortissimo*). There is also *mp* and *mf* indicating *mezzo* (half) *piano* and *mezzo forte*. *fz* or *sf* (*sforzando*) means that the one note or combination of notes is to *bite*. (The use of this direction is characteristic of Beethoven.)

These short tables of tempo and mood indications might be greatly extended, but enough have been given to show their purpose. It is obvious that the proper observance of these marks of expression, as they are called, is akin to the proper modulation of the voice in reading aloud.

" HEARING " MUSIC WITH THE EYE

To be able to read music at an instrument the technique of the particular instrument must be understood. If you do not know how to play the violin you cannot read its music at the instrument : nor can a pianist read a piece on the violoncello.

By exercising the imagination, aided by a knowledge of the Elements of Music and of the Theory of Music, anyone, granted a certain natural aptitude and musical intelligence, can read a piece of music, with little, or even no knowledge, of the finger technique of instruments.

Although, in reading a piece of music away from an instrument, it is extremely hard to " auralise " chords other than those in constant use, and harder still a succession of them, it is not by any means impossible to get the " feel " of a piece of music through the eye.

It would be very difficult, for instance, to mistake a hymn-tune for a waltz, or to confuse a march with a two-step. From your knowledge of what a hymn-tune is, you would know it must have a certain " look " on paper, and a " look " very different from that of a waltz ; you would know that a march does not look like a two-step. These are extreme cases, but it is only a step further to be able to see that one hymn-tune has a tune in the top part while the other parts are dull and uninteresting, and that another has two, perhaps even three, interesting parts, all moving at once.

A piece of music such as a march or a waltz is as easy to read as a hymn-tune. Even if you cannot hear inwardly the harmonic combinations, you can follow the feeling, the gist of the music. The habit should be fostered of memorising tunes and the " feel " or sound of the harmony. It is value-less picking up a tune " by ear." But to learn tunes by heart from the printed page is interesting and a valuable exercise.

A medical doctor of my acquaintance, naturally musical, as a child was not given the opportunity of learning an instrument. Having qualified, he felt the urge of music, and became an ardent concert-goer. Later on he realised he obtained com-paratively little mental satisfaction from concerts, although, he said, he found them stimulating emotionally. He deter-mined, fully knowing the mental effort required, to study the Theory of Music. This he proceeded to do, and pursued a course of training, starting with the Elements of Music, through Elementary Harmony to its higher realms, through two-part Counterpoint to Canon and Fugue. He studied the capabilities of the Strings, of the Wood-wind and Brass, and is now able, he affirms, to read a quartet or a full score with confidence, and with a keen reaction. But, he says, he still attends concerts, since no amount of " auralising " can re-produce the sensuous effect of sound.

READING FURTHER ABOUT MUSIC

AMONGST the large number of books dealing with music in one or another of its many aspects, two books which may be highly praised are *The Limitations of Music*, by Eric Blom (Macmillan), and *The New Music*, by George Dyson (Oxford University Press). Each is of outstanding interest, and original both in thought and in matter. Each is scholarly, and neither can fail to stimulate curiosity and research. Of a more historical and critical nature are George Dyson's *The Progress of Music* (Oxford University Press) and C. H. Colles's *The Growth of Music* (Oxford University Press). William Wallace's *The Threshold of Music* (Macmillan) and C. H. H. Parry's *The Art of Music* (Kegan Paul) have achieved the status of classics by reason of their vision, reality, and erudition. The Elements of Music are dealt with fully by Stewart Macpherson in his *Rudiments of Music* (Joseph Williams, Limited). Each detail is pursued with meticulous care and characteristic thoroughness.

ADVICE ON HOW TO WRITE MUSIC

THOSE whose interest in music leads them to try and write it for themselves will find Sir John B. McEwen's *Harmony and Counterpoint* (Ricordi) very useful and essentially musical. The bulk of the exercises presented are not merely a succession of harmonic combinations ; a number of the tunes and basses are of considerable beauty. Hymn-tunes and chants are entirely absent, and rhythmic variety is both sought and achieved. A portion of the book is devoted to strict Counterpoint—a subject not touched upon in the present article but one of mathematical precision and fine interest. It must be admitted that McEwen's book is not altogether suited to the requirements of the student or of the examination candidate working without the aid of a capable teacher. For such students Macpherson's *Melody and Harmony* and *Practical Harmony* are more helpful, and are, in fact, written for this purpose. Macpherson's *Studies in the Art of Counterpoint* and *Form in Music* are valuable, and are written in a more interesting manner than the normal text-book. They are less purely utilitarian in scope and outlook than his books on Harmony. All Stewart Macpherson's educational treatises are published by Joseph Williams Limited.

C. H. Kitson's *The Art of Counterpoint* (Oxford University Press) is absorbingly interesting and is the expression of a definite point of view, as is also, but in a lesser degree, his *Evolution of Harmony* (Oxford University Press). Two other books which may be recommended unreservedly are R. O. Morris's *Foundations of Practical Harmony and Counterpoint* and his book on Figured Bass (both published by the Oxford University Press). These, like Dr. Kitson's books, are original in scope and are of practical value. Adam Carse's *Counterpoint Exercises* (Augener) is a delightful compilation of exercises in rhythmical counterpoint, including Canon, together with short hints for working them. His two little books of *Harmony Exercises* are useful and written for examination candidates.

MUSIC AS A PROFESSION

by EDMUND RUBBRA

ROMANTIC novels and plays have for long fostered the idea that a composer is a superhuman being who, meditatively sitting on a hard garret chair, receives without visible effort floods of melody and harmony from some unknown but presumably divine source. Even if we have not studied the notebooks of Beethoven, a moment's reflection will convince us that this is far from being a true picture. Granted, however, that the music is divinely inspired, for we can always recall the case of Mozart, yet the spirit will not condescend to use our hands and fingers planchette-wise for the purpose of writing it down. The actual putting on to paper of music is a highly specialised work. Without this particularised knowledge the ideas would be valueless to others, for the written score is as necessary for musical communication as a written letter is for verbal communication. One can, of course, employ an amanuensis to write the copy down to dictation, but two minds are distinctly inferior to one in producing a piece of music, unless, as would rarely happen, the amanuensis were a mere will-less automaton.

PUTTING THE IDEA INTO SHAPE

COMPOSITION is a craft. A craft is a moulding of ideas into an assimilable form. As we cannot eat the Platonic Idea of a potato, or brew a cup of tea from a Platonic Essence, so we cannot listen to the amorphous Idea that is the starting-point of any piece of music. The idea must assume some kind of material form, and that will only happen if the receiver of the idea *thinks in terms of music*. Once the idea assumes a tangible shape for others to grasp, the composer becomes a species of gardener who, at every point in the growth of the music, prunes away all unnecessary shoots and directs it to a form which is satisfactory both to himself and to others. But both the gardener and the musician must, at some point in the growth, not necessarily at the beginning, have an image of what the ultimate form must be, otherwise the plant and the music will be but a rambling and incoherent improvisation. As life cannot be imagined without a limiting and defining form, so form is a necessary vehicle for successions of sounds. Form is the basis of even the individual sound, for experiments have proved that when a sensitive plate covered with a thin layer of sand is exposed to the vibrations of a musical note, the sand will form itself into a definite and balanced pattern. A noise creates a distorted and unbalanced pattern.

What then is form ? and how can the student discover what is its nature ? He can examine the works of the classical masters and find out the underlying formal principles. But what then ? Is this knowledge of service in the expression of *his own ideas ?* One ventures to think that the examination and analysis of the forms of classical works, however fascinating as a demonstration of the workings of other minds, is of doubtful value as a finger-post to the student's own imaginings, because form is not a ready-prepared receptacle into which we can pour our ideas : rather is it that *the ideas should build their own forms.*

HOW MUSIC SHOULD GROW

IT is an easy matter to analyse a Beethoven Sonata and say that its form consists of a first subject, a second and strongly contrasted subject, a development section, and then a return to the two principal ideas, but to reverse this procedure, to mould a piece of music to a form which in reality is an academic abstraction, is for the student a risky and unsatisfactory way of setting about composing. The two ideas of a Beethoven Sonata have an *organic* connection, that is, although they are contrasted, they have both sprung from one emotion, in the same way that both joy and sorrow are inherent in any single life-experience. The beginner, in composing a sonata, will most likely write strongly contrasted ideas with no inner connection ; so that, although the structure is, superficially, correct enough to place it in the category of a sonata, yet in reality it is but a patchwork of unrelated ideas, with no unity of purpose.

The soundest advice that can be offered to the student just beginning to put his ideas on to paper is to let the music grow and bud and flower according to its own nature. The policeman autocratically deflecting the traffic down a side street is not an exact symbol of artistic workings. There may, at first, be but blind growth : gradually, however, the shape and form will reveal itself. If the result is not the wished-for sonata, no matter, for the piece will have an organic unity of its own.

14

A Bach fugue or a Beethoven sonata is the result of the mind and imagination of Bach or Beethoven working in a particular way. *For them*, the Fugue or Sonata is the ideal form, but not necessarily for us.

TECHNIQUE : THE VEHICLE OF INSPIRATION

THIS, of course, is a counsel of perfection for the student wishing to become a composer in the real sense. Moreover, it pre-supposes a certain amount of technical proficiency, for technique is the vehicle of inspiration. If the aim is not so high, and limitations of expression are accepted, for the successful ballad-composer will rarely be successful in larger and more organically unified forms, then the technical demands are not so exacting. It is more an advantage than otherwise if the forms are simple and square-cut, for most popular music gains its effect by reiteration of easily assimilated rhythms and phrases, the actual make-up of the tune being to a large extent dependent, if a popular song, upon the words, if a dance-form upon the patterns of the actual dance.

Popular music does not, however, merely consist of a simply constructed and lyrical tune : to an increasing extent the resources of the modern harmonic vocabulary are used to colour the tune. Gone are the days of the *Daisy Bell* type of popular song : now we demand at least a passing acquaintance with the harmonic procedures of Debussy. Jazz in particular, by using the harmonic clichés of the last thirty years tries to keep up an illusion of modernity, but it is in reality one of the most reactionary movements in music. The composer of popular music must also have at his finger-ends the many tricks of orchestration whose only duty too often is to lash a semblance of life and energy into monotonous and uninspired tunes. Of course, the decision as to what kind of music the composer shall write must be made by himself. But whatever the decision, no harm is done by going through the usual period of training, for good craftsmanship, no matter in what strata of music it is found, is welcome.

WHERE THE COMPOSER CAN BE TRAINED

WHERE can this training in composition be obtained ? Usually it is best to go to a musical institution such as the Royal College of Music, the Royal Academy of Music, the Guildhall School of Music, or the Trinity College of Music. Not only is excellent instruction given by well-known teachers, but the student has opportunities for attending orchestral rehearsals and performances, opera, chamber music and choral concerts. This is invaluable, for no amount of statements on paper about the sounds and compasses of orchestral instruments and the effects of their combination, can take the place of aural apprehension. (If a book on orchestration is needed, no better work than Gordon Jacob's *Orchestral Technique* can be recommended. Forsyth's *Orchestration*, although excellent, is too detailed for a beginner). Institutional training has been often criticised because the students tend to form themselves into cliques, but in any case the young composer's work will be influenced by the almost inevitable hero-worship.

If the talent has already flowered into works of a fairly large scale, the student would be well-advised to enter for the free scholarship which is offered yearly by each of the above-mentioned institutions. The successful scholar is given at least three years' tuition in composition, and an instrument can be learnt as a second study. Facilities are given for the performance of any work the student may do. This is an invaluable experience for showing how difficult it is to equate intention with achievement.

After the period of apprenticeship is over, it is natural for the student to wonder what the prospects are of obtaining a livelihood by composition, or failing this, what are the opportunities for the performance of his works.

It may be said at once that the composer of serious music, unless he has independent means, will find it extremely difficult to live by his own creations. Looked at ideally, this is not a disadvantage, for the composer who earns his money entirely through his creative work will tend, however unconsciously, to cast an eye upon popularity. Under such conditions artistic verity is bound to suffer. One cannot, in the realm of art, choose a middle course : one must either live to create the music one feels without thought of monetary advantage, or be frankly commercial in one's output. If the former, the composer must, in order to live, have other strings to his bow.

BY-PATHS IN A COMPOSER'S CAREER

SUCH are the playing of other instruments, writing (criticism), conducting and lecturing. Many great composers, including Schumann, Hugo Wolf, and Debussy, have resorted to criticism as an ideal way of combining propaganda for their own artistic viewpoints with the earning of an income sufficient for their needs. If the propaganda is one-sided, its very enthusiasm makes it interesting reading. The young composer who is not drawn to instrumental playing as an additional means of expression—and composers are not notorious for being fine executive artists—would then be well-advised to develop any powers he may have as a writer. Classes in musical criticism can be attended at any of the before-mentioned institutions. The concentration that is needed to form a well-balanced judgment on either the performance or works of others has also valuable reper-cussions upon one's own work.

Conducting offers a fascinating by-path for the composer. The movements can be easily learnt from Dr. Adrian Boult's excellent *Handbook on Conducting*, and Wagner's essay *On Conducting* is full of interesting substance. But the learning of baton-movements, how to beat two, three, four or six in a bar, is only the first small step. The most important and most difficult task is to impress the body of players or singers with one's own reading of the music. The movements the conductor makes are symbols in space of a non-spatial music, a concentrated essence of the sound. In one sense, the conductor is a priest mediating between the music and the hearers, while the players or singers are the officiating clergy.

To be able to convey a clear image of one's intentions to a body of players demands years of experience, but a beginning can be made with small amateur groups. In every town there are singers and players who would welcome the oppor-tunity for combining and pooling their talents for the per-formance of concerted music. The advantages of such activity are equal on both sides, for the composer-conductor will from his experiences learn more about instrumental or vocal scoring than can be obtained through the pages of the best text-book or the instruction of a teacher.

IS THERE A SHORT-CUT TO FAME ?

ALL the above-mentioned activities pre-suppose that the initiator is to a certain extent known, otherwise his efforts would be fruitless. Is there a short-cut to this desirable state of affairs ? Circumstances of necessity differ in each case, but one piece of general advice can be offered to the young composer. Grasp every opportunity that comes for writing music, even if at the moment it seems to entail a lowering of the level of ambition. Craftsmanship is learnt by doing, not by waiting for inspiration. If one learns not to despise the smallest amount of music-making, all kinds of valuable connections will be made in the world of music, and a public interested in the composer's work will gradually be formed.

Unless the composer wishes to enter what are considered the more scholastic realms of music, the taking of degrees such as the Mus.Bac. and Mus.Doc. is not an absolute necessity. Indeed, a scholastic label is nowadays of far less value to the composer than it was in the Elizabethan era, when nearly all the famous composers were connected with the Church. (Byrd was organist at Lincoln Cathedral, Tallis at Waltham Abbey, Weelkes at Chichester Cathedral, and Gibbons at the Chapel Royal, London.) For lecturing, appointments to church organistships, or judging at musical competition festivals, the holder of a degree obtains more consideration. Many composers find the latter activity a useful adjunct to their own work.

GETTING THE COMPOSITION PERFORMED

OPPORTUNITIES for the performance of a composer's works are continually growing. There is the Royal College of Music Patron's Fund, the special functions of which are : the rehearsal and performance of works by British composers ; the assistance of performers, who are British subjects, in procuring a hearing in public ; and the provision of travelling scholarships and special grants to students ; also the publication of works.

Other information about this fund can be obtained from the Registrar of the Royal College of Music. The Contemporary Music Centre gives frequent concerts of new works, and an organisation called The First Performance Society, 22 Holland Park, London, W., was formed in 1934 for the especial purpose of giving first performances of new works. Again, the B.B.C. is doing a fine work in making known new compositions. These are some of the chief organisations, but there are numerous clubs, such as the Ballet Club, Notting Hill Gate, London, W., and the Federation of Music Clubs, which are only too glad to give performances of works by young composers.

The priority in importance of performance or publication could be debated at great length, but usually publishers are loth to risk publishing a new work which has not received some kind of public acknowledgment of its worth after a performance. In any case, composers should view publication as a means of widening the circulation of their music, rather than as a means of livelihood, for royalties are small unless the music has a big sale. The latter is a rare phenomenon, only to be met with in the sale of popular, classical, or instructional teaching music. The demand for good teaching music is continually expanding, and the composer who can express interesting ideas in the simplest terms, technically and musically, is sure of a ready market.

MUSIC REQUIRED FOR THE TALKING-FILM

A NEW and profitable field opening out for the composer is the provision of music for the talking film. Indeed, as Constant Lambert truly remarks in his book, *Music Ho!* much of the twentieth century output is film music straying in the alien grounds of abstract music. Its rhythmic pictorialism makes it a peculiarly effective background for underlining the dramatic situations.

AUGMENTING THE PERFORMER'S INCOME

C OMPOSERS then have a wide choice of activity, much wider than is offered by the more circumscribed life of the professional musician, by which is meant the performer. But the same difficulty arises with the latter as with the composer : unless the performer is particularly gifted, or perhaps it is truer to say, particularly popular, it is very difficult to gain a livelihood through playing engagements. Resort must often be made to teaching, privately and in schools, colleges, etc., and the wise performer will prepare himself or herself for this additional activity.

Teachers' training courses (including psychology) are given at all the well-known musical institutions, and through them or any of the scholastic agencies information about any vacant teaching post can be obtained.

A NEW POSSIBILITY FOR THE INSTRUMENTALIST

H ITHERTO three possibilities faced the instrumental player (the pianist is not included) : either to be a solo player, including concerted chamber music, an orchestral player, a teacher, or a combination of these. A fourth and growing possibility, and one which string players should quickly take advantage of, is the increasing popularity of music played on the viols. These were the predecessors, not the ancestors, of the violin family, and practically all the instrumental music up to the end of the seventeenth century and even later was written for what was known as consorts of viols, collections of viols of different sizes and different ranges in pitch, with or without the addition of other instruments, such as recorders.

Arnold Dolmetsch was the first important figure in advocating the necessity of hearing the old music on the instruments for which it was written, but other groups of players are now in existence (a club exists at 44A Loudoun Road, London, N.W.8) for educating the public to the smaller but sweeter voice of the old instruments in interpreting the early classical music. There is a growing demand in schools and colleges for such groups of players, and the student accustomed to the modern stringed instrument can rapidly adjust his or her technique to the requirements of the older instrument.

The current pessimism as to the state of affairs in the musical world is justified only if we persist in ignoring the changes that are rapidly taking place in its constitution. But if the student is adaptable, and does not expect the outline of his life to form the same contours as those of a generation ago, then there is every chance of his making a success. Destruction and new creation of forms is an eternal world-process.

THE GROWTH OF STAGECRAFT
THROUGH THE AGES

by BARBARA NIXON

THE style of drama is very considerably influenced by
the stagecraft of the age. The latter does not create
new style—that is the work of history, and of the
environment and circumstances of the writers—but the
technical craft can retard or advance it to a very great extent.
Those few really creative and imaginative artists who fight
for a new spirit or a new style have to direct a large part of
their struggle against the conventions of the practical side.
Tradition dies particularly hard in England. Ask an average
playgoer what his idea of a stage set is, and he will give you
a picture of a room, with a ceiling, and walls, and windows
and doors, as like an ordinary room as possible ; any suggestion of something less photographic he will class as " arty "
and peculiar. The expressionist and constructivist sets of
Germany and Russia are considered at best as highbrow, and
more usually as foreign eccentricities. Gordon Craig found
so little response to his new ideas at the beginning of this
century that he has been unable to work in this country for
a long time.

Yet the modern movement bears a very close resemblance
in many of its principles to the stage of the Greeks and
Romans, and to the Elizabethan theatre ; and there is little
reason to suppose that the stage of the eighteenth and nineteenth centuries with its elaborations is any " better " than
that of preceding or subsequent ages. Critics to-day complain
that there are few really great dramas ; but to build a grand
tragedy on a stage cluttered with sofas and ash-trays, pictures,
and all the naturalistic detail of to-day would have taxed the
powers of Shakespeare himself.

It is usually curtly stated that the Greeks and the
Elizabethans used no scenery. If by scenery is meant the
painted panorama of a seashore, or a canvas forest, it is true
enough. But the word " scenery " can be used in its wider
sense, to comprise the formal and constructional side of any
dramatic production—all that is not comprised by the words
and the movements of the actors. Stage decoration, however,

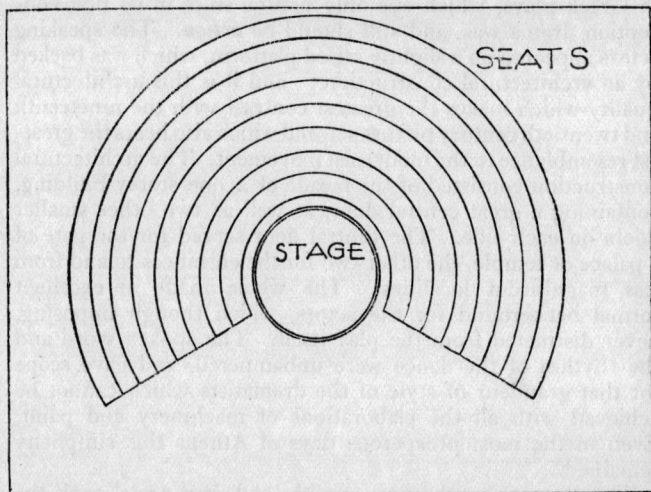

33. THE FINE SIMPLICITY OF THE GREEK THEATRE

The magnificent plays of Æschylus, Sophocles, and Euripides were all performed on a circular stage set in a semicircular auditorium. There was no scenery except the façade of a one-storeyed building with three entrances.

should always be subordinate to the play itself; it should be a background and a platform for the actor, and the designer who works for a burst of applause for his scenic effects on the rise of the curtain, misunderstands the whole meaning of both theatre and stage.

Drama is the most representative of all the arts, and therefore the formal side of this representation is of the greatest importance, and naturally exerts a very great influence over the style of both playwriting and acting.

THE IMPOSING SIMPLICITY OF THE GRECIAN SETTING

THE classical theatre was set in a semi-circular auditorium, and for that reason alone the painted vista as we know it was out of the question, since even if it had been desired, it would have blocked the line of visibility. The stage, or orchestra, was in the centre of this semi-circle, and it was here that the chorus danced. The dance performed a very large function in Greek plays, which was only natural since in its first conception drama was, and still should be *action*. The speaking actors appeared on a slightly raised platform, which was backed by an architectural construction ; and it is this architectural quality which makes the greatest contrast with the nineteenth and twentieth century picture set, and which also bears the greatest resemblance to the modernist movement. The architectural construction consisted of the façade of a one-storey building, containing a great central door, as well as two other smaller doors on each side. The central door served for the gate of a palace or temple, the other two for the entrances to and from less magnificent localities. The whole made an excellent formal background for the actors, which though imposing, never distracted from the play itself. The spoken word and the rhythm of the dance were unhampered, and gave scope for that grandeur of style of the dramatists which cannot be achieved with all the elaborations of machinery and paint. Even in the most prosperous days of Athens this simplicity remained.

The Romans, with more wealth and less taste, took the fundamental idea of the Greek theatre, and immediately began to elaborate it. The auditorium and the orchestra remained the same, but the background became more and more complicated. The single storey building became a double, or even treble storeyed affair, with pillars and porticoes, and all the ornate decoration that the architects could contrive. A formality remained, it is true, but the simplicity had gone, and the effect is at once visible in the plays. The dramatists had to over-write, and the actors to over-act, in order to make the play heard and understood in front of this overwhelming structure. Where Æschylus had one murder, Seneca had three or four, and ranting took the place of poetry in a desperate effort to achieve significance, and to keep the attention of the audience.

By the time of Augustus decoration had advanced even further. The three doors were no longer left as simple entrances or exits, but vistas of colonnades and inner courtyards were painted behind them on triangular pieces of machinery called " periacti." The triple-faced periacti of the Greeks were developed, more elaborate scenes were painted on each face, and the whole thing revolved as occasion demanded. These periacti never took up more than a small part of the stage, and in no sense resembled the modern backcloth. The paintings themselves were formal. Tragedy demanded pillars ; comedy, domestic interiors or ordinary houses ; satire, trees or bushes Perhaps the best description of the Roman stage can be found in Vitruvius. He writes :

> " The *scæna* displays the following scheme. In the centre are double doors decorated like those of a royal palace. At the right and left are the doors of the guest chambers. Beyond are spaces provided for decoration . . . places that the Greeks called περιακτοι because in these places are triangular pieces of machinery which revolve, each having three decorated faces. When the play is to be changed, or when gods enter to the accompaniment of sudden claps of thunder, these may be revolved and present a face differently decorated. Beyond these places are the projecting wings which afford entrances to the stage, one from the forum, the other from abroad."

THE STAGE TAKES SHAPE IN ENGLAND

THE early English drama inherited nothing in its beginning from the classical tradition. It began in the Church, where the raised altar, and later the porch with its architectural background, made an admirable and natural stage. When the plays were taken over by the guilds there was still no such thing as a permanent theatre. Bare platforms erected in market places, and, more frequently, carts and wagons, were used. The convention of locality was established as easily, though more crudely, as in the classical theatre. While the plays were still religious, Hell was assumed to be one side of the stage, the normal world in the centre, and Heaven at the other extreme ; and the progress of such moralists as Everyman was easily marked in his passage from right to left. Even when the plays became more advanced the added complications were more in the nature of properties such as Noah's Ark than decorative scenery. Each guild provided the necessaries for the various plays. The Goldsmiths gave the jewellery for *The Three Magi*, and the Glovemakers the gloves for God. The stage remained for the most part a bare platform, with the audience standing round three sides of it.

When plays moved from the market-place to the inn-yard, an important advance was made, and the artistic standard rose accordingly. All the Elizabethan theatres were modelled on these inn-yards in their construction. The square shape

and the balcony round were both kept. The stage jutted out
into the floor space, and where the balcony went behind the
stage, it was used for the walls of a city or a bedroom window.
The Elizabethans established a formality fundamentally
similar to that of the classical stage. The old " orchestra "
was now taken up by the audience, and accordingly dancing
never played such a large part as in the classical theatre.

Playwrights are necessarily bound by the technical possibilities open to them. Elizabethan dramatists knew that they
could use the upper balcony, the little space that could be
curtained off for an inner room, and the open platform stage
on which the main action took place. Nearly all their plays
use these three. But apart from them, stage decoration as we
know it barely existed. The inner stage may at times have
had a painted background hung in it, but the main platform
only had the more solid variety of " property," such as a
bench or table, or at most a tree. As the audience was on
three sides more was impossible, and the theatre remained
theatre in the truer sense of the word, a place in which to see
and hear and to participate in the action. Landscapes were
described in verse rather than depicted with paint on an
unsteady canvas. In the more decadent period which followed,
the lack of restrictions led to much the same standard, drama
almost becoming melodrama, which had existed in Seneca's
time.

The apron stage, jutting out into the auditorium, had an
enormous influence on the plays of the time. It provided a
very valuable contact between the actor and the audience.
There were no footlights and no proscenium arch to form a
barrier between them. The play was performed in the midst
of the spectators, and became more easily part of their actual
experience. To-day, both to the stalls and the gallery, a play
is something to be watched almost as detachedly as pictures
in the Royal Academy, or a horse show. Although we have
all the machinery to provide spectacular illusion, lighting
effects and elaborate scenery, we have lost the essential
illusion of something really vital taking place in our midst.

The soliloquy again, which seems such a cumbersome device
on the modern stage, was reasonable enough on the Elizabethan.
The actor could talk quite naturally to an audience which
was close to, and all around him, and could easily discuss his
real motives or his philosophy. He did not have to use the
full strength of his voice to reach a gallery almost beyond his

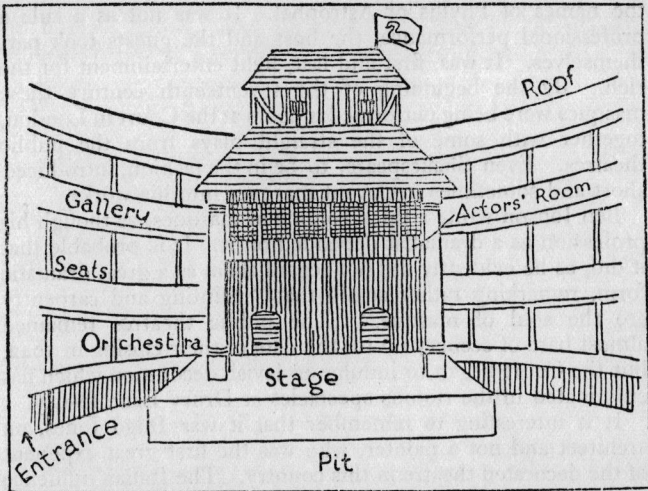

34. A GREAT THEATRE MODELLED ON AN INN YARD

By the time of the Swan Theatre, of which this is a diagram, the Elizabethan Theatre had developed its characteristic square stage jutting out into the auditorium. The balcony or gallery, derived from the inn-yards where plays were formerly performed, continued behind the stage and was used to represent the walls of a city or a bedroom window.

range, and at the same time pretend that his fellow actors, three feet away from him, could not hear what he was saying. Several of the masters of the modern theatre on the continent have experimented with types of stage similar in many ways to the Elizabethan, not for antiquarian reasons, nor from a sentimental interest in an ancient art, but from an attempt to establish this greater contact between the audience and the play.

PRETTY ENTERTAINMENTS PLAYED FOR THE RICH

THE masque in England began as an out-door recreation on occasions such as a royal visit to the country house of some earl or lord. It was intended as the lightest and prettiest entertainment, filled with charming compliments to both guest and host. Frequently it took the form of a classical pastoral with the noble visitors only thinly disguised under the names of Phyllis or Astrophel. It was not as a rule a professional performance, the host and the guests took part themselves. It was, first and last, light entertainment for the rich. By the beginning of the seventeenth century these masques were being performed indoors at the Court in London, together with some of the straight plays from the public theatres. Even Shakespeare, to be in the fashion, introduced short and sometimes irrelevant masques into his works.

Ben Jonson wrote a thick volume of masques, as though his profession as a dramatist depended on it. It is probable that it did, as he evidently did not regard them as a great dramatic form, remarking rather acidly that " painting and carpentry are the soul of masque." The public theatres remained almost bare of scenery up till the date of their closing in 1642, but the Court began to indulge in lavish decoration which has culminated in the riotous spectacles at Drury Lane to-day.

It is interesting to remember that it was Inigo Jones, an architect and not a painter, who was the first great exponent of the decorated theatre in this country. The Italian influence on literature had been very marked during Elizabethan days, but now in the seventeenth century their style of building was adopted too. In Italy the theatre had died during the Dark Ages, but when it revived again it was still based on the Roman model, as for instance in the case of the Palladian, constructed on the classical style but with a roof added. What the Romans had done to the Greek original, the Italians did even more to the Roman. Although they retained the single architectural background for all plays, they added further storeys and further rows of pillars. They enlarged the doorways and inserted even more extensive painted vistas behind them.

Inigo Jones brought these fashions back to England, including the newly discovered laws of perspective painting. He built sets with splendid colonnades and archways, and at the back he hung a cloth with further colonnades painted to diminish in an imaginary distance. As all his theatrical work was done for the indoor Court stage, he was greatly helped by the use of artificial light which can give the appearance of solidity to a two dimensional object.

These two innovations, artificial light and perspective painting, were the two most important technical achievements of the time, and they have both had far-reaching results. The first has progressed out of all recognition since the discovery of gas, and later electricity, although the second has remained essentially the same. Moreover the latter is still haunted by the same fundamental difficulty, that what may appear to be the most convincing perspective, in accordance with all the rules of actuality, from the centre of the stalls, cannot look anything but ridiculous from the side or the gallery. With the masque and the court play the engineer and the painter began to supersede the author. In Elizabethan days it was the playwright and the actor who mattered, now it was chiefly the technician. The actor, rant as he might with the new horror tragedies coming into vogue, was lost among the formidable array of constructions towering behind him. Drama was becoming mainly a matter of spectacle, and the original conception of the theatre was forgotten.

THE PURITANS ROB THE POOR OF THEIR PLAYS

In 1642 the Puritans closed the theatre. A few troupes of actors struggled on illegally, but for twenty years drama was practically dead. The effect of the Puritan ban lasted far longer than the actual period of its enforcement, in two ways particularly : it infused the idea into the growing middle class population that the theatre was immoral and wicked, an idea which died very hard at the end of the nineteenth century ; and even more important, it depopularised the theatre and drove it into the hands of the Court, so that it became primarily an upper class amusement.

When Charles II returned in 1660 he brought with him the French tradition which he had found in his exile. In France technical equipment had already made great advances. At one time the most famous theatre in Paris was known as " La Salle des Machines," on the strength of its complicated apparatus for moving scenery and producing effects. By 1689 the " flying " system was in existence, and with this every hope of restraining the extravagances of scene designers was gone. Inigo Jones had had to limit himself to one or two big scenes because it was clearly impossible to move his massive structures with any speed by hand. But now the new theatres were built with as much space above the proscenium arch as below, that is, with double the height of the stage as seen by the audience ; and a system of pulleys and ropes was put in so that most of the scenery could be raised or " flown " quickly out of sight. In England these ropes were hand-pulled for many years to come, almost until the present day ; but on the Continent and now here, the counterweight eliminates half the labour and more than half the waste of time.

In the building of Charles' new theatres, Dorset Garden and The Theatre Royal, the apron stage almost disappeared. Three or four feet remained jutting out and this space was used for asides and soliloquies, but the main production was pushed behind the proscenium and became a moving picture, a spectacle set in a heavy architectural frame. The frame still resembled the Roman pattern, but the Romans had used their architectural structure as a permanent background to all plays, and only put anything like the modern conception of scenery behind the doors. The Italian theatre of the sixteenth century enlarged these doors and the vistas behind them, but still kept the main structure. The new theatre kept only the roof and the supporting pillars, as it were, and what had been two small views became the whole stage. The theatres themselves were much larger, and the audience no longer participated in a performance going on in their midst, but went to see as many spectacles as the ingenuity of the carpenters and the engineers could contrive for them. There were attempts to build smaller theatres, but the authorities of the City of London refused permission.

WHEN A STAGE WAS ALL THE WORLD

MARLOWE and Shakespeare had used no scenery, and there was therefore no reason why their plays should not move from England to Persia, Italy, France and back again ; the bare apron stage could easily represent each of them equally well, as long as the actors said where they were supposed to be. The Elizabethan audience had to listen, it could not just sit back and watch. The continuity of the play was not broken by this multiplicity of scenes as long as they followed quickly after each other. An audience which could imagine that a bare stage was Persia, could just as easily imagine that it was England a few minutes later, if it remained bare, and if they were told of the change.

The first result of the introduction of scenery was to limit the number of scenes, and this coincided with the neo-classical movement which came to England from the Continent and took such a strong hold in the eighteenth century. The three unities of time, place, and action, which Shakespeare had successfully ignored, were insisted on, and there was a strict adherence to classical forms. It is important to remember that this classicism was based much more on the Roman pattern than on the Greek. Aristotle's critique was read, it is true, and his precepts were followed ; but the plays which were copied were those of Seneca rather than the greater masterpieces of Æschylus or Euripides—authors who tempered the austerity of their dramas with the beautiful poetry of the chorus.

In France, Racine and Corneille took the Roman model, not only in its dramatic form but in its verse style. The rhymed couplet with a stop at the end became " the correct thing," and when Racine carried on the sense of one line to the next without even a comma between, the whole French literary world was thrown into consternation. Pope and Dryden established this model in England as exactly as it was possible, regardless of the fact that the English language is far less formal than the French, and that the heroic couplet is rather unsuitable for any very lengthy recitation.

This formality both of matter and manner was, however, of assistance to the actor in his new position. The scene designer was still more of an architect than a painter and he decorated his stage with massive pillars and porticoes which towered above the actors and made them appear rather insignificant little puppets in a mass of masonry. The subtleties of Shakespearian verse, the quick and sparkling prose of the Restoration comedies were overpowered by the spectacle, and could not possibly be expected to reach to the distant gallery. The heroic rhymed couplet offered a solution, since it could be declaimed in the best oratorical manner. The increased formality of plays and the necessity for declamation produced an increased conventionalism in all sides of the theatre. Actors began to rant and over-act in a vain attempt to compete with the efforts of the carpenters, and the emotional quality of the plays became more strained and more false.

THE DRAMA UNDER ADVERSE CONDITIONS

IT is not, of course, fair to blame the scene designers for the corruption of the drama which immediately followed the eighteenth century. There were many reasons for this. First the Puritans had successfully stopped the theatre as a popular concern. It continued to exist as an entertainment for a small coterie, patronised and to a certain extent financed by the Court, but as the theatre is essentially a popular form of art it cannot thrive in such conditions. Moreover when the House of Hanover came to the throne even Royal support was withdrawn, and it was left with no vital support at all; it lost all pretence to having any intellectual appeal, and became a pleasure resort of rather a low level.

History did not produce a genius capable of dramatising the age. Sheridan and Goldsmith struggled to revive something of the glitter, superficial as it was, of the Restoration comedies; but after them, in an age as dramatic and more revolutionary than the Elizabethan, there was no one. The French Revolution, the Industrial Revolution with its strikes and its fierce struggles, offered magnificent dramatic material, but the theatre had become such an amusement for the idle that no one dared to put these problems on the stage. But the technical elaborations of the scene designers, though they cannot be held responsible, certainly contributed to a very great extent to the decay of the drama. Plays which had little plot and less characterisation could be made tolerable by the ingenuity of the painter. More and more devices were crowded into the thirty square feet of stage. Inigo Jones had built his massive pillars and built them square or round; now the false " wing " and " border " came into being, and with them the ascendancy of the painter was established.

By the later Victorian period painted scenery had so taken possession that stock sets were kept in theatres—and not only in the touring companies. Scenery had become almost as much of a convention as in the classical stage, though of an infinitely more shoddy and tawdry variety. Theatres kept their forest, their garden, their well-to-do interior, and their poor interior. Pictures as well as panelling were painted on the walls, even the furniture at times. Companies, for instance, would provide three chairs and a table for actual use, and then have another three chairs painted on the background, obviously of no utilitarian value, and of no decorative value either, merely to fill up a blank space. The Victorian mind hated emptiness, and every corner had to be filled. The chairs were painted as realistically as the artist's capabilities would allow, but even at their best they could only look convincing from one position in the house. Even the shadows were painted; they had to be, since there was now no solid structure which could throw a shadow. The whole theatre had become a nonsensical attempt at " let's pretend," at the same time leaving no scope for the imagination of the spectator.

Everything in the theatre became part of a " stock " concern—the plays, the leading rôles, the costumes, the scenery, even the gestures of the actors, all had to fit in to stereotyped rules. It is surely easier to imagine a landscape described on a bare stage, than to be really convinced by a mass of paint on an unstable backcloth. Defenders of the Victorian age say that despite its tawdriness and fantastic convention, the theatre had its charm. So perhaps have the wax-works at Madame Tussauds, but they cannot be compared with sculpture ; and in the same way when compared with the ages of great drama, much of the Victorian stage is best ignored.

DEVICES TO AID THE IMAGINATION

THE use of " wings " and " flats " was now universal. The word " flat " explains itself ; it is a piece of canvas stretched taut on a wooden frame, and painted to look as solid as possible, either with trees or pillars, or pictures, or whatever the scene of the play might require. These were placed alongside each other, secured with rope, and kept upright by means of wooden braces behind them ; the back wall was thus complete. The side walls were dealt with by the wings. Built on the same principle, they were placed one behind the other at intervals of three or four feet, from left to right of the stage. Each one masked the one behind, the audience was prevented from seeing the workings of the theatre at the side, and from at least one place in the house it could get a fairly convincing idea of a room. The ceiling, or sky, was contrived in much the same way ; " borders "—painted strips of cloth—were hung overhead in rows behind each other, and three would generally prevent the spectators from seeing above the set.

This method, though it may sound confusing in description, was simple to use and to move, if rather crude, and it maintained undisputed sway for half a century. Any scenic inventiveness was applied, not to altering the fundamental structure, but to elaborating the surface only. Exits and entrances were made between the wings, and as there were three gaps of this sort on each side the actors appeared and disappeared with a supreme indifference to any laws of architectural possibility or logic. The Victorian stage was a rather curious mixture of a conventional theatricality, and an irrational attempt at a false naturalism.

SCENERY REACTS TO THE REAL LIFE PLAY

AT the end of the century came the reaction. Belasco, Otto Brahm, and Antoine headed the new movement in decoration. They saw how ridiculous the Victorian convention had become and set out to introduce an almost photographic realism. Robertson, Pinero, in England, and above all Ibsen on the continent, were writing plays about real life on a life-size scale. They abandoned the false heroics, the tawdry emotions, and the pretentious language which had become tradition, and wrote in plain prose of people who might be met in ordinary life, of the problems which the codes of society forced on the individual, and of the struggles of the individual to assert himself against these iron laws. The old style of décor had done very well as a setting for heroines running mad, or other equally extreme forms of pathos and melodrama, but they were of no use for a production of *The Second Mrs. Tanqueray* or of *The Doll's House*. Ibsen gave detailed instructions for the sets of all his plays ; part of his study was curtained off as a stage, and he decided how many doors and windows there were to be, and how they were to be placed in relation to each other, and to the architectural possibilities of the house. The door at the left led to the bedroom, the door at the back to the hall, and actors could no longer wander on and off the stage whenever they liked.

One great change towards naturalism was achieved very easily. It is surprising that it had not been used before. On the Victorian stage the back wall at least had looked something like a back wall, but the sides had never looked like anything but what they were—wings. By placing these wings end to end up and down stage, instead of three feet apart and across it, the side wall immediately looked as convincing as the back. Naturally doors that opened and shut like actual doors had to be inserted, and having got thus far it was only a short step to do away with the old sky borders, lay a ceiling over the whole, and the modern box set was complete—a room as convincing as one's own rooms at home, except that the fourth wall which should have come across the footlights was not there, and the audience could see inside.

ACTORS BEGIN TO " USE ALL GENTLY "

THE new plays and their new settings had a marked effect on dramatic standards. The actors were now acting in a life-like room, and they had to abandon the old ranting and declaiming manner, and as it were, suit their voices and their gestures to the armchairs and the tables around them. Naturalistic expression became essential, as anything a little broader immediately looked laughable. Remarks had to be addressed to the other actors on the stage and not given directly and unashamedly to the gallery. To-day the vogue for naturalism has taken such a hold that often, even in West End theatres, an actor is so intent on holding a life-like conversation with his fellow actors that he is barely audible beyond the tenth row of the stalls.

The move towards naturalism was excellent in so far as it gave back to the stage some of the old reality and, consequently, importance. The theatre could now deal with current and contemporary problems, and it began to take its place again as the important social art form that it can be. But as was to be expected, the pendulum of reaction swung right to the other extreme. Naturalism of construction was followed quickly by naturalism of decoration. The late Victorian home was crowded with furniture and ornaments, until barely a few feet of floor and a few inches of plain wall were visible. Belasco brought all this decoration to the stage, down to the last antimaccassar and the last shelf of bric-à-brac.

One of the results was the same as the over-decorated pillared scenery of the eighteenth century—the actor was crowded off the stage. True, it was all very life-like, but it was not artistic, since one of the fundamental necessities of any art is selection. The actor's face was lost against a confused background of pictures, mirrors, shelves, and hangings, and his movements were limited by countless tables, chairs, carpets, and stools. He could still, it is true, imitate Mr. Everyman at home, but that for more than one act is a dull subject ; and when he was required to express deeper emotions or more imaginative actions he was too circumscribed to be able to do so.

Another result of this change to naturalism and the box set was that the number of scenes had again to be limited, because, with a ceiling and side walls, the difficulties of quick changes were far greater. The Elizabethans used no scenery and had a multitude of scenes. The eighteenth century used heavy and elaborate scenery and at once had to limit them. They were not content with saying that it was convenient; they quoted Aristotle and said that it was right. With the simplified system of wings and borders of the Victorian age the number of scenes crept up and up till it nearly equalled the Elizabethan. The naturalists brought this process to a dead stop, and dramatists had to write their plays with a maximum of three sets. If they were really ingenious, they contrived that the whole action should take place in one and the same room.

DRAMA AND ITS MODERN SETTINGS

IN dealing with the modern stage there are three main sections—the continuation of the naturalistic, the " colossal " show dependent on complicated machinery, and the more symbolic, expressionist, or constructivist setting. In England the naturalistic method still holds the floor, but a naturalism very much simplified, still using the box set, but eliminating a great deal of the extra decoration. This in interior scenes reflects no credit on the stage itself, but more on the progress of modern taste in architecture and furniture design, and the growing preference for a bare wall rather than one covered with flowered papers. In exterior scenes, however, an equally definite advance has been made; painted perspective has given way to partially solid sets, more often than not against a plain sky, and constructed as a decorative background to the action rather than as a decoration in itself.

At the turn of the century the three greatest figures of the modern theatre came into prominence—Gordon Craig, Appia, and Meierhold. Each wanted not only to change but to revolutionise the methods and style of stage presentation. They realised that not only the decoration and the presentation, but the whole theatre was in their way.

All three began from the same point. They realised the need for unity of the whole of a production—of the play, the scenery, and the action—and they insisted on the sub-ordination of the scene painter to the actor. Appia wrote in 1899 that the one essential of the *mise-en-scène* was the actor. " It is he that we come to see, it is to him that we look for the emotion, and it is this emotion that we have come to seek. Our business, then, is above all else to lay the foundations of the mise-en-scène in the actuality of the actor, and therefore to clear it of everything that is out of keeping with his presence."

Appia detested the sight of a living actor against a dead and painted cloth of trees or landscape. The actor was three-dimensional, and the scenery should also, he maintained, be three-dimensional. What scenery he did use he made solid, and the rest he achieved with light. He sought a completely different illusion from that which tradition had come to demand. He wanted to create " not the illusion of a forest, but only the illusion of a man in the atmosphere of a forest— spectators should see Siegfried bathed in light and living shadows, and not some stage ' cut-outs ' arbitrarily set in movement." In this Appia was far in advance of his time : he had none of the modern electrical equipment at his dis-posal ; but he gave to the operas of Wagner, which he chiefly produced, an atmosphere the audience had never known before.

THE POWER OF SUGGESTION TO TRANSLATE EMOTION

CRAIG'S greatest contribution to the stage was his insistence on unity, an insistence more abstract and at the same time more essential than that of Appia. The decoration, for want of a better word, and the whole production, including the movements of the actors, should express the essential quality of the play. In his book, *On the Art of the Theatre*, he writes : " I let my scenes grow out of not merely the play, but from broad sweeps of thought which the play has conjured up in me." He understood the great value of proportion, that height is only relative. Actuality, he asserted, had nothing to do with the stage : an actual scene even if desirable, was not possible as the lights could rob it of its chief qualities. He understood action to mean movement, and concentrated most on providing a space where the actors could move. He sought " the large and sweeping impression produced by means of scene and the movements of the figures." The theatre producer must " create a place which harmonises with the thoughts of the poet." Suggestion, he insisted, was of far greater importance than representation. " By means of suggestion you can bring on the stage a sense of all things . . . by means of suggestion in movement you may translate all the passions and the thoughts of vast numbers of people."

Craig made some beautiful settings which startled the whole theatre world. They were so revolutionary that many people could not even take them seriously. But settings in themselves were not enough ; he refused to separate the background from the whole movement of the play. He put his finger on the weakest spot of the organisation of the theatre itself, and pointed out the stupidity of having several masters in charge of departments that were kept separate and autonomous. A painter would not think of signing a work in which the sky had been painted by one friend and the figures by another. Craig created the rôle of the modern master producer, or to use a wider term, the *régisseur*.

The producer should not only control the movements of the actors, but also the creation of the scenery, the style of the costumes, the arrangement of the music, and the quality of the light required. " It is impossible for a work of art to be produced where more than one brain is permitted to direct ; and if works of art are not seen in the theatre this one reason is sufficient, though there are plenty more." But as Craig expanded both his theories and his practice he found that the old playhouses could no longer contain him. Their very shape and construction prevented him from expressing his ideas fully, and rather than work with bad material he left England.

THE LEADER OF PROGRESS IN RUSSIAN DRAMA

THE third of the three great theatre men of modern times, Vsevolod Meierhold, an exponent of ideas equally as revolutionary and fundamental as those of Craig, has had more scope for experiment and practice. Since 1898, when he joined the Moscow Art Theatre as an actor, he has continuously led the vanguard of the Russian theatre. The Moscow Art Theatre stood for the perfection of the naturalistic method. Stanislavsky trained his actors to an exceedingly high standard ; but after four years Meierhold tired of this emotional realism, and left to explore new fields on his own. Tchechov and Maeterlinck exercised a great influence on his early work. Like Craig, he was chiefly concerned with representing the essential qualities of the play. He selected the basic motif of *A Midsummer Night's Dream*, for instance, as lightheartedness, of Maeterlinck as religious mysticism ; and for one of the latter's plays he decorated the auditorium of the theatre as a church. Again, for Andreyev's *Life of Man*, he used grey curtains to increase the dream quality of the play.

Always he tried to give the actor prominence ; he made the stage shallower, and the background plainer, and tried several

methods of breaking down the barrier of the footlights. This
led him to the greatest problem of all, the relation between
the audience and the performance. He experimented with
many types of production, and after visiting Italy, and being
impressed with both the Commedia dell' Arte and the
Marionettes, he endeavoured for a time to reproduce them in
Russia. He insisted on a high degree of physical training for
the actor, so that the latter should be able to command the
fullest expression of movement and gesture as well as voice.
But always he came up against the barrier of the proscenium
and footlights. The audience still watched the performance
and was remote from it ; there was no atmosphere of partici-
pation such as there is in a church congregation for instance.
And, like Craig, he realised that the very shape of the play-
house was wrong. Unlike Craig, however, he was able to
change this, for the Revolution gave him every chance to
experiment.

Meierhold discovered the importance of different stage
levels not only to help point the play, but to assist the actors ;
finally, he devised the principles of the constructive set—a
set which was generally permanent throughout the play,
was expressionistically designed, and in which the different
levels, ladders, and steps served openly as platforms for the
grouping of the actors. He abolished scenery in the painted
sense and left the walls of the theatre undisguised, in an
attempt to focus concentration on the movements and words
of the actors, and to emphasise the essential meaning of the
plays. After the Revolution he experimented with plays
themselves as well as with their presentation. The theatre
was used as a commentary on the social problems of the time ;
during the Civil War it almost became a dramatised newspaper, the actors, and at times even the audience, making up
the " script." Meierhold used the auditorium for part of
the action, built the stage out, and used every means to secure
the co-operation of the audience instead of merely its attention for a spectacle. One of his pupils, Oklopkov, now has
stages and platforms built in several parts of the auditorium,
and, as in the Elizabethan days, the play is really performed in
the middle of the audience.

EFFORTS IN GERMANY TO OVERCOME REMOTENESS

PISCATOR in his Volksbühne Theater in Berlin was working
in the same direction, trying to break down the barrier of

unreality and remoteness produced by a spurious and un intelligent realism. He frequently used the cinema at the same time as the stage to bring out the universal significance of the plot and to give a wider and more general picture. These methods are not suitable for the bourgeois social dramas of the late nineteenth and early twentieth centuries, or for Restoration comedy, but they are of immense value for expressing the vital and fundamental problems of an age.

Max Reinhardt, probably the most famous theatre man to-day, has not the fundamental approach to drama of Meierhold and Craig. He is less of a theoretician and more of an excellent craftsman, with the qualities of the real showman. But he has contributed enormously to the technical advance of the modern theatre. The German stage, and very largely Reinhardt and Georg Fuchs, have been responsible for the new equipment. They introduced new methods of using and mixing light, the cyclorama, the revolving stage, the sinking and divided stage, and many other devices which have made possible the huge spectacles with which Sir Oswald Stoll and C. B. Cochran entertain us.

Each of these inventions has been of great importance. In lighting, it was found that by mixing red, blue, and green lamps alternately a white light was produced which had not the glare of the old uncoloured bulbs. Also where before 50 or 60 watt was the highest possible, they could now use lamps of anything up to 5000, thus enabling the light to be concentrated far more effectively, the most important parts of the stage to be picked out, and what was not needed to be left in shadow. And by the perfecting of the colour process, atmosphere could be created with one per cent. of the labour of the scene painter, and one hundred times its effectiveness.

The cyclorama is a smooth white wall built at the back of the stage, curved at the sides to meet the lines of sight from the auditorium, and again curved towards the top. This invention makes it possible to-day, using the three primary colours, to produce any colour of the spectroscope and any effects from a sunrise to a sunset. The curve gives an illusion of distance which cannot be achieved by the most skilful backcloth, and it also makes an excellent ground for shadow effects ; shadows of trees, or clouds, or buildings can be easily and cheaply thrown on to it. A six inch child's toy, connected on to the lighting system so that the wheels will revolve, and set in front of a projecting lamp, can give the impression over twenty square feet of a factory works.

The third invention, that of the revolving stage, naturally needs space, as only the centre of the stage can be made to revolve, but it vastly simplifies the changing of scenes, and is of great help when a large number of sets are required. Two or more scenes can be set at once, back to back ; and while the one in use is facing the audience the other can be reset behind, and then very quickly revolved into position. It can also be used not merely as a scene-shifting device but as part of the action. In a play of Fritz Von Unruh's at the Deutsches Theater in Berlin, the hero, a film actor, wanted to see the Director who was remote and inaccessible at the top of a long flight of stairs and through several offices. Normally this could only be done by a film, where the camera can follow the action ; but Reinhardt used a moving spiral stair-case, set four or more rooms with connecting doors on his turn-table, then put it in motion, so that the actor proceeded through room after room remaining all the time in sight of the audience. With a constructive set, or one made by blocks of units, curved surfaces and steps forming a permanent platform for the action, the revolving stage is again of great value, as by turning it different aspects and shapes of the central construction can be revealed.

The divided stage is more complicated mechanically. The floor is divided in the centre and can be moved back to left and right, and a second set, with its scenery ready, can be raised into sight from below. The new theatre at Stratford-on-Avon has been fitted in this way. But although elaborate sets can be arranged and no time lost in changes, it is a massive and cumbersome device, and even if the layman is awed by so much machinery in a theatre it does not really advance the cause of art, which can be much more effective when it depends on simplicity. It is suitable and advantageous for the large scale revue, but it is too ponderous for a genuine work of art. Again it encourages exuberant scenery, and the actor and the play are dwarfed. One is reminded again of Ben Jonson's complaint, " Painting and carpentry are the soul of masque " ; but to-day it is painting and machinery.

A REVIVAL IN FRANCE THAT BEGAN WITH PAINT

IN France the modern movement did not take so strong a hold as in Russia and Germany. The revolutions in 1917 and 1918 forced both these countries to make a break with the past, and create new forms. In France the first signs of revival were still in the painted tradition, but better painted. The Russian ballet under Diaghilev, with Bakst and Benois painting sometimes fantastic and sometimes gorgeous scenery, brought a new style of theatre painting into being. For the Ballet with its stylised movement this suited very well; but when Matisse, Picasso, Dérain, and other of the great French painters applied the principles of post-impressionism, cubism, or pointillisme to more straight plays they were not wholly successful—although Dérain's curtains for *La Boutique Fantasque* created a sensation. It was, of course, an enormous advance on the old painted " drop," because they were masters, but even such good paint was not the true medium : it remained a flat background for living actors.

Copeau and Jouvet with the Vieux Colombier theatre, however, deserve exception. They built a permanent architectural set, permanent not only for many scenes but for many plays. Steps led up from the auditorium, and in the middle of the stage was a raised platform, and at the back an arch, with more steps leading up each side and over the top. Parts were movable and interchangeable, but the main structure formed a permanent platform for all plays, with different levels for the acting. It was a modern reversion to the Greek formula for a theatre.

England has been little influenced by the continental innovations, and the theatre has advanced slowly along the regular course of naturalistic production. As in France the painted set has progressed in quality, and artists like Paul Nash, Rutherston, Wilkinson, Ricketts and Lovat Fraser, have introduced a far more artistic standard of fantasy and decoration. But the more modern movement has been confined to the Little Theatres. Miss Horniman at Manchester, and Granville Barker in London, were responsible for experimenting not only with new plays but also with new techniques.

Complete naturalism became a more suggestive type-naturalism, and the emotive quality of the plays was greatly increased. But the movement was in the hands almost entirely of the small theatres which could provide a more intimate atmosphere. There has been no really native attempt to break down the fundamental barrier between stage and audience, which lies at the root of the present barrenness of the stage. There have been productions of expressionist plays by Toller and Kaiser, one or two Russian plays have been performed, mostly by Sunday societies, and several modern American plays; but the majority of the latter are more in the style of Reinhardt and are over-mechanised rather than simplified. And all of these are apt to be regarded as foreign and eccentric. The modern movement even if it is sometimes admired is considered freakish, whereas actually it bears a great resemblance to the original and fundamental conception of theatre.

A QUALITY THE CINEMA CANNOT RIVAL

TO-DAY the theatre is suffering from the competition of the cinema; no doubt without the existence of the latter the stage would still be a profitable concern. But it is not just to blame the cinema *qua* cinema and, indeed, if it gives more universal satisfaction there is no reason why the theatre should not die out. There is no value in keeping it alive from an antiquarian point of view. But there is a very real difference between them. Because it uses real people, and if it uses real acting spaces and solids for them, and not the tawdry paint of the last generation, the theatre will always have a deeper and more urgent appeal than the cinema. The audience can be moved by a film to tears or even anger, but the film does not become part of its actual experience as a good theatrical production can.

Modern producers have introduced many cinema devices in an attempt to compete. In order to get more continuous action in *Grand Hotel* the whole of a hotel with several floors was presented, with the front façade knocked out so that the audience could see into all the rooms. The action went on in all of these rooms which were lit up alternately. It was ingenious but again too laborious for the theatre; it would have been better to have kept it as a film or to have condensed and simplified the action. A play and a film are two distinct art forms, as can be seen when screen versions of Shaw's plays are made, and they become merely poor cinema with their dramatic quality lost. There will be more profit to the theatre when producers and playwrights concentrate on discovering what is truly theatrical and how to represent it. The convention of the three-act play in its box set has become so firmly established that it will die hard, even though it has already had such a long life. But in England to-day it is the play even more than the presentation which is at fault ; there is no other way of putting on the kind of play written to-day.

A revival of the theatre must depend primarily on the plays ; but given these plays, and given an understanding of the function of the theatre by the playwrights, their successful presentation will be an easier matter.

BOOKS ON ALL ASPECTS OF THE STAGE

THERE are a number of books about acting and the history of the stage which may be consulted with profit and read with pleasure as a supplement to study at first hand by visiting the theatre. A reliable guide to the fundamental standards of good playing is afforded by G. H. Lewes' *On Actors and Acting*. The more sophisticated student will be intrigued and enlightened by Diderot's *Paradox of Acting* which carries its instruction a little further than Lewes' and provokes us on the ethics of acting, the morality of a player's feelings—his personal integrity. *The Old Drama and the New* is the complete book of the English theatre. Archer's rational, finely-reasoned history will appeal both to the reader who requires a general survey, easily understood, and to the serious student. An excellent book dealing with every aspect of the theatre is Ashley Duke's *Drama*, 600 B.C.–A.D. *1926* (Home University Library, Thornton Butterworth Limited).

Those who are interested in the future of the theatre should read C. E. Morgan's volume, *Tendencies of Modern English Drama*. In *The English Dramatic Critics, 1660-1932* James Agate presents a sequel of dramatic criticism from the earliest days of professional criticism. His researches go back to the seventeenth century, and then proceed through Addison and Steele to Leigh Hunt, Charles Lamb and Hazlitt. This is followed by the Victorians—Lewes, Clement Scott—and this again by C. E. Montague, Bernard Shaw, A. B. Walkeley, and the sequence ends with St. John Ervine and the leading critics of to-day. This anthology should certainly be studied; it will teach the interested reader more about the difficult art of appreciation than twenty text books.

STAGECRAFT FOR PLAYER AND PRODUCER

by EVAN JOHN

THERE are several ways in which the ordinary man may come into contact with dramatic art, several reasons for which he may desire to know more about it. There is first the ordinary playgoer who wishes to become an intelligent playgoer—to know why some productions give him great pleasure and others a vague discomfort, how plays come to seem as bad and as good as they do. There are others whose love of the drama leads them to believe that they can only be happy by devoting their whole lives to it (and to go on the stage for any other motive is, to say the least, extremely unwise). A very slight acquaintance with the theatre will convince anyone that no book can teach the art of acting ; it can only be learnt by experience—that is, by performing plays before an audience, whether it is an audience of applauding (or yawning) hundreds, or an audience of one, the teacher at a dramatic academy, who interrupts the performance to praise, blame, and advise.

There remains a third, a middle way. There are some people who are unwilling or unable to change their whole scheme of life in order to adopt the actor's precarious profession, and yet they are not content with merely sitting in an auditorium to watch others act. They feel something inside them which can only be expressed on a stage, and they itch to express it. They become amateur actors.

Their standards and their mode of procedure must differ from those of a professional production. Fewer performances are planned, less constant application to the work of rehearsal is possible. Generally there is far less money available for the initial expenses—though this is not always a handicap : many professional productions are swamped by a foolish and inartistic lavishing of money on their details. Finally, the performers will lack the experience and the technical skill of professionals. They will experiment where the professional *knows*, intend more than they can perform, feel more than they can express. Nevertheless there is a real and an important

place for the amateur in this, as in all arts.   Occasionally his
product is of real artistic importance.

THE AMATEUR ACTOR AND THE DRAMATIST'S STORY

I HAVE so far spoken as though the need for self-expression
were the only motive behind amateur productions. There are
many others. There is mere vanity. There is the desire for
a new type of social intercourse; it is a dangerous one, for
unless the performers are co-operating for some end that
appeals to higher instincts, amateur theatricals shatter more
friendships than they cement. There is the hope of raising
funds for some charitable object. There is the desire to
brighten life in one of the duller places of the earth. But the
need, or at least the wish for self-expression, must also be
present, and it is from this angle we shall proceed. The most
crucial matter to be discussed from this point of view is the
choice of plays. The reader's indulgence is asked if I seem to
go a long way round in order to discuss it.

A play is a dramatist's highly complicated method of telling
a story—or rather of getting others to tell it for him. He may
help in the telling himself, as did Molière in leading rôles and
Shakespeare in small ones. He may coach the other actors.
More generally, he hands the business over to a company and
its producer, and returns to his desk to write another play.
He needs interpreters as much as the musical composer, and
acting is primarily, though not entirely, an interpretative art.
There is a need for high technical skill in the interpretative
artist, and room for genius. There is also need for a somewhat different quality, which is sympathy with the creative
artist. The story which the dramatist is trying to get
told must not only be intelligible to his actors, it must
also fire their imagination and kindle a desire to help in
the telling.

This sympathy with the creative artist, which is the actor's
form of imaginative power, is not an uncommon quality. It
must be latent, in some degree, in the audience, or they will
have wasted their money. It must be nearer the surface in
the actor, roused by rehearsal or by mere study of the play's
script—or he had much better leave the stage and try the
Stock Exchange. It can be cultivated, to a certain extent, by
experience and effort, though far less so than the actor's
second requisite, his technical skill in telling the story. It is
more likely to be present in equal degree in amateurs and

professionals : it is not unlikely that, of the two, the amateurs may have more of it.

IMAGINATION VERSUS TECHNIQUE

Now it is quite reasonable, as well as quite practical, to classify plays in the light of these facts. There are plays, and great plays, whose main virtue is to give the amplest scope to the actor's technical skill. There are others which depend for their effect on the force and width of the imaginative vision which prompted their writers. Shakespeare's plays, written by an actor who was also a man of almost ununbearable imaginative power, unite both virtues in a quite unique degree. Sheridan's, though not lacking in vision, are more remarkable as channels for the actor's artistry.

The untrained actor, however much he may be in sympathy with Sheridan's intentions, may be quite incapable of carrying them out ; his lack of experience and skill may make the plays seem ineffective, artificial, and even dull. This is still truer of the majority of modern drawing-room comedies, which derive some of their inspiration from the tradition which Sheridan recreated, some from the personal foibles of the particular actors and actresses for whom most of them were written. At the other end of the scale stands Greek tragedy. It demands, as do all plays, clear speaking and appropriate gesture. But it depends infinitely less than most upon technical skill and experience, infinitely more upon imagination, sincerity, and honesty of purpose.

Here a difficulty immediately suggests itself. The majority of modern plays are written expressly for professional actors, and not only take their technical skill for granted, but trade, as it were, upon that skill. During the last two centuries, this tendency has grown more and more unmistakable. By recommending the imaginative rather than the technical, the poetical rather than the smart, I seem to be condemning the amateur to rummage among the works of our remoter ancestors for his plays, and adding to his other burdens the great one of speaking a language partly out of date, and imitating manners, or even emotions, that are unfamiliar in the modern world. The difficulty is a real one, and must be faced. I must plead that the larger emotions, with which imaginative plays are principally concerned, alter exceedingly little from one century to another.

15

MODERN PLAYS WHICH DEMAND IMAGINATIVE ACTING

APART from this, there are many plays written to-day which demand imaginative power rather than technical skill. Some amateur societies have begun to find their own local playwrights, and this is perhaps the happiest solution of all. But it is not the only one. There is the work of Masefield and of Gordon Bottomley. If Shaw's *You Never Can Tell* is largely dependent on the technique of its actors, his *Saint Joan* or (if a more modern setting is required) his *Showing Up of Blanco Posnet* demand sincerity and imagination, and can be made effective by these qualities alone.

Nor would it be in the least true to say that plays of which professionals have made a great commercial success are necessarily unsuitable for amateurs. But it is worth while stopping to think what principally contributed to such a success. I believe that by thinking along the lines I have suggested, amateurs will be led, and wisely led, towards *R.U.R.*, *Abraham Lincoln*, *The Likes of 'Er*, or *Journey's End*, rather than to the plays of Sutro, Somerset Maugham, or Noel Coward. There was until recently a very strong tendency for amateur theatricals to be concerned only with the latest smart drawing-room comedy. It looks so easy because it is " like ordinary life " : and it is so easy to make it as dull as most of ordinary life.

HOW THE ACTOR CASTS HIS SPELL

FOR good or ill, the play is chosen : it remains to get it acted. We know that at a certain date in the future, a certain (and we hope a large) number of people will assemble to hear a story told. It is our business to tell it in such a way as to excite, amuse, or at least interest them. Every play has a slightly different appeal, but there is one supreme necessity for all. The audience must be " held." A spell must be cast. It is better to avoid the word " illusion," which leads to endless and rather barren controversy.

I do not myself believe that, in any form of play, however " realistic," an actor should attempt to create an illusion of reality, and trick his audience into thinking that they are not sitting in a theatre, but are actually watching, in some mystic fashion, an incident in ordinary life. Surely it is rather his task to interest them so profoundly in the dramatist's story that they have neither time nor inclination for remembering where they are ; to lead their minds into an atmosphere where the distinction between " Actual " and " Imaginary " is utterly unimportant.   Drama, even in its most sophisticated forms, appeals to a primitive, and, one might say, a childish part of us.   It is the essence of a child's enjoyment that he does not know the difference between imagination and reality, and certainly does not stop to ask whether there are real pirates or real Red Indians at the end of the garden.

The word " spell " is quite unscientific ; but we are dealing with matters impossible to classify scientifically, and it has the advantage of calling two things to mind—hypnotism and magic.   The actor's power over his audience is not unlike the hypnotist's.   It is exercised on willing victims, who have paid for the pleasure of being bewitched.   And it needs something akin to magic to take such hold of another's mind that only a tiny and half-conscious part of it is aware of the discomfort of his seat, and the loudness of his neighbour's wheezing, while its larger and more active part is completely absorbed in the doings of a set of people he has never seen before—in their triumphs and disasters, their loves and hates, or the exquisitely funny things that they are doing and saying.

MAGIC THAT MUST BE KEPT ALIVE

IF this is the spell that the actor must cast, it will be seen that his work is different from the painter's or the novelist's in two important particulars.   He must start at a prescribed moment, keep his magic active so long as the curtain is up, and not allow anything to break, or even slacken it.   He cannot leave his work lying about, to be picked up and put down at will. He must even dictate to his audience at what pace they should listen to the various parts of the play, rather than leave it to their discretion or the quickness of their eye ; and experience shows that this matter of " timing " is almost as vital as it is in music, and possibly more difficult to master.

Secondly, his spell, like an orchestra's, is a communal one; it is cast, not by one artist, but by many ; and these artists are working in mediums more different than the various musical instruments.   There is a company of actors, each fitted to a different rôle, whose effectiveness lies in a certain measure of contrast.   They have been coached and directed by a producer, who roughly corresponds to the conductor. And since acting, unlike music, appeals to eye as well as ear, their attitudes and movements must be aided by the costume designer, the scenic artist, and the electrician.

If anyone of these neglects his work, or is incompetent to perform it, the total effect will suffer, and the dramatist will not get his story told in the most effective way. If, with all the goodwill and competence in the world, the communal efforts are not directed to a single end, if each co-operator is trying to enforce a different idea of the play in hand, then no story at all will be told, and the audience will be distracted, confused, and finally bored.

It may be true to say that drama is the impurest of all the arts : it is certainly true to say that it is the most complicated. The perfect production (could there be such a thing) would present a series of stage pictures as beautiful as Leonardo's, constantly changing with a rhythm as pleasing as a ballet's ; meanwhile the spectator's ear would be charmed by perfect words perfectly spoken, and his mind completely satisfied in its sense of character, its sense of artistic truth, and (probably) its sense of humour. It is obvious that such perfection must be left until Kingdom Come. It is equally obvious that no approach to it can be made without a great deal of organisation, far more organisation than any other art demands, except possibly architecture. It is time to see what forms that organisation has taken in the modern theatre.

THE CAST LIKE AN ARMY UNDER COMMAND

ODDLY enough, the problem is not unlike the military one, though danger to life or limb has become a very small factor in the theatre. There is the same need for harmonising apparently disconnected activities : there is the same slow and careful preparation for spasms of swift and irrevocable action ; there is the same training of individuals by instructors who cannot be present, and certainly cannot be giving constant advice, when the crisis arrives. We have all read of mediæval armies with their feudal levies, nominally under one command but actually liable to embark on any adventure that offered, even the adventure of disbanding and returning home. Time and necessity have replaced them by a very delicate organisation, in which every member is directly or indirectly responsible to a commander-in-chief ; his general aim is prescribed by government, while its details are, or should be, left to his discretion. A somewhat similar evolution has taken place in the theatre, and produced a similar result.

The business manager decides general policy, and fixes the amount of money available. The actual planning and working of the play is left to the producer, who is given a stage-manager to be his chief of staff and see that his orders are carried out. The producer deals directly with the actors. He should have some voice in the casting of them. He should have the last word on all matters of scenery and costume, though he may be unwise to use it against a competent designer. He is unquestionably supreme over the electrician and the stage-hands, to whom he gives orders through his stage-manager. His authority, generally speaking, ends as soon as the play is running satisfactorily ; the stage-manager remains to see that everything continues roughly as it was planned at rehearsal.

Of course there must be much more give-and-take than there can be in an army. With the best will in the world actors are more " temperamental " than soldiers, and cannot give of their best if they are treated with rigid tyranny. A wise producer will listen to much more suggestion from below than an officer can afford to do. He will be slow to force unwilling actors to do anything, without persuading them, at any reasonable expense of time, that it is the right thing. It is even possible that minor revolts against his authority, or pressure on him from the management above in matters of detail, may improve the production—though such things can prove exceedingly dangerous precedents. Within certain limits, mainly financial limits, it is probably wisest to leave him monarch of all he surveys. He may not be a genius, he may make a great number of blunders ; but he should at least achieve some sort of unity, and without unity the production is foredoomed.

THE QUALITIES THAT MAKE A PRODUCER

IN spite of its many disadvantages this limited dictatorship has become the rule in most professional theatres. It is almost essential for amateurs. Amateur societies generally contain a single member marked out for the position of producer by his greater experience, his thoroughness and energy, or his authority over others. If there is no such single person, the society may experiment with different producers for different plays. Their respective worth will soon show itself. One may be found more suitable for one type of play, another for another. One may have a *flair* for handling crowds, another may be a brilliant coach of single actors in intimate scenes. Some plays require specialised qualifications, a knowledge of music, an artist's talent for scenery and costume, or a particular ingenuity in inventing " comic business."

A thousand such considerations will govern the choice, but, once it is made, the wisest course is generally to invest the producer with authority similar to that enjoyed by his counterpart in the professional theatre, to hamper him with no restrictions except the financial ones, and to offer him as little unasked advice as human nature permits. His responsibilities will be so all-embracing that one can discuss three-quarters of the subject of drama in terms of the producer's duties. This is in some ways the most convenient method, and, for the most part, it will be followed here.

It is fairly safe to say that no play can be satisfactorily put on the stage without some little adaptation. The majority of plays are altered, some slightly, some almost beyond recognition, during the rehearsals that precede their first production ; it is often in this altered form that they first appear in print. Sometimes the business ends here, and subsequent productions use much the same text, and even stage directions. But there is usually great advantage to be gained by further adaptation, dictated by the size and shape of the stage, the nature of the audience, and, particularly, the capacity and characteristics of the actors. For instance, amateurs generally play a scene rather more slowly than professionals, and there are instances when this lack of pace should be compensated for by " cutting."

Cutting is an art, and a very difficult one. The story must be left intelligible, the balance between the various characters must be roughly preserved. In the case of Shakespeare, old-fashioned people prefer to cut out whole scenes and play other scenes intact ; the new fashion is to cut few scenes entirely out, but to blue-pencil so many lines out of each. In other words, the admiration for Shakespeare as a writer of splendid scenes is giving way to the appreciation of him as a magnificent architect of plays. The Victorians (ignorant of cinema technique ahead of them, burdened by the long tradition of the " well-made play " behind) had no grasp of Shakespeare's queer but brilliant construction. They even played *The Merchant of Venice* in four acts, of which Act I consisted of a selected number of the early Venetian scenes, and Act II of the scenes in Belmont. The extraordinary ingenuity with which the two atmospheres are alternated so as to heighten each other was sacrificed to the necessity for elaborate scenery and the influence of a dramatic convention utterly alien to the play.

WHAT TO CONSIDER WHEN CUTTING A PLAY

An amateur producer, if he wishes to catch the modern ear, is probably wiser to make his acting version in imitation of recent " Old Vic " productions, rather than of Tree's or Irving's. He may do better still to make one in imitation of nobody : to sit down and soak himself in the play, decide for himself what is the relative importance of each character and each scene, what is the " shape " of the play with its main and its secondary climaxes, and discover how best to preserve that shape in a shortened version. The Elizabethan dramatists told their stories in somewhat leisurely fashion. The modern producer must decide what to sacrifice in order to get the same story told in two or two and a half hours ; intervals and pauses accounted for, he cannot allow himself much more.

Whatever cutting the producer does, he must do it with an eye to his particular stage and performers, preferring to sacrifice those scenes which demand greater scenic elaboration than he can obtain, and those which would be unintelligible or distasteful to the kind of audience he expects. He would also do well to cut down those rôles which he is forced to give to his less talented actors, and to emphasise those which he feels are in more competent hands.

This process of settling the " acting-version " of the text should be complete in its main lines before rehearsal begins. Small changes can sometimes be made with advantage up to, or even after, the dress rehearsal. It is not unusual to find that a scene which seemed satisfactory at rehearsal appears tedious when played before an audience, and the fault may be rectified after the first performance by cutting a few lines.

What is true of Shakespeare and his contemporaries, is true in lesser degree of modern dramatists. A few plays need no editing at all, and would suffer by any attempt to edit them in view of a particular production. Most require slight alterations. For instance, it may be absurd to leave one's most talented actress unemployed, because she is rather tall and the play contains a line in which its only female character is described as short. If the author saw his heroine as short, the play will be slightly damaged by a tall one. But it will be far more damaged by an incompetent actress in a leading part ; and, unless this question of stature is an important one, on which some essential feature of the story depends, it is much better to cut the line. The silliest method of all is to use the tall actress, leave the line in, and hope the audience will not notice it.

Again, modern plays are sometimes written with an eye to the scenic designer, and to an audience which will be attracted by the hope of seeing sumptuous scenery changed every few minutes. The scene of action is made to shift rapidly about with no particular advantage to the dramatic intention of its author. An amateur society may have few scenic resources or (worse still) no adequate method of shifting scenery quickly. The producer must decide whether the play may not be more seriously damaged by shoddy attempts to vary the scenery or long pauses between short scenes, than by the cutting of a few lines which indicate a change of locality. He must remember that the original author may even have been persuaded against his judgment to a frequent change of scene by some commercial manager, and that his play may be actually improved by scenic simplification.

STAGE-DIRECTIONS WHICH MAY BE IGNORED

UNLESS the producer knows something of the art of play-writing, cutting the text, however necessary, is a difficult business and calls for great caution. With stage-directions a far greater latitude must be taken. Here the case is reversed, for the playwright is really intruding onto the producer's ground. Many of the best playwrights leave the whole thing to their producer and allow no stage-directions to appear except those which are absolutely necessary to make the story intelligible to a reader. The greatest of all dramatists seldom went beyond *Enter*, *Exit*, and occasionally *Dies* : and we are told nowadays that he left most of these to the printer's devil.

Since Elizabethan times, the habit of writing long stage-directions has grown to inordinate proportions. They are supposed to make a play more readable, though even this is a very doubtful proposition. Barrie has certainly brought the thing to a fine art and added great charm to his plays, considered merely as reading matter. Other writers are less successful, and their lengthy directions are therefore apt to hamper a producer instead of helping him.

Again and again their stage-directions will be found impracticable on any stage ; often they turn out to be inconsistent with each other, so that characters rise before they have sat, and walk Left to a door already described as Right. Many stage-directions are not the work of the author at all, but are merely taken from the " prompt copy " of the first London production. The original producer, shall we say, decided that the villain should exit L and then re-enter L disguised as a Chinaman ; there happens to be a quick-change room on the left side of the Grassmarket Theatre stage. It is obviously ridiculous that future producers should be bound by such a stage-direction merely because it has got into print.

Similar situations arise from the peculiarities of the particular actors and actresses who first played the parts. Actors differ enormously in their method of expression, some using an exactly contrary gesture to express the same feeling. If Sir Herbert Tree walked round the stage or ran his hands through his hair at one point of a play, it by no means follows that such is the right action for his successors in the same part. Amateur acting would be far more entertaining and instructive for the actors, far more effective for the audience, if it could shake off the burden and tyranny of stage-directions.

It is questionable whether a producer's best method is not to read through the play, skipping everything in italics and only going back to them where he finds the story unintelligible. Strange as it may seem, this is often the best method of getting at the author's true intention. Having formed his own picture of the play, the producer must go back and carefully reread the text with its stage-directions. He will find many of them extremely helpful, and can adopt them at once. Others can be left to be tried at rehearsal. Others again can be rejected at once as impracticable, or less well adapted to the particular production in view than the producer's own ideas.

There remains the melancholy case of the producer without ideas, or, what is commoner, without confidence in his own ideas. His best chance is to insist on the choice of some play published with full stage-directions taken from some professional presentation, to supply their deficiencies, and, as far as possible, reconcile their inconsistencies. This means the surrender of his own judgment to another man's enigmatically expressed ideas (for nothing can be so inscrutable in intention as a printed stage-direction) ; the result will probably be a workable compromise ; but it is hardly production. .

MOVING THE PIECES ON THE STAGE CHESS-BOARD

THE question of stage-directions has insensibly led us to the most important of all the producer's problems, the problem of " positions." A stage may be likened to a chess-board, on which the pieces are constantly moving as their mutual relations or the twists of the story demand. These movements, especially in a modern play, appear to the audience to be governed by the furniture on the stage and the doors and windows represented or suggested by the scenery. It is not a bad thing that the actors themselves should think of their movements as so governed. Only the producer fully realises that to state the matter thus is to put the cart before the horse. The position of furniture, exits, and so forth should be worked out before rehearsals begin, and should not be changed unless unforeseen difficulties arise. But it should be worked out with one principal object in view—to give the actors the maximum of appropriate positions at the most important moments of the play, so that the big crises of its story, emotional or comic, are facilitated and emphasised by grouping and posture.

In this matter there are no general rules. It is obviously necessary to avoid what is called " masking " an important actor at an important moment—that is, placing him so that his face is hidden from a large part of the audience by other actors, or by a tea-table. On the other hand, it is a great advantage to an actor at such important moments (and especially for long speeches) to be more " upstage " than the person to whom he is talking—that is, farther away from the footlights. A good actor's power is directed like a search-light's beam. Other actors, playing with him, can feel it being directed upon them. One can see it sweeping round an audience, or broadening out to embrace the whole auditorium. It is possible to project it backwards by an expressive posture of the back, while the voice (to change the metaphor) hits the back wall of the stage and ricochets into the target of the audience.

The secret of doing this seems to be a rediscovery of modern times, which have rejected the old rule, " Never Turn Your Back on an Audience." To make your leading actor assume such a position at one or two of the play's big moments may be to vary and so intensify his power over his hearers. But it is a device to be used sparingly. There was much sense in the old rule, if not in its rigid application. It is generally impossible to get the full effect out of a long speech with one's face turned away from the audience ; prolonged ricochets soon cease to be as penetrating as the direct hit. In comedy especially, the back and even the side view quickly become tiresome. And it is unfair to demand of an actor that he should play too long a scene deprived of one of his principal weapons, facial expression.

PLACING THE CHARACTERS IN POSITION

WHEN an actor is alone on the stage he can often be left to find his own positions and vary them at his own will. But even here the producer, seeing things with the eye of an audience, can make valuable suggestions. Nowadays many actors demand definite instructions from their producer, even for soliloquies, and are puzzled or angered at any vagueness or any suggestion of " I leave it to you."

When it is a question of two people on the stage, the problem is generally a fairly easy one, even in a long unbroken scene. They can be placed roughly level and still bring their full force to bear on the audience without spoiling the suggestion that they are addressing each other. Where it is very necessary to make one more important than another, one can generally find some excuse to move him or her into a more emphatic position. The real difficulties begin when the stage is filled with a number of people, and increase when it becomes necessary to bring pairs or groups of them together at certain moments and then recombine the groups as the nature of the scene alters. Here the chess-board may become infinitely complicated.

The broad rule, to be constantly broken and yet never quite forgotten, is to decide who is the most important character in any given scene, and put him slightly " upstage " of those whom he is addressing. As they must not " mask " him for long while he is speaking, they must generally be put somewhat to the side of him ; or they can be made to sit, kneel, and lie while he stands over them ; or they can be kept on the level of the stage-boards while he mounts steps or stands on some raised platform or balcony. It is also clear that his face should usually be as well lighted, or better lighted, than the other faces.

The old-fashioned solution of the problem was the actor-manager's. If he was a selfish man, he planted himself well upstage of his employees, talked down to them (that is, towards the audience), and forced them to talk up to him. The system left no doubt who was the principal character in the play. When he found himself in a muddle, for instance when the play demanded his speaking an aside to someone he had placed ten yards away, he would sometimes call on his stage-manager to rearrange the tangle; but the re-arrangement left him still upstage and still near the centre. The audience naturally thought him the most remarkable artist on the stage, and may even have enjoyed the play all the better for its being a " one-man show." Of course, many actor-managers behaved less selfishly, would often come down towards the footlights, and so give the play those delightful twists whereby minor characters become the centre of interest.

In most theatres to-day, the stage-manager has nothing to do with positions except to record them in the prompt book and see that they are roughly maintained throughout the run of the play. The leading actor as well as the rest of the cast takes his orders from a producer. The producer will naturally put him in emphatic positions far more often than he puts minor characters. But he will be strictly on guard against such groupings becoming ineffective through constant repetition.

MANŒUVRING THE PLAYERS ROUND TABLES AND CHAIRS

IT is with such considerations in mind that the producer must arrange the exits and entrances to his chess-board, the points (tables, chairs, windows, or fireplaces) towards which his pieces must be constantly moved, and the obstacles round which they must manœuvre; for furniture is an obstacle as well as a point of approach. He must read through the play and decide which are the most important crises, tragic or comic, of the plot, the points where Romeo bursts in to the Capulet's tomb, or Charlie's Aunt pours tea into a top hat. He must decide how his characters should be grouped to give the greatest effect to such moments; how doors, windows, and furniture can be placed so as to get the entrances most easily leading up to such groupings, and the movements or exits leading out of them again.

He must take some half-dozen or dozen of such situations, reconcile their various demands for entrances, exits, sitting-places, or hiding-holes, and then quarrel with his scenic designer until some compromise is reached between the necessities of the acting and the need for artistic shape in the scenery.

Mere chance, or what appears to be mere chance, will again and again come to his aid. He decides to put the door to the hall at Centre Back, so that when it is opened the audience can look through it and see the postman speaking his few lines in the first act—without the unnatural business of bringing a postman into the drawing-room. He suddenly discovers that this makes a magnificent entrance for the end of Act III, when the Husband returns unexpectedly, throws open the door, and stands dominating Faithless Wife and Unprincipled Lover. If the said Lover a few moments before has left his paramour on the luxurious sofa (close to fireplace Down L.) to pour himself out a drink at the side-board (Down R.), the triple group may have an impressive symmetry.

The producer next discovers that it is quite possible to put the hall on a slightly higher level than the drawing-room, so that the Husband finds himself at the top of a few steps when he enters. The same platform which represents the hall floor in Acts I and III can be left standing for Act II, and become a walled terrace which greatly assists the grouping of the garden-party scene.

This apparent chance is the queerest and yet the commonest of theatrical phenomena. It is noticeably more frequent when one is dealing with well-written plays than with bad ones. It is most frequent of all in the works of playwrights who were primarily men of the theatre, Shakespeare, Molière, and even Ibsen. For, behind all its complexities, theatrical art has a unity, and that unity is constantly reasserting itself when it is least expected.

THE DELICATE TASK OF CHOOSING THE PLAYERS

WHILE the producer is planning scenery and stage movements—and before he has had a chance of experimenting with the latter at rehearsal—there is the difficult business of casting to be done. It is here that he feels, rightly or wrongly, most need of despotic power. It is just here that he is most hampered and dictated to by others. Mr. So-and-so will not act unless he has the hero's part : the committee is convinced that Miss Whatshername would be ideal for the villainess, but has heard a rumour that her mother will only allow her to act " nice " parts. Lady Thingummy is a principal subscriber to the society, and disaster threatens unless her niece (who cannot act at all) is provided with an important rôle.

In the face of such difficulties the producer may be glad to share his responsibility with others—for instance, with the committee. But it is only just to consult him at every turn of the casting, and generally wise to give him a veto. Though some good producers are curiously bad at casting, and many too fanciful in their choices, it is unjust to ask anyone to rehearse with actors whom he regards as incompetent, unteachable, or unsuited to their parts.

On the question of suitability there is endless war. The old-fashioned view was that it is best to give the largest and most important parts to the best or most experienced actors. The more modern opinion is that the most important thing is to find the right " type " for each particular part. The old view is probably the safer, except in the matter of age : we have all suffered from Romeos and even Juliets bearing the burden of forty summers. " Casting to type " may have a serious effect on the general level of acting, providing everyone with a part that he thinks he can do easily, and denying him the opportunity for pretending to be something different from what Nature designed. But, as always, hard-and-fast rules are only made to be broken, and systems must be combined with apparently inconsistent systems to achieve the highest practical success.

PRODUCER AND DESIGNER LEARN FROM EACH OTHER

BEFORE the producer has got far with rehearsals, probably before he has begun them, he must give his mind to a number of people who will never appear on the stage at all. Scene-painting and costume-making are lengthy businesses, and the designers may need instructions weeks before the production. Here everything depends on the personal factor. Some producers are perfectly competent to design their own scenery, and design or choose the costumes. Some producers even have time to do so. But the majority lack this specialised gift, or the opportunities for developing it. Some designers know how to create beautiful things in general, but do not know how to adapt them to the stage. There are others with a good working knowledge of the theatre who cannot judge from the script of the play what forms of beauty are appropriate to it.

It may be true of every art, it is certainly true of the theatre, that the words " beautiful " and " ugly " could be dropped from discussion and the words " appropriate " and " inappropriate " substituted. It is a matter of chance and personality whether designer or producer has the surer eye for the appropriate. The only way of hitting the best distribution of work between them is by constant discussion of the play, often apparently aimless, and (if possible) by collaboration over a series of plays.

It is often found that the designer can begin the game by suggesting a general style to which costumes and scenery should conform. He may produce a few rough sketches, or he may put forward a name, suggesting that *Antony and Cleopatra* be done in the style of Rubens' classical pictures, or the first two acts of *Milestones* according to the idiom of Leech's and Du Maurier's drawings in *Punch*. If he is worth his salt, " Period " will not be enough for him. Different artists saw their own periods with very different eyes, and archæological exactitude on the stage is a very doubtful virtue.

No one denies that Lovat Fraser's designs for *The Beggar's Opera* were immensely successful, with their queer insistence on butterfly shapes and their preference for broad patches of even colour, most uncharacteristic of the besprigged, bepatterned eighteenth century. Turn from *The Beggar's Opera* to some play that emphasises, instead of the gaiety, the sordidness, cruelty, and oppression of the same period. If the designer has no immediate ideas of his own, a glance at Hogarth's engravings may be an excellent stimulant for his imagination ; and the designer's experience generally makes him more able to make such suggestions than the producer.

On the other hand, the producer is usually in a better position for suggesting how costumes and scenery can be made to tell the dramatist's story. He should know more of the social position and mutual relation of the characters, and should have ideas for making these plain to an audience. He may suggest how the important characters can be made to stand out, not necessarily by being more gorgeously, but by being differently costumed from the rest ; and this is a point on which many good designers are curiously at fault. He will also know when characters most need a change of dress, to indicate a change in their fortunes or their occupations —when they must grow more or less ragged, buckle on armour, or get into evening dress.

MOODS AND CHARACTERS EXPRESSED IN COLOURS

THE instinct which produced totem-poles and heraldry, uniforms and trade-marks, can be exploited and greatly extended on the stage. Since broad effects are always needed, the badge is less important than the livery. To dress servants in similar, if dowdier, colours to those of their masters is only a beginning. A whole colour-scheme can be worked out, to tell the audience which of the characters are friends, followers, rivals, and enemies. There may even be changes of costume when friends quarrel or servants betray. History sometimes supplies a scheme ready-made : symbolism may suggest a basis for constructing one. The audience may be unconscious of it and yet find the play far more intelligible than it is when read.

If I might take a somewhat crude example, I would suggest *Julius Cæsar*. If Cæsar himself appears in purple or gold, his wife Calpurnia and his slaves can be dressed in varying shades of deep red. When he is dead, Octavius, coming to supply his place, could wear an exact replica of his costume. Antony in scarlet and gold is clearly their ally, and the colours seem appropriate to his character. Opposite shades must be found for their enemies, royal blue for Brutus, green for Cassius (it is the colour of envy), and other blues, greens, or greys for Casca and his fellow-conspirators. White could be kept for the neutrals, Cicero and Popilius, black for the Soothsayer and Artemidorus. When the confusing battle-scenes begin, they can be made less confusing if Titinius has only to enter in a green cloak to proclaim that he is Cassius's man, and if the defeat of the conspirators' army is an affair of reds and browns slowly ousting the greens and blues from the stage.

It is obvious that we have here an excellent method, though a crude one of telling the story. It is less obvious that such a logical colour-scheme will sometimes (again by what seems chance, and is something more) produce the most striking colour effects in the stage pictures.

Here a difficulty suggests itself. The professors tell us that every Roman gentleman wore a white toga edged with purple, and that any other colour-scheme is definitely *wrong*. It may be remarked, to begin with, that the Roman period is one of very few in which such a difficulty arises ; colour has generally been a matter of personal preference. It may also be remarked that the professors are (as usual) at odds with each other.

Many tell us that the white *Toga Prætextata* was a purely formal affair only worn for occasional high ceremonies. But there are times when no such arguments serve us, and we must face the question : should theatrical effect be sacrificed to historical accuracy—even to the extent of making a confusing scene more confusing by dressing the whole cast in one uniform ?

The question is a more difficult one than appears at first sight, especially with writers like Shakespeare, who was under the impression that Romans wore doublets. Nowadays we have a few playwrights indifferent to historical details, and a great number whose work is based on historical research. Feuchtwanger's *Warren Hastings*, an essay on government (though an excellent play into the bargain) was played in Germany in vaguely Victorian clothes ; it probably did not suffer at all. *Clive of India* is a play about the eighteenth century, and would be meaningless in any other costume.

Even more important than the playwright's intention is the state of mind in the audience. No one nowadays could stand Abraham Lincoln in a powdered wig. Yet no one thought it odd when Garrick played King Lear in one. The big change came a century ago and was inaugurated by the great actor Talma. He refused to play Greeks and Romans in a costume reminiscent of Louis XIV ; attempting accuracy, he was at first derided for " dressing up like an old statue." His contemporary, Walter Scott, was meanwhile completing the conversion of novel-readers to a sense of period. Since their time we have grown yearly better instructed about the petty details of our ancestors' lives.

HEALING THE BREACH BETWEEN HISTORY AND DRAMA

WE are left with three possible solutions. There are the historical purists, whose argument is stronger than it appears at first sight ; the best of all designers is Fashion ; an exact reproduction of any period will be in itself a unity, and a beautiful unity ; any amount of research that can perfect it is artistically justified. At the other extreme are those who think that the historical sense is definitely an enemy to the dramatic. They hope to kill it at one blow by playing historical plays in the purest fancy dress, reminiscent of no particular period. They go further, and play *Hamlet* in modern costume. This is a perfectly defensible policy, though sometimes difficult to apply. It makes *Henry V* very

difficult to play, and would banish *Saint Joan* to theatres
where eccentricity is a virtue.

The middle way is more usually adopted and is perhaps the
most defensible of all. The defence may be based on the
principle that artistic demands must always override archæology, provided that the word "artistic" is used in its widest
sense. It is surely inartistic to disturb and distract an audience
from the play by introducing well-known anachronisms. It
is equally inartistic to handicap a production, and empty the
treasury, in order to give a somewhat pedantic pleasure to a
few specialists. Research in museums is always worth while,
for it may always suggest interesting ideas. But if archæology
is a good servant, it can be a very bad master.

The problem of accuracy becomes rather different when
we are dealing with the history of our own day. Here the
minutest details are so well known to the audience and the
slightest incorrectness will distract them so much that there
seems no room for design. The case seems most desperate
in the matter of costume, though not so desperate as it was
thirty years ago, when fashion decreed that all men must
dress in clothes of uniform cut and some variation of mud
colour. But a good artist is awake to the variety which
underlay this apparent monotony, and to-day the monotony
is rapidly breaking down.

If he cannot invent the artist has at least a wide field to
select from, and the subtleties of modern dress give scope
for a certain degree of symbolism (for instance, the rather
obvious "white for innocence") as well as for immense talent
in securing that appropriateness to character which is dramatic
beauty. Even scenes in which every male character must
appear in evening dress can be helped by a clever producer
or designer. In some plays a dramatic point can be made
of the actual uniformities of modern life, especially plays of
what is called the "expressionistic" type such as *The Adding
Machine*. In others, the variety still permitted in women's
clothes can be used to tell the story and emphasise its dramatic
points.

THE STANDARD OF BEAUTY SET FOR SCENERY

MUCH the same considerations apply to scenery, furniture,
and properties. Their principal standard of beauty is
appropriateness to the play ; modern plays often leave the
designer nothing to do except reproduce an ordinary room in

an ordinary house. But we have seen that the last word about the placing of doors and furniture must rest with the producer : rehearsal at the dictation of a designer generally ends in rebellion.

Poetic plays demand less background, or at least a vaguer background, than others : fewer places to sit, less definite doors for entrance and exit, fewer " properties " for the actors to handle. Poetry generally deals with the larger aspects of life, and dramatic poetry in particular is careless of its smaller details. The scenery need not be so meticulously painted, and there is no need for the host of teacups, ash-trays, and photographs that swell up the property-list of a modern play.

Oddly enough, the most unrealistic of all plays—that queer form called farce—demands a wealth of realistic detail. Here the dramatic effect is that of ordinary life run mad. The actors take some familiar object, a soda-water syphon or a baby's pram, and proceed to do the most fantastic things with it. They enter a drawing-room, and behave as if they were in a zoo. Farce is one of the most delightful of all forms of art, because it is perpetually reminding us of ordinary life, and then turning it upside down, releasing us from the petty tyranny of familiar things. Instead of wearily washing up the crockery, people begin to throw it at each other. Instead of sitting in an office to add up figures, they suddenly start to crawl under the desks, hide behind the ledgers, and put the waste-paper baskets on each other's heads. All that is childish and primitive in us rejoices at the outrages committed against the solemn objects which dominate our lives with their stupid demand to be used for a rational purpose.

It is noticeable that old farces such as Shakespeare's *Merry Wives of Windsor* or *The Taming of the Shrew* need a far larger list of properties than his poetic plays—buckbaskets, plates, dishes, and riding-whips. We probably get less fun from them than our ancestors, because they have to have a vaguely Elizabethan shape and so do not give us the same sense of escape from ordinariness.

Romantic plays give the producer one clear advantage. The scenery can be simple and even cheap. A sky cloth, a set of curtains, and a few steps will see you through most poetic plays. But if the settings are simple, they can be immensely significant. Certain shapes and colours suggest or enhance certain emotions, and they can be built up with the simple equipment I have suggested. The modern living-room, or its rough equivalent on the stage, gives far less opportunity. Like costume, it can express the character of its occupier, but it is difficult to make it emphasise the emotional effect of what happens within its three walls. But the producer has one ally, more potent in romantic plays but not to be despised in the most realistic forms of drama. This is the electrician.

DARKNESS AND LIGHT

FOR stage purposes nothing has any shape, nothing is there at all, until you turn light upon it. Everything can be altered, and even altered in the middle of a scene by the quality of the light so turned. The most realistic representation of a vulgarly furnished hotel lounge can become impressive, tragic, or sinister by a scarcely perceptible change of light. Smooth and efficient " dimmers " for working such changes during a scene are not always provided in places where amateurs act. But even if the lights must be set while the curtain is down and not altered during the action, there are still great possibilities to be explored. The lighting of scenes to enhance their emotional effect is an extraordinarily complex art, but it has its elementary rules which should be firmly grasped. Only long experience will show where and when to break them.

Some of the most ghastly things in history, certainly the majority of violent deaths, have taken place under a bright sun. Some of the funniest things have happened in the dark. Yet the emotional effect of bright light evenly distributed is triumphant, pleasant, or jocose. The emotional effect of broken light, alternate patches of brightness and dark, is serious, tragic, and sometimes lurid. The thumb-rule based on this holds good in nine cases out of ten : in most comedies and in all farces, turn on all the light you can, distribute it equally over everything, actors, scenery, and furniture, and keep it on for three-quarters of the play : in most tragedies, detective-plays, and plays of horror, distribute your light as unevenly as possible.

The theatre being what it is, your brightest patches should generally be the actors' faces and bodies, and those places on the stage where they most frequently sit or stand. The darkest will be the corners where they do not go, the space above their heads, and the scenery behind them. If Rembrandt had not lived in a country like Calvinistic Holland, and in an age before electricity was invented, he would have been a wonderful producer of tragedy and even of crook-plays. A study of his paintings will help a producer to learn how ordinary rooms can be made to look dramatic. If the scene demands daylight, let that daylight appear to come through windows that concentrate or distribute it for a dramatic purpose. If it is night, then the opportunities are unlimited. Lamps, candles, and even firelight can be so placed as to make a pattern which is at once plausible and dramatically effective. Long scenes in serious mood can be played with no light but a red glow through the fireplace. A single candle can suggest romantic love, a lantern hideous plots.

One word more. The reader may wonder why I have dealt with all these matters before I have touched on the crucial question of acting. Acting becomes what it is at rehearsal. But the producer must have worked out most of his positions before rehearsal starts. He must know roughly where his scenery is to stand, and what furniture he needs. It is less obvious, but also true, that he should have a rough idea of the lighting resources of his stage, and of how he proposes to use them. If he gets far with rehearsals and accustoms his actors to their positions before he has given a thought to lighting them, he may be storing up incurable trouble for the dress rehearsal.

SOME HINTS ON MAKE-UP

THERE remains one other matter for which it may be wise to make plans ahead—the matter of make-up. Amateurs sometimes hire an expert from a shop to paint the faces of the whole cast : sometimes they save their money by asking a professional actor to come in and help them—or, at least, to advise. It is probably wise to do something of the sort. The art of make-up resembles that of portrait-painting, and is almost as complicated : different kinds and colours of lighting multiply the complications.

Make-ups are often divided into two classes, " straight " and " character." In the first category comes the business of emphasising the features of an actor's face so that it can be seen as clearly as possible from the back seats ; the chief difficulty, even in a small theatre, is that of making movements and expressions of the eye visible at a distance. It is hardly possible to do this without giving the front seats an unpleasant sensation of " plastered " faces, and there is no satisfactory solution of this problem. "Character" make-up (the categories are elastic, not rigid) deals more with the problem of changing an actor's face to suit his part : the commonest problem is to add to—or subtract from—his age. It is easier for men than for women, largely because the male face can be changed out of recognition by the use of false hair—beards, whiskers, and moustaches. But age is only one of many changes. Grease-paint and hair can make the mild look irritable, the poetic military, and the ordinary distinguished.

It is particularly legitimate for amateurs to call for outside help in this matter. Needless to say, it is quite useless to discuss it in print, except in a book where diagrams and photographs outweigh the letterpress. Professionals rarely learn from books ; they learn from experience—and from "tips" supplied by fellow-actors. For in this art the tricks are far more numerous than the principles.

WHEN THE CURTAIN GOES UP ON THE PLAY

IF we have left the subject of acting till last, it is from no desire to underrate its importance. It is the one essential thing. Theatres in the past have done without scenery, without artificial light, without special costumes, without stage-managers and producers. The Commedia dell' Arte practically dispensed with the dramatist, leaving the actors to make up their dialogue as they went along. But it is quite impossible to do without acting (manipulation of puppets is only an indirect form of acting), and good actors can compensate for a lack of everything else. Nor can the best producer, except in rare instances and with unusual types of plays, make a successful production without good actors, or, at worst, actors that he can teach to act well. It has been said that a theatre can consist of four boards and a passion. It can also consist of four boards and a sense of humour. But the delineation of passion and the manipulation of jokes is the centre round which everything else in the theatre revolves.

TAKING LEAVE OF THE PRODUCER

HERE it may be best to cease looking at things through the producer's eyes. It is true that the coaching, teaching, and restraining of actors is far the most important part of his duties. It is true that he is in command at all rehearsals, that he must set the atmosphere of the play, and keep the acting in key with it. He arranges his actors' positions so as to give their talent its maximum scope. He is the defender of the self-sacrificing and humble against the conceited and self-centred. To do all this successfully, he must have been an actor himself (though not necessarily a good one), just as he should have been a stage-manager and have had some personal experience of electric switchboards, painting-frames, and carpenter's benches. But in order to discuss acting it may be better to say good-bye to this paragon of all virtues who has engrossed our attention for so long.

ACTING CANNOT BE TAUGHT

I HAVE given a few reasons for postponing the problem of acting to the last. But there is one more which must be faced before we start. To teach a particular person how to act a particular part may not be a very difficult matter ; but it is extremely difficult to put anything into conversation, let alone print, on the subject of acting in general. There is hardly any helpful suggestion made at one moment which, if taken to heart, may not cramp an actor's style at another. To repeat what has already been repeated to the point of boredom, there are no rules in the theatre except those made to be broken. This applies to acting, the soul of theatrical art, even more than to its outward organisation. One cannot teach anyone to act, one can hardly suggest how he can learn. One can only say, " Get some lines by heart, stand on a platform before an audience, and see what happens."

It is a custom in many amateur societies, and rather a good one, to discuss the choice of a play among those who will have to act in it. It is frequently found that most of them feel more competent to tackle a modern and a realistic play than a romantic or poetic one. I have given some reasons for believing this to be a misplacing of confidence. To illustrate the point a little more may be a good introduction to a talk about acting.

Every play is written in a certain style or convention. And it is customary—though not very satisfactory—to classify these conventions according as they are more or less " like Real Life." To write a play in blank verse is obviously to lessen its superficial resemblance to the surface of life, and to use rhymed verse carries the process a step further. Thinking along such lines, the amateur naturally feels that he can best depict something resembling his own daily experience. He feels himself liker to a Galsworthy character than he is to Othello, and thinks that by going on the stage and behaving, roughly, as he would in ordinary life, he will acquit himself better than he would by spouting poetry.

THE DIFFICULTIES OF "REAL LIFE" PLAYS

HE has forgotten at least three difficulties. First, it is one of the hardest things in the world to behave naturally with five hundred pairs of eyes trained upon one ; it requires years of practice. And the difficulty is greater than this ; it is not to behave naturally but to *appear* to be doing so, while raising the voice to a quite unnatural pitch and doing the smallest actions so clearly and decisively that they can be seen thirty yards away. Secondly, his task is not so much to imitate life, or to imitate anything, as to *entertain*. People do not pay for their seat in order to see a piece of real life which they could see better in their neighbour's drawing-room. They come to be entertained, and the art of entertaining them by speaking blank verse, or even by standing on one's head, is often an easier one than the art of entertaining them dressed in ordinary clothes and doing things which constantly remind them of the monotonous round from which they have come to the theatre to escape.

And there is a final, and often unrecognised, difficulty. The art of realistic acting involves the extremely difficult feat of coming on to a stage for ten minutes and making clear to an audience what manner of man one is supposed to represent without doing anything which would seem unusual in real life ; yet in real life such a man might remain inscrutable to his closest acquaintances after six months of daily intercourse.

It is worth while considering whether the old playwrights did not set the actor an easier task. Richard III can tell his audience, straight from the shoulder :

" I am determined to prove a villain."

The modern actor has to convey the same impression by his manner of lighting a cigarette. He may have to do it very quickly. I have suggested ten minutes because minor characters often get less and major ones who have not established themselves in the audience's mind by that time have probably ruined the dramatist's chances of conveying an intelligible story to the audience.

To sum up a point that I have perhaps laboured unduly,

it is quite reasonable to say that one distrusts romance, detests poetry, and believes that there is more fun to be had by acting realistic plays. But it is not quite so reasonable to suggest that it is easier for the amateur to choose such plays, and to prevent them from seeming unnatural, unintelligible, or dull.

MAKING THE PERFORMANCE "ONE HARMONIOUS WHOLE"

WHATEVER the choice, the most important thing is to preserve the convention of the play chosen : to keep it, as some would say, all at the same distance from real life : to tell the story, as I would prefer to put it, all in the same style. Now that we have said good-bye to the producer, we can hardly call him back into the discussion to preserve this unity, though it is principally his business to do so. But whether he is there or not, it is essential that the actors should watch each other, and use roughly the same methods.

One frequent cause of disunion is that some members of the cast play more " broadly " than others. The term needs a little explanation, though the phrase " broad farce " is common propetry. It is generally necessary on the stage to do everything more deliberately and certainly more decisively than in ordinary life, and to speak louder, or at least more penetratingly. How far this exaggeration should be carried is largely a matter of the play, and of the convention in which it is written. But it is essential that some harmony should be established between the various actors. Among amateurs, the most usual difficulty is to make the inexperienced actors play broadly enough, speak their words with sufficient deliberation, and avoid fogging their actions by indecisive fumbling. There is also, at times, the difficulty of preventing the more experienced from playing too broadly.

Acting may be compared to a game in which the players toss the ball to each other. The ball is the attention of the audience, which, while the dialogue proceeds, is generally focussed on the speaker, sometimes on the person spoken to, more rarely on a third person. During silences it generally rests on some particular actor or group of actors. The perfect game is achieved when each player holds the ball and juggles with it for the exact space of time demanded by the situation, not hurrying and slurring his tricks, nor dragging them out, before he passes it on to the next man. The self-assured tend to hold on to the ball as long as possible, to bore the spectators with unwanted exhibitions of dexterity, and to hold back the swing of the game for the sake of a single performer.

This fault is common among professionals, and it often succeeds in its selfish purpose of attracting undeserved admiration. It is not unknown among experienced or conceited amateurs. But it is commoner to find amateurs suffering from the opposite defect, the natural desire of an inexperienced and nervous player to pass the ball on as soon as he decently can, without doing anything with it. He gets too interested in the other players, and not enough in himself. He forgets how many eyes are focused on him in the hope of being entertained, interested, or thrilled by what he will do ; or if he remembers it, he grows nervous and is so afraid of spoiling the game by his own lack of dexterity that he spoils it by lack of self-confidence. A cast which contains performers of both kinds (and most casts do) may upset the balance of the whole game, and spoil both the dramatist's purpose and the pleasure of the audience.

The proper way to play the game is a matter that cannot be taught and is only learnt by long experience. Self-confidence, self-assertion, one might almost say " cheek " are necessary to success. Some temperaments are so unsuited to the stage that they can never acquire it. Some develop it easily and misuse their power to make themselves more important than the play warrants. This danger is not so great in well-written plays as in bad ones. Good writers tend to give the smallest characters their little share of the audience's attention, and so do not tempt them to seize and hold on to the ball when they ought to be passing it on.

Badly written plays are filled with minor characters, little more than names, who are only put in to save the playwright trouble, and to do what is called the " feeding " of the main parts. They speak lines for the hero to cap. They do business which he can outdo with more conspicuous business. They bring messages which are his cue for outbursts of horseplay or emotion. Every part contains a certain amount of " feeding " : Hamlet must feed Osric and the Gravedigger. But there are few parts in Shakespeare, or another good dramatist, that do not get their chance of showing their mettle at some moment. I have seen an amateur performance of Hamlet in which the First Sailor (Act IV. scene 6—generally cut) stood out for his little minute, and made a definite and delightful contribution to the play.

IMMOBILITY THAT MAY BE SPELL-BINDING

IT has been suggested already that the audience's attention is not always focused upon the speaker, and the point needs a little elaboration. The voice is perhaps the easiest method whereby an actor casts his spell upon the audience : it is generally the first which an amateur learns to use with full effect. But the body, whether in motion or frozen into some significant posture, is equally important. To learn this one has only to watch a ballet or a silent film. It is not always easy to keep the attention of an audience by pose or movement during a silence ; it is sometimes harder still to do so while another actor is speaking ; and yet plays again and again demand that it should be done. Watching professional actors, especially good ones, is no way to learn the business ; the art has become so complex that it completely conceals itself. It is better to start at the beginning and learn the elements. Talent and ingenuity can do what it pleases upon this foundation.

It is difficult to stand rigidly in one position through a long scene without attracting an audience's attention. Soldiers, guards, and flunkeys can do so, partly by virtue of their uniform ; they become part of the scenery rather than of the cast—a background against which the actors act. Otherwise absolute rigidity tends to draw the eye. It is a trick—though a difficult one to maintain—for the leading actor. I have been told that Guitry played the first act of *Le Misanthrope* thus, hardly moving any part of himself except his lips, whilst *Philinte* manœuvred round the stage. Actors on whom it is undesirable to fix the audience's attention should take an easy and natural position and change it slightly, without fuss, every minute or so. Then, when their turn is coming to be the centre of attraction, they can either take a significant posture and hold it until the eyes of the audience begin to focus on them or they can achieve the same result by waiting their time and suddenly making larger and better-defined movements than the other people on the stage.

PERFORMANCES SPOILT BY FIDGETY ACTORS

WHAT is most damaging of all to amateur performances is the enormous amount of non-significant movement, sometimes thoughtless, more often nervous ; little fidgetings of the fingers, little wrigglings of the body, and, worst of all, constant shifting on the feet. Movement on the stage can be of immense value and significance : its value must not be frittered away by any motion for which there is no good reason. The more one actor understands the art of stage-movement (which is largely the art of economy in movement) the more intolerable it is to see his efforts thwarted by his colleagues' fidgetings. Luckily good acting casts its spell on the stage as well as on the audience, induces other actors to remain still, or hypnotises them into making the appropriate movement at the appropriate moment.

The actor who is holding the audience's attention needs to exercise a similar economy. If his voice is expressing something, his feet and hands must either express the same thing, or divert attention from themselves by keeping still or moving inconspicuously. The emotion he is expressing, the joke he is trying to " put across," may at any moment demand any part of him to help in the expression. It is better for the beginner to keep everything still until the moment arrives when it can be of assistance. Then, and then only, the finger waggles, the feet move to carry their owner into a new posture, the arm waves, or the eyebrows shoot up. The professional actor devotes all his time to his art, so that if necessary he can remain in constant motion and yet constantly express the simple or the complicated thing which he is trying to convey to the audience. The untrained amateur (unless he is that rare phenomenon, a natural mover with movements unspoilt by self-consciousness) will do well to reduce his motions to the fewest and most significant.

Here is another reason why light comedy is beyond most amateurs ; it demands a constant flow of natural but ex-pressive movement, which can only be carried out by actors who have trained themselves to do it unconsciously. Tragedy, melodrama, and detective plays on the one hand, farce on the other, admit of much broader movements such as can be studied and taught at rehearsal. Dead pauses and frozen postures are succeeded by the kind of large and significant movement which would smash the atmosphere of light comedy to pieces.

I have said that it is difficult to teach acting in general, and almost impossible to write usefully about it. There is nothing absolutely right or absolutely wrong upon the stage. Even inarticulate mumbling can be effective, and clumsy shuffling may be extremely funny, or infinitely pathetic. But the cardinal difficulty is that what one does often matters less than the pace at which one does it. " Timing " is the governing factor in all acting, hardly less important than it is in music. It owns no principles, but differs with every line of every play.

It is obvious that some scenes must be played faster than others, and a good playwright will generally offer his actors little opportunity or temptation to speak them slowly. Beyond the written dialogue of each play there is no sure guide. One cannot even say that comic scenes necessarily need brisker timing than serious ones ; some types of humour—for instance, those emanating from Yorkshire—depend on slow speech for their effect. Tragedy demands briskness wherever it verges, as tragedy always does, on melodrama ; and at other times it calls for the torrential rapidity of Hamlet assailing Laertes by Ophelia's grave, or Hibbert gibbering his cowardice in the dug-out. Apart from the general pace of the scene there is the pace of every speech to be considered ; emphasis can be laid on the crucial speeches by making them faster or (more usually) slower than the rest.

Most important of all is the pace at which cues are to be taken up. Here experiment at rehearsal may produce astonishing results in bringing apparently dead matter to life. It cannot really begin until all the actors have learnt their parts, and learnt them thoroughly. They must know as soon as they finish each speech how their next one will start, and this knowledge must become so unconscious, by practice, that the sound of the actual cue presses a button and releases an instantaneous spring. Then the scene can be gone through again and again until it obtains its full effect. A cue may be the signal for a definite pause, prolonged or momentary. On the other hand, it may call for so immediate a reply that there is no check in the sound of the dialogue. Occasionally, but far more often than amateurs suppose, the second speaker should cut in upon the last few syllables, or even words, of the preceding speech.

DISASTROUS RESULTS OF LEARNING LINES TOO LATE

INDEED, if there is one fault which particularly besets amateurs it is that of slow timing on cues. It is mainly the product of imperfect learning of lines—and of learning them too late in rehearsals. In the professional productions of London theatres, where the rehearsals continue daily for three weeks or more, the actors should know their lines thoroughly before the last week begins ; some prefer to arrive word perfect at the first rehearsal, and their performances generally benefit.

Amateurs sometimes think that it is enough to know their lines by the dress rehearsal. This is laziness, and its results are disastrous. It is like training for a boat-race and never troubling to change into the proper clothes, or row as one intends to row in the race, until the day before. Lines learnt are spoken quite differently from lines read in a book. One needs practice in so speaking them. More still, the other actors need to know in good time how they are going to be spoken before an audience. There is no other way of getting the correct timing throughout a cast.

REHEARSELS, THOUGH FEW, SHOULD BE FREQUENT

HERE a word must be said on the peculiar and inevitable difficulty with which all amateurs have to struggle. If their productions are inferior to those of professionals, it may not be merely a question of lack of experience. Sincerity, freshness, and the power to choose better plays may be an ample compensation, and put the amateur in a stronger position than all but the best professionals. It is not even a question of time for rehearsals ; hour for hour, many amateurs can spend far longer on a play. It is rather that these hours may be spread out over a period of many weeks, or even many months, while professionals, rehearsing for one week, for a fortnight, or perhaps for a month, can rehearse daily. Where rehearsals are scattered, with long intervals between them, the first hour or two of Wednesday's rehearsal may be spent in recapturing the smoothness, the briskness, or the emotional effect, which was achieved last Saturday. It is quite possible that with actors tired, or unable and unwilling to concentrate, one may not have caught up with Saturday's achievement when the time arrives for going home ; the production may be going backward instead of progressing.

Societies should strain every nerve and cancel every social engagement in order to crowd their rehearsals together towards the end. A production is like a leaky can. Filled to the brim one day, it is left alone for a week and then found inexplicably and distressingly empty. The leakage is caused by all the other interests or duties which prevent an amateur concentrating all his waking attention on the play, by forget-fulness, by mere lapse of time, and by lack of constant practice. Only continual pouring will repair the waste and keep the play alive.

The record of our repertory theatres proves that anything can be done in a week of daily rehearsal, even though the rehearsers are acting another play at night. But nothing that is worth doing can be done by one rehearsal a week over a period of six months or even a year. Unfortunately those who are acting the smallest parts may be just as important for the re-creating of the *ensemble* as those who are getting most of the fun. But drama is an art, and demands sacrifice : it is a communal art, and demands a heartless inequality of sacrifice.

LITTLE FAULTS THAT DISPEL THE CHARM

ONCE unity has been achieved in movement, it can still be broken by inappropriate tones and inflections of the voice. Here the smaller parts have sometimes a harder task than the leading actors ; after standing silent for a long time on the stage they are suddenly required to produce a line or two in harmony with the general music, without previous practice before an audience.

But the spell cannot only be broken by thoughtless movement or inharmonious inflections, it can also be destroyed by considered but injudicious attempts to enhance it. It can be broken by over-emphasis. Here professional actors are often worse than amateurs — delivering unimportant lines with the slow and portentous manner of an unskilful parson, or drawing a cork as if the fate of empires depended on the action. This is like attacking the audience with a bludgeon, instead of using the enchanter's wand. In most plays there are times when the bludgeon is needed ; some even demand the letting off of firearms on the stage, and most farces contain moments when everybody yells at the top of his voice. But a constant succession of such belabourings will soon reduce an audience to inattention, resentment, or active hostility.

THE LIFE-BLOOD OF THE THEATRE

FINALLY—and it is the most insidious of all dangers— monotony will destroy the whole spell, gradually but more irretrievably than anything else. Variety is necessary to every art : it is the life-blood of the theatre. Contrasts must here be sharper and—it is the only possible word—more dramatic than anywhere else. Some plays rely less on sudden twists of the story than others ; they must obtain their contrasts by sharper distinctions and conflicts of character, or by the constant variety in the style of the dialogue. In some plays, and Greek drama is the best example, the variety is obtained by development. There are no surprises, no sudden changes, and yet the final curtain finds everything changed—and irrevocably changed.

There is great artistic pleasure to be had in watching the gradual unfolding of an inevitable destiny. But it must unfold. The actors must make it do so. They must act differently, more slowly or more rapidly, with more emphasis or with less, as the story proceeds. They must work for the smaller crises which contribute to the main development. They must make it quite clear where the grand climax comes, and their acting must have as much " shape " as the play.

We have said that there is nothing in itself wrong upon the stage ; but to this rule there is one universal exception. It is always wrong to be dull. It is possible for a work of history to be dull, and usual for a scientific treatise : yet their dullness does not prevent them from exercising a great and valuable influence. A play obeys other laws. It can be a good play—though perhaps not a great one—while remaining unreal, grotesque, untruthful, immoral, and disgusting. But if it is dull, or if the actors have made it so, there is no more to be said. They are bad artists, and they have cheated the audience of their money.

BOOKS THAT PRODUCER AND PLAYER SHOULD READ

THE literature of the theatre, and even of the amateur theatre, is extensive, and seems to increase hourly. I can do no more than suggest a few books that I have found useful myself.

PRODUCTION.—A simple and business-like book for amateurs is John Fernald's *The Play Produced* (Deane and Sons) : its practical directions are good, even when the reasons given are questionable. Frank Vernon's *Modern Stage Production* (published by *The Stage*) is also short, simple, and direct, though not addressed particularly to amateurs. Martin Browne's *The Production of Religious Plays* (Philip Allan) deals with a single field, but deals with it in an instructive and forceful way.

DESIGN.—I know of no single book on theatrical design

except those of Gordon Craig, for instance, *The Art of the Theatre* (Heinemann) : they are excellent reading and well illustrated, but supply ideas rather than practicable advice. Collections of photographs and designs are often the most useful, as, for instance, those of Robert Edmond Jones (Theatre Arts Inc., N.Y.) and the beautiful collection of George W. Harris (Nisbet). The illustrations to K. Macgowan's *The Theatre of To-morrow* are interesting.

COSTUME.—Books on costume abound : for completeness and arrangement, none supersede Planché's *Cyclopedia of Costume* (Chatto and Windus, 1876). Dion Clayton Calthrop's *English Costume* (Black) is better written than most ; the line drawings are excellent, much better than the coloured plates. M. and C. H. B. Quennell's *Histories of Everyday Things— in England—in Roman Britain*, etc. (Batsford), are excellent and most useful. Most of the illustrations to Köhler's *History of Costume* (Harrap) are good, and patterns are provided for the cutter.

ACTING.—I know of no general book that is much use, except perhaps Louis Calvert's *Problems of the Actor* (Simpkin Marshall). Much can be picked up from such books as G. B. Shaw's *Dramatic Opinions and Essays* (Constable). Talma's *Reflexions on the Art of Acting* (published with Irving's Introduction by Columbia University) is quite masterly. Many books of Memoirs make good reading, a few are really useful, as, for instance, Sarah Bernhardt's (Bles). Stanislavsky's *My Life in Art* (Bles) is widely praised.

LIGHTING.—C. H. Ridge's *Stage Lighting for Little Theatres* (Heffer and Sons) is excellent, comprehensive, and extremely intelligible.

MAKE-UP.—The best book is perhaps Cavendish Marton's *The Art of Theatrical Make-up* (Black).

The best library for books on drama, particularly amateur drama, is that of the British Drama League. In fact, this society gives valuable help to amateurs in all directions.

16

THE ART OF PHOTOGRAPHY : CAMERA AND SCREEN

by VERNON J. CLANCEY, A.R.C.S.

Discussion of cameras and photography conjures up thoughts of the family album and the agonies of looking at " our holiday snaps." These little monstrosities of " me and my pal on the breakwater " are the justification of the scoffers who deny that photography can have the slightest affinity to art. That such photographs are inartistic is, of course, only too true ; but a little consideration and skilful manipulation can produce results in photography sufficient to rout these scoffers and definitely to establish that there is an art of the camera. Perhaps the greatest handicaps to the progress of photographic art are the ease with which the camera produces some sort of a result and the fact that so many people are satisfied with anything in a photograph, so long as they can recognise the persons or places it records.

Many amateurs only require of their cameras that they should produce records—not too libellous—of their infants, their friends, and the scenes of their holidays. There is, however, no reason why such records should not also be pleasing pictures worthy of their space in the album. In this section it is intended to outline an approach to this end, to suggest certain lines of thought and to indicate how the technique of photography may be applied as a medium of artistic expression.

WHAT SHOULD WE EXPECT OF A PHOTOGRAPH ?

The photographer should first establish clearly in his own mind what it is that one looks for in a photograph ; then he will know just what he is setting out to obtain, and he will have a standard by which to criticise his results. Similarly those who look at photographs need to know the principles on which the art of photography depends. We are all familiar with the praise : " It's just like her," and the corollary : " She doesn't photograph well," as the critical formulas of our friends. Likeness, evidently, is the first criterion by which they judge photographs. Faithfulness of reproduction both in portraits and scenes is placed in front of everything else. Since this is simply a matter of correct handling of the apparatus and mastery of the mechanical technique, it gives an entirely false basis of criticism, from an artistic standpoint, and leads to a misuse of the medium.

When we look at a photograph, there are certain things we should look for beyond this degree of naturalistic accuracy. In the first place the photograph should present to us a pleasing arrangement of lights and shades, of masses of tones, in exactly the same manner as a drawing in monochrome ; in fact it should, at first glance, draw us to study it further. Secondly, the subject-matter should be presented in an interesting and satisfying manner so that we are told something more in the picture than a bare record of the scene ; the photographer himself must contribute a viewpoint or interpretation of the subject. Thirdly, technical perfection must play its part, considered both as purely technical work and in terms of its contribution to the other two aspects of photographic art.

These considerations will form the basis of our theory of camera art. If we learn to look at photographs from these points of view we shall establish a definite critical faculty which must help to give us a knowledge of what we wish to obtain and a method of constructively criticising our efforts.

WHERE DRAWING AND PHOTOGRAPHY ARE ALIKE

IN their main principles, the laws of the graphic arts apply to the finished photograph. In so far as we are dealing with a graphic representation in a gradation of tones of monochrome, the laws of composition, and so on, in a photograph are identical with the similar laws of drawing ; though certain natural modifications arise owing to the peculiar nature of a photograph and to the degree and nature of the control which is exercisable in the production of the picture.

There are certain specific and well-defined characteristics of the photograph which may be considered as its special qualities giving it its own potentialities and sphere distinct from the graphic arts. The most important of these derive from the mechanical and physico-chemical methods by which the picture is obtained.

Everyone is familiar, in a general way, with the typical qualities of a photograph, and there is no difficulty in recognising the photograph as such. (We are excluding here certain " stunt " and trick imitative work whereby its nature is concealed or modified.) Such general recognition is, however, not sufficient ; we must make a closer examination in order to find the fundamental characteristics.

The photographic process, if uncontrolled, produces and can only produce a certain kind of rendering of that which lies before and in the field of the lens. This rendering is entirely determined by the chemical laws of the effects of light of differing colours and intensities on the sensitive materials. Thus photography is bound to a type of naturalistic representation of the selected subject-matter of the picture, and this naturalism is only modified by photographic processes. If we examine a photograph of a landscape we shall obtain some idea of the effects of this and of its importance in establishing the broader principles of camera art.

HOW THE CAMERA RECORDS LIGHT AND SHADE

PROBABLY the first thing we notice is the way in which colour and light are recorded. The whole range of the spectrum and the whole range from darkness to the most intensely bright light of the scene are transformed into a series of tones from black to the pure white of the paper on which the picture is reproduced. The camera cannot distinguish between green with a certain amount of light on it and blue with proportionately less light on it. Consequently the photograph cannot, as can the artist, make a picture in terms of light and shadows only—the colours in the subject are inextricably involved. Thus we see fundamental limitation of the medium, to combat which certain steps can and must be taken. This factor, although a limitation, must be considered also as one basis from which the photograph works.

On this basis are created the pictorial results of photography, with the additional aid of a number of conventions. It is patent that, as in the graphic arts, conventions are essential. We do not need, here, to enter into the general question of, say, the convention of three dimensional representation or the reduction of the light scale from the range of nature to the range from black to white paper, and so on, as these properly belong to the theory of the graphic arts and are common to them.

But it is important that we realise that these conventions, to which we have become educated, play a most vital part in the picture, raising it from an abstract arrangement of masses of tones to a picture with subject interest, and ultimately a viewpoint or impression of the subject. That they do play such a vital part is shown by the reactions of, say, an un-educated Indian who, on first being shown a photograph, will frequently hold it upside down and quite fail to recognise what it portrays.

OUR EYES AND THE CAMERA'S ACT ALIKE

RETURNING to our consideration of a photographic land-scape, we shall notice that while it deals only in tones, it definitely conveys to us an idea or impression of surface qualities of textures. For example, a grass meadow, while it may be rendered by exactly the same tone of grey as a cottage wall, differs quite definitely in texture. Generally the differ-ence is emphasised by our imagination and knowledge derived from the subject—thus we are familiar with the flat expanse of a field, and we know that cottages are built with plastered walls—yet there is a definite absolute difference in the quality of the two tones in our picture. Here again the photographer is at a considerable advantage over the graphic artist. The reason for this lies in the similarity between the mechanism of our eyes and the lens and sensitive plate of the camera.

An examination of this similarity will show the unique position of photography as a representational art. The lens of the camera acts in precisely the same manner as the lenses of our eyes—in one case an image of the scene is projected on to the sensitised plate ; in the other case the image is projected on to the sensitive retina. Our eyes, however, possess two qualities superior to the camera—the nerves of the retina are individually sensitive to three colours, thus giving the power of colour vision ; and the co-ordination by the brain of the two viewpoints, one of each eye, gives the impression of depth.

Consequently, if we take into account the conventions of monotone rendering of colour and of two dimensional per-spective, it is apparent that the camera must give a closer rendering of the scene than can the artist. For example, in the case of texture rendering already mentioned, the camera portrays the infinitely minute lights and shades of the grass surface, whereas the artist must rely on the artificial use of brush work, texture of his pigment, and so on—thus intro-ducing further conventions to overcome the limitations of his craft.

Another instance of this is in the matter of " atmosphere " in a picture. The artist—note that I am using this word in the rather narrow meaning of common usage—is prone to claim that he alone is capable of putting atmosphere into his work. It is patent that if there is any atmosphere in a scene capable of being appreciated by our eyes then it must also be apparent to the eye of the camera, and it is up to the photographer to appreciate it and ensure its rendering in his finished picture.

Thus we see that, in so far as we are considering the problem of transferring a scene from nature on to paper or any other flat surface, the photographer starts with an advantage. However, while this advantage is considerable, it is also the greatest limitation of the medium.

WHY PHOTOGRAPHY IS DISCREDITED AS AN ART

THE nature of certain of these limitations is obvious. For example, the loss of colour particularly affects the range of possibilities of the medium. Probably the most important, however, is due to the naturalism of the picture in combination with the fact that the " eye " of the camera is unselective. If, for the moment, we ignore any possibility of control in the processes after the actual taking, we find that the camera will only give us a picture of exactly that which is within range of its " vision " and that this picture will include everything within that range. Thus it is impossible to eliminate the unnecessary or undesirable, or to emphasise or reduce in importance the components of the picture ; and far less is it possible to distort our subject—in fact, we are denied in the camera, all the " licence " of the artist. This, incidentally, is the main reason why photography is discredited as an art and condemned as a mere mechanical method of portrayal.

If, however, we realise its special possibilities as well as its limitations we can define a method which will capitalise the one and overcome the other and which will elevate photography to the position of being truly an art. In so doing we must remember that any art form should be founded on its own special qualities—employing them for their own peculiar effect and purpose—and that it must work within its own powers ; above all, we must not attempt to imitate the effects of, or trespass into the realms of other and foreign art forms.

HOW ARTISTIC THEORIES CAN BE PUT INTO PRACTICE

LET us now consider how these theories affect the practice of photography. We are not concerned here with the technicalities of producing photographs but rather with the bearings of artistic theory on the various phases of the medium.

First, we must consider why we take photographs and the purposes they are intended to serve, for this governs our whole approach to the actual technical work. The vast majority of photographs taken are primarily intended as records of personal interest—records of ourselves on holidays, our children and our friends at times and places of personal interest, and of places that we visit. These, kept in our albums serve as reminders of happy days and bring back in retrospect our travels and our sightseeing. Generally, they are of little interest to anyone but the photographer himself ; but this need not be so if some thought and care is given to their making.

If we do not allow the subject interest alone to outweigh every other consideration we can add other interests which will not only appeal to others, but also will add greatly to our own pleasure. We all know how boring it is to see a lot of pictures of groups of people sitting or standing in rows on beaches and cliffs when we do not know who they are; but if there is also a pictorial interest in the photograph and if the people are doing interesting things, or if the picture tells a story, then we can be pleased by it, although we may know nothing of the people themselves.

Closely allied to this type of photograph is the portrait. Here again the principal reason for its making is primarily to record a subject usually also of personal interest. Similarly, this need not be only a record, a catalogue of features—item two eyes, item one nose. In fact, it must be more than this if it is to be truly a portrait ; it must convey character, the artist's eye must govern the mechanical functions of the camera.

In general, we may define the reasons why we take a photograph as being to record some scene, event, etc., *plus* to produce a " picture "—that is, an artistic and interesting interpretation of the scene, event, etc. It is apparent that the balance between these reasons will vary in each case. At one end of the scale the record will vastly preponderate—as in scientific, documentary records, and so on, and also in the majority of "news" pictures, which are taken under uncontrollable conditions and are intended simply to satisfy the transient interest of a casual public. At the other end the " pictorial " value will outweigh the record—as in much of the work shown in photographic exhibitions to-day, and more particularly in the so-called "abstract" photographs and examples of "photo-montage."

THE PHOTOGRAPH THAT CONVEYS A MOOD

"ABSTRACT" photographs are the final result of subordinating subject interest to the pictorial, thus lying at the farthest end of the scale from the documentary photograph. Their object is not to portray the natural world but to use the photographic medium to produce patterns of light and shade so arranged as to convey impressions and moods. The "abstract" photograph tries to free itself from that naturalism which has always hampered the artistic recognition of the medium. Closely allied to this aim is that of "photo-montage." In this method a composite picture is built up from related fragments, each of which may or may not be naturalistic, and the result produced is cumulative, both subjectively and objectively.

The "abstract" photograph and "photo-montage" are worthy of considerable attention ; but it is impossible to deal here with their theory and practice. They are new and comparatively unexplored realms. While many conservative minds are inclined to consider them as monstrosities comparable with the efforts of the "cubists" of pre-War days, they undoubtedly can and will play a most vital part in the future development of the art of photography. They bear a very definite relation to modern ideas and conditions. Although, as is always the case in new movements, there is a tendency to subordinate everything to mere technical achievement and novelty, it is probable that, when the exaggerations are toned down by experience, there will emerge from these experiments the photographic school of the next decade.

THE ART OF THE SCREEN

WHEN to the method of photography is added the potentiality of rendering movement there is opened up an enormously vast field which is only slightly represented by the cinema of to-day. The possibilities of this field are so great and its method so in its infancy that we can only begin to see its perspectives as the child, just acquainted with his primer, can glimpse the oppressive vistas of literature.

This analogy, while it serves to indicate the resemblance between words and the moving picture—from one is built the much ramified edifice of the world of letters, of drama, and thence the theatre; from the other is now growing up a literature, a cinematic theatre—this analogy does not adequately express the ultimate possibilities of cinema, it suggests limits where there is no apparent horizon.

If photography has done nothing else but make the motion picture possible, it has generated the most important and vital new art form and method of expression since man first evolved words from his primitive bestial grunts. While we are making this comparison, let us remember that we are comparing the product of ten thousand years of progress with the rather naïve and precocious utterings of an infant of about thirty years—remember this, and imagine what we may expect cinema to become in the future.

Hitherto, the progress of cinema—(Note: I use the word " cinema " as analogous to " literature ")—has been governed by certain commercial considerations. This fact is generally lamented by writers on the theory of cinema; but consideration will show that these financial aspects and their effects are in reality the great urge which has produced such enormous advances in the art—advances which would have been much slower and probably less direct if the sole impulse had been an æsthetic curiosity felt by a few experimentalists.

THE MISTAKE OF COMPARING DIFFERENT KINDS OF FILMS

AN appreciation of literature takes into account form, style, and subject-matter; cinema must be classified in a similar way, thus providing a basis for criticism and understanding. We should not think of comparing a sonnet with, say, a Dickens novel, or the most brilliant piece of journalism with, say, a Shakespearian drama, yet such impossible and ridiculous comparisons are often made in discussions of films. We have all heard such comparisons, which can only be made by those who totally lack understanding, realisation of the great variety of film forms possible, and the vital differences between them.

In the first place, we may class films as prose films or poetic films—using a direct analogy. The great majority of films to-day are definitely prose films; that is plain statements in the units (words) of cinema without regard to rhythm. In fact, our story-telling films are very much in the primitive " Once upon a time there was a beautiful princess who lived in a great castle " stage. Occasionally, however, we do see films which show some simple poetic form—" an emotional expression generally in some metrical form," according to the dictionary. For example, Grierson tends towards the blank verse of Carl Sandburg; Robert Flaherty became lyrical in *Moana*; Walt Disney uses the simple rhymes and rhythms of the nursery; while Eisenstein endeavours towards an epic poem in his treatment.

HOW THE FILM MAY USE SOUND

IN addition to these, cinema can claim a third form beyond the realms of literature. By its use of sound, the film has the additional potentialities of aural expression. In the majority of films the sound is used either as conversations are used in novels or as speech is used in the theatre. There is, however, a further use of sound which makes it a more intimate part of the presentation so that the picture is incomplete without the sound. The closest analogy to this is to be found in ballet, but whereas, in its traditional form, ballet is a matter of pantomimic expression with music, cinematic ballet need not be pantomimic; it may be vocal and naturalistic, and the music may be replaced by other sounds.

This is a field which has not as yet been explored, and therefore we can give no examples beyond some little known experiments. Perhaps the easiest to conceive would be a ballet of machines—shots of wheels and cranks, of throbbing steel and vibrant power, in which the beat and throb, the hum and pulse of a factory are welded together into emotional rhythms expressive of an artistic interpretation of machinery. The nearest approach to this form is to be found in the *Mickey Mouse* cartoon films—and it is because of this that they are so frequently acclaimed to be " the most pure form of cinema." There is in them, however, a certain vital difference in that the sound is rather in the position of being an accompaniment to the picture.

Further, to employ the analogy to literature, we can subdivide cinema again into forms corresponding to the novel and biography. Prose films may tell a story as Wellsian prose creates a romantic novel, or George Arliss may create a cinematic biography; or, again, the film may in its prose style correspond to a travel document; it may reach out further into the regions of the epic in prose—whether it be the epic of a railway, or of the conquest of the West, *Turksib*, or *The Covered Wagon*.

Thus the whole world of cinema must be considered as we consider the world of literature. Before venturing on criticism we must define the class to which the particular film belongs ; then we may establish standards for each class, a basis from which to argue its qualities.

THE PRINCIPLES ON WHICH ALL FILMS ARE BASED

BEFORE we proceed further, let us consider the fundamental methods of the film, the mechanics of this form of expression. There are certain things which are common to every kind of film, as the word and sentence is common to every form of literature.

As the individual words are employed by the writer so are pictures used by the film maker—he builds up his phrases from individual pictures which by juxtaposition grow in meaning into an effect greater than the sum of their individual values. Thus a series of static pictures in juxtaposition will create a movement on the screen which was not apparent in any of the individual pictures. This building-up from individual photographs is the meaning of Pudovkin's theory of " montage."

Now, in theory, each of these component pictures may be considered as we consider a still photograph. When we say that the photography of a film is good, we mean that each component picture satisfies our requirements of composition, and so on ; but we must remember that this has as much bearing on the quality of the film as the style of the type has on the quality of a book. Correctly, we should assess the picture on its value and appropriateness in its particular position, just as we may like a certain word by itself, but must still judge whether it is correctly placed in a given sentence and whether it gives the right contribution to the meaning.

THE PICTURE A GENIUS AT TERSE DESCRIPTION

WE should notice here that if we adhere too strictly to the word analogy we shall get into considerable difficulties, since there are very obvious limitations in the comparison. Thus the picture tells more than a word—it may qualify the word, but it will always remain essentially substantive. For example, we may state pictorially *a man* or *a tall man with grey hair in a smoking-jacket standing in a library*, thus in one picture giving the equivalent of a whole paragraph of descriptive writing.

Now, beyond the individual pictures we can, as we have seen, so arrange them as to create movement. In general, we

may consider such movements as being the verbs for our
picture nouns—thus we can state that our *man walks across
the library and sits down at the table*. Thus a film " shot "—
that is a number of individual pictures conveying a scene and
movement therein—may be compared to a sentence.

It is beyond our present scope to pursue this theory at
length, but I would suggest that here is an interesting field
for thought, since along these lines the reader may evolve for
himself a cinematic theory. We must here content ourselves
with indicating certain lines of thought. We may, for example,
consider the question of movement in the abstract. As we
require in a still picture a certain composition, so we may
require a composition of movements in a cinematic scene.

We may work out a theory of movement balance corresponding with a balance of masses of tone. I would suggest here
that the laws which will become established for this will be
very closely related to the laws of mechanics—that a good composition will only be attainable by balanced movements, such
as two equal and opposite or three or more which balance each
other in a circular or other geometric form. Further, we may
deliberately use unbalanced movements to convey special
effects, such as a succession of undirectional movements to
give a processional effect or a series of converging movements
to give a piling-up effect. It is evident that here is to be
found an almost unexpected field for research in cinema
technique.

PROBLEMS OF PRESERVING THE RHYTHM IN FILMS

WHEN we come to consider the theories of cinematic
sentences, of complete scenes, we introduce a whole
host of new problems. For example, the question of rhythms
of picture and action and, particularly in the case of cinematic
verse, of picture and action rhymes. Some indication of the
use of pictorial rhythms was given in Grierson's *Drifters* and
more recently in the cartoon films of Disney. I am not aware
of any use having been made yet of pictorial rhymes except
the very elementary form of repetition of a picture in some
of the Russian films.

All this is a consideration of the film method in the abstract
—dissociated from the subject content of the pictures. When
we come to include this we reach the stage of comparison
with literature when we consider its subject-matter. We have
the further analogies of dramatic construction, of story-telling,

of the possibilities of pictorial metaphors, of the film's relations with the theatre method, and so on.

Since to all this we must add the possibilities and problems of sound in conjunction with the pictures, it is evident that cinema offers a vast field for theory and research. By such research and all its incumbent experimental work a cinema technique will presently be evolved which will justify cinema's claim to be an art that incorporates the possibilities of literature, of the theatre, of music, indeed of nearly every form of artistic expression.

THE TYPES OF FILMS THAT ARE MADE TO-DAY

LET us now survey briefly the various types of films which are made and shown to-day in the light of this theory; thus we may obtain some evidence of the lines on which progress is being made and some indication of the vast possibilities of future development. For this purpose we may employ a classification based on subject matter, since the contents of the films have, to a large extent, governed the evolution of the different forms.

RECORDS.—Films have to some extent been used to make exact records of events, for scientific, classroom, and general educational purposes and also as an aid to research. The high-speed camera, for instance, has been used to analyse movements of machines. These films, however, in that they are merely specialist uses of the mechanism of cinema, do not come properly under our consideration.

NEWS-FILMS.—The position of news-films is essentially the same as that of newspapers; they are the journalism of the cinema, and are subject to the requirements and the latitudes of journalism. Nevertheless, the majority of news-films exhibited in our cinemas show lack of appreciation of this fact; any editor who consistently filled his front page with such banal stories of ship launchings and civic receptions would promptly be sacked. It would be well worth while for news-film producers to employ journalists with proved Fleet Street ability to tell them what is news and how a story should be presented. In this connection it is interesting to note that the proprietors of an American periodical have recently launched what they claim to be a revolution in news-films. This is *The March of Time*, which dramatises current events— a definite advance in the bald recording of facts.

INTEREST FILMS.—In this category we must include the majority of travel films, portrayals of industries, and all films which rely for their appeal mainly on the reproduction of interesting actualities. They are little better, from a cinema art point of view, than the record films, and have not even the excuses of the news-film. They correspond with those little paragraphs of general knowledge which used to appear in some magazines and which, mercifully, have faded away. Let us hope that these films will do the same. They can either revert to their proper sphere of records to be used in the classroom or else grow up into the type of films to be described next.

DOCUMENTARY FILMS.—This name has been coined to indicate a special type of film which may be defined as a dramatised interest picture, but it is here used in a broader sense to mean any film which creates a dramatic or other form out of the material of actualities as distinct from the artificial creations of the studio. Thus, under this heading, we may include Grierson's drama of the fishing fleet, *Drifters*; Cooper's romance of a jungle, *Chang*; Flaherty's poem of the South Sea Islanders, *Moana*; Ruttman's blank verse symphony of a city, *Berlin*; and Basil Wright's and Arthur Elton's epics of industries.

The most vital school of documentary production is to be found in Great Britain. Grierson was the originator, and in the E.M.B. Film Group (now transferred to the G.P.O.) formed in a Government office the most revolutionary film production unit in the world. It would seem that he has studied the methods of Flaherty and the Russians, and has learnt from *The Covered Wagon* the pitfalls to be avoided. To the results of his observation of the work of others he has added his own vision to originate a definite film-form which is still developing and has now reached beyond the results of his earlier prototypes. He has found a cinematic form of drama which is independent of any necessity for drama in his subject-matter—thus he dramatises a telephone exchange or makes a sonnet of flowers in the park and an epic of an æroplane. It is impossible here to explain his technique; the best thing to do is to study his work and that of his pupils, especially Elton, Wright, and Rotha.

STUDIO FILMS.—Under this heading is included the vast majority of the films shown in the cinema to-day. We may define them as being films for which the subject-matter is

artificially created—while we use the term " studio," it is
evident that this does not eliminate such subjects as are
artificially created " on location " away from the studio.
These films are unique in that the producer and his co-authors
create everything—thus being in a similar position to the
novelist and the dramatist.

By reason of its entertainment requirements and associations,
the films of this class are practically universally an adaptation
of theatrical methods. They are in fact theatrical productions
recorded and slightly adapted to the mechanics of the screen.
We see dramas, and melodramas, comedies, and musical
comedies which really belong to the world of the theatre.
Certainly there is a greater freedom of action, since on the
screen we are not limited to a few scenes, or to one point of
vision. There is a greater lavishness of legs in the musical
comedies, and the sea is more real than the undulating backcloth, but it all belongs to the methods of the stage. The
scenes are played in a stage manner before the camera so that
they may be reproduced on the screen to the audience. All
that has been added is a degree of ingenuity in the mechanics
of getting the stage on to the screen.

THE THEATRICAL FILM A CLASS BY ITSELF

THEORISTS are inclined to argue that such films are not
pure cinema. They are definitely cinema; but they are
a very specific branch which we may call theatrical cinema,
just as the drama itself is a very definite branch of literature.
It is important to remember this lest we be inclined to judge
the whole of the cinema from this one branch.

Everyone is aware of the progress that has been made in
this field—the gradual evolution of a special acting method,
all the technical tricks such as the " fade out " to indicate
passage of time, the " dissolve " as a continuity device, the
" vision " and the " flash back "—but despite all this the
studio film still remains of the theatre. The " fade out " is
the curtain between scenes ; the " vision " belongs to the
theatre ; even the much publicised " narratage " method is
only a version of the old Greek chorus. Though much
progress in technique has been made, these films still consist
of scenes acted on a stage ; they are still essentially linked to
the theatre.

There are, however, certain indications that the studio film
is evolving into a form beyond the stage. Occasionally we

find a little sequence hemmed in by the masses of theatrical
treatment which brings a breath of freshness, of novelty,
showing possibilities beyond those of the theatre. They
suggest whither theatrical cinema is advancing. It will have
all the powers of the stage without its limitations. Even now
the portrayal is becoming more selective ; the old lavish
detail of De Mille has passed, and the value of elimination
and simplification is being realised.

Evidence of this will be found by an examination of the
better of recent films and a comparison with earlier examples.
Thus *David Copperfield*, when compared with previous
pictures of the same subject, shows an enormous improvement and development ; the work of Bergner, Arliss, Laugh-
ton, of Joan Crawford, Robert Donat, and the other " stars "
of to-day show how the acting technique is turning further
from the stage. The musical productions of Warner's—such
as *Forty-Second Street* and *Dames*—show a technique far
beyond the realms of the theatre ; certain recent M.G.M.
productions—beginning with *The Thin Man*—show a new
economy of statement ; the London Film Productions—
from *Henry VIII.* to the *Shape of Things to Come*—show the
breadth of range of the studio film.

ABSTRACT FILMS.—Not many examples of this group have
been shown to the general public, although a considerable
number have been made, particularly on the Continent, and
are shown privately to film societies. A few years ago a
series of short films were shown which endeavoured to interpret music by means of changing designs on the screen.
More recently, Len Lye's *Colour Box* (made for the G.P.O.)
carried on the same idea, with the addition of colour.

THE FUTURE OF SCREEN ART

AT intervals the pundits of the commercial cinema give
great publicity to what they are pleased to call revolutionary advances. The one really important advance was the
addition of sound to the silent picture. The two things
which are " boosted " by them now are colour and stereoscopic pictures. Neither of these seem to me to be revolutionary from the art point of view, but rather to be technical
improvements in the presentation.

The latest concern with colour has arisen because the
American Technicolour Company have invented a new process
and sponsored the production by it of *Becky Sharp*. Other

processes—such as Gaspacolour and Spicer-Dujay—are also trying to promote general interest. It seems that it would be a pity if colour, which artistically is very poor still, is to be foisted on our infant which has not yet learned to express itself fully in black and white. However, the evidence seems to show that this is only a passing phase, and that colour will, as it has done before, sink back into oblivion.

At first sight, stereoscopic pictures would seem to open up a great new territory. If, however, we remember that the present two-dimensional films are, by reason of accepted conventions, viewed by the spectator as being in three dimensions, it will be realised that this is not to be a revolution in cinema art. While it will certainly be an advantage to dispense with an artificial convention, there is a great danger in this technical development—a danger common also to the advent of colour—that cinema will be increasingly tied to naturalism in its portrayal, thus adding to the inherent difficulty of photography.

WHAT TO READ ABOUT CAMERA AND SCREEN

THERE are a very considerable number of books available dealing with the technique of the camera and the screen. The photographer will welcome such as *Making a Photograph*, by A. Adams (Studio), but the artist will gain much more by an intelligent study of such collections as *Photograms of the Year* (Iliffe) and *The Year's Photographs* (R. Photo. Soc.). The amateur film-maker, who wishes to test out his theories, should refer to such works as *Film Craft*, by Adrian Brunch (Newnes), and *Cine-Photography for Amateurs*, by J. H. Rayner (Chapman and Hall), while many interesting viewpoints on film art are to be found in *Celluloid*, by Paul Rotha (Longmans), *Film Technique* and *Film Acting*, by Pudovkin (Newnes), *Film*, by Rudolph Arnheim (Faber and Faber), and *This Film Business*, by Rudolph Messel (Benn), all of which are in their way the "classics" in this connection. C. A. Lejeune, in *Cinema* (Maclehose), gives the most effective review of the world of commercial cinema.

MAKING A LIVING ON THE STAGE

by BARBARA NIXON

THE advice of any professional actor or actress to the aspirant who asks how best he or she can get on the stage, is: "Keep out of it, and don't try." This, though it sounds brutal, is not jealousy on the part of the old of the younger generation, nor, generally, selfishness and a desire to keep the secrets and the glamour to themselves. It is, for at least two reasons, very sound advice. First, the stage is not only the romantic and glamorous place the public imagines. As a profession it is the worst organised in the whole labour market, and the most overstocked, since so many overestimate their histrionic abilities. It is one of the grossest cases of casual methods of employment with all its attendant evils in this country; it entails long hours of rehearsing, with bad tempers and often worse manners, gross injustices, often bad pay, *and no security at all.* Secondly, so many young people think that they would like "to act" rather than sit in an office, when they have in reality few qualifications other than their good looks, that it is certainly the wisest course to deter them as far as possible. If they still persevere and overcome all the obstacles that are put in their way, then they have possibly a true theatrical bent, and even if they are not "successful" will have justified themselves and their profession.

Few people realise what an amount of work goes into a play, not only on the production and stage-management side, but on the part of the actors themselves. Rehearsals are not a matter of just running through the play once or twice. With a scrupulous producer every two pages may be gone over again and again, and then the whole scene taken through a second or third time on end. Actors often have to wait, sitting in the stalls where it is too dark to read half the day, and then not be needed at all. Then, after three weeks of such work, with half-pay for the lower-paid artists and none for the higher, the show may only run for three days or a week. Apart from the financial side the insecurity is a great nervous strain.

Despite this blacker side of the picture, however, the stage still has its attraction. For the actor there is always the

WHERE TO OBTAIN A GOOD TRAINING 499

pleasure, to him, of being someone else ; there is the piquant delight of the mixing of unreality in the wings and the apparent reality to the audience of the stage picture, of the back of the scenery, with its braces and lamps and ropes, and the front looking solid and convincing. There is the per- petual excitement of the curtain going up, and the rather mysterious contact between actor and audience. Even the insecurity, though it frays the nerves, yet works as an excitant like gambling to many ; even for the more pessimistic in temperament present bad luck may always turn. Finally, there is the appeal of artistic expression to the artist. And just as many famous painters have lived in penury in their youth, and gone without food to buy canvas and brushes, so a true actor will endure bad conditions for the sake of the need within him to create his form of art.

WHERE TO OBTAIN A GOOD TRAINING

IT is often said that English actors are inferior to their continental fellow-artists. It may be true, but it is to a very large extent due to a lack of efficient training. There is the Royal Academy of Dramatic Art (and a few private schools) which gives a good teaching in elocution and other branches of the art, but the whole training is nothing like so extensive as that received in many continental schools and academies.

Possibly the best training in this country can be had by joining a repertory company. It is hard work, rehearsing one play all day, playing in another at night, and with one eye on the play for the following week, and this continued week after week. But it provides very wide experience, a chance to progress from small to larger parts, to gain variety from comedy one week to serious drama the next, and above all to see how a theatre works, to gain a sense of production as a whole and the relation of the component parts of a play. This cannot be learned in occasional and spasmodic engagements in London, where too often the actors, small and great, think of their own scene as the be-all and end-all of the performance.

London is regarded as the Mecca of any actor, the goal to be attained at any cost, quite out of proportion to the facts. Wages of course are higher, except for the small parts, but it is ridiculous to suppose that the London audience, though it is more sophisticated, is either more intelligent or more appreciative than provincial audiences. One virtue at least of the late Victorian stage was that there was not this metropolitan emphasis; the greatest stars—Irving, Tree, and Ellen Terry—invariably toured the country for part of the year. The facilities of transport which have increased the visiting population of London, and the modern star salaries have almost killed this habit. Touring companies still go out, but they are invariably regarded as inferior, and from many points of view they are. They are badly paid, conditions are not good, and the standard of acting has inevitably suffered. The folly of touring managers in sending out so many third-rate companies has rebounded on to their own heads, as the provincial public naturally prefers a well-acted film to a badly acted play. Unfortunately it is not only the managers who suffer, but also the whole acting profession.

The Repertory and Little Theatres have been mainly responsible for what modern movement there has been in this country. Manchester, Liverpool, Birmingham, Cambridge for a time, and Hull, have done excellent work; and the general standard of acting and of the whole production has often been higher than that in London, if not so gorgeously put on. These productions form excellent training for the beginner, as well as providing a kinder audience on which to practise.

On the Continent a system similar to the repertory has been in existence to a far greater extent. The Compagnie des Quinze in the Vieux Colombier Theatre in France was a permanent company whose members therefore got to know each other's work; consequently they achieved greater unity in their productions, which were harmonious wholes, not a series of performances and incidents strung together. Reinhardt kept a dramatic school attached to the Deutsches Theater in Berlin, and the students were in the fortunate position of being part of a living theatre instead of training in a remote school. They acquired experience by crowd work and later by small parts. In Russia the system has been developed further still and almost perfected. The actor there does not have to look for a job in our haphazard way through completely unco-ordinated agencies; he works at one theatre, and can give his best work because he knows that in due course he will be advanced. Schools are attached to all the principal theatres, their members are part of the permanent staff, and there is extensive training in the art of the theatre, and of acting, as well as courses in physical training, history, and political economy. The training is as thorough as that of medicine in this country. The theatre is a science as well as a profession, and is not treated as a romantic and somewhat scatter-brained pastime as it is apt to be here.

SALARIES THE ACTOR MAY EXPECT

WAGES in the theatre are not systematised and regulated as in most other professions, neither are there any laws of promotion or increased pay by seniority. In London the three pounds a week minimum for a speaking part is adhered to, but in touring some beginners, who can afford to, go for less, thus making impossible conditions for those of the profession who have to earn their livelihood and have no other means of doing so. An actor with a small part can, and generally does, increase his salary by understudying. The rates of pay up to ten pounds a week are to a certain extent determined by the size of the part. An actor who gets more than ten pounds receives no money for rehearsal, and in these cases the salary is generally settled by the actor's fame and his powers of bargaining. A well-known actor will earn from fifteen to thirty or forty pounds a week, a star from seventy to one hundred or even two hundred pounds. A cinema celebrity like Maurice Chevalier can ask and receive twice that amount for a stage appearance. Those, however, who enter the profession hoping for these large salaries would be wiser to take to bookmaking : they are hard to get, and hard to keep, and even some of our most famous stars, though they may be in four or five shows in the year, may only get four or five weeks paid work.

Most English actors now act for the films as well. The latter naturally pay higher rates. They use the actor for only two or three weeks, but the film itself may travel for a year or more, and the artist has every right to expect a higher salary. Film and stage acting require very different techniques, and it is one of the faults of the English cinema that it is too stagey, though this is more the fault of the director than of the actor.

PROTECTING THE PROFESSION AGAINST ABUSE

THE Actors' Association and the Stage Guild were the first attempts on the part of actors to secure a fair deal and protect themselves against the abuses of some managers— the bogus managers who would put on a play when they had not sufficient capital to pay the artistes' salaries would gamble on a very hypothetical success, and after obtaining their services free for three weeks' rehearsing and a week's run would take the play off and not pay the artists a penny. Even worse abuses occurred with companies touring the colonies : actors and actresses would get stranded in South Africa, for instance, with no money and without even a return ticket. In England, again, touring managers would also be partners in agencies and split the commission extorted from actors they had themselves engaged. As a result of the work of these unions a standard contract was drawn up with a minimum salary, and half-pay for rehearsals. Agitation was carried on, successfully, to enforce colonial touring managers to give the artists return tickets. But these unions were not strong enough to be really effective : the membership was not sufficiently comprehensive, and the existence of two unions split the ranks of the actors. Though there was the new contract, and the reputable managers agreed to use it, it could not be enforced.

British Actors Equity has amalgamated the other two, and has made great strides to safeguard actors, despite the carping criticism of the Press and of such critics who assert that an actor's duty is to the public first rather than to his fellow-actors or himself. The membership has now become large enough to demand a closed shop, and insist that no member should act with anyone who was not a member. To-day the whole of the London acting profession is enrolled from star to chorus, and though it has not yet achieved a strong foothold in the provinces, there is every hope that it will do so very soon. The majority of the managers have little against it, as they dislike the bogus managers almost as heartily as do the actors. A new contract has been drawn up, very similar to the previous one, and very moderate in its demands, but the great difference with this is that with one hundred per cent. union membership behind it, it can be enforced.

There are, of course, the other departments of the theatre—costume and scenery designing, stage managing and producing—but these do not properly come within the province of this article ; although acting experience is helpful to the latter two, they need other qualifications also, and other training.

INDEX AND PRONOUNCING GLOSSARY

Compiled by L. M. MONT-CLAR.

How to use this index.—In order to facilitate immediate reference to the principal entry on a particular subject, the page number for this entry is set in italics, thus : *258*. Subsidiary references to the subject which occur elsewhere in the book are indicated by numerals in roman type, thus : 387. References to illustrations are indicated by numerals in roman type surrounded by square brackets, thus : [156]. Cross references given in the index refer only to the index pages.

The pronouncing glossary.—Where the pronunciation of proper names and technical terms is not immediately understood from the spelling, or where the spelling may be misleading, a separate pronunciation is given after the first index entry. In simple cases a hint may be considered sufficient ; in all doubtful cases a complete phonetic re-spelling is given. The word is broken into syllables as it is spoken, and an accent mark (′) follows the syllable on which the stress is placed. The notation used for the phonetic re-spelling is as follows :

ā	mate	a	pat	ė	there	th	thin
ē	mete	e	pet	á	father	TH	thine
ī	mite	i	pit	ę	her	zh	leisure
ō	mote	o	pot	aw	awl	ch	church
ū	mute	u	nut	oi	oil	g	get
ōō	boot	oo	foot	ow	owl	j	jam

The French nasalised *n* is denoted by italicising the vowel and the nasal concerned, thus : u*n*, b*on*, vi*n*. The German modified ö and the similar French sounds are denoted by *oe*, the German soft ch and g by *ch*, and the guttural ch (as in Scots " loch ") by CH. The French *u* and the German modified *ü* are indicated by ü.